Oil and Terrorism in the New Gulf

D1713584

Oil and Terrorism in the New Gulf

Framing U.S. Energy and Security Policies for the Gulf of Guinea

James J. F. Forest and Matthew V. Sousa

LEXINGTON BOOKS

A division of
ROWMAN & LITTLEFIELD PUBLISHERS, INC.
Lanham • Boulder • New York • Toronto • Plymouth, UK

LEXINGTON BOOKS

A division of Rowman & Littlefield Publishers, Inc.
A wholly owned subsidiary of The Rowman & Littlefield Publishing Group, Inc.
4501 Forbes Boulevard, Suite 200
Lanham, MD 20706

Estover Road
Plymouth PL6 7PY
United Kingdom

British Library Cataloguing in Publication Information Available

The hardback edition of this book was previously catalogued by the Library of Congress
as follows:
Forest, James J. F.
  Oil and terrorism in the new Gulf : framing U.S. energy and security policies for the
Gulf of Guinea / James J. F. Forest and Matthew V. Sousa.
     p. cm.
  Includes bibliographical references and index.
  ISBN-13: 978-0-7391-0989-2 (cloth : alk. paper)
  ISBN-10: 0-7391-0989-8 (cloth : alk. paper)
  ISBN-13: 978-0-7391-1995-2 (pbk. : alk. paper)
  ISBN-10: 0-7391-1995-8 (pbk. : alk paper)
  1. United States—Foreign relations—Africa, West. 2. Africa, West—Foreign
relations—United States. 3. United States—Foreign relations—Middle East. 4. Middle
East—Foreign relations—United States. 5. Petroleum industry and trade—Political
aspects—Guinea, Gulf of. 6. Petroleum industry and trade—Political aspects—Middle
East. 7. Energy policy—United States. 8. Terrorism—Government policy—United
States. I. Sousa, Matthew V., 1970– II. Title.
JZ1480.A56F67 2006
333.8'2320973—dc22   2005037705

Printed in the United States of America

♾™ The paper used in this publication meets the minimum requirements of American
National Standard for Information Sciences—Permanence of Paper for Printed Library
Materials, ANSI/NISO Z39.48–1992.

Contents

List of Tables and Figures

Preface

Our intention in producing this volume was to create an easily accessible, practical, yet scholarly source of information about a topic of increasing importance to the United States: our relationship with the oil producing nations of West and Central Africa. By examining in depth the lessons learned from our relationship with the oil producing nations of the Middle East and exploring the current landscape of noticeable trends and challenges in the Gulf of Guinea, the book offers an integrated policy framework for how we should pursue our energy security and national security goals in tandem. U.S. national security and energy security are inexorably intertwined, particularly when considering the multiple state and non-state actors who can wreak considerable havoc on our economy based solely on our significant dependence on foreign oil. Ensuring unfettered access to Middle East oil has sustained U.S. economic growth, but has also contributed to less desirable outcomes, such as the spread of anti-U.S. sentiments that fuel radical terrorism. Despite its oil wealth, the quality of life in the Arab World is considerably lower than in many Latin American and East Asian developing countries—a condition which Osama bin Laden and other Islamic radical terrorists have noted in their continual exhortations for the Muslim world to take up violence against the U.S. and its allies.

This volume argues that lessons learned from our experience in the Middle East should be applied to our burgeoning energy security interests in western and central sub-Saharan Africa. Particularly, the Gulf of Guinea presents some unique opportunities, quite distinct from the Middle East. Oil is plentiful, but there are many challenges to overcome before the people of the region can truly benefit from the revenues this oil will bring. There are numerous security challenges throughout the region that must be addressed before good governance can truly be achieved. Unfortunately, because of the authoritarian regimes, corruption, and other challenges discussed in this volume, there are a range of broad political, social, and economic grievances that create a climate of unrest and dissatisfaction in the region. Overall, the research provided in this book suggests that long-term national security for the U.S. will prove elusive unless our energy security interests are pursued alongside coordinated efforts to increase state legitimacy and good governance in oil-producing countries worldwide.

The discussion begins with an analysis of how oil plays an integral role in our national security and economic stability, followed by a review of emerging U.S. energy security and national security interests in West and Central Africa. Because the U.S. is so dependent upon imported oil, and because of the threat of increasing political instability throughout the Middle East, our policymakers have recently turned their attention toward the oil-rich countries of sub-Saharan Africa. The next three chapters of the volume thus examine the opportunities and challenges faced by the countries of the strategically important Gulf of Guinea region—specifically, Angola, Cameroon, Chad, the Republic of Congo, Equatorial Guinea, Gabon, Nigeria, and São Tomé and Príncipe. Along with individual (albeit necessarily brief) profiles of each country, Chapter 2 offers a comparative analysis that highlights similar patterns of political violence—including attempted and successful military coups—indicating that this is certainly a tough neighborhood in which to maintain peaceful, good governance. In addition to local and regional violence, the major governance challenges can be generally grouped into a small handful of categories: authoritarian regimes, corruption, and underdevelopment. A brief analysis of each reveals important considerations for U.S. energy security policy.

Chapters 3 and 4 then delve into specific security challenges that result from a climate of political instability, porous borders, corruption, and resource exploitation. In short, there are a host of security vulnerabilities throughout this region that can be exploited by both criminal networks and terrorist organizations. Because the oil-rich, authoritarian countries of the Middle East have become the birthplace of today's global jihadist terrorism movement, there is a growing concern that the U.S. over-reliance on oil from this region has created a serious vulnerability to our national security. Thus, U.S. energy security and national security objectives are more intertwined in the 21st century than ever before. From this perspective, Chapter 5 argues that the if United States is going to get more involved in the Gulf of Guinea, we should examine the history of U.S. relations with key oil-rich states in the Middle East, and identify the "mistakes" we should avoid in our emerging relationship with the countries of West and Central Africa. The analysis of U.S.-Middle East history provided in this volume reveals disturbing realities that are directly connected to the extraction of oil: political corruption, lack of political and social development, critical levels of economic dependence on a single national resource, and increasingly dissatisfied young populations with limited prospects for a brighter future.

Following this discussion, Chapter 6 reviews contemporary U.S. policies in the Gulf of Guinea, highlighting both successes and challenges. Then chapter 7 reiterates our initial argument that African energy development requires synchronized involvement in neo-liberal development, democratization, and other dimensions of human development. The chapter also introduces a policy framework for U.S.-Africa relations that may be useful for planning and implementing a coherent and effective policy in the future. This framework is structured around three essential foundations for U.S.-Africa policy: security, economic development, and democratization. Security is an absolute prerequisite for both economic development and democratization. Economic development is the second priority after human security, and is arguably more important to most citizens of underdeveloped countries than is democracy. Democratization, adapted to local culture and unique national factors, is what will guarantee stability by institutionalizing peaceful mechanisms for political compromise and thereby strengthening the relationship between the society and the state. Three requirements for effectively implementing this framework—interagency coordination, public-private partnerships, and multilateral cooperation—are also identified in this chapter. Together, these elements will determine the nation's ability to realize our core energy security and national security goals. Following this discussion, the remaining chapters of the volume explore in depth each of these essential foundations and implementation requirements, and a concluding chapter offers an integrative summary of the analyses, arguments, and recommendations presented in the volume.

In sum, the observations and analyses presented in this volume lead to a single conclusion: the U.S. must adopt a long-term, integrated strategy for achieving the nation's energy and security goals in sub-Saharan Africa. Long-term national security for the U.S. will prove elusive unless our energy security interests are pursued alongside coordinated efforts to increase state legitimacy and good governance in oil-producing countries worldwide. This argument is particularly salient when building our relationships with the oil-rich countries of West and Central Africa, especially in the Gulf of Guinea, where a complex history of external and internal factors have led to an overall decline in the standard of living for most people. Based on an historical analysis of oil extraction in the Middle East—where the overall standard of living has also declined dramatically, despite the region's oil wealth—it becomes clear that securing unfettered access to oil for multinational extraction corporations without commensurate investments in socioeconomic and political improvement does not bode well for achieving long-term energy security and national security goals. Thus, as the U.S. moves forward in developing the energy extraction industry in the Gulf of Guinea, it must demand transparency in public financial transactions, respect for human rights, and a social and economic environment governed by the rule of law. An integrative and forward-thinking approach, guided by fundamental U.S. values, must serve as the basis for both policymakers and corporate leaders when dealing with the developing world. If we fail to learn from the past, we are destined to repeat our mistakes in the future.

Please note: The views expressed throughout this volume are those of the authors and not of the Department of Defense, the U.S. Military Academy, or any other agency of the U.S. Government.

Acknowledgments

Many colleagues and friends have supported this effort. To begin with, we extend our sincere thanks to the faculty and staff in the Department of Social Sciences at West Point who have inspired and encouraged us, particularly Colonel Mike Meese, Head of the Department, and Colonel Cindy Jebb, Deputy Head. The cadets at West Point have also been a source of inspiration, particularly those who enrolled in the Politics and Development of Sub-Saharan Africa course that each of us taught during the past few years. Our discussions with these creative learners, and with each other, are largely responsible for our writing this book.

In conducting our research, we were privileged to interview a number of key experts and national leaders, both in the U.S. and in several African countries, and we are indebted to the kindness and candid insights they provided. Most importantly, to Alicia and Veronique, we offer our sincere appreciation for the incredible patience and support you have shown us throughout this project. We could ask for no better partners in this incredible life journey. Finally, we wish to dedicate this volume to Second Lieutenant Englebert Eric Mbog-Hob. An international exchange student from Cameroon, Eric graduated from the U.S. Military Academy in 2004 and inspired us with his genuine desire, commitment, and ability to make a difference along the lines of the topics addressed in this volume. Tragically, Eric's life was cut short, and the Gulf of Guinea will miss the impact of his hard work and leadership.

James J.F. Forest, West Point, NY
Matthew V. Sousa, Washington, DC
October 1, 2005

Chad

Nigeria

Cameroon

Equatorial Guinea

São Tomé
and Príncipe

Congo

Gabon

Angola

The Gulf
of Guinea

Chapter 1
Oil and Security: An Introduction

Oil is one of the world's most sought-after resources. Today oil supplies about 40% of the world's energy and 96% of its transportation energy. Militaries around the world rely upon oil for a variety of transport vehicles and weapons systems, while airlines, commercial shipping, and other enormous industries require dependable access to a vibrant global oil market. From the heat in our homes to the fuel in our cars, oil is clearly an important part of our daily lives. According to the *2005 BP Statistical Review of World Energy,* global oil consumption grew by almost 2.5 million barrels per day (3.4%) from the previous year, the most rapid rate since 1986.[1] The strongest increase was in the Asia Pacific region, where Chinese oil consumption rose by nearly 900,000 barrels per day, or just under 16%. U.S. consumers lead the world, accounting for nearly 25% of the world's oil consumption. A review of global patterns of oil consumption also indicates that for the past ten years, Africans and Latin Americans have consumed the least amount of oil, while China and India—which together account for a third of the world's population—have seen enormous growth in oil consumption (please see the tables in Appendix A).

According to the Institute for the Analysis of Global Security, world oil consumption will rise by about 60% between now and the year 2020,[2] while a more conservative estimate by the U.S. Energy Intelligence Administration indicates global demand for energy will increase by over 50% by the year 2025.[3] Transportation will be the fastest growing oil-consuming sector. By 2025, the number of cars will increase to well over 1.25 billion from approximately 700 million today. As a result, global consumption of gasoline could double.[4]

The U.S. Department of Energy estimates that by 2020, the U.S. will need to import 17 million barrels of oil per day, 6 million more than it does now.[5] By 2020, China's oil consumption will match that of the U.S., leading many to forecast an eventual global struggle between a small handful of countries over access to oil in places like the Caspian Sea basin, Russia, Africa, and Latin America, as well as in the Middle East.[6] Given that China's oil consumption is expected to grow at a rate of 7.5% per year and India's 5.5% (compared to a 1% average growth for the industrialized countries), it will clearly be strategically imperative for these countries to secure long-term access to oil.[7] Access to oil is

1

clearly a vital national interest for the U.S. as well, as it meets two basic criteria: the first criterion is that the United States has committed or is likely to commit significant public-sector resources to advance or protect it; the second is that it is a major foreign policy end in itself, not simply a contributor to a larger objective.[8]

Thus, as the U.S. consumes about a quarter of the world's oil production, and imports over half of what it consumes, the importance of oil cannot be overstated. Our nation's reliance on a robust petroleum industry is a key point of many contemporary economic and political debates, where it is often argued that a relationship of dependence—particularly for heating and the transportation sector—on this singular resource is a worrisome security issue. For example, in a recent *Foreign Affairs* article, Wirth, Gray and Podesta (2003) observed that "the intensity of oil use in the transportation sector makes the American economy vulnerable to the actions of other states . . . every economic recession in the past 40 years has been preceded by a significant increase in oil prices."[9] Energy security thus plays a central role in U.S. foreign relations, not only in the oil-rich Middle East but in other parts of the world as well. For example, Canada is the leading exporter of oil to the U.S., providing over 1.8 million barrels per day. Nigeria, Mexico and Venezuela are also among the top suppliers of oil to the U.S.[10]

On the global level, however, today's energy security environment is dominated by a relatively small handful of countries, particularly members of Organization of Petroleum Exporting Countries (OPEC). The global supply of oil is currently estimated at over 1,000 billion barrels, and nearly 75% of it is owned by OPEC member states. Of the trillion barrels currently estimated, nearly 62% are in the hands of Middle Eastern regimes, most notably Saudi Arabia (22%), Iran (11%), Iraq (10%), Kuwait (8%), and the United Arab Emirates (8%). According to the Institute for the Analysis of Global Security, by 2020 83% of global oil reserves will be controlled by Middle Eastern regimes.[11] As a result, a handful of Middle East countries are poised to gain a greater ability to manipulate oil prices and world politics, and can use their oil revenues to increase their military expenditures, fuel an arms race and undermine regional stability. As described later in this volume, corrupt and oppressive regimes in oil-rich countries will likely continue to use oil revenues as a means to maintain their power, while a number of increasingly violent political groups look for ways to overthrow these governments. Overall, it is clear that reliance on a single energy resource that is unevenly distributed throughout the world produces a variety of energy security and national security concerns for the U.S., concerns that will be intensified as demand for oil grows. These concerns frame the discussion provided throughout the next several chapters.

To meet the world's demand for oil, production is on the rise. Global oil production exceeded 80 million barrels per day for the first time in 2004. OPEC member states produced 32.9 million barrels per day (an increase of 2.2 million from the previous year), thus accounting for over 41% of the world's daily oil production. In Saudi Arabia alone, output reached a record 10.6 million barrels per day. Oil production outside OPEC increased by 965,000 barrels per day in 2004. Russia was the leading producer, with output rising by nearly 750,000 barrels per day (to reach an average production level of 9.3 million barrels per day). Angola, Chad, Ecuador, Equatorial Guinea and Kazakhstan all registered growth of more than 100,000 barrels per day. The largest declines in production during 2004 were seen in the U.K., down by 230,000 barrels per day, and the U.S., down by 160,000 barrels per day.[12] In fact, production declines in the U.K. and U.S. can be seen over the last two decades.

Overall, the Middle East is the largest producer of oil for the global market, and thus can have an enormous impact on the global supply (and, by extension, the price) of oil. As any basic course in economics will explain, the price of oil is a result of both supply and demand. Given that demand is high and growing, as described earlier, if the production of oil does not also increase, the price of a barrel of oil increases. A recent example of this reveals the power that oil-rich countries can wield in the global marketplace. During the summer of 2005, oil prices rose to over $70/barrel, and were expected to climb even higher. Responding to pleas from the U.S. and other Western countries, the Saudi Arabian government agreed to increase its daily output, and as a result the price of oil began to decrease slightly. However, experts are forecasting increasing oil prices for the future, for the simple reason that growth in global demand for oil has outstripped growth in supply, drastically limiting spare production capacity. Indeed, currently Saudi Arabia is the only country with significant spare production capacity—an asset which the House of Saud has found useful in its foreign policy negotiations with the U.S. and other countries.

In sum, the world's oil supply is largely concentrated in the hands of a small handful of Middle Eastern countries. Given the rise of anti-American sentiment throughout this region—as measured both by public polls and by terrorist group statements and attacks—our dependence on these countries for such an important resource has created a national security challenge. In responding to this challenge, as described throughout this volume, the Bush administration has been actively seeking ways to increase the diversity of supply and reduce U.S. dependency on Middle East oil. As an outgrowth of this effort, sub-Saharan Africa has over the past few years come to be seen as an increasingly important strategic resource region for the U.S. This is the starting point from which the research and policy recommendations provided in this volume are framed.

Alternatives to Oil

While we have chosen in this book to focus on better ways for the U.S. to pursue the extraction of foreign oil, this is certainly not meant to dismiss the vital importance of developing new, alternative and renewable sources of energy. Indeed, our nation's dependence on oil is a deeply worrisome national security challenge. Former CIA Director James Woolsey notes that "we live in a world in which a terrorist attack in the Middle East could push oil well over $100 a barrel and send the world economy into a tailspin."[13] As a recent Baker Institute report observed, "the strategic and economic reality of U.S. dependence on Middle East oil is costing the United States dearly in terms of military operations and national security."[14] Because of rising demand for energy and depleting reserves elsewhere, the U.S. will become even more reliant on Middle East oil by 2025. As a result, "it will be imperative to have prepared for new energy sources that do not derive principally from oil or gas."[15]

Recent efforts to do so have explored a variety of options, including solar power, clean coal, ethanol, hydrogen, wind, fuel cells, batteries, and hybrid vehicles. For example, in 2005 the British firm Intelligent Energy unveiled a new fuel cell-powered motorbike which, according to news reports, will go 100 miles on just five ounces of hydrogen.[16] A subsidiary of Intelligent Energy is working on several devices that would produce hydrogen from natural gas, while the company's vice president Andy Eggleston envisions portable fuel cells, similar to that used in the motorbikes, being able to power anything from personal watercraft to a small home.

Research and development of alternative energy sources—and particularly their adaptation to private consumers—requires significant and long-term investments. Richard Russell, associate director for technology in the Office of Science and Technology Policy in the Executive Office of the President, notes that the Bush administration has pledged over $1.7 billion over the next five years to fund new energy initiatives such as the National Nanotechnology Initiative, the Freedom Car, the Hydrogen Fuel initiative, and the International Thermonuclear Experimental Reactor project.[17] Organizations like the Energy Future Coalition and the Set America Free Alliance are putting pressure on Congress and the White House to do more in the way of promoting the development of alternative energy programs.

However, despite all these efforts—which we fully respect and endorse—this volume is driven by a conviction that renewable, alternative energy programs are long-term endeavors, while the nation's increasing physical presence in West Africa and the Gulf of Guinea is driven by short-term realities. Hybrid vehicles (which combine a conventional gas-powered engine with rechargeable batteries) are currently available. However, the car that runs completely on batteries or solar power, yet performs comparably to a gas-powered car, is still many years in the future. According to most observers, oil will have continuing importance to America's economy and security for at least the next two decades. Thus, we have chosen to explore ways in which the U.S. can more effectively pursue its immediate energy security agenda, with West Africa and the Gulf of Guinea as our geographic region of focus. Before doing so, however, it is first necessary to highlight the sources and patterns of conflict that are common to most oil-rich nations.

Oil and Political Conflict

A range of international relations theories highlight the role of resources—particularly, the determination of one or more states to control important resources—in explaining regional and global conflicts. Whether it is water, land, gold, diamonds, oil, etc., many wars have been fought over control of resources that are perceived as valuable sources of power and wealth. It is thus no coincidence that the handful of countries which dominate the world's oil supply are also places where political conflicts have simmered and boiled throughout the last half century. By itself, oil is neither a creative nor a destructive force. However, it does seem to encourage government leaders to make particularly bad decisions, and has served as a motivating factor behind a number of conflicts over the past four decades. In 1998, Richard Cheney—then CEO of Halliburton—observed, "The problem is that the good Lord didn't see fit to put oil and gas reserves where there are stable governments."[18] According to a recent World Bank study, countries that export oil are forty times more likely to be engaged in civil war than countries that do not.[19] Border disputes and offshore territorial disputes are also exacerbated as neighboring countries vie for control of the underlying reserves.[20] Further, as reported in a study prepared by the Royal Institute of International Affairs in London, nearly 40% of the world's oil production comes from countries where human rights, as defined by UN conventions, are either not recognized or are seriously and frequently violated.[21] For example, in June 2005, the United States criticized Kuwait, Qatar, Saudi Arabia and the United Arab Emirates for doing little if anything to stop forms of "modern slavery" within their borders.[22]

As author and noted resource conflict expert Michael Klare has observed, "oil is closely associated with conflict and violence because its possession is viewed by many states as a matter of national security."[23] Indeed, in most cases the state claims exclusive ownership over valuable natural resources, producing a centralized receipt of revenues that encourages corruption and cronyism.[24] Government leaders, rebel and guerilla movements, and even neighboring states all view these large revenue streams as something worth fighting for. Oil is thus linked to conflict and violence through its role in generating immense wealth for those who receive the royalties and other rewards derived from the exploitation of a nation's petroleum reserves.[25] In the Middle East, the flow of funds to certain oil-producing states has financed widespread corruption, perpetuated repressive regimes, funded radical anti-American fundamentalism, and fed hatreds that derive from rigid rule and stark contrasts between rich and poor. The accumulation of wealth by those who control disbursement of the nation's petroleum income invariably produces resentment on the part of those in a society who are excluded from the economic benefits of oil production.[26] For example, in Nigeria the percentage of revenue allocated to regions of oil extraction declined from 50% in the 1960s to a low of 1.9% in the 1990s.[27]

In general, a majority of the political conflicts associated with oil-rich countries can be said to have a direct correlation with how the oil wealth is managed. A review of the historical record shows that natural resource endowment has not been positively correlated with economic development and social progress. Instead, international statistics show that countries rich in natural resources have had a performance that is markedly poorer than those countries that have possessed few natural resources.[28] In other words, oil revenue in these countries has rarely been used for investment in economic diversification or the development of human capital. The reasons for this pattern vary from country to country, but there are several important similarities. Weak governance structures undermine a country's ability to ensure that oil extraction is undertaken in a way that promotes wider social development. Further, a country's possession of natural resources encourages political underdevelopment, creating a vicious circle of negative outcomes.[29] According to industry observer Philip Swanson, "Large investments in natural resource exploitation and export tend to give rise to a number of negative dynamics in the economy, government and society of the host country . . . with consequences for social stability."[30] These dynamics can be generally grouped into one of two categories: economic effects and political effects.

Negative Economic Effects

Governments typically receive oil wealth via several different routes, including bonuses, royalty payments and income tax. In many cases, a combination of these payment methods is used. Together they can be used to obscure the direction and volume of oil revenue flows. Revenues from oil extraction activities often account for over half of the country's GDP, giving a false sense of economic security that undermines the need for economic and fiscal management.[31] As a result, most oil exporting countries have no significant market economy, but rather a protected concessionary and distributive economy that is directed by the government.[32] Oil represents 90-95% of total Saudi export earnings, 75% of state revenues, and about 35-40% of GDP.[33] Oil accounts for about 80% of the Nigerian government's budget, while in Angola its contribution has fluctuated between 70% and 90%.[34] Access to easy oil wealth can undermine efforts to mobilize resources in other sectors of the economy. This is because the relative ease of collecting large revenues from oil production makes the more difficult collection of relatively small revenues in other sectors hardly worth the effort.[35]

A number of economic effects can take place in an economy where significant investments have been made in natural resources intended for export. Collectively, they are usually referred to as "Dutch disease" after the economic problems faced by the Netherlands following the development of that country's large gas fields in the 1960s and 70s. The typically large investments involved in petroleum development, followed by increased government spending of petroleum revenues, tend to drive up prices for services and inputs in the economy, undermining the competitiveness of other export-oriented businesses. They also lead to an appreciation of the local currency, which penalizes non-commodity exporters, as well as manufacturers of goods competing against imported products.[36] The Dutch disease phenomenon goes far beyond the exchange rate effects of a large oil sector. Possibly more important are the economic consequences that arise from the effects of oil wealth on the vision and attitudes of a country's rulers. Angola provides a particularly striking example of this. High and rising oil revenues have tended, despite the occasional adverse price shocks, to encourage complacency about the dismal state of the rest of the economy.[37]

Given the increased dependence on a single exported natural resource, a nation's economy may also become subject to severe cycles of boom and bust related to the changing world price of that commodity. Historically, most governments of oil-rich developing countries have been unable to resist significant spending increases in boom periods, often supplemented by borrowing on the security of future revenues. Since it becomes politically difficult to curtail a high level of spending, such governments typically have developed heavy debt problems, especially once oil prices have fallen.[38]

Negative Political Effects

Several recent reports have shown a correlation between civil conflict, dependence on primary commodity exports and low national income.[39] In fact, in countries where oil is plentiful, it has rarely helped promote peace, progress or prosperity. As described earlier, the limited excess capacity and high demand are the cause of high crude oil prices, which affects what we pay at the gas pump and for heating oil. When oil prices are high, oil-exporting countries become flush with revenue, and therefore one would expect the people of these countries to enjoy a reasonably high standard of living. The truth, however, is dramatically different for most.

Saudi Arabia, with the world's largest oil reserves, is a debtor nation. Significant proportions of the population live in poverty, while the members and close allies of the ruling House of Saud enjoy an incredibly lavish lifestyle. Current demographic trends will encourage Saudi Arabia to seek higher oil prices for domestic political reasons. Per capita income in the Kingdom has fallen since 1980 and is expected to continue, while the population continues to grow. Thus, the House of Saud will need increasing amounts of money to meet basic social services. Failure to do so could certainly contribute to the increasing social and political unrest already seen elsewhere in the region, where the governance challenges are similar. For example, in neighboring Yemen, riots erupted in late July 2005 after the government implemented a budget cut in subsidies. In the country's worst political violence in more than a decade, rioters clashed with security forces, burned cars and buildings, and left 16 people dead. What began as anger over a crumbling economy turned into a rare open expression of fury at Yemen's leadership, with rioters demanding the government's ouster and burning pictures of top officials. Security forces launched tear gas canisters, beat demonstrators with batons, and opened fire on stone-throwing protestors outside government buildings—including the oil ministry—in Yemen's capital city, San'a.[40]

In Iraq, Saddam Hussein plundered his country's oil wealth over two decades, distributed it among his family and friends, and used it to build an army of loyalists to himself and the Ba'ath party (which then helped him crush any opposition to his rule). Hussein also launched a war against neighboring Iran, invaded Kuwait, and was generally a source of concern throughout the Persian Gulf. Oil has also been associated with poor governance, political instability and violence in other parts of the world. For example, Nigeria—the world's 17th poorest nation, according to a recent World Bank report—saw its oil wealth plundered by a series of military dictators, including Ibrahim Babaginda and Sani Abacha (whose family now enjoys an estimated $20 billion in overseas banks).[41] Venezuela is, in the words of the World Bank, "blessed with the largest petroleum reserves in Latin America and the Caribbean but plagued by a prolonged economic and political crisis, high levels of crime and violence, and long-term social ills such as extreme inequality and poverty."[42] Overall, most oil-exporting countries have not successfully transformed their natural endowment into a means for self-sustaining, stable paths of development. Further, in many cases oil has been directly linked to political turmoil, government corruption, environmental degradation, and violent conflicts.

In particular, the relationship between oil wealth and corruption has been widely documented, and is a key source of political opposition groups— including those of a more militant Islamic orientation—throughout the Middle East, Southeast Asia and Africa. Large amounts of oil revenues in a non-transparent system invites corruption, in turn creating incentives to further limit transparency and accountability. Indeed, among most oil exporters, a lack of transparency in the management of oil revenues is at the heart of the weakness in economic governance.[43] Under such conditions, significant amounts of oil wealth have disappeared into off-budget accounts. Such "looting" of a country's natural resources by its governing elites can provide the incentive and means to remain in power. Further, given a regime's dependence upon oil revenues for its power, any threat to such revenues is likely to be met with significant resistance, in some cases leading to the brutal treatment of citizens (like the Ogoni tribe in the Niger Delta region) who are opposed to oil industry activities.[44] A number of NGOs, as well as missions by the United Nations and various governments, have reported numerous allegations of violent human rights abuses committed by government forces in and around oil producing regions in a number of countries.

According to the *2004 Corruption Perceptions Index* (CPI), corruption is one of the most significant problems facing many oil-rich nations. Peter Eigen, chairman of Transparency International, explains that "in these countries, public contracting in the oil sector is plagued by revenues vanishing into the pockets of western oil executives, middlemen and local officials."[45] A similar report produced by Transparency International, the *2004 Global Corruption Barometer*, reveals how corruption is particularly widespread among the political parties—both those in office and in opposition—as well as among the police and security forces of several oil-rich countries.[46]

The role of oil in this endemic corruption is similar throughout these countries: revenues from oil have enabled a variety of regimes to build up powerful armed forces and huge personal bank accounts while sustaining a political system of patronage that benefits only those loyal to the country's ruler.[47] In fact, as described later in this volume, oil-financed patronage has been a fundamental part of the strategy pursued by many of these countries' leaders for the consolidation and conservation of power.[48] Countries where this takes place can be characterized as "predatory" states rather than "developmental" states, because the revenues from oil are used primarily to safeguard the interests of the elite and finance their ability to remain in power (through massive expenditures on security and patronage), rather than to promote social and economic development.[49] As Claude Ake of the Brookings Institution has observed, "predatory states and Hobbesian politics have ruined the prospects of development by spreading alienation, resentment, inefficiency, and corruption. Politically disenfranchised and set upon by state violence, the people are no longer available for supporting the state or its development project. Some of them have retreated to ethnic or communal identity and local concerns. Political repression has forced highly educated and talented people to become political or economic refugees in other countries, their talents lost to the cause of national development."[50]

At the very least, the vast flow of oil revenues into historically impoverished and underdeveloped countries has the *potential* for being an agent of government corruption on a massive scale. Complicit in this pattern are oil firms who provide these vast revenues to corrupt regimes while turning a blind eye toward how the monies are used. Oil companies typically offer "signing bonuses" to states as an incentive to guarantee exclusive access to oilfields, and in many cases these bonuses have been a source of funding that can be easily diverted into personal bank accounts. In countries with authoritarian, corrupt leaders, there is little accountability over whether the revenues paid for the nation's oil actually make it into the national treasury. For example, oil giant Shell recently admitted (in an independent report commissioned by the company in 2003) that it had inadvertently fed corruption, poverty and conflict through its oil activities in Nigeria.[51] Since 1970, Nigeria has earned about $400 billion from oil, and yet the country consistently ranks among the poorest in the world. Meanwhile, a small number of Nigerians own some of the finest properties in some of the world's best cities, and swell some of the world's biggest bank accounts.[52] According to the United Nations Office on Drugs and Crime, many wealthy patrons in politics exhibit enormous wealth that has no obvious origin.[53]

Another prominent example of oil-related corruption can be seen in the recent Riggs Bank scandal, involving the new oil-producing country Equatorial Guinea and its president, Obiang Nguema Mbasogo. In 2003, both the *Los Angeles Times* and *CBS News* reported that American oil companies had been depositing hundreds of millions of dollars in oil royalties into an account controlled by President Obiang at a branch of the Riggs Bank in Washington, D.C.[54] A Congressional investigation, launched shortly thereafter, revealed that the embassy banking division of Riggs had allowed Obiang, one of its largest customers, to siphon oil revenue into his personal accounts. Despite the fact that Obiang and his wife made cash deposits of nearly $13 million over a three-year period into their Riggs accounts, the bank never filed a single suspicious activity report to federal regulators as required by law.[55] At one point, Equatorial Guinea's "oil account" at Riggs held $700 million.[56] The report of the Permanent Sub-Committee on Investigations of the U.S. Senate Committee on Government revealed that most of the payments into the Riggs accounts came from activities related to the country's oil resources. As Senator Norm Coleman (the chairman of the Investigations Sub-Committee) observed, "most of the oil wealth appears to be concentrated in the hands of top government officials."[57]

According to the Congressional investigation into the Riggs scandal, millions of dollars moved through various accounts owned by Obiang's family and friends, and at least $35 million was moved offshore to countries with bank secrecy laws.[58] In short, a considerable sum of money that oil companies have paid for access to Equatorial Guinea's oil reserves will never make its way to supporting projects that improve the country's infrastructure, despite the enormous need for better water, sewage, electricity, roads, schools, and more. The country of Equatorial Guinea may have wealth, but—as is the case with so many so-called "petro-states"—the majority of the country's citizens remain largely impoverished.

The corporate dimensions of this pattern cannot be overlooked. As Scott Pegg recently observed, "Conflict-ridden countries would initially appear to be unappealing locations for foreign investment. Poor enforcement of property rights and inability to guarantee physical and legal protection of assets effectively bar entry for most service and manufacturing firms."[59] However, such concerns do not apply when it comes to transnational oil companies, whose extraction operations are typically self-contained enclaves with limited interaction with local markets or people. "Their basic requirements are just secure working facilities and access to ports or airports from which their products can be transported to the global marketplace."[60] This ability to cordon off operations from problems in the local economy, combined with the fact that oil companies must go wherever the oil is, allows these companies to bear political risks of a different order of magnitude than other firms will consider.[61] Hence, their direct involvement in many zones of conflict over the past four decades, in some cases providing a stable flow of cash through the region which thugs and criminals use to support their activities, and in other cases bringing local populations into direct confrontation with security forces.[62]

Transnational corporations have a long history of involvement with weak states (where, ironically, much of the world's natural resources are located), and their relationship with these states helps increase their profits. However, because these states typically lack both fiscal transparency and accountability, the financial windfall these corporations have provided has all too often enriched only the ruling elite. Further, in order to protect these profits, transnational corporations have turned to a variety of efforts to provide security, from hiring private mercenary firms to bribing local police and military officials to ensure men with arms are available to keep would-be troublemakers at bay. In Nigeria, for example, oil companies have directly requested assistance from government security services on several occasions, resulting in the deaths of nonviolent protestors.[63] When asked in May 1999 whether Chevron would officially demand that the Nigerian military not shoot protestors at its facilities, the company's chairman and chief executive officer gave a one-word response: "No."[64]

In the Republic of the Congo, General Denis Sassou-Nguesso seized power as president in 1979 and again in 1997 after a civil war in which control of oil revenues played a central role, and the armies on both sides received considerable funding from U.S. and French oil companies.[65] However, most international oil companies have taken a "neutral" stance on the nature of host country regimes, noting that companies should not get involved in politics. For example, Unocal states on its website that it has a "legal and ethical obligation to remain politically neutral."[66] TotalFinaElf similarly mentions a duty to "abstain from all intervention in the political process of host countries."[67] However, companies are not powerless actors. They make choices that directly affect the security or insecurity of local populations.[68] Thus, as described later in this volume, we believe that it is in the best interests of multinational corporations to actively support strong public-private partnerships in order to counteract these trends of oil-related corruption and political violence. A recent example of a worthwhile model is the global "Publish What You Pay Campaign," sponsored in part by George Soros and the Open Society Institute, which has called on oil, gas and mining companies to reveal the extent of their payments to resource-rich countries.[69] Initiatives like this are vital to creating an environment of transparency in which government corruption is far more difficult.

However, while transnational corporations have clearly played some role in the problems faced by these states, the responsibility for addressing these problems lies squarely on the shoulders of the governments and their leaders. Multinational companies have no political or social authority to address the kinds of problems that can significantly curtail corruption. Further, there is a natural reluctance for foreign oil firms or countries to be overly critical of oil-rich countries' leaders, in order to avoid potential obstacles to the continued extraction of oil. An additional fear is that these countries could disrupt the flow of oil (much like OPEC did in the 1970s), creating a negative impact on the global economy. More discussion on the relationship between oil, corruption and conflict is provided in the next four chapters of this volume. Overall, it is important to note that, based on our research, it is our conviction that U.S. foreign policy has an important role to play in compelling the kinds of change that will improve the management of oil revenues in the new oil-rich nations of the Gulf of Guinea.

Corruption in oil-exporting countries has been one, but certainly not the only, source of conflicts associated with oil. The Japanese attack on Pearl Harbor had its origins, at least in part, in a decision by the United States to limit oil exports to Japan in 1941, in response to the Japan invasion of China. Japan was almost entirely reliant on imported oil, mainly from the U.S., and it needed oil for its navy. It concluded that if the American tap was going to be turned off, it would have to get its oil elsewhere, and this was a factor in its decision to invade the oil-rich Indonesian islands.[70] In another example, explored later in this volume, oil played a major role in the 1953 coup in Iran as well as a series of military conflicts in the Persian Gulf. Overall, the combination of domestic corruption, increasing global demand for oil, and a host of other geopolitical realities are critical for informing our understanding of oil in today's global security environment.

Oil and Terrorism

As this brief analysis of the global energy situation reveals, there is a worldwide vulnerability which terrorists could exploit. With global oil consumption at 80 million barrels per day and spare production capacity gradually eroding, the oil market has little wiggle room. As a result, supply disruptions can have a devastating impact on oil prices—as terrorists well know. Take for instance the tremendous jump in gasoline prices observed in the aftermath of hurricane Katrina which interrupted oil production and transport through the U.S.' Gulf coast. U.S. Energy Secretary Spencer Abraham has repeatedly warned that "terrorists are looking for opportunities to impact the world economy" by targeting energy infrastructure. In recent years, terrorists have targeted pipelines, refineries, pumping stations, and tankers in some of the world's most important energy reservoirs, including Iraq, Nigeria, Saudi Arabia, and Yemen.[71] James S. Robbins, a terrorism expert at the National Defense University, recently noted that "The terrorists understand that they can influence oil markets through directed violence, and thus exploit a critical U.S. vulnerability."[72]

Particularly vulnerable to oil terrorism is Saudi Arabia, which holds a quarter of the world's oil reserves and, as the world's leading exporter, accounts for one-tenth of daily oil production. Al Qaeda is well aware that a successful attack on one of the kingdom's major oil facilities would rattle the world and send oil prices through the ceiling. In the summer of 2002, a group of Saudis was arrested for plotting to sabotage the world's largest offshore oil-loading facility, Ras Tanura, through which up to a third of Saudi oil flows. More recently, in May 2004, jihadist gunmen opened fire on foreign workers in Yanbu, Saudi Arabia's petrochemical complex on the Red Sea, killing five foreign nationals. Later in the same month, Islamic extremists seized and killed 22 foreign oil workers in the Saudi city of Khobar. All of these attacks caused major disruptions in the oil market and a spike in insurance premiums, bringing oil prices to their highest level since 1990. As of this writing, the price of oil exceeds $60/barrel and is projected to climb even higher, despite a new commitment by Saudi Arabia to increase production by a million barrels a day.

As described later in this volume, attacks on oil pipelines are tactically easy, as there are long stretches of unguarded pipelines; since pipelines are relatively easy to repair, oil companies have often invested little in their protection.[73] The desire among terrorists to do so is evident in statements made by Osama bin Laden in which he called on his cohorts to take their holy war to the oil industry and to disrupt supplies to the U.S from the Persian Gulf.[74] The relationship between politics and terrorism in the oil-rich countries in the Middle East has produced a powerful incentive for the U.S. to look elsewhere and to look for other partnerships to meet its increasing oil needs. Clearly, our dependency on imported oil demands an energy security strategy that addresses greater diversity in the sources of our oil. Thus, in the past several years we have seen a growing interest in the Gulf of Guinea.

The Gulf of Guinea on the Horizon

On his way home from the World Summit on Sustainable Development in Johannesburg, 2002, U.S. Secretary of State Colin Powell visited both Gabon and Angola. It was the first-ever visit by a U.S. secretary of state to Gabon, which has traditionally been seen as falling within France's sphere of influence.[75] In late 2002, President Bush met with the leaders of Cameroon, Congo-Brazzaville, Gabon, Equatorial Guinea, Chad, and Sao Tome and Principe, and visited Nigeria in July 2003.[76] This flurry of activity is not surprising given that the greatest increase in oil production worldwide in the next decade is likely to come from Africa.[77] Today, nearly 18% of U.S. oil imports come from sub-Saharan Africa—almost as much as from Saudi Arabia. According to projections by the National Intelligence Council, that proportion will likely reach 25% by 2015. The vast majority of it will come from a stretch of western Africa's coastline between Nigeria and Angola called the Gulf of Guinea, where an estimated 50 billion barrels of oil reserves are located.[78] Already, Nigeria is the fifth largest supplier of U.S. oil, Angola is the ninth largest, and countries like Equatorial Guinea, Gabon, and the Republic of Congo are becoming increasingly important to U.S. energy security interests.

The Department of Energy's International Energy Outlook 2003 asserts that "several West African producers (Angola, Cameroon, Chad, Congo, Gabon, and Ivory Coast) are expected to reap the benefits of substantial exploration activity," in several cases becoming capable of producing a million or more barrels per day.[79] According to Edmund Daukoru, Nigerian Presidential Adviser on Petroleum and Energy, "With the recent advances in deep water oil and gas production technology, particularly submersible production facilities, that have extended the reach of oil and gas production to water depths of 3,000 meters, the Gulf of Guinea has become one of the most prolific hydrocarbon provinces of the world."[80]

As described in the next chapter of this volume, the Gulf of Guinea presents some unique opportunities, quite distinct from the Middle East. Oil revenues dominate most of these African countries' economies, but radical Islam plagues almost none of their political systems.[81] Of all the countries in the Gulf of Guinea, only Nigeria is a member of OPEC. Although sub-Saharan Africa will likely never replace the Middle East as an important strategic resource region for the U.S., it will significantly increase diversity of supply and reduce U.S. dependency on Middle East oil. As a result, sub-Saharan Africa has become an increasingly important U.S. foreign policy consideration.

Congressman Ed Royce, chairman of the U.S. House of Representatives Africa Sub-Committee, recently underlined the benefits of the region: "West African oil doesn't have the strategic bottlenecks that other nations have. We generally have good political relations with African oil producers. And if it lessens our dependence on a particular section of the world, that's good."[82] Robert Murphy, an economic specialist with the State Department's Office of African Analysis, commented in 2003 that "political discord or dispute in African oil states is unlikely to take on a regional or ideological tone that would result in a joint embargo by suppliers all at once."[83]

In May 2002, Vice President Dick Cheney outlined another benefit of West African oil. "African oil tends to be of high quality and low in sulphur, giving it a growing market share for refining centers on the east coast of the U.S."[84] Stephen Ellis, of Britain's Royal Africa Society, agrees with Cheney. "The quality of Nigerian crude oil in particular is especially well adapted for use in U.S. refineries."[85] It thus comes as no surprise to see the rapidly growing presence of multinational oil corporations throughout the region. In 2003, huge oil firms like ExxonMobil and Chevron-Texaco—along with lesser-known ones such as Amerada Hess and Ocean Energy—invested over $10 billion in West Africa's oil. Further, ChevronTexaco's chief executive David O'Reilly announced plans in 2003 to invest up to $20 billion over the next five years in Africa-related energy projects, much of it in West Africa.[86] According to Ken Evans, ExxonMobil's Vice President for Africa, the company's 12 projects in Nigeria, Angola, Equatorial Guinea and Chad will boost oil production capacity by 1 to 2.3 million barrels per day by 2006.[87] Evans recently noted that the continent was well positioned to benefit from the expected 3% growth in global oil demand over the next 10 years, which will see total demand grow from 120 million to 160 million barrels/day by the end of the decade.[88] Shell, which has invested over $16 billion in Nigeria alone in the last four years, has in three years added over 700 million barrels of oil to its reserve base, according to the company's regional vice president Ebbie Haan.[89]

On July 15, 2004, energy expert David L. Goldwyn—a former U.S. assistant secretary of energy for international affairs—testified before the Senate Foreign Relations Committee's Subcommittee on International Economic Policy, Export and Trade Promotion that the African nations of the Gulf of Guinea are critical to U.S. energy security and could one day provide the United States with up to 20% of its energy needs.[90] Furthermore, he explained, the non-OPEC nations in this area (all of them except Nigeria) provide a counterweight to OPEC's monopoly power. "While OPEC countries cut production, countries from the Gulf of Guinea provided one out of every four barrels of new oil that came on the market last year."[91] These nations, he added, are rapidly growing as suppliers because they have opened their economies to Western investment. Even though most of the world's oil reserves are closed to international oil companies, the Gulf of Guinea has offered nearly 15% returns on investment and is expected to attract $30-$40 billion in investment this decade. From a geological and investment perspective, the region's prospects are "quite bright," he said. "New technologies, competitive investment frameworks and the availability of reserves for exploration by international oil companies have produced outstanding results, and much of this oil is the kind of low-sulphur crude oil that U.S. refiners need to produce gasoline that meets our environmental requirements," he explained.[92]

J. Stephen Morrison, director of the Africa Program at the Center for Strategic and International Studies (CSIS), was also asked to testify to the Subcommittee, and concurred with Goldwyn's analysis. He argued that as oil-producing nations in the Gulf of Guinea become more important, the United States needs to develop an effective energy policy that takes these countries into account. Such a policy, he suggested, should contain certain key elements: "It must be long-term, it must be built upon sustained partnerships with African counterparts, and [it] must feature a two-pronged, regionally coordinated approach." It should also address "serious deficiencies in the internal governance of key African oil-producing states at the same time that it systematically addresses the shared, external security threats these states face."[93] Finally, transparency, accountability, improved human rights, and greater democracy within the African oil-producing nations are also essential to ensure that oil revenues are tied to sustained and equitable economic growth in those countries.[94]

In sum, the interplay between energy security and national security in the Middle East is quite obvious, and there is growing concern over the potential parallel challenges in the oil-producing nations of Africa. Countries in Africa are poor, and too often they are also poorly governed—according to a recent World Bank study, 38 out of 46 countries on the continent were ranked as both poorer than the world average and also exhibiting worse governance than the world average.[95] According to industry analyst Stephen Ellis, "While oil will greatly increase the strategic importance of the region, it will also raise the stakes in the national politics of the states, many of whom have a worrisome record (at best) when it comes to political stability and good governance. The increase in oil royalties to the governments of the new Gulf's small island states—Sao Tome and Principe and Equatorial Guinea—is likely to more or less destroy their current economic production, leaving them as rentier states in the manner of some Persian Gulf emirates."[96] As described later in this volume, most Gulf of Guinea regimes are "neither stable nor democratic, and oil development in that context is likely to buttress authoritarian rule and foster corruption, instability and environmental destruction."[97] The role of oil in spawning and nurturing authoritarian regimes is clear, but perhaps a lesson the U.S. has not yet fully learned.

Learning from the Past

The analyses by Daukoru, Murphy, Royce, Goldwyn, Morrison and others have led us to write this book. Clearly, the oil resources of West and Central Africa will be increasingly vital to our nation's energy security. However, we believe that Africa is important to the U.S. for a host of reasons. Beyond the energy and other resources that are discussed in this volume, the U.S. has a clear interest in promoting democratization and improved security throughout the continent as a component of its Global War on Terror. To this end, we are convinced that there are lessons to be learned from our historical involvement with the oil-rich nations of the Middle East—specifically, by failing to adequately promote democratization and improved security throughout the region, our policies have contributed to the present-day challenges in the global security environment. As James Robbins observes, "the more money the United States sends to the [Middle East] region purchasing energy, the more is available to underwrite the terrorists and their beliefs by their state sponsors and other supporters in the region. This is an enduring pattern; since the oil shocks of the 1970s, the United States has sent uncounted billions of dollars into a region that has converted them into weapons of mass destruction programs, globally networked terrorist groups, and a hostile, internationally promoted anti-Western ideology."[98]

As we build new partnerships with the nations of West and Central Africa in the Gulf of Guinea, it is critical that we learn from that past if we are to avoid contributing to the rise of the same kind of conflict-prone "petro-states" that we have seen in the Middle East. As Congressman Ed Royce argues, "If done right, the development of Africa's energy resources will improve our nation's security, benefit our economy, and help lift African economies."[99] Just like the Middle East, issues of national security and energy security are closely intertwined in Africa, where recent oil discoveries combine with an emerging terrorist threat to warrant a new, integrated policy approach. Thus, in order to enhance energy security in Africa, this volume argues that lessons must be learned from what has gone wrong in the Middle East, and applied to our future efforts in the Gulf of Guinea.

Chapter 2 begins our analysis by exploring the potential this region holds in terms of increasing the global supply of energy. This is followed by a chapter focused on the challenges of governance and political stability that have historically plagued the region, and another chapter focused on the emerging terrorist threats in West Africa. Chapter 5 expands the core argument of this volume—if the United States is going to get more involved in the Gulf of Guinea, it "must not repeat the mistakes of the Persian Gulf"[100]—by exploring in detail the history of U.S. relations with key oil-rich states in the Middle East, and highlights some of the "mistakes" we should avoid in our emerging relationship with the countries of West and Central Africa.

The analysis of U.S.-Middle East history provided here reveals disturbing realities that are directly connected to the extraction of oil: political corruption, lack of political and social development, critical levels of economic dependence on a single national resource, and increasingly dissatisfied young populations with limited prospects for a brighter future. Following this discussion, Chapter 6 reviews contemporary U.S. policies in the Gulf of Guinea, highlighting both successes and challenges. The next chapter presents the argument that African energy resource exploitation requires synchronized improvements in human security, neo-liberal economic development, and democratization. The chapter also introduces a policy framework for U.S.-Africa relations that may be useful for planning and implementing more coherent and effective policy in the future.

The framework proposed in Chapter 7 is structured around three essential foundations for U.S.-Africa policy: security, economic development, and democratization. Security is an absolute prerequisite for both economic development and democratization. Economic development is the second priority after human security, and is arguably more important to most citizens of underdeveloped countries than is democracy. Democratization, adapted to local culture and unique national factors, is what will guarantee stability by institutionalizing peaceful mechanisms for political compromise and thereby strengthening the relationship between the society and the state. Three requirements for effectively implementing the framework—interagency coordination, public-private partnerships, and multilateral cooperation—are also identified in this chapter. Together, these elements will determine the nation's ability to realize our core energy security and national security goals. Following this discussion, the remaining chapters of the volume explore in depth each of these essential foundations and implementation requirements, and a concluding chapter offers an integrative summary of the analyses, arguments, and recommendations presented in the volume.

Conclusion

In a recent keynote address at a conference on West Africa's offshore petroleum industry, Nigeria's President Olusegun Obasanjo remarked that "as we continue to take giant strides in the oil and gas industry, it is my belief that issues which hold the promise to add value to our national economies, through harnessing of our human capacity and materials resources, should be actively debated. This should ensure that we reap the abundant blessings of this transforming resource, while avoiding its damning curses of corruption, rent-seeking and indolence, factors as relevant to Nigeria as they are to be pondered by our sub-regional neighbors that are yet to join the club of major producers."[101]

This volume argues that the U.S. must play an active role in this evolving and important effort, as opposed to our history of being more passive bystanders—or worse, enablers of forces which prevent real economic and political development. Our research indicates that long-term national security for the U.S. will prove elusive unless our energy security interests are pursued alongside coordinated efforts to increase state legitimacy and good governance in oil producing countries worldwide. This argument is particularly salient when building our relationships with the oil-rich countries of West and Central Africa in the Gulf of Guinea, where a complex history of external and internal factors have led to an overall decline in the standard of living for most people.

Based on an historical analysis of oil extraction in the Middle East, it becomes clear that securing unfettered access to oil for multinational extraction corporations without commensurate investments in socioeconomic and political improvement does not bode well for achieving long-term energy security and national security goals. Thus, as the U.S. moves forward in developing the energy extraction industry in the Gulf of Guinea, it must demand transparency in public financial transactions, respect for human rights, and a social and economic environment governed by the rule of law. Further, the U.S. must be prepared to take decisive action when states fail to make progress in these areas. We have already seen what happens when an over-reliance on a particular region's petroleum results in a lack of commitment to such basic principles.

Indeed, the annals of oil extraction are an uninterrupted chronicle of naked aggression, exploitation, and the violent mores of the corporate frontier.[102] Decades of oil extraction in the Middle East have resulted in a widespread image of the U.S. as a global parasite, feeding off Middle Eastern petroleum reservoirs and propping up malevolent and greedy autocratic states, and this has undoubtedly contributed to the challenges of global terrorism. The U.S. did not demand transparency or infrastructure development in the Middle East, nor was there much visible policy integration or interagency cooperation. Various security-related initiatives, particularly in Saudi Arabia and Kuwait, were not pursued alongside a democratization agenda. Overall, as the past several years have demonstrated, the goals and objectives of U.S. national security have to some degree been jeopardized by the achievement of our energy acquisition goals.

This is not a call to closely regulate the oil industry's activities in Africa. Nor is this a treatise for interfering in the affairs of the sovereign state governments of sub-Saharan Africa. Rather, we offer a rationale for ensuring that the transactions of U.S. oil companies and the approaches by the U.S. government's energy policy communities in Africa do not lead to long-term negative impacts on U.S. national security. Given some of the lessons learned from the recent history of the Middle East, it is clearly in the nation's best interests to do so. Throughout sub-Saharan Africa, a combination of economic failure, high birth rates, disease, corruption, and crumbling infrastructure threaten social disintegration and governmental collapse. And yet, this is the century in which we will witness great political, social and economic advancements throughout the African continent. The U.S. can and should be a vital and supportive partner in this process. The current situation in sub-Saharan Africa offers a significant opportunity to avoid repeating the mistakes made in the Middle East that have contributed to the current environment of global insecurity. The extraction of oil should no longer result in the same patterns of theft, greed, corruption, and authoritarianism. This is not an opportunity to be lost; this is a chance to get it right.

Notes

1. *BP Statistical Review of World Energy, 2005.* Available online at: http://www.bp.com/genericsection.do?categoryId=92&contentId=7005893

2. Institute for the Analysis of Global Security, "The Future of Oil," 2003. Available online at: http://www.iags.org/futureofoil.html

3. Daniel L. Goldwyn, "Extracting Transparency," *Georgetown Journal of International Affairs* (Winter/Spring 2004): 7

4. Institute for the Analysis of Global Security, "The Future of Oil" (2003), 1

5. David R. Francis, "Fueling War," *Christian Science Monitor,* 5 December 2002.

6. For example, see Michael T. Klare, *Resource Wars: The New Landscape of Global Conflict* (New York: Henry Holt and Company, LLC, 2001).

7. Institute for the Analysis of Global Security, "The Future of Oil," 2003.

8. Dan Henk, "U.S. National Interests in Sub-Saharan Africa," *Parameters* (Winter 1997-98): 95-96.

9. Timothy E. Wirth, C. Boyden Gray, and John D. Podesta, "The Future of Energy Policy," *Foreign Affairs* 82, no. 4 (July/August 2003): 134.

10. Stephen Ellis, "West Africa and its Oil," *African Affairs* 102 (January 2003): 135

11. Institute for the Analysis of Global Security, "The Future of Oil," 1.

12. *BP Statistical Review of World Energy, 2005.*

13. Unmesh Kher, "Breaking that Dirty Oil Habit," *Time Inside Business* (July 2005), A8

14. James A. Baker III Institute for Public Policy, "Energy and Nanotechnology: Strategy for the Future," Baker Institute Study no. 30 (April, 2005), 2

15. Baker Institute, "Energy and Nanotechnology," 2

16. Bill Griffith, "A Motorbike 167 Years in the Making," *Boston Globe,* 24 July 2005, J1.

17. Baker Institute "Energy and Nanotechnology," 4.

18. Richard Cheney, Speech at the Cato Institute, 23 June 1998.

19. Paul Collier and Anke Hoeffler, *Greed and Grievance in Civil War*, Policy Research Working Paper 2355, World Bank Development Research Group (May 2000).

20. Molly Farneth, "Powering Foreign Policy: The Role of Oil in Diplomacy and Conflict," Energy Security Initiative Report (New York: Physicians for Social Responsibility, October 2004), 7.

21. John Mitchell with Koji Morita, Norman Selley and Jonathan Stern, *The New Economy of Oil: Impacts on Business, Geopolitics and Society* (Royal Institute of International Affairs/Earthscan, London, 2001).

22. Joel Brinkley, "U.S. Faults 4 Allies Over Forced Labor," *New York Times,* 4 June 2005

23. Michael T. Klare, "The Deadly Nexus: Oil, Terrorism, and America's National Security," *Current History* (December 2002): 415, 417, 419.

24. Scott Pegg, "Globalization and Natural Resource Conflicts," *Naval War College Review* 61, no. 4, (Autumn 2003): 87.

25. Klare, "The Deadly Nexus," 415.

26. Klare, "The Deadly Nexus," 415.

27. Pegg, "Globalization and Natural Resource Conflicts," 87.

28. Helge Bergesen and Torleif Haugland, "The Puzzle of Petro-States: A Comparative Study of Azerbaijan and Angola," unpublished paper cited in cited in Tony Hodges, *Angola from Afro-Stalinism to Petro-Diamond Capitalism* (Bloomington: Indiana University Press, 2001), 2.

29. For more on this, see Mick Moore, *Political Underdevelopment*, paper presented at the 10th Anniversary Conference of Development Studies Institute, London School of Economics, London, 7-8 September 2000; and United Nations Development Program, *Promoting Conflict Prevention and Conflict Resolution through Effective Governance: A Conceptual Survey and Literature Review* (New York: United Nations, 1991). Online at: *http://magnet.undp.org/Docs/crisis/mapexercise.htm.*

30. Philip Swanson, *Fueling Conflict: The Oil Industry and Armed Conflict,* Fafo Report 378, (Oslo, Norway: Program for International Cooperation and Conflict Resolution, Fafo Institute for Applied Social Science, March 2002), 7.

31. Swanson, *Fueling Conflict,* 7

32. Oystein Noreng, "The Predicament of the Gulf Rentier State," in *Oil in the Gulf: Obstacles to Democracy and Development,* edited by Daniel Heradstveit and Helge Hveem. London: Ashgate, 2004), 11.

33. U.S. Department of Commerce, National Technical Information Service (NTIS), "Saudi Arabia Interim Country Commercial Guide, FY 2005." Online at: http://strategis.ic.gc.ca/epic/internet/inimr-ri.nsf/en/gr126392e.html

34. Swanson, *Fueling Conflict,* 14

35. Terry Lynn Karl, *The Paradox of Plenty: Oil Booms and Petro-States* (Berkeley: University of California Press, 1997), 213.

36. Swanson, *Fueling Conflict,* 15

37. Hodges, *Angola,* 135

38. Swanson, *Fueling Conflict,* 15

39. See for example, *Petrostates - Predatory or Developmental?* Report by ECON Centre for Economic Analysis and Fridtjof Nansen Institute, Norway, October 2000; and Paul Collier, *Economic Causes of Civil Conflict and their Implications for Policy,* World Bank Development Research Group, 15 June 2000.

40. "Rioting Continues over Cuts in Subsidies," *Boston Globe,* 22 July 2005, A10.

41. Arthur A. Nwankwo, *Nigeria: The Stolen Billions* (Enugu, Nigeria: Fourth Dimension Publishers, 1999).

42. World Bank, *Country Brief: Venezuela,* 2003. Online at: http://lnweb18.worldbank.org/external/lac/lac.nsf/Countries/Venezuela

43. Hodges, *Angola,* 4

44. Swanson, *Fueling Conflict,* 7.

45. Transparency International, "Corruption is rampant in 60 countries" (Press release accompanying Corruption Perceptions Index 2004), released October 20, 2004. Online at: http://www.transparency.org

46. Transparency International, *Report on the Transparency International Global Corruption Barometer 2004,* December 9, 2004. Online at: http://www.transparency.org

47. Tony Hodges, *Angola from Afro-Stalinism to Petro-Diamond Capitalism.* Bloomington: Indiana University Press, 2001, p. 4.

48. For example, see Tony Hodges' description of this in Angola, in *Angola from Afro-Stalinism to Petro-Diamond Capitalism* (Bloomington: Indiana University Press, 2001) including p. 139-140 and other sections, and A.A. Nwankwo's description of this in Nigeria, in *Nigeria the Stolen Billions* (Enugu, Nigeria: Fourth Dimension Publishing Co., 1999).

49. Helge Bergesen and Torleif Haugland, "The Puzzle of Petro-States: A Comparative Study of Azerbaijan and Angola," unpublished paper cited in Hodges, p. 171.

50. Claude Ake, *Democracy and Development in Africa* (Washington, DC: Brookings Institution, 1996), 117.

51. BBC News, "Shell Admits Fueling Corruption," June 10, 2004.

52. Anthony Goldman, "Who Benefits from Africa's Oil," BBC News, March 9, 2004.

53. United Nations Office on Drugs and Crime, "Transnational Organized Crime in the West African Region," June 2005, 7.

54. Bob Simon, "Kuwait of Africa?" CBS News, November 14, 2003. Online at http://www.cbsnews.com/stories/2003/11/14/60minutes

55. Terrence O'Hara and Kathleen Day, "Ex-Riggs Manager Won't Testify About Accounts," Washington Post, July 15, 2004.

56. In May 2005, FBI agents arrested Simon Kareri, the former senior vice president at Riggs who was in charge of all the Equatorial Guinea accounts. He and his wife were arraigned in federal court on charges of fraud, conspiracy and money laundering, making them the first individuals held accountable for what has become known as the Riggs Bank money laundering scandal. Meanwhile, Riggs has closed all its Equatorial Guinea accounts (see the Written Statement of Riggs Bank N.A., to the Permanent Subcommittee on Investigations of the Committee on Governmental Affairs of the U.S. Senate, July 15, 2004).

57. U.S. Senate Probe Reveals Massive Theft of Oil Revenue, UN Integrated News Networks, July 16, 2004.

58. Terrence O'Hara and Kathleen Day, "Ex-Riggs Manager Won't Testify About Accounts," Washington Post, July 15 2004.

59. Scott Pegg, "Globalization and Natural Resource Conflicts," *Naval War College Review* 61(4), (Autumn 2003), 89.

60. Pegg, "Globalization and Natural Resource Conflicts," 89.

61. Pegg, "Globalization and Natural Resource Conflicts," 89.

62. Pegg, "Globalization and Natural Resource Conflicts," 90.

63. Scott Pegg, "The Cost of Doing Business: Transnational Corporations and Violence in Nigeria," Security Dialogue (December 1999), pp. 475-479.

64. Bronwenn Manby, "The Role and Responsibility of Oil Multinationals in Nigeria," *Journal of International Affairs* (Fall 1999), p. 298, cited in Scott Pegg, "Globalization and Natural Resource Conflicts," *Naval War College Review* 61(4), (Autumn 2003), 91.

65. Daniel Volman, *Oil, Arms and Violence in Africa.* African Security Research Project, Washington, DC, February 2003.

66. http://www.unocal.com/responsibility/humanrights/hr4.htm, cited in Swanson, p. 25.

67. *Code of Conduct,* TotalFinaElf, 2000, cited in Swanson, 25.

68. Pegg, "Globalization and Natural Resource Conflicts," 90.

69. Ibid.

70. Paul Reynolds, "Oil and Conflict: A Natural Mix," BBC News, April 20, 2004.

71. Anne Korin and Gal Luft, "Terrorism Goes to Sea," *Foreign Affairs* (November/December 2004).

72. James S. Robbins, "No Blood for Oil," National Review Online, July 12, 2005. Online at: http://www.nationalreview.com/robbins/robbins200507120857.asp

73. For more on oil pipeline vulnerabilities and attacks, see: http://www.iags.org/n0328051.htm

74. From an audiotape address released on Islamic websites on December 16, 2004, as transcribed by and posted at http://www.jihadunspun.com on December 24, 2004. See also, the al Qalah website: https://www.qal3ah.org/vb/index.php? This address is discussed in greater detail in chapter 3 of this volume, and an English transcript is provided as an Appendix to this book.

75. Neil Ford, "U.S. Targets West African Oil," *Energy Economist,* London August 2003, #262, 1.

76. Bush also visited Uganda, Algeria and South Africa in July 2003. Neil Ford, "U.S. Targets West African Oil," *Energy Economist,* London August 2003, #262, 1.

77. *Africa Policy Outlook 2004*, Booker and Colgan; http://www.fpif.org.

78. Center for Strategic and International Studies (CSIS), estimates taken from "West Africa Petroleum Sector: Oil Value Forecast and Distribution" , prepared by PFC Energy and included as Appendix A in *Rising U.S. Stakes in Africa*, a CSIS Panel Report, 2004.

79. U.S. Department of Energy's International Energy Outlook 2003, accessed on the web at: http://www.eia.doe.gov/oiaf/ieo/oil.html.

80. Edmund Daukoru, "Address on the Occasion of the Signing of the Production Sharing Contract (Psc) in Respect of Block 01 in the Nigeria-Sao Tome and Principe Joint Development Zone," February 1, 2005.

81. Nigeria is the obvious exception, with a large, active Muslim minority. However, this population is almost entirely located in the north of the country, far from the oil and gas producing regions in the Niger delta.

82. Neil Ford, "U.S. Targets West African Oil," 1.

83. Neil Ford, "U.S. Targets West African Oil," 1.

84. Neil Ford, "U.S. Targets West African Oil," 1.

85. Stephen Ellis, "West Africa and its Oil," *African Affairs,* 102 (Jan 2003), p. 135.

86. Neil Ford, "U.S. Targets West African Oil," *Energy Economist,* London August 2003, #262, p. 1.

87. Jacinta Moran, "Three Majors Promise to Continue Push in African Upstream," Platt's Oilgram News, New York, Oct. 23, 2003, Vol. 81, Issue 205, 2.

88. Moran, "Three Majors Promise to Continue Push in African Upstream," 2.

89. Moran, "Three Majors Promise to Continue Push in African Upstream," 2.

90. Charles W. Corey, "Gulf of Guinea of Increasing Importance: West African Nations Critical to U.S. Energy Security," *The Washington File,* July 22, 2004 (Bureau of International Information Programs, U.S. Department of State). Online at: http://usinfo.state.gov.

91. Charles W. Corey, "Gulf of Guinea of Increasing Importance."

92. Charles W. Corey, "Gulf of Guinea of Increasing Importance."

93. J. Stephen Morrison, "The Gulf Of Guinea and U.S. Strategic Energy Policy," Testimony before the Subcommittee on International Economic Policy, Export and Trade Promotion, Committee on Foreign Relations, United States Senate, July 15, 2004. Available Online at: http://foreign.senate.gov/testimony/ 2004/MorrisonTestimony040715.pdf

94. Morrison, "The Gulf Of Guinea and U.S. Strategic Energy Policy."

95. Daniel Kaufmann, Aart Kraay, and Massimo Mastruzzi, *Governance Matters IV: New Data, New Challenges.* Washington, DC: The World Bank, May 2005.

96. Stephen Ellis, "West Africa and its Oil," *African Affairs,* 102 (Jan 2003), p 136.

97. Terry Karl, political science professor at Stanford University, as quoted by Ken Silverstein, "U.S. Oil Politics in the 'Kuwait of Africa'," *The Nation,* vol. 274, no. 15, (April 22, 2002).

98. James S. Robbins, "No Blood for Oil," National Review Online, July 12, 2005. Online at: http://www.nationalreview.com/robbins/robbins200507120857.asp.

99. Representative Ed Royce (R-CA), Chair of the House Subcommittee on Africa, June 12, 2002. Statement prepared for the "African Oil Policy Initiative Group." Online at: http://www.royce.house.gov/News/DocumentSingle.aspx?DocumentID=855

100. A paper of symposium proceedings, "African Oil: A Priority for U.S. National Security and African Development," is available online at: http://www.israeleconomy.org/strategic/africatranscript.pdf

101. Olusegun Obasanjo, "Capacity Building and the Challenges of Realizing and Enhancing the Potentials of Nigerian and West African Offshore Petroleum Industry,"

Keynote Address at the Offshore West Africa Conference and Exhibition, March 17, 2004.

102. Douglas *et al.*

Chapter 2
A Region of Opportunities and Challenges

During the Cold War, several nations of Africa were seen by many U.S. policy-makers as quasi-battlegrounds in the global ideological struggle between democracy and communism. After the Cold War, Africa appeared to lose its strategic value to the United States, which began withdrawing its presence from the continent throughout the early 1990s. By 1993, the State Department's Bureau of African Affairs had lost more than 60 posts, with similar staff reductions the Africa desk for USAID and other agencies. In 1996, the U.S. Institute for National Strategic Studies noted that "the United States has essentially no serious military/geostrategic interests in Africa any more, other than the inescapable fact that its vastness poses an obstacle to deployment in the Middle East and South Asia."[1] In 1999, renowned African scholar George Ayittey observed that "the United States has all but disengaged from Africa. It resolutely refused to send peacekeeping troops to Liberia . . . . Donor governments have become fed up with Africa's incessant crises, onerous misrule, and grotesque mismanagement and have been reducing their Africa aid budgets."[2]

However, as observed in the previous chapter, the U.S. now has a renewed interest in Africa, specifically those countries that have the potential for helping us achieve our nation's energy security and national security objectives. An ExxonMobil advertisement that appeared on the Op-Ed page of the *New York Times* on November 1, 2001, entitled "Africa: A Wealth of Opportunity," was timed to influence the third biennial United States-Africa Business Summit in Philadelphia, a meeting of industry and government leaders on American business opportunities in Africa.[3] The Departments of Energy and Commerce have supported U.S. oil interests with official trade missions and ministerials, while executive branch officials have made unprecedented trips as well, like Senator Chuck Hagel's 2004 visit to Angola, and President Bush's 2003 visit to Algeria, Nigeria, South Africa, and Uganda. In fact, President Bush has met with over 20 African heads of state since 2001, and over a half-dozen of his cabinet members have visited Africa.[4] The U.S. recently broke ground on a new embassy in the

25

Angolan capitol, Luanda, and re-opened its embassy in Equatorial Guinea, which had been closed since the mid-1990s.

Overall, sub-Saharan Africa has become an increasingly important U.S. foreign policy consideration, and the subcontinent's strategic importance to the U.S. in the realm of energy security has been widely documented. For example, Robert Murphy, an economic specialist with the State Department's Office of African Analysis, noted in 2003 that "under current projections, we will import 770 million barrels of African petroleum in 2020."[5] The continent's importance to the U.S. in the realm of national security, particularly as a strategic partner in the global war on terror, will be discussed in later chapters of this volume.

Africa in the early years of the 21st century offers an array of both challenges and opportunities to most observers. Among the most critical challenges is the impact of widespread poverty: the continent contains 32 of the world's 48 poorest countries, and the number of people estimated to be living in extreme poverty has doubled in the last two decades.[6] Indeed, British Prime Minister Tony Blair recently observed that Africa is the only continent to have grown poorer in the last 25 years.[7] Poor governance is partly to blame. The economies of Africa have experienced little structural transformation, one manifestation of which has been limited export diversification. Most countries of the region remain highly dependent on primary production and export. In many cases, export earnings are dominated by one or two commodities—for example, coffee is the most dominant, or one of the two most dominant, export commodities in several countries. As a result, Africa's economic and political stability are extremely vulnerable to a variety of shocks, both internal and external. In virtually all the countries of Africa—including those with a healthy endowment of oil or other resources—the infrastructure (power supply, roads, telecommunications, health services, etc.) is in significant need of improvement. Africa has the lowest primary school completion rates of any continent today, while average life expectancy has declined from 50 to 46 years since 1990.[8] Recurrent droughts and famines stalk the countryside. In short, a history of civil war, political corruption, and a variety of both natural and man-made catastrophes frame our contemporary view of Africa's future.

And yet, the promise of a new, more positive African story is emerging. The African Union recently launched a new Peer Review Mechanism, an initiative meant to promote good governance, and a new Peace and Security Council, aimed at the prevention, management and resolution of conflict in the continent.[9] In the past several years, some (but certainly not all) elections that have taken place throughout Africa can be considered significantly democratic. In 2005, Africa's economy grew by 5%—the best performance in eight years—although only a small handful of countries are expected to meet the United Nations' Millennium Development Goals of reducing poverty, hunger, disease, illiteracy, environmental degradation, and discrimination.[10]

Writing of his experiences leading a World Bank project in Equatorial Guinea during the 1980s, Robert Klitgaard observed that "Africa is the world's basket case. But it also has smiles and guitar solos and an awesome ability to persevere."[11] Indeed, bright spots do exist throughout the continent. The push for democracy has seen a variety of African countries holding multiparty elections in the last five years, while several nations have seen health and education budgets significantly increased, and 24 nations saw economic growth in excess of 5% in 2003.[12]

The wealthy countries of Asia, Europe and North America are showing increasing interest in promoting a better future for Africa. At the July 2005 G-8 Summit,[13] the leaders of the world's most industrialized countries agreed to an unprecedented $50 billion aid package for the developing world—the majority of it targeted toward the nations of Africa. These nations also agreed to cancel the multilateral debt of the 18 poorest countries of the world; all but four of them are in Africa.[14] Some observers of these policy decisions argue that they are motivated not by a renewed sense of humanitarian generosity towards Africa, but rather, because recent discoveries of oil and natural gas have propelled the states of sub-Saharan Africa into the limelight for enterprising private sector firms and government agencies throughout the West and Asia.[15] Clearly, as Table 2.1 indicates, the oil-producing countries of West Africa will play an important role in the world's oil markets.

Table 2.1: Reserves and Production, 2004

	2004 Reserves	2004 Daily Production
	Billion barrels	Barrels
Algeria	11.8	1,933,000
Angola*	8.8	991,000
Chad*	0.9	62,000
Cameroon*	0.4	168,000
Rep. of Congo (Brazzaville)*	1.8	240,000
Egypt	3.6	708,000
Equatorial Guinea*	1.3	350,000
Gabon*	2.3	235,000
Libya	39.1	1,607,000
Nigeria*	35.3	2,508,000
Sudan	6.3	301,000
Tunisia	0.6	69,000
Other Africa	0.5	92,000
Total Africa	**112.2**	**9,264,000**

Source: BP Statistical Review of World Energy, 2005.
Note: * Indicates country is located in western Africa, most of which border the Gulf of Guinea.

Jeff Shellbarger, ChevronTexaco's general manager for asset development in southern Africa, has stated that his company plans to invest $20 billion in energy-related projects in Africa over the next five years, after investing a total of $5 billion in the past five years. The company already has significant operations in eight Africa countries including Nigeria, Angola, and Equatorial Guinea. "By 2010, one out of every five barrels of oil consumed globally will come from west and south Africa," Shellbarger said.[16]

The importance of Africa to meeting the energy needs of the United States is clear—nearly 18% of our oil comes from the region. As seen in Table 2.2, the majority of African countries from which the U.S. imports oil are located in the west of the continent, particularly along the Gulf of Guinea.

Table 2.2: Net Imports of Oil (Crude and Products) into the U.S. from African Countries, January through April 2004

	Imports (barrels) per day
Algeria	400,000
Angola*	309,000
Cameroon*	30,000
Chad*	34,000
Congo Brazzaville*	13,000
Democratic Republic of Congo*	6,000
Egypt	5,000
Gabon*	134,000
Ivory Coast*	2,000
Nigeria*	1,130,000
Tunisia	1,000
Total African Imports	2,030,000
Total U.S. Global Oil Imports	11,405,000
African Percentage of Total Oil Imports	17.8%

Note: * Indicates country is located in western Africa, most of which border the Gulf of Guinea.

Source: John R. Brodman, Statement to the Subcommittee on International Economic Policy, Export and Trade Promotion, Committee on Foreign Relations, U.S. Senate, July 15, 2004.

Indeed, according to Daniel Yergin, chairman of Cambridge Energy Research Associates, "there is a lot of excitement about West Africa [in the oil industry]. . . . Its politics may be complex, but the transportation and logistics are easier [than in the Persian Gulf]."[17] Robin West, chairman of the Petroleum Financing Company (a consulting firm for the oil industry), agrees: "West Africa in the near to medium term will be a more important source of oil to international markets than Russia."[18] And according to John Brodman, Deputy Assistant Secretary in the U.S. Department of Energy, "West Africa is the source of light, sweet crude oil critical for U.S. refining needs, and a key replacement for declining North Sea oil production."[19] The United Nations Conference on Trade and Development (UNCTAD) estimates that Angola will be exporting 3.28 million barrels per day and Nigeria 4.42 million, by 2020.[20]

Since 1999, oil discoveries off the western coast of Africa have been profound. According to Dr. Rilwanu Lukman, Secretary General of OPEC, "The hundreds of thousands of square kilometers of the sub-region's largely under-explored ultra-deep waters (that is, depths of 1,000 meters or more) would seem to make West Africa the crown jewel, as the most sought-after new frontier in the offshore industry."[21] Further, because most of the oil in this region is "light and sweet"—in other words, it is easy to pump and refine because it more fluid and has a low sulfur content—it is highly desirable to international oil companies. Since 1996, at least 21 oil discoveries in Angola have been made, and the country's reserves have jumped from 1.5 barrels per day in 1995 to 10.5 barrels per day in 2003.[22] Clearly, these countries will be of increasing strategic importance to the U.S. in the coming years.

However, despite the optimism focused on this region, oil industry executives have their reservations about the Gulf of Guinea—it is much more costly to lift, develop, drill, and gather oil and gas in offshore African locations than in the Middle East. Further, there are currently a limited number of oil rigs capable of extracting oil from deep water reserves. Granted, the technology in this area will dramatically improve within the next twenty years, and the proximity and high quality of the oil in the region are very attractive. But due to the significant capital expenses and technical difficulties projected, along with comparably lower proven reserve amounts, African oil will never replace the Middle East oil.[23] Nonetheless, given the politically volatile situation in the Middle East, many major multi-national energy companies have stepped up investment and exploration in this region over the last few years. Exxon-Mobil and Chevron-Texaco already have substantial investments in deep-water crude oil productions off the Angolan coast.[24] Houston, Texas is rapidly becoming the American gateway to West Africa, with non-stop flights to places like Malabo and Luanda, the capitol cities of Equatorial Guinea and Angola.

Other nations are also looking to this region to help address their own energy needs. For example, each day at least 1.3 million barrels of West African crude oil are being shipped to Asia, where demand is being driven largely by explosive economic growth in China. The region's oil imports have risen steadily over the past several years, and Chinese firms such as Kanqi, Unipec and Sinopec have increased their presence throughout West Africa. Thus, as the U.S. seeks greater energy security, it will have to do so in the context of a global market.[25]

As one of many oil-consuming nations, U.S. foreign policy has the greatest potential to affect global energy security through building bilateral relations with governments of oil-producing states and encouraging these nations to engage in good governance.[26] The remainder of this chapter thus sets out to explore the governance challenges that warrant consideration by policymakers and industry leaders. We begin by briefly reviewing significant political, social and economic issues in each country of this unique and complex region, and how their governments have used revenues derived from the activities of the global oil industry. This discussion will be followed by a comparative analysis of the contemporary governance challenges in this region, and will highlight key areas of interest to the central argument that U.S. energy security warrants a fresh look at how we build a mutually beneficial relationship with these countries.

Angola

Only two men—from the same political party, the Popular Movement for the Liberation of Angola *(Movimento Popular de Libertação de Angola* or MPLA)—have ruled Angola, a country which from 1975 to 2002 was embroiled in one of the world's longest and bloodiest civil wars. [27] In all, up to 1.5 million lives may have been lost and 4 million people displaced during the quarter century of fighting. The government has also struggled to contain a separatist movement in the oil-rich Cabinda province. Similar to the Niger Delta region of Nigeria, political tension and violence in Cabinda stems from demands among the province's population for a greater share of oil revenue. These longstanding conflicts have had a lasting impact on Angola's economic and political history, and are particularly important when examining the country's relationship with the oil industry. Indeed, since the mid-1970s, oil production in the region—led by Gulf Cabinda, a subsidiary of Gulf Oil Corporation—helped support the MPLA government in their fight against guerilla movements and separatists, as described in Chapter 3 of this volume.

Oil in Angola

Sub-Saharan Africa's second largest oil producer (behind Nigeria), Angola has estimated oil reserves of between five and nine billion barrels, although these estimates have been rising with new offshore discoveries. A country nearly twice the size of Texas, much of Angola's potential resource endowment remains unexplored. Angola is not a member of OPEC, and thus has comparatively more autonomy than other oil-rich countries in adjusting its current production output of 1.07 million barrels per day.[28] In fact, the country's stated goal is to increase oil production to 2 million barrels per day by 2008—a goal they are predicted to reach when new deep-water production sites begin operating at higher levels.[29]

Oil production began in Angola in 1955, following the discovery of oil onshore in the Kwanza basin. This was followed, during the 1960s, by the discovery and development of oilfields off the coast of the Cabinda province, where production began in 1968. By 1973, oil had become the country's largest source of export earnings, overtaking coffee.[30] In 1976, the Angolan government established a national oil company, SONANGOL (*the Sociedade Nacional de Combustiveis*), and passed a petroleum law in 1978 which made the state the sole owner of the country's petroleum deposits. This law also established SONANGOL as the exclusive contracting agent for oil exploration and development, while permitting the state company to enter into associations with foreign companies to obtain the resources needed for oil exploration, development and production.[31]

During the 1980s and 1990s, successful shallow water exploration, particularly by Chevron in Cabinda and by Elf and Texaco off the estuary of the Congo river, led to substantial new investments in development and a steady rise in production. The application of new deep water technology, pioneered in other oil extraction zones like the North Sea, was particularly successful in locating and extracting resources even further off the Angolan coast. Overall, during the 1990s, Angola was the most successful non-OPEC country in the world for oil exploration, raising its proven reserves almost fourfold.[32] By 2000, Angola's production was approaching 800,000 barrels a day, or almost six times higher than it had been in 1980.[33] However, with the exception of about 40,000 barrels per day that is delivered to the country's sole refinery in Luanda, all oil production is exported.[34]

Today, Angola provides 4% of U.S. oil imports, and the United States buys more than half of all the oil that Angola produces.[35] ChevronTexaco now pumps 60% of Angolan oil, and plans to invest $4 billion in Angolan development projects through 2008.[36] British Petroleum (BP) is set to increase their output of Angolan oil from 50,000 barrels per day to 250,000 in 2007, after winning a large concession from SONANGOL of six offshore fields in the northwest region of Angola. Much of the country's oil wealth lies in the province of Cabinda, where a decades-long separatist conflict is simmering—a conflict driven not by cultural or ethnic differences (as found in most of the world's separatist movements) but rather, driven by a demand for greater control over the region's vast oil wealth. Although Cabinda accounts for nearly all of Angolan foreign exchange earnings, the province receives only 10% of taxes paid by ChevronTexaco and its partners operating offshore Cabinda. Since the 1960s, separatist groups like the *Frente para a Libertação do Enclave de Cabinda-Renovata* (FLEC-R; Front for the Liberation of the Enclave of Cabinda) have demanded that a greater share of oil revenue remain in the poverty stricken province, often kidnapping foreign nationals to draw attention to their cause.

In response, the government has sent thousands of troops to subdue the rebellion in the province, which does not share a border with the rest of Angola. The strategic importance of Cabinda, as the source of about 70% of Angola's current oil production,[37] is almost certainly the main motive for separation and also an iron-clad reason why Angola's government would never consider letting

the province secede. For the Cabindans, the material benefits of secession would
be quite staggering. With a population of only about 110,000 and oil exports of
$2.5 billion (1995-1997), Cabinda would be one of the richest countries in the
developing world in per capita terms. Its net annual earnings from oil might well
be close to $11,000 per capita, making it sort of a tropical mini-Kuwait. This
dazzling prospect is almost certainly a far more powerful motive for secession
than any sense of ethnic identity or economic injustice. [38]

Governance in Angola

According to African scholar Tony Hodges, "one of the best resource endowments in Africa has been associated not with development but with years of conflict, economic decline and human misery on a massive scale." In describing the
"terrible, shocking paradox" of Angola's experience with huge oil reserves (as
well as diamonds), Hodges notes that "if these resources were managed properly, Angola's economy would be among the most dynamic in the developing
world. Its people would be among the best fed, best educated and healthiest on
the African continent." Instead, he notes, Angola is a deeply-indebted nation,
heavily reliant on imported goods and at the mercy of fluctuations in oil market
prices. "Social services such as health and education are in a state of advanced
decay, resulting in widespread illiteracy and appalling health conditions. Angola
now has the second highest child mortality rate in the world: Almost a third of
children die before they reach the age of five." [39]

Despite the current production of just over a million barrels of oil a day, the
vast majority of Angola's 11 million people live in poverty, and only 15% have
access to electric power. Telephone lines reach only five out of every 1,000 Angolans, and roads—many of them filled with landmines—have not been repaired
for decades. According to a recent UN Development Report, unemployment is
estimated at over 50%, and more than half the population is malnourished, lacking access to clean water or health services. [40] Angola's external debt in 2004
was estimated at over $10 billion, the highest of any country in the Gulf of
Guinea. [41] Overall, as reflected in Table 2.3, by many standards Angola can
clearly be considered a poor, developing country.

Much of the government's challenges stem from over 30 years of civil war;
a conflict that destroyed much of the nation's infrastructure, economy, and
workforce, and has only subsided in the last few years. However, another source
of tension is a widespread perception of government incompetence and corruption. Government officials and oil executives live in villas behind security walls
and barbed wire, while most Angolans—even in the capital city of Luanda—
stay in crumbling cement-block huts without electricity or running water.

Table 2.3: Important Facts about Angola

Population	11,190,786 (July 2005 est.)
Median Age	18.12 years
Avg. Life Expectancy	36.61 years
GDP	$35.1 billion (2004 est.)
GDP Per Capita	$2,525 (2004 est.)
GDP Growth, 2004	11.7% (2004 est.)
Population below poverty line	70% (2003 est.)
External Debt	$10.45 billion (2004 est.)
Literacy [1]	42%
UN Human Development Index Ranking [2]	166
Probability at birth of not surviving to age 40 (% of 2000-2005 cohort)	49%
Population without sustainable access to an improved water source	62%
Physicians per 100,000 people [3]	5
Malaria cases per 100,000 people	8,733
Public Expenditures:	
on education (2001)	2.8%
on health (2001)	2.8%
on the military (2002)	3.7%
on debt service (2002)	7.7%
Armed Forces (2002)	100,00

Sources: *2005 CIA Factbook*, 2004 UN Human Development Index, and U.S. Department of State, Bureau of Africa Affairs.

Notes:
[1] Defined as the percentage of the population age 15 and over who can read and write.
[2] A total of 177 countries are ranked in the 2004 UN Human Development Index. Higher numbers indicate poorer performance on a collection of indicators. http://hdr.undp.org/reports/global/2004
[3] By comparison, a typical industrialized country has 200-300 physicians per 100,000 people.

The petroleum industry in Angola is an extreme case of an enclave sector, with minimal linkages to the rest of the economy, except through the redistributive mechanisms of government revenue and expenditures. As a capital-intensive industry, it creates few local jobs: in all, it employs about 10,00 Angolans, half of whom work for SONANGOL.[42] Angola's public revenue has been allocated primarily to military expenditure, the running costs of the public administration (government consumption) and transfers for subsidies to keep ailing state companies afloat or to subsidize official prices, notably for petroleum products, water and electricity. During the late 1990s, annual expenditure on defense and internal security accounted for 32% of total government expenditure. When the war resumed in 1999, this rose to 41%.[43]

Each year, a large portion of Angola's oil wealth goes unaccounted for. The International Monetary Fund claims that $4 billion of oil revenue disappeared from Angola's treasury between 1997 and 2001, accusing the state oil company, SONANGOL, as the largest source of diverted funds.[44] Recent reports by the World Bank and by Transparency International both rank Angola as one of the worst countries in the world for corruption.[45] As seen in many other oil-rich countries, President dos Santos has astutely cultivated his political base and built alliances, through forms of legalized patronage, or what some have termed "clientalist redistribution."[46] Cronyism, through which part of the oil revenues is transferred (legally or illegally) to the elite, thus provides an important incentive to maintain the lack of transparency. For example, when British Petroleum recently announced its intention to make public its various payments to the Angolan government, the Dos Santos regime reportedly threatened the company with the loss of its oil concessions.[47]

The lack of transparency in government finances is intertwined with a system of oil-collateralized financing of imports, under which loans and credit lines for the government are tied to future shipments of oil by the state oil company, SONANGOL. This complex triangular relationship between SONANGOL, the Treasury, and the central bank has created what Hodges calls a "black hole" for the country's oil revenues, making it virtually impossible to know who has grown rich from Angola's oil, or by how much.[48] Angola's oil revenues have basically been used to finance large military expenditures and sustain basic government operations, while providing minimal services and subsidies for the country's largely unproductive but swollen urban regions and thus helping to maintain social peace in the cities. During the late 1990s, annual expenditure on defense and internal security accounted for 32% of total government expenditure. When the war resumed in 1999, this rose to 41%.[49] By contrast, very little public money has gone to investments in infrastructure and human capital, which are critical for development and economic diversification.[50]

Corruption and mismanagement has dramatic implications for the continued impoverishment and political unrest of the Angolan people. According to Stephen Ellis, of Britain's Royal Africa Society, "In Angola, oil has helped produce a wealthy elite living in enclave settlements, and a government that heavily invests in military forces while leaving the social services and welfare needs of its populations in the hands of international agencies." [51] Instead of social services and infrastructure development, revenues from oil wealth—running at well over $2 billion a year—finance the military and a government patronage system. Budgetary allocations for the social sectors have been far lower than in most African countries, or for investment in physical infrastructure, such as roads, railways, ports, electricity supply and water systems, all of which are in a critical state. Both public investment and non-oil private investment are extremely low relative to GDP. The poor physical infrastructure and low levels of human capital combine with other factors that discourage private sector investment, such as the unstable macroeconomic environment, the maze of bureaucratic regulations, a primitive financial services sector, the lack of safeguards resulting from a weak judicial system and the effects of an overvalued exchange rate on competitiveness.[52]

Compounding these challenges in Angola, the government's available resources fluctuate wildly when oil prices rise and fall. Over the past several decades, the government has become almost exclusively dependent on revenue from oil production: Angola's oil sector has accounted for over 80% of export earnings since the 1980s and for well over 90% of exports throughout the 1990s, except in 1998. The sector accounts for over 40% of gross domestic product (GDP) and 90% of government revenues.[53] There have been two particularly severe external shocks to Angola's economy in the past two decades. The first, in 1985-86, which marked the end of the period of high oil prices ushered in by OPEC in the 1970s, caused a 38% drop in Angola's oil sector exports in 1986, plunging the country into a debt trap from which it has yet to recover. Previous levels of borrowing had been premised on a level of oil prices that proved unrealistic. The country began building up external arrears from 1986, destroying its previously high credit rating in international financial markets and creating the situation which led to the mortgaging of oil resources for import financing in the 1990s.[54]

A similar external shock occurred in 1998, when the average price of Angolan crude fell to $12 a barrel and the value of oil exports fell by 33%. International reserves were almost completely exhausted by the beginning of 1999, when prices briefly dipped below $10 a barrel, and it became difficult for the government even to meet its commitments for the servicing of its oil-collateralized loans. This happened at a particularly bad time, as the country was returning to war and the government was engaging in major new military procurement contracts. The situation reversed in 1999, however, as a result of the dramatic recovery in oil prices, which rose above $30 in mid-2000, and the timely windfall that accrued to the government in the form of signature bonuses from the leasing of the first ultra-deep water blocks.[55]

Today, the external debt situation is one of the most significant challenges to the Dos Santos regime. Modest until the early 1980s, when it amounted to less than $3 billion, Angola's external debt rose rapidly between the mid-1980s and the mid-1990s, reaching more than $11 billion by 1995. At first, the main factors driving this surge in debt were the large loans negotiated with the former USSR in the 1980s for military procurement and ill-conceived capital projects. Later, after Angola began to default on its debt-service payments from the late 1980s, the stock of debt increased further as a result of the capitalization of interest arrears and the use of oil collateralized credits to finance imports of military equipment and consumer goods.[56]

By the late 1990s, almost all the oil physically available to the government through SONANGOL (amounting to almost half of the government's total oil revenue) was committed to the servicing of oil-guaranteed loans.[57] Thus, despite Angola's oil wealth, the government has had to borrow heavily on international markets, preferring to avoid IMF financing, presumably due to the governance conditions attached to such loans. A significant amount of future oil revenue has been used as collateral. This debt burden, compounded by mismanagement, corruption, the civil war and low oil prices, apparently eventually gave the Angolan government an incentive to work with the World Bank and IMF. In April 2000, the IMF and the Angolan government agreed on a Staff Monitoring Agreement, which set financial, fiscal and reform targets that the government must achieve in order to qualify for loans under the Enhanced Structural Adjustment Facility. This agreement included an "Oil Diagnostic" program to monitor the government's oil revenues between July and December 2000, by comparing export, tax and other earning from oil activities with deposits into the Central Bank of Angola. This program's limited scope means that it was not able to investigate discrepancies found, nor monitor how income was spent. The program also had to rely on the information that the Angolan government and the international oil companies were willing to supply. Information emerging from this program suggests that nearly $1.4 billion (about one-third of Angola's income from oil revenues) was unaccounted for in the year 2000.[58]

Overall, the intersection of oil and governance in Angola offers a striking example of the challenges that exist throughout the Gulf of Guinea. Here, the state relies heavily upon revenues derived from foreign extraction of a single, vital natural resource, and as a result, little attention is paid to diversifying the economy or fostering self-sufficient or entrepreneurial ventures. In this environment, control of the state is seen by individuals and groups as the primary means to a comfortable lifestyle, as opposed to any real desire to improve the living conditions for all the state's citizens. Unfortunately, a similar story is told in other countries of this important region.

Cameroon

Similar to Angola, Cameroon began its independence with a bloody insurrection and has been ruled by only two men from the same political party.[59] Oil extraction has played a vital role in Cameroon's national economy, and is controlled by the state oil company, the National Hydrocarbons Company. However, unlike Angola, the country benefited from considerable investment in agriculture, education, health care and transportation during the 20-year reign of President Ahmadou Ahidjo. In 1982, Mr. Ahidjo was succeeded by his prime minister, Paul Biya, who has remained in power—and has won several multi-party presidential elections—ever since. While Biya has continued much of his predecessor's policies, he has also sought to modernize the government, to include privatizing the state oil company.

Oil in Cameroon

Roughly the size of Montana and Wyoming combined, Cameroon has estimated oil reserves of 400 million barrels, and has been an important supplier to European energy markets. Reserves are located offshore in the Rio del Rey Basin of the Niger Delta, offshore and onshore in the Douala/Kribi-Camp basins on Cameroon's western coast, and onshore in the Logone-Birni basin in the northern part of the country.[60] The country is sub-Saharan Africa's sixth largest oil producer, but daily oil production has been in steady decline over the past few years. Oil production in 2005 is estimated at 50,000 barrels per day, down from 84,800 barrels per day in 2000.[61] If no major oil fields are discovered, current major oil fields will be depleted by 2010. However there are several areas of the country that have yet to be explored, including the offshore Logone Birni and Douala basins. But more significantly, two recent developments involving Cameroon's neighbors offer some hope to its future economic fortunes.

First, a massive oil field was discovered in the Doba basin of Chad, Cameroon's French-speaking neighbor to the northeast. However, because Chad is land-locked, a 663-mile pipeline was built through Cameroon in order for this oil to make its way to international markets. The pipeline runs from the Doba basin through southern Chad to the Cameroon border, where it continues through the Logone Birni Basin until it reaches the port of Kribi for export. Roughly 85% of the pipeline is located in Cameroon. Export facilities in Kribi include an onshore-pressure reduction station and a subsea pipeline connected to a floating production storage and offloading vessel (FPSO). The Tchad Oil Transport Company (TOTCO) and the Cameroon Oil Transport Company (COTCO) have respective ownership of each country's portion of the pipeline. The capacity of this new underground pipeline, which officially began operation in July 2003, is estimated at 225,000 barrels per day; production exceeded 200,000 bbl/d at times in 2004.[62] Cameroon will earn an estimated $0.46 on every barrel of oil transported through the pipeline, more than $500 million during the 25 to 30-year lifetime of the pipeline.[63]

Another positive development came in October 2002, when a ruling by the International Court of Justice (ICJ) awarded sovereignty of the oil-rich Bakassi peninsula to Cameroon. Ownership of this strategically important resource had long been claimed by both Nigeria and Cameroon, and the countries fought a border war in 1994 (and again, briefly, in 1996) over this disputed region. Following these skirmishes, Nigeria's forces (far larger and better-equipped than those of Cameroon) have occupied the peninsula for the past decade. By September 2004, Nigeria had failed to meet the deadline for the handover, and declared its rejection of the ICJ ruling.[64] Still, it is assumed that because the court ruling is recognized by the international community as valid and final, an eventual resolution to this situation will leave Cameroon in control of a new and important means by which to boost its declining oil industry.

Governance in Cameroon

Compared to most of the African continent, Cameroon's population of roughly 16 million have enjoyed relatively stable political and economic development, with real GDP growth averaging 4.5% annually over the last six years.[65] As Table 2.4 indicates, Cameroon also has one of the best literacy rates in Africa, and spends a higher level of public resources on education than any other Gulf of Guinea country.

Table 2.4: Important Facts about Cameroon

Population	16,380,005 (July 2005 est.)
Median Age	18.6 years
Avg. Life Expectancy	47.84 years
GDP	$30.17 billion (2004 est.)
GDP Per Capita	$1,900 (2004 est.)
GDP Growth, 2004	4.9% (2004 est.)
Population below poverty line	48% (2000 est.)
External Debt	$8.46 billion (2004 est.)
Literacy [1]	79%
UN Human Development Index Ranking [2]	141
Probability at birth of not surviving to age 40 (% of 2000-2005 cohort)	44%
Population without sustainable access to an improved water source	42%
Physicians per 100,000 people [3]	7
Malaria cases per 100,000 people	2,900
Public Expenditures:	
on education (2001)	5.1%
on health (2001)	1.2%
on the military (2002)	1.4%
on debt service (2002)	3.9%
Armed Forces (2002)	23,000

Sources: *2005 CIA Factbook* and 2004 UN Human Development Index.

Notes:
[1] Defined as the percentage of the population age 15 and over who can read and write.
[2] A total of 177 countries are ranked in the 2004 UN Human Development Index. Higher numbers indicate poorer performance on a collection of indicators. http://hdr.undp.org/reports/global/2004
[3] By comparison, a typical industrialized country has 200-300 physicians per 100,000 people.

However, despite the relatively positive indications that the country is on the right path, Cameroon's continued development is hampered by a level of corruption that is among the highest in the world.[66] Corruption is particularly rampant in the country's two natural resource export sectors: logging and oil. At the turn of the century, Transparency International classified Cameroon as "the most corrupt country in the world" for two consecutive years—a dubious distinction that even the government of Cameroon has recently come to acknowledge. According to Jean Marie Onana, the head of the Anti-Corruption Unit at the Ministry of the Economy and Finance, "When Cameroon topped the chart as the world champion of corruption, the entire nation was disturbed and traumatized. Some citizens considered it a betrayal or even a show of hatred for our country by certain donors or super powers. A closer look would, however, reveal that many indicators seem to confirm the classification in almost all sectors of national activity."[67] A rather peculiar sigh of relief was heard in some quarters when Transparency International's 2003 corruption survey ranked Cameroon 124 out of 133 countries, indicating either modest improvement here or a dramatic increase in corruption elsewhere. But real progress was seen in January 2005, when the government published the names of 73 top civil servants accused of embezzling public funds in local newspapers to spotlight its new anti-corruption drive.[68] Most of the doctors, prison directors and other prominent officials were said to have pocketed sums ranging from a modest 80,000 CFA francs (US $158) to 42 million CFA francs (US $83,000), in addition to equipment totaling 126 million CFA francs (US $249,000). The government naturally relieved these officials of their positions, and there is growing hope that the country is heading towards a greater, corruption-free era.[69]

In sum, Cameroon is a country that appears to be turning several corners at once. On the positive side, the government is investing in education and confronting a legacy of corruption. On the negative side, its economy is poised to suffer declining revenues as the country's oil resources dry up. Further exacerbating Cameroon's economic woes (and not unrelated to widespread corruption) is a tremendous external debt burden (an estimated $8.64 billion in 2004), the second highest in the Gulf of Guinea. Its recent partnership with neighboring Chad is thus not only good diplomatic cooperation; it is an economic necessity.

Chad

While technically not a Gulf of Guinea country, Chad relies on the Gulf as the sole means by which its vast oil fields in the Lake Chad basin (in the country's southwestern region) can be connected with the world's energy markets. Chad's landlocked status and geographic location thus requires significant cooperation with its Gulf neighbors, and faces many of the same governance and development challenges faced by all the countries in the Gulf of Guinea. For these reasons, Chad is included in this discussion.

Oil in Chad

Given the country's estimated 1.5 billion barrels of oil reserves, there is a rapidly growing amount of interest, development and investment in Chad.[70] As described above, the World Bank helped finance the construction of a $3.7 billion, 663-mile pipeline to transport Chadian oil through Cameroon and into ports along the Gulf of Guinea. This pipeline is the largest single private investment in Africa.[71] The cost of transporting Chadian oil through the pipeline and onto the global market consumes nearly 30% of the total oil revenues generated. A major portion of these transportation-related costs goes to recover the investments made by the shareholders of the pipeline companies. In fact, nearly 60% of the project's construction cost went to building the export system—with its pipeline, pumping stations and marine terminal—and roughly half of the project's day-to-day costs go to operating this system.[72]

Chad began producing oil for the first time in July 2003, and is currently producing over 200,000 barrels per day.[73] The U.S. is now receiving approximately 34,000 barrels per day of oil from Chad that did not exist just a few years ago.[74] In November 2003, the country received its first oil payment about into an account at Citibank London for dispersal according to World Bank expenditure terms, and by the end of 2004 Chad had received a total of $149 million in royalties from the sale of roughly 70 million barrels of oil.[75] While these royalty allotments will be closely watched, another $100 million is collected annually from taxes and customs, and is entirely at the government's discretion. Chad is expected to receive $3.5 billion in revenues during the first ten years of exporting oil through the pipeline, increasing annual government revenues by more than 50%. Recent increases in worldwide oil prices will likely increase Chadian revenues, offering the government its first real opportunity to dramatically improve the lives of its roughly 10 million citizens.[76]

Governance in Chad

One of the poorest nations of the world (and the fifth largest country in Africa), Chad has recently seen its GDP virtually double overnight with the opening of the aforementioned oil pipeline through Cameroon to the Gulf of Guinea. In 2000, when it granted its development loan for the Chad-Cameroon pipeline, the World Bank imposed strict conditions on the use of oil revenues by the Chad and extracted promises from the government that the money would be used for economic development and social services. Chad was the first country to accept such a conditional loan from the World Bank, and in 1999 adopted a Petroleum Revenues Management Law (PRML) as a prerequisite for World Bank financing, outlining the planned allocation of new oil revenues. According to this plan, 80% of Chad's oil revenues are to be allocated to health, education, rural development, environmental concerns, and other social services. The remaining 20%

will be divided between government expenditures (15%) and a supplement to the Doba region (5%). The government has also declared its intention to use oil revenues to improve Chad's infrastructure, including construction of paved roads from N'Djamena to Abeche and Bisney to Bokoro.[77]

Few countries in the world have greater need for these oil revenues—Chad ranks 165th of 173 countries on the United Nations Human Development Index. In southern Chad, where the country's oil reserves are located, local residents live in abject poverty, without access to piped drinking water or electricity. Less than half the population is functionally literate, and the average Chadian can expect to die before his 45th birthday (see Table 2.5).

Table 2.5: Important Facts about Chad

Population	9,826,419 (July 2005 est.)
Median Age	16.02 years
Avg. Life Expectancy	47.94 years
GDP	$15.66 billion (2004 est.)
GDP Per Capita	$1,600 (2004 est.)
GDP Growth, 2004	38% (2004 est.)
Population below poverty line	80% (2001 est.)
External Debt	$1.1 billion (2000 est.)
Literacy [1]	47.5%
UN Human Development Index Ranking [2]	167
Probability at birth of not surviving to age 40 (% of 2000-2005 cohort)	43%
Population without sustainable access to an improved water source	73%
Physicians per 100,000 people [3]	3
Malaria cases per 100,000 people	197
Public Expenditures:	
on education (2001)	2.0%
on health (2001)	2.0%
on the military (2002)	1.4%
on debt service (2002)	1.5%
Armed Forces (2002)	30,000

Sources: *2005 CIA Factbook* and 2004 UN Human Development Index.

Notes:
[1] Defined as the percentage of the population age 15 and over who can read and write.
[2] A total of 177 countries are ranked in the 2004 UN Human Development Index. Higher numbers indicate poorer performance on a collection of indicators. http://hdr.undp.org/reports/global/2004
[3] By comparison, a typical industrialized country has 200-300 physicians per 100,000 people.

Unfortunately, despite the dire need for economic and social development, the government of Chad has not always demonstrated the kind of good governance decisions that observers had hoped for. For example, despite the PRML agreement restrictions discussed above, when the first World Bank loan disbursement of $25 million was made to the government of President Idriss Deby in November 2000, it was disclosed that the Deby government had instead spent $4 million of the money on arms to fight insurgent forces (perhaps following the example set by Angola throughout previous decades).[78] Chad has been plagued by insurgency and conflict since it became an independent nation in 1960, and unfortunately, the acquisition of oil revenues promises to prolong Chad's civil war and reduce the likelihood of a peaceful resolution. The government has also demonstrated a repressive tendency that is cause for concern. For example, shortly after the pipeline project's official inauguration in October 2003, the government closed down the country's only independent radio station (FM Liberte), which had argued against the development of the pipeline until the government had established the capacity and legal frameworks to ensure environmental protection and transparency in how the revenues would be managed.

As with Angola and Cameroon, corruption is also a major problem in Chad. According to the government oversight committee established to monitor the use of the World Bank funds and the oil revenues, money has already been spent refurbishing ministers' offices, while one ministry tried to buy rice and millet at twice the market price, and another wanted six off-road vehicles. The committee blocked many of those requests, but critics point to the fact that President Idriss Deby, a military ruler who has twice been elected president, recently appointed his brother-in-law to this oversight committee.[79] Indeed, according to one analyst, it may be foolhardy to expect a leadership dominated by one ethnic group (the president's) and with a record of repression and mismanagement to do anything but use its new wealth to crush opponents.[80]

Thus, as seen in Angola and (to a lesser degree) Cameroon, the government of Chad has yet to utilize oil revenues to effectively provide a better life for its people. Through a combination of corruption and negligence, this African nation appears to be following a pattern that has a predictable outcome. However, optimists hope that time and increased international pressure will change the course of Chad's development toward a more positive, secure, democratic, and prosperous future.

Congo

The Republic of Congo (or Congo-Brazzaville) is one of the most urbanized countries in Africa, with 70% of its total population living in Brazzaville, Pointe-Noire, or along the 332-mile railway that connects them in the southwestern portion of the country.[81] The country is also one of the continent's largest petroleum producers, with significant potential for offshore development.[82] Like other Gulf of Guinea countries, Congo's economic fortunes are closely tied to this one resource. And, as observed in the earlier discussion on Angola, the state is largely seen as the primary means for acquiring wealth, which under-scores the numerous military coups and civil wars that have taken place in the country.

Oil in Congo

The Republic of Congo is sub-Saharan Africa's fifth largest oil producer, with current production of roughly 243,000 barrels per day (a significant increase from the level of 65,000 barrels per day in 1980). Congo has estimated oil reserves of 1.5 billion barrels, but there are significant areas of the country (which is almost the size of Montana) that have yet to be thoroughly explored. Like other Gulf of Guinea countries, the majority of Congo's crude oil production is located offshore, which is also considered to have significant potential for additional exploration.[83] Although Congo's national oil company, the Société Nationale des Pétroles du Congo (SNPC), regulates oil extraction in the country, a number of production sharing agreements (PSAs) have been used primarily since 1994 to insure a constant minimum flow of revenue to the government, commensurate with similar agreements between other regional oil exporting states and major oil companies. Under Congo's PSAs, foreign partners carry out exploration and development during an agreed period of time (usually three years for each phase), financing all investment costs and recovering investments when production begins. Because all major operators in Congo have signed PSAs for their respective field developments, approximately one-third of the oil produced goes directly to the government and is sold by SNPC on the state's behalf.[84]

Economic dependency on the oil sector in Congo mirrors that of other oil-rich countries. Since the 1980s, the oil industry has provided the major share of government revenues and exports—nearly 50% of the country's GDP and about 95% of export earnings.[85] The oil sector is dominated by the French oil company TotalFinaElf (which produces approximately two-thirds of all Congolese oil output) and the Italian oil firm Agip, while ChevronTexaco (in partnership with TotalFinaElf) is the primary American oil company active in petroleum exploration or production.[86] Oil is exported through Congo's main port, Pointe-Noire, and is destined for Western Europe (mainly France) and the United States.[87]

Governance in Congo

Denis Sassou-Nguesso first seized power in a coup in 1979, and remained in office until his defeat in a multi-party presidential election in 1992. For the next five years, tensions simmered between Sassou supporters and those of newly elected president Pascal Lissouba. When President Lissouba's government forces surrounded Sassou's compound in Brazzaville with armored vehicles on June 5, 1997 Sassou ordered his militia to resist. Thus began a 4-month conflict that destroyed or damaged much of Brazzaville. In early October, Angolan troops invaded Congo on the side of Sassou and, in mid-October, the Lissouba government fell. Soon thereafter, Sassou declared himself President again—a position he still holds today.

The governance challenges faced by Sassou include poverty, lack of infrastructure, budgetary shortfalls and economic mismanagement. GDP per capita is less than half that of neighboring Cameroon, and nearly half the population is without reliable access to clean drinking water. The average Congolese can expect to die before reaching the age of 50, and nearly a third will likely not reach their 40th birthday (see Table 2.6).

Table 2.6: Important Facts about Congo

Population	3,039,126 (July 2005 est.)
Median Age	20.7 years
Avg. Life Expectancy	48.97 years
GDP	$2.324 billion (2004 est.)
GDP Per Capita	$800 (2004 est.)
GDP Growth, 2004	3.7% (2004 est.)
Population below poverty line	n/a
External Debt	$5 billion (2000 est.)
Literacy [1]	83.8%
UN Human Development Index Ranking [2]	144
Probability at birth of not surviving to age 40 (% of 2000-2005 cohort)	32%
Population without sustainable access to an improved water source	49%
Physicians per 100,000 people [3]	25
Malaria cases per 100,000 people	5,880
Public Expenditures:	
on education (2001)	3.2%
on health (2001)	1.4%
on the military (2002)	n/a
on debt service (2002)	0.8%
Armed Forces (2002)	10,000

Sources: *2005 CIA Factbook* and 2004 UN Human Development Index.

Notes:
[1] Defined as the percentage of the population age 15 and over who can read and write.
[2] A total of 177 countries are ranked in the 2004 UN Human Development Index. Higher numbers indicate poorer performance on a collection of indicators. http://hdr.undp.org/reports/global/2004
[3] By comparison, a typical industrialized country has 200-300 physicians per 100,000 people.

Further, Congo is plagued by air pollution from vehicle emissions, water pollution from the dumping of raw sewage, and deforestation. While the country's literacy rate is considerably higher than most of its neighbors, it also has one of the region's highest rates of malaria infection. To meet these and other governance challenges, a large public sector has evolved. In fact, throughout much of the last few decades, Congo's major employer has been the state bureaucracy, with 80,000 employees on its payroll—enormous for a country of Congo's size. During the mid-1990s, the World Bank and other international financial institutions pressured Congo to institute sweeping civil service reforms in order to reduce the size of the state bureaucracy and pare back a civil service payroll that amounted to more than 20% of GDP in 1993.[88] The country has made some progress in this area over the last ten years, but by most accounts there is still much further to go.

As a result of these huge public expenditures, along with slumps in world oil prices (1998-1999) and armed conflicts (1997, 1998-1999, and 2002), Congo has also experienced several budgetary shortfalls over the last decade. To further complicate matters, corruption has undermined the effectiveness of the government and weakened the Congolese public's confidence in their leaders—a pattern seen in other Gulf of Guinea countries. Because the Congolese government is frequently accused of misusing oil revenues, the International Monetary Fund (IMF) recently urged the country to enforce transparency and improve public finances. In response, Congo pledged in October 2004 to adhere to the Extractive Industries Transparency Initiative (EITI), a voluntary scheme designed to increase transparency in the oil and mining sectors.[89] Congo's Paris Club creditors then forgave $1.6 billion of the country's debt in December 2004, and rescheduled another $1.5 billion. As a result, Congo's debt to the Club was reduced from approximately $3.7 billion to $770 million. The lenders also agreed to raise the country's debt cancellation rate to 90% when the IMF accepts Congo into its Highly Indebted Poor Countries (HIPC) initiative.

After clearance of its outstanding external debt arrears and the December 2004 release of an independent audit of SNPC, the IMF approved a three-year, $84.4 million Poverty Reduction and Growth Facility (PRGF) to support a three-year economic reform program targeting 5.5% GDP growth, 2% inflation, and an average current account surplus of 1.5% of GDP. The World Bank also approved a $30 million Economic Rehabilitation Credit (ERC) for Congo in December 2004, to be repaid over 40 years with a 10-year grace period. In the same month, the African Development Bank (ADB) approved a $51.1 million grant to finance an arrears clearance program. A $10.7 million loan from the African Development Fund (ADF) has also been earmarked to support Congo's IMF-approved Policy Reform Program.[90] So, in short, the future has begun to look brighter for the Republic of Congo—let us hope their leaders do not squander the rare opportunity they have been given.

Equatorial Guinea

For its entire existence, the tiny country of Equatorial Guinea has been ruled by two men—from the same family—who have been described by a variety of human rights organizations as among the worst abusers of human rights in Africa.[91] After 190 years of Spanish rule, the country (formerly known as Spanish Guinea, and the only Spanish-speaking-country in Africa) gained its independence in 1968, with Francisco Macias Nguema as its president. In 1972, Nguema declared himself president for life, but seven years later his nephew—Teodoro Obiang Nguema Mbasogo, at the time a Lieutenant Colonel and a close advisor to the president—led a military coup which overthrew him. Shortly thereafter, Macias Nguema was tried and executed for a variety of corruption and human rights abuses: an estimated 100,000 of the country's population had been forced to flee the country during the 1970s, and another 50,000 were reportedly executed by his repressive regime. Obiang has ruled the country for over two decades, and today the country lives under the uncertainty of which direction its autocratic family-based rule will evolve.[92]

Oil in Equatorial Guinea

Roughly the size of Maryland, Equatorial Guinea is comprised of five inhabited islands in the Gulf of Guinea and a relatively small (by African standards), square piece of coastal property on the mainland wedged between Cameroon and Gabon. The discovery of large deposits of oil and gas in the mid-1990s transformed Equatorial Guinea into Africa's fastest-growing economy and into the third largest oil producer in sub-Saharan Africa. It is also the third largest recipient of U.S. investment in Africa.[93]

Equatorial Guinea's total proven oil reserves are estimated at 1.28 billion barrels, and production is expanding rapidly, averaging 371,700 barrels per day in 2004.[94] Oil production increased more than tenfold between 1996 and 2002,[95] and oil revenues increased dramatically from $3 million in 1993 to $725 million by 2003.[96] Gross domestic product (GDP) growth was strong at 23.7% in 2004, and it is expected to be as high as 26.8% in 2005.[97] Oil production accounted for nearly 90% of GDP and export earnings in 2002, having made no contribution only a decade earlier.[98] Today, Equatorial Guinea pumps more oil per person than Saudi Arabia.[99] Three U.S. oil companies are primarily responsible for Equatorial Guinea's oil production: ExxonMobil, Amerada Hess, and Marathon.[100] Equatorial Guinea holds a record number of oil prospecting permits, and over the next 20 years could well see production increase to 740,000 barrels a day.[101]

Governance in Equatorial Guinea

During the mid-1980s, Robert Klitgaard—a former Harvard professor—led a World Bank development project in Equatorial Guinea. His memoirs of the time spent in the tiny African country illuminate the depth of corruption, impoverishment, crumbling infrastructure, and repressive government for which the Obiang regime has become infamous. Following an attempted coup, one of Klitgaard's employees on the World Bank project was snatched and severely tortured for weeks as part of the government's "investigation." While the man was eventually deemed innocent, his broken collarbone took months to heal.[102]

"Equatorial Guinea is one of the most backward countries in the world," Klitgaard wrote at the time.[103] Indeed, by all available indicators of economic performance, this is still one of the poorest, most underdeveloped countries in the world. Its population of just over a half million suffers from one of the world's highest per capita rates of malaria infection. Although roughly two-thirds of Equatorial Guinea's land area is covered with forest and woodland, increased agricultural production has led to deforestation and environmental erosion, and clean drinking water is extremely scarce. According to a recent U.S. Senate committee report, "three out of four Equato-Guineans suffer malnutrition" and yet "between 1997 and 2002, Obiang spent just over one percent of his budget on health."[104] Over a third of the population can reasonably expect not to live to their 40th birthday (see Table 2.7).

By virtually any standard, Equatorial Guinea can be considered a poor, developing country, and a legacy of corrupt, authoritarian rule is much to blame. According to Susan Rice, Assistant Secretary of State for African Affairs during the Clinton administration, Equatorial Guinea can be considered "a poster child of undemocratic practices."[105] Despite growing international pressures, President Obiang has no interest in providing greater financial transparency, insisting that how much money his government earns from oil is nobody else's business.[106] When asked recently in a BBC interview why so much of his country's public oil money had apparently disappeared, he replied that this was a state secret, and that he did not have to tell anyone where it had gone.[107]

The government of Equatorial Guinea has been routinely charged with engaging in excessive corruption, human rights abuses and political repression. There has also been strong evidence in Equatorial Guinea of government misappropriation of oil revenues, in particular, for lavish personal expenditures. For example, despite his country's widespread poverty, President Obiang owns a couple of mansions in the Washington, DC area, including one which he bought for $2.6 million in cash.[108] Obiang's first son, Teodoro Jr., is the minister of infrastructure, but he prefers spending his days in Paris, Rio and Hollywood over his country's capital, Malabo.[109] The country's oil industry in the hands of the president's son Gabrial; the president's cousin is inspector general of the

Armed Forces, and his brother runs the security services (though interestingly, the president imports his own security force of bodyguards from Morocco).[110]

Table 2.7: Important Facts about Equatorial Guinea

Population	535,881 (July 2005 est.)
Median Age	18.83 years
Avg. Life Expectancy	55.56 years
GDP	$1.27 billion (2002 est.)
GDP Per Capita	$2,700 (2002 est.)
GDP Growth, 2004	20% (2002 est.)
Population below poverty line	n/a
External Debt	$248 million (2000 est.)
Literacy [1]	85.7%
Unemployment rate	30% (1998 est.)
UN Human Development Index Ranking [2]	109
Probability at birth of not surviving to age 40 (% of 2000-2005 cohort)	36%
Population without sustainable access to an improved water source	56%
Physicians per 100,000 people [3]	25
Malaria cases per 100,000 people	2,744
Public Expenditures:	
on education (2001)	0.5%
on health (2001)	1.2%
on the military (2002)	n/a
on debt service (2002)	0.2%
Armed Forces (2002)	2,000

Sources: *2005 CIA Factbook* and 2004 UN Human Development Index.

Notes:
[1] Defined as the percentage of the population age 15 and over who can read and write.
[2] A total of 177 countries are ranked in the 2004 UN Human Development Index. Higher numbers indicate poorer performance on a collection of indicators. http://hdr.undp.org/reports/global/2004
[3] By comparison, a typical industrialized country has 200-300 physicians per 100,000 people.

According to Frank Ruddy, U.S. Ambassador to Equatorial Guinea during the Reagan administration, Obiang's administration is a "corrupt, rotten government. The people there deserve better than that crooks they've got."[111] Television and radio are controlled by the president and his family.[112] Oil company compounds are built on land owned by the president, and leased from him for large sums.[113] John Bennett, U.S. envoy to Equatorial Guinea from 1991 to 1994, received a death threat because of his outspokenness against the government's abuses of power, and the U.S. closed its embassy in 1995 because of concerns over corruption and human rights.[114] And of course, the recent corruption investigation into Riggs Bank, described in chapter 1 of this volume, indicates a deep and troubling pattern of corruption among Equatorial Guinea's leaders.

Yet, despite what some might call a blatant disregard for international norms, Obiang's administration has recently enjoyed increasing attention from the U.S. and other industrialized countries. U.S. investment, almost exclusively in the oil/energy sectors, has increased dramatically since 1996, and the World Bank resumed lending to Equatorial Guinea in April 2002 after severing its relationship with the country in 1993. The U.S. reopened its Embassy in Equatorial Guinea in October 2003. President Obiang recently visited the U.S. and met with Secretary Abraham at the Department to discuss bilateral energy issues, and was entertained lavishly by several U.S. oil companies.[115] In 2000, Louisiana Representative William Jefferson led the first-ever Congressional delegation to Equatorial Guinea, taking along representatives from Baton Rouge-based Shaw Global Energy Services.[116]

In essence, largely because of its new oil wealth, Equatorial Guinea enjoys a great deal of positive attention from countries that are quick to condemn government corruption and abuses elsewhere in the world. As described later in this volume, this also has been a common trend in U.S. foreign policy relations with the oil-rich countries of the Persian Gulf, where we have enabled a whole variety of corrupt, authoritarian regimes. One would hope that our country's policymakers are able to learn lessons and avoid repeating mistakes of the past. Very recently, President Obiang has expressed a renewed commitment to using Equatorial Guinea's huge surge in oil wealth to dramatically improve the country's human development conditions. Only time will tell if these pledges are actually realized.

Gabon

Like other Gulf of Guinea countries, only two autocratic presidents have ruled Gabon since it gained its independence from France in 1960. Gabon's current president, El Hadj Omar Bongo Ondimba—one of the longest-serving heads of state in the world—has dominated Gabon's political scene for almost four decades. Gabon has a per capita income that is at least four times the average of sub-Saharan Africa, largely thanks to its oil and mineral wealth and to the fact that it has a relatively small population of 1.3 million. But the country is largely dependent on the exploitation of its mineral resources, particularly oil, and thus its economic fortunes fluctuate according to world prices.

Oil in Gabon

Africa's fourth largest producer and exporter of crude oil, Gabon's production averaged nearly 250,000 barrels per day in 2004.[117] A country about the size of Colorado, it has 2.5 billion barrels of oil reserves, most of it along the coast and offshore. Petroleum production, which stood at 56.8 million barrels annually in the late 1980s, was declining due to depletion of reserves until a major new field was tapped, and production subsequently increased to a high point of 370,000 barrels per day in 1997.[118] However, without the discovery of new fields, current production will deplete Gabon's oil reserves by 2012.

Gabon officially left OPEC in 1996, citing the organization's high annual dues, and thus currently has greater flexibility over its production than do OPEC members.[119] However, the country is also largely dependent on oil revenues to fund its economy. Exports of crude oil account for approximately 60% of the government's budget and more than 40% of GDP.[120] Over half of Gabon's crude oil shipments are exported to the United States, with much of the rest going to Western Europe and occasionally the Far East.[121] Thus, like other countries in the Gulf of Guinea, there is an obvious relationship between Gabon's economic fortunes and U.S. foreign policy.

Governance in Gabon

By the standards of central and western Africa, Gabon has remained comparatively peaceful since gaining its independence from France in 1960.[122] The continued presence of French troops in the country—which in 1964 reinstated President Leon Mba after he had been overthrown in a coup—may have something to do with this. Further, the government controls the country's main broadcast media. In 1968, Mba's successor, Omar Albert-Bernard Bongo, declared Gabon a one-party state, a status that it retained until 1991. Opposition parties have failed to pose a serious challenge to the president's Democratic Gabonese Party.[123] While many would rightly call this an authoritarian state, it has resulted in a level of political stability that is rather uncommon throughout Africa.

This political stability has helped make Gabon a wealthy nation compared to the rest of sub-Saharan Africa. However, over half the population of Gabon lives below the poverty line, and access to potable water is a problem even for many who live in the poorer suburbs of the capital Libreville (see Table 2.8). The country is entirely reliant on imports for even the most basic of goods and services (nearly 50% of Gabon's trade is with the U.S.), and its external debt of nearly $4 billion results in a significant drain on the government's annual revenues.

According to the U.S. Department of State, approximately 5% of Gabon's population accounts for over 90% of the country's wealth.[124] The fairly regular stream of oil rent, coupled with a lack of incentive among the wealthy elites to diversify the country's economy, has led to great concern over what will happen once these oil reserves are gone. Further, according to a recent *Economist* report, "decades of oil revenues have corrupted society and eroded the work ethic . . . Citizens aspire to soft billets in the civil service, and turn their noses up at menial jobs like taxi driving or shop keeping, which they leave to immigrants from poorer places like Togo and Mali. Agriculture in Gabon, as in Equatorial Guinea, is all but dead. The elite in Libreville, Gabon's capitol, buy French bottled water, French milk and gourmet cat food. The country's president, Omar Bongo—who has been in power since 1967—helps French companies keep competitors out, and France thanks him by stationing 600 soldiers next to one of his palaces, and neglecting to criticize him when he wins rigged elections."[125]

Table 2.8: Important Facts about Gabon

Population	1,389,201 (July 2005 est.)
Median Age	18.57 years
Avg. Life Expectancy	55.75 years
GDP	$7.966 billion (2004 est.)
GDP Per Capita	$5,900 (2004 est.)
GDP Growth, 2004	1.9% (2004 est.)
Population below poverty line	n/a
External Debt	$3.804 billion (2004 est.)
Literacy [1]	63.2%
UN Human Development Index Ranking [2]	122
Probability at birth of not surviving to age 40 (% of 2000-2005 cohort)	28%
Population without sustainable access to an improved water source	14%
Physicians per 100,000 people [3]	n/a
Malaria cases per 100,000 people	2,148
Public Expenditures:	
on education (2001)	3.9%
on health (2001)	1.7%
on the military (2002)	n/a
on debt service (2002)	8.3%
Armed Forces (2002)	5,000

Sources: *2005 CIA Factbook* and 2004 UN Human Development Index.

Notes:
[1] Defined as the percentage of the population age 15 and over who can read and write.
[2] A total of 177 countries are ranked in the 2004 UN Human Development Index. Higher numbers indicate poorer performance on a collection of indicators. http://hdr.undp.org/reports/global/2004
[3] By comparison, a typical industrialized country has 200-300 physicians per 100,000 people.

Gabon has also earned a poor reputation with the Paris Club and the International Monetary Fund (IMF) for the management of its debt and revenues. Successive IMF missions have criticized the government for overspending on off-budget items (in good years and bad), over-borrowing from the central bank, and slipping on the schedule for privatization and administrative reform.[126] Overall, as with the other Gulf of Guinea countries, Gabon faces a host of complex governance challenges, although the situation here may not be as dire as in Angola, Equatorial Guinea, or Nigeria.

Nigeria

Many Nigerians see their country as Africa's superpower.[127] According to Stephen Ellis, of Britain's Royal Africa Society, "A calm and prosperous Nigeria would be a guarantor of peace and stability [while] an unstable Nigeria creates great tension and does nothing to fill the power vacuum apparent in the region."[128] With an estimated population of 129 million, Nigeria is the most populous African state—one of every five Africans is Nigerian.[129] Further, Nigeria's oil reserves of over 35 billion barrels are the second largest in Africa (behind Libya's 39 billion barrels), and the country is Africa's largest oil producer. Nigeria accounts for just over 50% of the Gulf of Guinea's oil production and 70% of proven reserves.[130] The majority of Nigeria's crude exports are destined for markets in the United States and Western Europe, with Asia and Latin America becoming increasingly important as well. The state is also a key player in African regional security, most recently in Sierra Leone and Sudan.

As a result, as Princeton Lyman—a fellow at the Council on Foreign Relations and a former Ambassador to Nigeria—recently argued, what happens in Nigeria matters to Africa, to the relationship between Africa and the United States, and to the hopes for peace and prosperity on the continent.[131] Nigeria's relationship with the U.S. is particularly important, as it is currently the source of 10% of U.S. oil imports (averaging 1.1 billion barrels per day). In December 2004, President Obasanjo announced his intentions to increase this amount to 15% within the next few years.[132] Thus, it should come as no surprise that Nigeria is the most important destination for an estimated $50 billion investment in Gulf of Guinea oil production within the next few years.[133]

Oil in Nigeria

Oil has played a major role in Nigerian foreign and domestic politics since its independence in 1960. With crude oil production averaging 2.5 million barrels per day in 2004, Nigeria is the world's seventh-largest exporter and the fifth largest supplier of crude oil to the United States. Oil production began in 1958, but did not become Nigeria's main export commodity until 1970.[134] Today, Nigeria is the only West African country with spare production capacity, estimated at 200,000 barrels/day, although as a member of OPEC it has limited flexibility in how it uses this capacity.[135] Nigeria has estimated oil reserves of 35 billion barrels, and plans to expand its proven reserves to 40 billion barrels by 2010.[136] The majority of reserves are found along the country's coastal Niger River Delta, with the majority of oil located in approximately 250 small (i.e., less than 50 million barrels each) fields. At least 200 other fields contain undisclosed reserves; Nick van Ooyen, of Shell Nigeria, estimated in 2003 that there could be several billion barrels in the Niger Delta alone.[137]

The largest producer is Shell Petroleum Development of Nigeria Ltd (SPDC), which produces nearly half of Nigeria's crude oil, averaging 1.1 million bbl/day.[138] Nigeria has six export terminals—the most of any country— including Forcados and Bonny (operated by Shell), Escravos and Pennington (ChevronTexaco), Qua Iboe (ExxonMobil), Brass (Agip), and Bonny Island LNG (Nigeria LNG).[139] Shell's Bonny terminal is currently undergoing a $600 million expansion and will export 1.5 million bbl/d after its completion in 2006. Shell's $2.7 billion, deepwater Bonga field, estimated to hold reserves of 1.2 billion barrels, is due to begin production in mid-2005. In August 2004, Shell announced plans to invest $9 billion in Nigerian oil and natural gas projects over five years, including investments in the NLNG Train Six, the Soku natural gas plant expansion, and the Bonga oil field. ExxonMobil, currently producing around 570,000 bbl/d in Nigeria, plans to invest $11 billion in the country's oil sector between 2003 and 2011, increasing production to 1.2 million bbl/d. The majority of the increase will occur at the 150,000-bbl/d Erha development, slated to come online in 2006. In addition, ExxonMobil's 400 million barrel Yoho field began initial production of 90,000 bbl/d in February 2003.[140] And in October 2004, ChevronTexaco announced that it would invest $2.5 billion in Nigeria in 2005, developing the Agbami field, which is scheduled to come online in late 2007, and a number of natural gas projects.

In August 2004, Nigeria's finance minister announced an ambitious goal of raising production capacity to 4 million barrels of oil per day by 2010.[141] According to a recent International Energy Administration report, "such aspirations have led to disputes with the Organization of Petroleum Exporting Countries (OPEC), as the country frequently exceeds its production quotas. Although OPEC increased Nigeria's production quota three times in 2004, the Nigerian National Petroleum Company (NNPC) has recently announced increased pressure from multinational oil companies for Nigeria to leave the organization. The multinationals see Nigeria's OPEC production quota as the main hindrance to increased production at several deepwater fields."[142]

Meanwhile, as part of this strategy for expansion, the government announced in 2005 that it would hold its first fully open oil rights auction. Hundreds of oil firms from Asia, the U.S. and Europe bid on the right to explore new plots, stretching from Lake Chad in the northeast of the country (not far from where the country of Chad began to export oil in 2003) to the Gulf of Guinea. These companies will have to pay "signature bonuses" of between $500,000 and $50 million per land parcel before they can begin exploring these potentially oil-rich areas. Such huge sums of money offer an important means for the government to address its widespread poverty and infrastructure challenges—but there is also concern that these funds are more likely to support the mismanagement and corruption for which Nigeria has become famous.

Governance in Nigeria

Most of Nigeria's oil is pumped from the wells sunk into the swampy forests of the coastal Niger River Delta—a region that stands at the crossroads of contemporary Nigerian politics—and from platforms offshore in the Gulf of Guinea.[143] Despite recent growth in the distribution of revenues to the oil producing Delta states, the region remains desperately poor and has benefited the least from the oil extraction industry. Only 27% of the Delta's people have access to safe drinking water, and only 30% of households have electricity. The figure of only one doctor per 82,000 people in the Delta is more than three times worse than the national average.[144] Many schools in the Niger Delta region have no teachers or books, hospitals and health centers are ill-equipped to deal with malaria and other equatorial diseases that are rife, and many communities have no electricity. Unemployment is 80% or more in some places, sanitation is almost non-existent, housing is atrocious, and the death rate amongst children is very high.[145]

As a result of these trends, tensions are high in this region, led by separatist groups demanding a greater share of oil revenue. The inhabitants of the Niger Delta complain that during the past four decades, the government has taken the oil money generated from these wells but has left the region poor, undeveloped and polluted.[146] After years of campaigning by activities and delta communities, a 3% share of oil revenue was restored to Nigeria's 11 oil producing states in the late 1980s. This was later increased to 13% under the 1999 constitution that returned Nigeria to democracy after 15 years of military rule. Currently, 17% of the nation's oil revenues are now conceded to the delta states.[147]

Despite massive oil revenues, a number of problems—including corruption, mismanagement and a lack of government accountability—has prevented Nigeria's oil wealth from improving the lives of its ordinary citizens.[148] The paradox is striking: although it is Africa's leading oil exporter, Nigeria is considered one of the least developed nations in the world. A 1992 World Bank report rated Nigeria as the 17th poorest nation in the world,[149] while according to the 2004 UN Human Development Index: 90% of the population earns less than $2 a day; one out of ever three people is illiterate; and more than 60% of the population lives in poverty (see Table 2.9).[150] Nearly half of Nigerians are younger than 15 years, and by 2025 the population is projected to grow to 206 million. Nigeria has no state-supported system to provide for the health and welfare needs of its citizens. Medical care is provided to government employees and to most workers in large industrial and commercial enterprises, but it is rare among the rest of the population. Many Nigerians lack access to primary health care, in large part because the great majority of treatment centers are located in large cities. As a result, less than 50% of the children in Nigeria are immunized against measles, and malnutrition affects more than 40% of children under the age of five. 20% of Nigerian children die before the age of five, primarily from treatable diseases such as malaria, measles, whooping cough, diarrhea, and pneumonia.

Table 2.9: Important Facts about Nigeria

Population	128,771,988
Median Age	18.63 years
Avg. Life Expectancy	46.74 years
GDP	$125.7 billion (2004 est.)
GDP Per Capita	$1,000 (2004 est.)
GDP Growth, 2004	6.2% (2004 est.)
Population below poverty line	60% (2000 est.)
External Debt	$30.55 billion (2004 est.)
Literacy [1]	68%
UN Human Development Index Ranking [2]	151
Probability at birth of not surviving to age 40 (% of 2000-2005 cohort)	35%
Population without sustainable access to an improved water source	38%
Physicians per 100,000 people [3]	27
Malaria cases per 100,000 people	30
Public Expenditures:	
on education (2001)	n/a
on health (2001)	0.8%
on the military (2002)	1.1%
on debt service (2002)	3.4%
Armed Forces (2002)	79,000

Sources: *2005 CIA Factbook* and 2004 UN Human Development Index.

Notes:
[1] Defined as the percentage of the population age 15 and over who can read and write.
[2] A total of 177 countries are ranked in the 2004 UN Human Development Index. Higher numbers indicate poorer performance on a collection of indicators. http://hdr.undp.org/reports/global/2004
[3] By comparison, a typical industrialized country has 200-300 physicians per 100,000 people.

According to African policy analyst Dianna Games, "fundamental structural problems [in Nigeria] include corruption; the poor state of the infrastructure, most notably in the power sector; skewed government spending priorities; neglect of potentially lucrative sectors; massive urban decay; a 'get-rich-quick' mentality that pervades much of business and even government; and a complex and weighty bureaucracy which still dominates the economy."[151] Economic dependency is another of the Nigeria's most pressing challenges.[152] For example, while oil comprises just 13% of the country's GDP, it supplies more than 80% of the federal government's revenues. This dependence on oil revenues means that Nigeria's income fluctuates with global market prices. Further, while Nigeria exports some 1.86 million barrels of crude oil a day, it then imports the refined product at a far higher price.[153] President Obasanjo stated in 2004 that his administration intended to refine 50% of Nigeria's national crude oil production by the year 2006, but few observers now believe this target will be met.[154]

Power shortages and similar shortcomings in infrastructure are another serious source of concern and a long term one. Nigeria has for far too long allowed its power sector to be badly managed. For example, while Nigeria is roughly twice the size of California, and the need for electricity is considerable, no new power stations were built during the 1990s despite the country's increased wealth from oil exports. From one account, in 2005 only 19 of 70 power generating plants were operational.[155] As a result, Nigeria today, with a population of perhaps 130 million people, produces little more than 10% of the power produced in South Africa, which has 40 million people. The World Bank recently estimated that the power shortfall in Nigeria adds 16% to the cost of production here. In an increasingly globalized economy, that almost puts Nigeria out of the running in many sectors. Already a flood of consumer goods from Asia is challenging domestic production and leading to the shutdown of key industries. The government projects a doubling of power generation over the next several years, but even if that is achieved it is not necessarily enough.[156]

Corruption has also been a huge problem in Nigeria for many years.[157] Corruption persists throughout the public and private arenas, ranging from 'signature bonuses' on large contracts to getting imported goods through Nigeria's ports. Nigerian taxi and bus drivers keep a wad of small-denomination notes handy to pay off police officers manning frequent roadblocks.[158] However, it is in government, and even at the ministerial level, that the most serious complaints about corruption are heard.[159] Major General Ibrahim Babangida, who seized power in a 1985 military coup, looted Nigeria's oil revenues for eight years, and at the turn of the century was worth an estimated $30 billion; while at one point more than 3,000 members of his administration had Swiss bank accounts.[160] His administration was followed by the equally corrupt—and far more brutal—military dictator Sani Abacha, who is accused of personally stealing $2.2 billion during his five years in office.[161] Overall, between 1973 and 1998, roughly $80 billion of Nigeria's oil revenues found its way to private bank accounts in Switzerland, North America, Western Europe and other places far from Africa.[162]

Within the last five years, Nigeria's government has begun to tackle the problem of corruption. In March 2005, Nigerian President Obasanjo fired his education minister in response to serious corruption allegations. Minister Fabian Osuji was accused of withdrawing nearly $410,000 from government coffers, and using this to bribe the leader of the senate and six other members of parliament in an attempt to smooth the passage of his annual budget. As President Obasanjo noted "it is a disheartening event that the number three man in the government hierarchy in the country is involved in this sordid matter" (referring to the Senate President Adolphous Wabara, who was criticized for accepting the bribe).[163] In a separate case, Maurice Ibekwe, a member of Nigeria's Federal House of Representatives, was arrested for financial fraud, forgery and conspiracy. Ironically, he had served as Chairman of the House sub-committee on Police Affairs.[164] While these and other arrests signify a commitment from the government to address this widespread problem, Nigeria is still ranked one of the world's most corrupt countries. Unfortunately, as this chapter highlights, government mismanagement and corruption are common throughout the entire Gulf of Guinea.

São Tomé and Príncipe

São Tomé and Príncipe is a multi-island country which has the potential to become one of Africa's largest oil producers. The main island of São Tomé lies approximately 180 miles from the coast of Gabon, while Príncipe is 160 miles from the coast of Equatorial Guinea. Both these islands are fairly mountainous and form part of a chain of extinct volcanoes and other small islands. With the land mass of all islands combined, São Tomé and Príncipe is barely more than five times the size of Washington, DC, making it the smallest country in Africa.

Discovered and claimed by Portugal in the late 15th century, São Tomé and Príncipe gained its independence in 1975. Coups and countercoups characterized the years up to 1990, but then a new constitution was established providing for opposition parties and multiparty elections and restricting the presidential period of office to two terms.[165] Free elections were held in 1991, but the political environment has been one of continued instability with frequent changes in leadership and coup attempts in 1995 and 2003. Further, because of the size and historical insularity of the country, the politics of São Tomé and Príncipe are based largely on personal agendas, kinship and patronage rather than on programmatic or ideological platforms.[166] Within this political climate, the recent discovery of oil in the Gulf of Guinea is having a significant impact.

Oil in São Tomé and Príncipe

São Tomé and Príncipe lies in the center of the Gulf of Guinea. Although no oil reserves have been proven to date, several major oil discoveries have been made in the Gulf over the last 10 years—including the new offshore fields of Nigeria, Equatorial Guinea, and Gabon—leading many to assume that it is only a matter of time until similar discoveries are made here as well. In fact, the twin islands of São Tomé and Príncipe are believed to be sitting on about two billion barrels of crude oil. As a result, the country has attracted growing attention from multinational oil companies and countries like the United States and Nigeria.

The U.S. government has recently promoted plans to extend the runway of São Tomé's small airport and build a new deep-water port on the island at an estimated cost of U.S. $500 million—as much as the entire country would earn from 100 years of cocoa exports, its traditional foreign exchange earner. If built, this deep-water port could serve as a possible U.S. Navy base to protect growing Western oil interests in West Africa.[167] Further, in July 2002, General Carlton Fulford (at the time, a member of the U.S. military command in Europe, which has responsibility for Africa) visited São Tomé and Príncipe to explore the possibility of setting up a regional military command center there, similar to the one in South Korea.[168]

Meanwhile, in February 2001, Nigeria signed a Joint Development Zone agreement with São Tomé and Príncipe, resolving a longstanding maritime boundary dispute.[169] Through this formal arrangement, the two countries agreed to share the proceeds of any oil found in an offshore zone where their territorial waters overlap, with 60% going to Nigeria (which has the infrastructure for offshore oil development) and 40% to São Tomé and Príncipe. Several multinational companies (including Royal Dutch/Shell Company, ExxonMobil Corporation, ChevronTexaco Corporation, ConocoPhillips and Devon Energy Corporation) participated in a competitive bidding process to obtain exploration rights to areas (called oil blocks) of the São Tomé-Nigeria Joint Development Zone. The first block was awarded to a consortium led by Exxonmobil in February 2005, which plans to start drilling in 2007 and is already putting up a new office block among the Portuguese colonial style buildings that grace São Tomé's city center.

Governance in São Tomé and Príncipe

São Tomé and Príncipe is one of Africa's poorest countries, where excessive reliance on one single export commodity (cocoa) since 1975 has led to economic stagnation; in recent years, production has declined substantially because of drought and mismanagement. The country must import all fuels, most manufactured goods, consumer goods, and a substantial amount of food.[170] In addition, corruption, poverty and underdevelopment have severely affected the livelihoods of the majority.[171] The average income stands at about $280 a year, and over half of the population live in poverty (see Table 2.10). Within this context, the promise of oil has raised hopes and expectations among the 187,000 inhabitants of this former Portuguese colony.

São Tomé and Príncipe's external debt stands at over $300 million, and it spends a higher percentage of its annual budget on debt service (over 12%) than any other country in the Gulf of Guinea. Over the years, it has had difficulty servicing its external debt and has relied heavily on aid and debt rescheduling. São Tomé and Príncipe benefited from $200 million in debt relief in December 2000 under the Highly Indebted Poor Countries (HIPC) program, but lacking a formal poverty reduction program with the IMF, it has not benefited from subsequent HIPC debt reductions.

Table 2.10: Important Facts about São Tomé and Príncipe

Population	187,410 (July 2005 est.)
Median Age	16.12 years
Avg. Life Expectancy	66.99 years
GDP	$214 million (2003 est.)
GDP Per Capita	$1,200 (2003 est.)
GDP Growth, 2004	6% (2004 est.)
Population below poverty line	54% (2004 est.)
External Debt	$318 million (2002)
Literacy [1]	79.3%
UN Human Development Index Ranking [2]	123
Probability at birth of not surviving to age 40 (% of 2000-2005 cohort)	10%
Population without sustainable access to an improved water source	n/a
Physicians per 100,000 people [3]	47
Malaria cases per 100,000 people	n/a
Public Expenditures:	
on education (2001)	n/a
on health (2001)	1.5%
on the military (2002)	n/a
on debt service (2002)	12.1%
Armed Forces (2002)	n/a

Sources: *2005 CIA Factbook* and 2004 UN Human Development Index.

Notes:
[1] Defined as the percentage of the population age 15 and over who can read and write.
[2] A total of 177 countries are ranked in the 2004 UN Human Development Index. Higher numbers indicate poorer performance on a collection of indicators. http://hdr.undp.org/reports/global/2004
[3] By comparison, a typical industrialized country has 200-300 physicians per 100,000 people.

In July 2003, declaring that the government was corrupt and had no solution to the nation's problems, a military junta seized power (while President Fradique de Menezes was visiting his Nigerian counterpart, President Olusegun Obasanjo), announcing that they had acted in response to the "continuing social and economic decline of the country." Both Angola and Nigeria—countries with close ties with São Tomé and Príncipe—reacted swiftly to President Menezes' unofficial requests for military assistance. Angolan President Eduardo dos Santos issued a strongly worded statement condemning the coup and called an emergency meeting of the Council of Ministers to discuss possible military intervention in the islands, while President Obasanjo demanded that the democratically elected government be returned to power.[172] As a result of mounting international pressure, the leader of the coup—Major Fernando "Cobo" Pereira—agreed to negotiations, and the Menezes administration was eventually returned to office.

Afterwards, Major Pereira described the coup as a cry for help for the international community to recognize the rampant corruption and poor life standards of the tiny West African islands.[173] As described in the next chapter of this volume, military coups have been all too common throughout the Gulf of Guinea, and have often been justified by their leaders in the name of tackling corruption and poverty. However, as many observers of the region have noted, these governmental takeovers are frequently driven more by a desire to obtain control over the state and its monopoly of natural resources—particularly oil. In essence, the combination of state-controlled oil extraction and endemic poverty produces a toxic brew that can undermine any hope of good governance. Thus, there is a good chance that whether or not significant amounts of oil are found in São Tomé and Príncipe, this will not be the last coup attempt we shall see in the Gulf of Guinea.

Governance Challenges in the Gulf of Guinea: A Comparative Analysis

Although each of these countries faces their own unique challenges, this brief overview reveals important patterns and common themes that impact U.S. energy security interests throughout the region. In each case, significant oil wealth is flowing (or is about to flow) into the coffers of underdeveloped governments that may be classified as illiberal democracies at best and authoritarian and blatantly illegitimate at worst. Institutions that support the rule of law are weak or absent, and private and public elites operate in a system that is not transparent or accountable. Militaries are by and large unprofessional and civil-military relations are tenuous. The gap between the state and the society is significant and destabilizing, and will only grow more profound with the introduction of enormous cash flows into the hands of the elites.

In the past, rather than serving as a platform from which to strengthen civil society and sustain economic development, in almost all cases, oil has played a double role in providing both a stake for conflict and money to fight it out.[174] As one analyst has described it, an oil-rich country in this region can be seen as "a land cursed by its wealth."[175] The picture for the future is not much better. According to Daniel Volman, of the African Security Research Project, "Given the instability and lack of democracy in most African countries and the difficulty of solving political problems by peaceful means, possession of oil is certain to continue to promote the militarization of African countries and to provoke both internal and inter-state violence."[176] From authoritarianism to corruption to poverty and economic dependency, the similarities among most of these countries are striking. When combined with regional demographic trends, the spread of Islamic fundamentalist terrorism, and indications of emerging political violence and social unrest, the implications for U.S. energy security interests are alarming.

In addition to the countries profiled above, there have also been significant new offshore discoveries in Mauritania, Côte d'Ivoire, Namibia and South Africa, most of which are in deep sea oil fields that can now be exploited by the same new technology as that used in the Gulf of Guinea.[177] Côte d'Ivoire, a country roughly the size of New Mexico, also contains an estimated 1.1 trillion cubic feet of natural gas reserves, and is poised to become a major natural gas supplier throughout the region, although the current political environment remains a cause for some concern. Here, too, the operating environment poses a variety of governance challenges that impact any long-term energy security objectives. For example, when President Robert Gueï (who led a military coup in 1999) saw that he was likely to lose the 2000 elections, he dissolved the official election commission and declared himself the winner, sparking widespread protests and violence. Although Gueï was forced to step down, an attempted military coup in 2002 led to increased violence, which lasted throughout most of 2003 until a fragile, externally mediated peace accord between the government and three ethnic-based rebel groups was reached.

Similar patterns of political violence have been seen throughout West and Central Africa—including attempted and successful military coups—indicating that this is certainly a tough neighborhood in which to maintain peaceful, good governance. In addition to local and regional violence, the major governance challenges can be generally grouped into a small handful of categories: authoritarian regimes, corruption and mismanagement, and underdevelopment. A brief analysis of each reveals important considerations for U.S. energy security policy.

Authoritarian Regimes

As noted African scholar George Ayittey once observed, "What keeps Africans poor is their powerlessness to rid themselves of predatory governments or force existing ones to adopt the right policies in a peaceful way."[178] The analysis of African countries provided earlier in this chapter reveals striking patterns of state-sponsored centralization of wealth and power, where a very small handful of people benefit from systems of patronage and corruption while the majority suffer a variety of ills related to poverty and underdevelopment. Further, in many countries the state is subsumed by the dominant party and elections simply become a focus for misuse of government expenditure. In some African states there are no rules on expenditure at all. This anomalous situation can result in the "abuse of incumbency," whereby dominant parties will attempt to change constitutional terms of office/control the media/outlaw political activity and engage in coercive or violent electoral campaigns.[179] As a result, the people of these countries have little opportunity to compel government change without resorting to violent means.

Unfortunately, examples of authoritarian governments abound in the Gulf of Guinea. In many cases, political dissent has been outlawed or otherwise prevented by government forces. For example, in Nigeria—a country which emerged in 1999 from a long history of military dictatorships—the president recently deported the correspondent of the respected news agency *The Economist*, after weeks of complaining about the lack of coverage on his country, and on April 1, 2004 all local radio and televisions stations in the country were banned from relaying foreign news broadcasts live (a move to restrict the access of Nigerians to global news services like CNN and BBC).

In most of the countries described above, only one or two men have ruled, virtually unchallenged, over the last four decades. Teodoro Obiang Nguema Mbasogo has been president of Equatorial Guinea since 1979 when he seized power from his uncle. He survived an attempted coup in the spring of 2002, and staved off another in August 2004. His legacy of authoritarian rule includes a litany of accusations about corruption and oppression. In the Republic of the Congo, General Denis Sassou-Nguesso first seized power in 1979, lost the presidency in a multiparty election in 1992, and then seized power again in 1997. Other countries continue to suffer from the deleterious political and economic effects of sultanism and statism[180] as many of Africa's "big men" refuse to share control over oil revenues. Jose Eduardo Dos Santos has been president of Angola since 1979, and the last quarter century of civil war was largely funded by oil and other mineral wealth.[181] El Hadj Omar Bongo has been president in neighboring Gabon since 1967, a country which has experienced 24 years (albeit a relatively peaceful tenure) of one-party rule. Cameroon's president Paul Biya has been in power since 1982, and is only the second man to lead the country. In late 2003, the media rights organization Reporters Without Borders criticized the closures of around a dozen private radio and TV stations in the country, and warned that Cameroon risked becoming one of the most repressive countries in the region with regard to freedom of expression.[182]

In sum, most observers will agree that there is an enormous need for political reform throughout Africa. As described in the next chapter of this volume, authoritarian regimes are often correlated with a history of conflict, political violence, and endemic insecurity. In many of these cases, the government of a resource-rich nation aligned itself with foreign companies and governments willing to pay handsomely for these resources, even at the expense of those citizens who have entrusted these government leaders with their well-being. As the

U.S. pursues greater involvement in the Gulf of Guinea, we must be cautious about enabling these types of authoritarian regimes—through massive influx of oil revenues—to strengthen their capacity for repression and corruption.

Corruption and Mismanagement

According to UN Secretary General Kofi Annan, corruption is found in all countries—big and small, rich and poor—but it is in the developing world that its effects are most destructive. Corruption hurts the poor disproportionately by diverting funds intended for development, undermining a government's ability to provide basic services, feeding inequality and injustice and discouraging foreign aid and investment. Corruption is a key element in economic underperformance and a major obstacle to poverty alleviation and development.[183]

Oil money has the potential to support enormous corruption—or at the very least mismanagement. According to David Goldwyn, former Assistant Secretary of Energy for International Affairs, "the majority of the world's resource-rich governments are also the world's most corrupt and ineffective."[184] In Africa, a corrupt elite—not the general population—benefits from oil resources.[185] Further, nearly all the oil-producing countries on the continent are (or are rapidly becoming) heavily dependent on the oil sector of their economies, accounting for 80-95% of export revenues in some cases. African governments know that the West desires their oil, and more than a few government leaders in the region appear committed to controlling the development of the oil extraction industry in order to ensure the largest potential revenue stream (and, at least in some cases, ensuring greater personal wealth for the corrupt government elite).

Corruption by wealthy elites is also problematic, because much of this graft is immediately invested outside the continent. About 40% of all African private portfolios are held overseas, and this share is likely to be even greater when the funds were obtained through corruption.[186] For example, illegal accounts belonging to (former Nigerian President) Abacha's friends and families were unearthed and frozen in Switzerland ($750 million), Liechtenstein ($100 million), Luxembourg ($630 million) in addition to the $1 billion voluntarily handed over by Abacha's family and associates. Investigators still believe that there are vast amounts of money to be unearthed in accounts held in the UK, US, the Channel Islands, British Virgin Islands, France and Germany amongst others.[187]

As Robert Klitgaard has argued, corruption is a natural result of a monopoly of decision making held by a small number of individuals, enormous discretion in how that monopoly is used, and a lack of oversight and accountability. Thus, it is hardly surprising that it affects many African states.[188] Indeed, in many African countries, the mechanisms of participation and accountability are neutralized by patrimonial structures and practices, by personal rule and clientelism, and by a significant disconnect between the state and society.[189] Oil-financed patronage has been a fundamental part of the strategy pursued by many of these countries' leaders for the consolidation and conservation of power. According to a recent Congressional Research Service report, "in many cases, corruption is a natural outgrowth of the social and cultural practices that characterize the patrimonial state in Africa—a type of organization in which personal and/or patron-client ties, rather than prescriptive criteria or elections, determine the allocation of resources (and often of public office)."[190] According to a recent report by the Royal Institute of International Affairs, political parties in the countries like Nigeria "exercise clientelist relationships with the electorate. Local, national and foreign patronage is largely blamed for the crisis in the country's politics. Parties tend to be based on individuals and in a society in which there is much poverty, vote-buying has become commonplace.[191]

Another way elites can be favored in corrupt regimes is through tax avoidance. Due to longstanding patronage networks, many African countries have tax regimes that favor the wealthy and powerful, and corruption exacerbates this effect.[192] The effect of all this macro and micro corruption is predictable. When the public faces ongoing demands for bribes, witnesses high level embezzlement, and knows that the rich avoid taxation, there remains very little incentive to support the government.[193] As a recent UN report indicates, "the cumulative effect of public corruption is to destroy respect for the law and the state. This profoundly undermines democracy, as many citizens come to regard the state as an adversary rather than a representative body."[194] Overall, corruption and mismanagement is rampant throughout West and Central Africa, and undermines the potential that oil wealth offers for dramatic improvement in the lives of the region's inhabitants.

Underdevelopment

As the data tables for these countries indicate, there is widespread poverty throughout the Gulf of Guinea.[195] Even in Angola and Nigeria, two of the most oil-rich countries of western Africa, there are high levels of unemployment, poverty and external debt. In many cases, governments have not been able to respond effectively to health crises like the spread of malaria or HIV/AIDS, and as a result are viewed as incompetent, unable to protect or care for the very citizens for whose lives they are entrusted. Malaria is the leading cause of death in many countries, and is likely to remain so because of the growing resistance both of the malarial parasite to drugs, as well as of the malaria-transmitting mosquito to insecticides. Large segments of the populations in the Gulf of Guinea have no access to clean drinking water, and instead rely on water infested with a range of bacteria, sometimes even poisonous.

Other preventable ills that governments have been unable to halt include measles, whooping cough, polio, cerebrospinal meningitis, gastroenteritis, diarrhea, tuberculosis, bronchitis, waterborne infectious diseases such as schistosomiasis, and sexually transmitted infections. Human immunodeficiency virus

(HIV) infections, which cause acquired immunodeficiency syndrome (AIDS), are becoming more and more prevalent, and have ravaged the military and police forces of many African countries, with alarming implications for their ability to provide security.

History has repeatedly demonstrated how poverty is often associated with political instability, and this offers a less than optimistic prognosis for the countries of West and Central Africa. According to a recent document prepared by the New Partnership for Africa's Development (NEPAD), "Africa faces grave challenges and the most urgent of these are the eradication of poverty and the fostering of socio-economic development, in particular, through democracy and good governance."[196] The fact that many of the countries discussed here are rich in oil resources adds an important dimension to the challenge of tackling poverty. In most oil-producing countries of the world, a general friction exists between the Western-oriented extraction of hydrocarbons, facilitated by national governments, and the local populations who see the oil and gas as their sovereign property but often receive no direct benefits from their exploitation. Large, inefficient governments absorb all the revenues without providing the services needed by their citizenry, and this can lead to anger towards both national governments and Westerners involved.[197] Just like the Middle East, the people of oil producing countries in Africa do not see the benefits of the oil extraction industry. However, unlike the Middle East, resentment and anger related to the oil industry appears to be currently focused on the corruption and incompetence of their national governments, rather than against the U.S. (More details on political instability and security is provided in Chapter 3 of this volume.) Still, this brief examination of current conditions in the Gulf of Guinea clearly reveals the volatile context of these oil-rich nations, and the potential for political instability in any African oil-producing country has significant implications for U.S. energy and security policy.

The Good News: An Emerging Commitment to Good Governance

Despite the governance challenges identified in this brief overview of the Gulf of Guinea nations, a brighter future is emerging on the horizon, driven by both internal and external forces. For example, in June 2005 a national conference was held in Abuja, Nigeria to craft a new constitution that would help resolve the nation's longstanding dispute over how to distribute the country's immense oil wealth.[198] Good governance is obviously critical to the successful future of West and Central Africa; it is also vital for the long-term viability of Western country's investments in the oil extraction industries of this region.

Good governance has multiple features, including the enforcement of the rule of law; political stability and competence; fiscal and economic competence; a free press for the open exchange of ideas; and transparency in governmental activities, through which citizens can gain the information necessary to hold their leaders accountable. Unfortunately, this latter item poses a significant challenge in the energy sector. According to an index maintained by Transparency International, the oil and gas industry is the world's third most corrupt industry.[199] Susan Hawley, author of *Exporting Corruption: Privatization, Multinationals and Bribery*, argues that unless both the oil exporting nations and the wealthy countries who import this oil agree to new, higher standards of transparency and proactive monitoring protocols, corruption and mismanagement will continue to plague regions like the Gulf of Guinea.[200] The dimension of proactive monitoring—in concert with legal prosecution of bribery cases—is particularly important; as Michael Wiehen of Transparency International observes: "Simply sitting still, doing business as usual and waiting for a legal judgment of bribery means that the sanction comes much too late to have any impact or relevance."[201]

At the World Summit on Sustainable Development in Johannesburg, September 2002, British Prime Minister Tony Blair announced the Extractive Industries Transparency Initiative (EITI), which calls for greater transparency both from companies on their payments to governments and government-linked entities, and from the host country governments over revenues.[202] This initiative also seeks to ensure that resource revenues are properly accounted for and contribute to sustainable development and poverty reduction. EITI is part of a G-8 initiative to fight corruption more effectively, particularly in extractive industries, and has its roots in the "Publish What You Pay" campaign championed by George Soros' Open Society Foundation and a range of non-governmental organizations.[203] Although true government transparency involves many dimensions—including accountability of expenditures, the development of policies, laws and regulations, and administration—EITI focuses on resource revenue transparency as a manageable, meaningful starting point. As described later in this volume, requiring transparency among the governments of the Gulf of Guinea is a key element of a robust U.S. foreign policy toward this region. Transparency increases accountability and reduces the risk of waste and corruption. It fosters democratic debate, improves macroeconomic management, and enhances the public's access to finances. As a result, transparency offers a unique opportunity to renew the public's trust in its government—a critical challenge seen throughout the Gulf of Guinea.

West and Central African countries participating in EITI include: Angola, Cameroon, Chad, Democratic Republic of Congo, Equatorial Guinea, Gabon, Ghana, Nigeria, Republic of Congo, and São Tomé and Príncipe.[204] Some of these countries are only beginning to launch the process, while others have published revenue and payments data. For example, Nigeria signed a "Compact to Promote Transparency and Combat Corruption: A New Partnership Between the G8 and Nigeria," and recently passed the Nigeria EITI Bill, calling for mandatory annual revenue/tax audits of the extractive industries sector. Oil companies will be legally required to disclose payments, and a recently established Oil Revenue Monitoring unit will be made independent of the Finance Ministry.[205] In Angola, the Ministry of Finance provides data on oil exports on its website, and recently produced a widely-available report on oil related earnings and expenditures. In Chad, as described earlier, a conditional loan program by the World Bank compels the government to ensure that 80% of its oil revenues are allocated to health, education, rural development, environmental concerns, and other social services.[206] São Tomé and Príncipe also adopted a new law for governing the receipt, investment, and use of oil funds. The law established a national oil fund to be held by an international custodial bank, and withdrawals from the account are limited to a single annual transfer to the budget. The country is not permitted to borrow against the account, and expenditures are to be made only for national development, poverty reduction, and the strengthening of good governance. In essence, some countries are putting in place extensive requirements for openness and transparency that go beyond the minimum requirements of the EITI.

In another sign of the emerging commitment to good governance on the continent, Nigeria's President Obasanjo proposed the creation of a new regional organization called the Gulf of Guinea Commission. As stated in a draft treaty prepared in 1999, the purpose of the Commission is to: achieve mutual trust and confidence amongst member states; create an atmosphere of mutually beneficial economic cooperation in the region; provide a framework of monitoring and control of environmental degradation to harmonize the exploitation of natural resources, including petroleum, minerals, and fisheries; and coordinate and articulate common positions related to peace and stability in the region. Several countries have agreed to become members of this commission, but thus far only Nigeria and São Tomé and Príncipe have ratified the proposed treaty. Once in full operation, this Commission has the potential to serve as a mechanism to prevent and resolve conflicts emerging from the economic and commercial exploitation of natural resources in the region.[207]

Obasanjo has also sent into retirement a number of so-called "political officers"—members of the Nigerian military with political ambitions—and has worked to root out corruption and mismanagement. By one account, an audit of a government ministry helped identify and weed out 5,000 ghost workers from the payroll.[208] According to Princeton Lyman, a fellow at the Council on Foreign Relations and a former Ambassador to Nigeria, "there has been real progress on reform in Nigeria in transparency of budget allocations, in improved revenue collection, in fiscal discipline, and pending reform of the financial sector. Steps are being taken to monitor government contracts and to bring to justice those engaged in financial crimes. Plans are under way to audit the entire oil sector, as a prelude to Nigeria meeting the criteria of the Extractive Industry Transparency Initiative, to which Nigeria was an early signatory."[209] During his first term in office, president Obasanjo established the Niger Delta Development Commission (NDDC) to plough some oil money into roads, schools and training for the region's inhabitants.[210]

Further, in order to reduce poverty and increase employment in his own country, Obasanjo established the National Economic Empowerment Development Strategy (NEEDS). The NEEDS initiative lays out a program of fiscal reform, transparency, countering corruption, investment in badly needed infrastructure, revival of agriculture, investment in health, and opening opportunities for the private sector.[211] Several of Nigeria's state governments have also launched similar programs (dubbed "SEEDS" for State Economic Empowerment Development Strategies) as well. The IMF has endorsed these efforts, and helps with quarterly monitoring. It is important to note that government corruption and mismanagement in Nigeria is not a phenomenon exclusive to the national policymaking arena. To the contrary, the most important fight against corruption in the country is taking place at the local and state government level. Information about how successful these governments have been is incomplete at best, but with continued national leadership and sustained commitment, there is hope.

Key dimensions of the NEEDS/SEEDS agenda include redefining the role of government in the economy, creating an enabling environment for private sector growth (including enforcing the primacy of the rule of law), and improving the delivery of social services. As we argue later in this volume, the U.S. should do all it can to support such local and national initiatives, while also providing the means for ensuring human security for the country's population. Other reforms put in place by the Obasanjo administration seek to foster macroeconomic stability and fiscal discipline; improve public expenditure management; implement public revenue reforms, tax reforms and customs restructuring; improve public resource management/utilization; establish a due process mechanism for government procurement contracts; improve oil sector transparency (EITI audits are scheduled to be launched in 2005, and Nigeria is a signatory to the recent G-8 Transparency Compact); ensure the rule of law and address local security problem through proper means of law enforcement; improve the efficiency, responsiveness, and delivery of services in the public sector; and rebuild the country's physical and social infrastructure.

Recent years have also seen a growing commitment to addressing the questions of good governance in Angola. In December 2002, President dos Santos named a new economic team to oversee new economic reform efforts, which has succeeded in decreasing overall government spending, rationalizing the nation's currency exchange rate, closing regulatory loopholes allowing off-budget expenditures, and capturing all revenues in the state budget.[212] Although attempts at transparency by BP and Shell resulted in government threats to withdraw their Angolan concessions. Angola elected in May 2004 to participate in the IMF's General Data Dissemination System (GDDS), created to improve the release of official statistics. That same month, the Angolan government announced that an oil deal signed with ChevronTexaco would bring the country $300 million—an important revelation that until recently would have been considered a state secret.[213] Angola is also participating in the UK's Extractive Industries Transparency Initiative (EITI), ostensibly to increase transparency by encouraging energy companies to voluntarily provide details of contracts.[214] Also, addressing its separatist rebel problem, the Angolan government announced in June 2004 that a $370 million cash injection into Cabinda would be used for improving infrastructure and social services.

Gabon has also recently taken steps toward good governance, in order to improve the investment climate and attract more interest in the energy sector. It also recently settled a territorial dispute with Equatorial Guinea that will allow oil exploration and development to proceed in a previously disputed offshore area.[215] In Gabon, President Bongo is unique among his regional counterparts not only in his longevity but also in his approach to governance. In 1993, after winning election to a 7-year term, the opposition party claimed that the balloting had been rigged, and began staging violent demonstrations. Determined to prove that he was not an autocrat who relied on brute force for his political survival, Bongo entered into talks with the opposition, negotiating what became known as the Paris Agreement in a successful attempt to restore calm. When Bongo won the second presidential elections held in 1998, similar controversy raged over his victory. The president again responded by meeting some of his critics to discuss revising legislation to guarantee free and fair elections.[216]

Finally, in 2005, members of the New Partnership for Africa's Development (NEPAD) issued a "Declaration on Democracy, Political, Economic and Corporate Governance" in which they announced their intention "to combat and eradicate corruption, which both retards economic development and undermines the moral fabric of society." They also committed themselves to "work with renewed determination to enforce the rule of law," emphasizing their determination to secure "equality of all citizens before the law and the liberty of the individual; individual and collective freedoms, including the right to form and join political parties and trade unions, in conformity with the constitution; equality of opportunity for all; the inalienable right of the individual to participate by means of free, credible and democratic political processes in periodically electing their leaders for a fixed term of office; and adherence to the separation of powers, including the protection of the independence of the judiciary and of effective parliaments."[217] The document also specified four courses of action that NEPAD members plan to take in support of promoting good governance: "adopt clear codes, standards and indicators of good governance at the national, sub-regional and continental levels; maintain an accountable, efficient and effective civil service; ensure the effective functioning of parliaments and other accountability institutions in our respective countries, including parliamentary committees and anti-corruption bodies; and ensure the independence of the judicial system that will be able to prevent abuse of power and corruption."

Together, these initiatives are welcome signs of movement in a positive direction. It is clearly in the best interests of the U.S. to do all it can to support these efforts, particularly in support of our energy security objectives. However, it also important to note that the promotion of good governance throughout Africa also contributes to the goals and objectives of the U.S.-led War on Terrorism, and supports our national security policy more generally.

Conclusion

To summarize this review of the Gulf of Guinea's opportunities and political challenges, it is useful to reflect on the example of South Africa, where a popular term "masakane" (roughly meaning getting together and working together) symbolizes a spirit of overcoming significant and historically pervasive challenges to create a bright future. The Gulf of Guinea has lots of oil, but lots of challenges to overcome before the people of the region can truly benefit from the revenues this oil will bring. Working together—through collaborative organizations like the Gulf of Guinea Commission, the African Union's Peer Review Mechanism and Peace and Security Council, the G-8-sponsored Extractive Industries Transparency Initiative, and the NEPAD declaration—is a necessary element of a broader, comprehensive strategy for creating a brighter future for West and Central Africa.

In addition, as the next two chapters will explore in greater detail, there are numerous security challenges throughout the region that must be addressed before good governance can truly be achieved. Unfortunately, because of the authoritarian regimes, corruption, and other challenges discussed in this chapter, there are a range of broad political, social, economic grievances that create a climate of unrest and dissatisfaction in the region. As individuals become dissatisfied and angry with their regimes, some resort to violence. Weaker, smaller states—particularly those in which oil discoveries are relatively recent—are particularly vulnerable to instability. Equatorial Guinea, São Tomé and Príncipe, and Chad are countries of significant concern to most observers. Here, a huge influx of cash in local markets will offer new, tempting targets for theft and corruption. As the U.S. is poised to be the main provider of this influx of cash, we must take into account the way in which these challenges (and our potential for exacerbating them) could undermine our energy security objectives. This is the focus of the remaining chapters of this volume.

Notes

1. *The Economist,* "A Survey of Sub-Saharan Africa." 7 September 1996,(Supplement), 4, cited in George B. N. Ayittey, *Africa in Chaos* (New York: St Martin's Press, 1999), 347.

2. Ayittey, *Africa in Chaos,* 347.

3. Meredeth Turshen, "The Politics of Oil in Africa," *The Scholar and Feminist Online,* 2, no. 2 (Winter 2004).

4. Jonathan Stevenson, "Africa's Growing Strategic Resonance," *Survival* 45, no. 4 (Winter, 2003): 166.

5. Jim Fisher-Thompson, "U.S. Officials Cite Importance of African Oil to U.S. Economy," U.S. Department of State, Washington File, 1 February 2002.

6. Jagdish Bhagwati and Ibrahim Gambari, "Political Will, Not Just Aid, Can Lift Africa Out of Despair," *Financial Times,* 5 July 2005.

7. Mark Doyle, "Blair Unveils Africa Action Plan," *BBC News,* 27 February 2004.

8. Bhagwati and Gambari, "Political Will, Not Just Aid."

9. Bhagwati and Gambari, "Political Will, Not Just Aid."

10. See the UN Millennium Goals website, at: http://www.unmillenniumproject.org

11. Robert Klitgaard, *Tropical Gangsters: One Man's Experience with Development and Decadence in Deepest Africa* (New York: Basic Books, Inc., 1990), x.

12. Roger Thurow, "Africa's Problems Move to Top of Global Agenda," *Foreign Policy,* 9 June 2005, A1.

13. The "G-8" is the nickname for the group of eight major industrialized nations: Canada, France, Germany, Italy, Japan, Russia, the U.K., and the U.S.

14. The debt relief agreement must be approved by the IMF before it can be implemented. Also, it is important to note that while this agreement focuses on multilateral debt, it does not address the bilateral debt. In many African countries, particularly Nigeria, the majority of debt is actually bilateral.

15. For example, see the full report of the Institute for Advanced Strategic and Political Studies, Oil Policy Initiative Group, *African Oil: A Priority for U.S. National Security and African Development* (July 2002) available online at http://www.israeleconomy.org/strategic/africawhitepaper.pdf

16. Jacinta Moran, "Three Majors Promise to Continue Push in African Upstream," *Platt's Oilgram News* 81, no. 205, 23 October 2003, 2

17. James Dao, "In Quietly Courting Africa, U.S. Likes the Dowry: Oil," *New York Times,* 19 September 2002.

18. Dao, "Quietly Courting Africa."

19. John R. Brodman, Statement to the Subcommittee on International Economic Policy, Export and Trade Promotion, Committee on Foreign Relations, U.S. Senate, 15 July 2004.

20. Neil Ford, "U.S. Targets West African Oil," *Energy Economist* (London) #262, August 2003, 1

21. Comments by Dr. Rilwanu Lukman, Secretary General of OPEC. London: Times Publications, accessed 2 January 2004, available at: http://www.times-publications.com/publications/corporate_africa/articles/rich_reserves3.html

22. Jacinta Moran, "Three Majors," 2.

23. Andrews, Jim, Vice President for International Business Development, KBR, Halliburton, telephone interview, 6 October 2003.

24. According to Jerry Kepes, managing director of the Petroleum Finance Company (PFC). See Jessica Lawrence, "U.S. Senate Hosts Discussion Of Countering The Causes Of Terrorism In Africa," U.S. Department of State, Washington File, 11 December 2002. Available online at: http://usembassy.state.gov/nigeria/wwwhp121102a.html.

25. Jessica Krueger, "U.S. Oil Stakes in West Africa," 3.

26. Jessica Krueger, "U.S. Oil Stakes in West Africa," 3.

27. More details on this conflict are provided in the next chapter of this volume.

28. John R. Brodman, Committee on Foreign Relations, U.S. Senate, July 15, 2004.

29. International Energy Agency (IEA), U.S. Department of Energy, Angola Country Brief, January 2005. Online at http://www.eia.doe.gov/emu/cabs/angola.html

30. Tony Hodges, *Angola from Afro-Stalinism to Petro-Diamond Capitalism* (Bloomington: Indiana University Press, 2001), 124.

31. Tony Hodges, *Angola,* 124.

32. Tony Hodges, *Angola,* 125.

33. Tony Hodges, *Angola,* 124.

34. Tony Hodges, *Angola,* 129.

35. Daphne Eviatar, "Can Profits Promote Democracy in Africa?" *New York Times,* (December 4, 2003).

36. IEA Angola Country Brief, January 2005.

37. "Angola" *International Petroleum Encyclopedia,* Oil and Gas Research Journal, Online Research Center, 2001. http://orc.pennet.com

38. Tony Hodges, *Angola,* 137-138.

39. Tony Hodges, *Angola,* 1.

40. *United Nations Human Development Report, 2004.* Online at http://hdr.undp.org/reports/global/2004; See also, UN Human Development Report, 2002; Special Angola Report, http://www.washingtonpost.com; and *Angola Peace Monitor,* vol. 6 (9), 14 May 2000.

41. EIA Country Report, Angola, January 2005, 1.

42. Tony Hodges, *Angola,* 129.

43. Tony Hodges, *Angola,* 136.

44. Justin Pearce, "IMF: Angola's Missing Millions" BBC October 18, 2002. Also, see "Angola's Elusive Oil Riches," *New York Times,* June 15, 2004.

45. Daniel Kaufmann, Aart Kraay, and Massimo Mastruzzi, *Governance Matters IV: New Data, New Challenges,* The World Bank, May 2005; and Transparency International, Corruptions Perception Index, 2005. Online at http://www.transparency.org.

46. C. Messiant, "Social and Political Background to the 'Democratization' and the Peace Process in Angola," Paper presented at the Seminar on Democratization in Angola (Leiden, the Netherlands, 1992) cited in Hodges, 53.

47. Swanson, p. 17, citing International Peace Academy (NY) and Fafo (Norway), 2001, "Private Sector Actors in Zones of Conflict: Research Challenges and Policy Responses," 8.

48. Tony Hodges, *Angola,* 124.

49. Tony Hodges, *Angola,* 136.

50. Tony Hodges, *Angola,* 123-124.

51. Stephen Ellis, "West Africa and its Oil," *African Affairs,* 102 (Jan 2003), 137. See also, Christine Messiant, "The Eduardo dos Santos Foundation; or, How Angola's regime is taking over civil society," *African Affairs,* 100 (2001), 287-309.

52. Tony Hodges, *Angola,* 170-171.

53. EIA Country Report, Angola, January 2005, 1.

54. Tony Hodges, *Angola*, 133-134.

55. Tony Hodges, *Angola*, 134.

56. Tony Hodges, *Angola*, 140.

57. Tony Hodges, *Angola*, 142.

58. Swanson, p. 16, citing Reuters, 12 December 2001, reported by Global Witness Press release of 13 December 2001.

59. BBC Country Profile: Cameroon, 4 August 2005. Online at: http://news.bbc.co.uk/1/hi/world/africa/country_profiles/1042937.stm

60. EIA Country Report, Chad-Cameroon, December 2004. Online at: http://www.eia.doe.gov/emeu/chad_cameroon.html

61. EIA Country Report, Chad-Cameroon, 2.

62. EIA Country Report, Chad-Cameroon, 2.

63. EIA Country Report, Chad-Cameroon, 2.

64. BBC Country Profile: Cameroon.

65. BBC Country Profile: Cameroon.

66. BBC Country Profile: Cameroon.

67. Kini Nsom, "Government Admits Cameroon Merited Corruption Champion," *The Post* (Buea, Cameroon) 25 August, 2005. Online at: http://allafrica.com/stories/200508260218.html

68. "New Government Embarks on Anti-Corruption Drive," *IRINnews.org,* UN Office for the Coordination of Humanitarian Affairs, 20 January 2005. Available online at· http://www.irinnews.org/print.asp?ReportID=45165

69. "New Government Embarks on Anti-Corruption Drive."

70. EIA Country Report, Chad and Cameroon, 2,

71. Somini Sengupta, "The Making of an African Petrostate," *New York Times,* 18 Feburary 2004.

72. *Chad Cameroon Development Project, Report No. 17,* Esso Exploration and Production Chad, Inc., (2004), 76.

73. EIA Country Report, Chad and Cameroon, 2.

74. John R. Brodman, Committee on Foreign Relations, 2004.

75. *Chad Cameroon Development Project*

76. EIA Country Report, Chad and Cameroon, 2.

77. EIA Country Report, Chad and Cameroon, 2.

78. Daniel Volman, *Oil, Arms and Violence in Africa.* Report prepared for the African Security Research Project, February 2003, available at: http://www.prairienet.org/acas/military/oilandarms.pdf

79. Somini Sengupta, "The Making of an African Petrostate."

80. Somini Sengupta, "The Making of an African Petrostate."

81. Department of State, African Affairs Bureau website: http://www.state.gov/p/af

82. *CIA Factbook, 2005*

83. John R. Brodman, Committee on Foreign Relations, 2004.

84. EIA Country Report, Congo. June 2005. Online at: http://www.eia.doe.gov/emeu/cabs/congo.html

85. EIA Country Report, Congo, 2.

86. U.S. State Department, Congo country profile, 2005. Available online at; http://www.state.gov/r/pa/ei/bgn/2825.htm.

87. EIA Country Report, Congo, 2.

88. U.S. State Department, Congo country profile.
89. EIA Country Report, Congo, 2.
90. EIA Country Report, Congo, 2.
91. BBC Country Profile, Equatorial Guinea. 5 May 2005. Online at: http://news.bbc.co.uk/1/hi/world/africa/country_profiles/1023151.stm
92. David L. Goldwyn and J. Stephen Morrison, *A Strategic Approach to Governance and Security in the Gulf of Guinea,* CSIS Report on Gulf of Guinea, July 2005.
93. Goldwyn and Morrison, CSIS Report on Gulf of Guinea.
94. EIA Country Report, Equatorial Guinea, May 2005. Available online at: http://www.eia.doe.gov/emeu/cabs/eqguinea.pdf
95. Briony Hale, "Africa's Oil Star Strives to Shine," *BBC News,* 13 November 2002.
96. Equatorial Guinea EITI Implementation Update. Available online at: http://www.eitransparency.org/countryupdates/equatorialguineacountryupdate.htm
97. Ken Silverstein, "U.S. Oil Politics and the 'Kuwait of Africa.'"
98. Equatorial Guinea EITI Implementation Update.
99. *The Economist,* "What Oil Can Do to Tiny States," 23 January 2003.
100. Norm Coleman, Chairman; Carl Levin, Ranking Minority Member, "Money Laundering and Foreign Corruption: Enforcement and Effectiveness of the Patriot Act Case Study Involving Riggs Bank," Report prepared by the Minority Staff of the Permanent Subcommittee on Investigations, Committee on Governmental Affairs, 14 July 2004. Available online at: http://govt-aff.senate.gov.
101. Jean-Christophe Servant, "The New Gulf Oil States," *Le Monde Diplomatique,* January 8, 2003.
102. Robert Klitgaard, *Tropical Gangsters,* p. 246-252.
103. Robert Klitgaard, *Tropical Gangsters,* p. ix.
104. Norm Coleman, Chairman; Carl Levin, Ranking Minority Member, "Money Laundering and Foreign Corruption."
105. Ken Silverstein, "U.S. Oil Politics and the 'Kuwait of Africa.'"
106. *The Economist,* "What Oil Can Do."
107. Nicholas Shaxson, "Equatorial Guinea's Great Survivor," *BBC News,* March 17, 2004.
108. Bob Simon, "Kuwait of Africa?" CBS News, November 14, 2003. Online at www.cbsnews.com/stories/2003/11/14/60minutes
109. Bob Simon, "Kuwait of Africa?"
110. Bob Simon, "Kuwait of Africa?"
111. Ken Silverstein, "U.S. Oil Politics and the 'Kuwait of Africa,'"
112. Bob Simon, "Kuwait of Africa?"
113. Bob Simon, "Kuwait of Africa?"
114. Ken Silverstein, "U.S. Oil Politics and the 'Kuwait of Africa.'"
115. John R. Brodman, Committee on Foreign Relations, 2004.
116. Ken Silverstein, "U.S. Oil Politics and the 'Kuwait of Africa.'"
117. John R. Brodman, 2004.
118. *BBC News,* Country Profile, Gabon, May 6, 2005.
119. EIA Country Analysis Brief, Gabon, November 2004, p. 2. Online at: http://www.eia.doe.gov/emeu/cabs/gabon.html
120. EIA Country Analysis Brief, Gabon, 2004.
121. EIA Country Analysis Brief, Gabon, 2004.
122. EIA Country Analysis Brief, Gabon, 2004.

123. BBC News, Country Profile, Gabon, 2005.

124. Department of State, Bureau of Africa Affairs, Background note, Gabon, April 2005.

125. *The Economist,* "What Oil Can Do."

126. Department of State, Bureau of Africa Affairs, Background note, Gabon, April 2005.

127. Joseph Winter, "Obasanjo's Thankless Task," BBC News Analysis, October 7, 2004. Online at http://news.bbc.co.uk/hi/world/africa/3724520.stm.

128. Stephen Ellis, "West Africa and its Oil," 137.

129. Population data referenced in this chapter are from the *CIA 2005 Factbook,* online at: http://www.cia.gov/cia/publications/factbook/index.html.

130. Goldwyn and Morrison, CSIS Report on Gulf of Guinea.

131. Princeton Lyman, "Nigeria's Economic Prospects: An International Perspective," Address to the Nigeria-U.S. Investment Conference, September 16, 2004. Online at: http://www.cfr.org/bio.php?meetv=&id=2373&puby=2004.

132. Goldwyn and Morrison, CSIS Report on Gulf of Guinea.

133. Goldwyn and Morrison, CSIS Report on Gulf of Guinea.

134. "Constitutional change conference deadlocks over oil dispute," IRIN News.org, UN Office for the Coordination of Humanitarian Affairs, July 8 2005.

135. Jessica Krueger, "U.S. Oil Stakes in West Africa," 2.

136. Oil reserve and production data referenced in this section are from the International Energy Administration's Country Analysis report on Nigeria, April 2005. Online at: http://www.eia.doe.gov/emeu/cabs/nigeria.html.

137. Neil Ford, "U.S. Targets West African Oil," *Energy Economist,* London August 2003, #262, p. 1

138. International Energy Administration, "Nigeria," Country Analysis Report (April 2005), p. 2. Online at: http://www.eia.doe.gov/emeu/cabs/nigeria.html.

139. International Energy Administration, "Nigeria," 2005, p. 2

140. International Energy Administration, "Nigeria," 2005, p. 2

141. John R. Brodman, 2004.

142. Oil reserve and production data referenced in this section are from the International Energy Administration's Country Analysis report on Nigeria, April 2005.

143. "Constitutional change conference deadlocks over oil dispute," *IRIN News.org,* July 8 2005.

144. Meredeth Turshen, "The Politics of Oil in Africa," *The Scholar and Feminist Online,* 2(2), Winter 2004.

145. John Vidal, "Oil rig hostages are freed by strikers as mercenaries fly out," *The Guardian* (UK), May 3, 2003. Online at: http://www.guardian.co.uk/oil/story/0,11319,948743,00.html

146. "Constitutional change conference deadlocks over oil dispute," *IRIN News.org,* July 8 2005.

147. "Constitutional change conference deadlocks over oil dispute," *IRIN News.org,* July 8 2005.

148. Michael Peel, "Why Africa Keeps Fighting Over Oil," *The Christian Science Monitor,* 1 October 2004, referenced in Molly Farneth, "Powering Foreign Policy, p. 11.

149. A.A. Nwankwo, *Nigeria the Stolen Billions* (Enugu, Nigeria: Fourth Dimension Publishing Co., 1999), p. x.

150. "Constitutional change conference deadlocks over oil dispute," *IRIN News.org,* July 8 2005.
151. Dianna Games. *An Oil Giant Reforms: The Experience of South African Companies Doing Business in Nigeria.* Pretoria: The South African Institute of International Affairs, 2004. p. 2-3.
152. Joseph Winter, "Obasanjo's Thankless Task.".
153. Joseph Winter, "Obasanjo's Thankless Task."
154. Olusegun Obasanjo, "Capacity Building and the Challenges of Realizing and Enhancing the Potentials of Nigerian and West African Offshore Petroleum Industry," Keynote Address at the Offshore West Africa Conference and Exhibition, March 17, 2004.
155. Ngozi Okonjo-Iweala, "Anti-Corruption Reforms in Nigeria," paper presented to the Topical Seminar on Energy and Security in Africa (Abuja Nigeria, March 2005).
156. Princeton Lyman, "Nigeria's Economic Prospects," 2001.
157. "Nigerians Wary of Corruption Crackdown," *BBC News,* May 2, 2005.
158. "Nigerians Wary of Corruption Crackdown," *BBC News,* May 2, 2005.
159. Dianna Games. *An Oil Giant Reforms,* 2004.
160. A.A. Nwankwo, *Nigeria the Stolen Billions,* 1999, p. 43-47.
161. "Nigerians ware of corruption crackdown," *BBC News,* May 2, 2005.
162. A.A. Nwankwo, *Nigeria the Stolen Billions,* 1999, p. vii.
163. "Obasanjo Fires Education Minister for Bribing Senate Leader," *IRIN News.org,* 23 March 2005. Online at: http://www.irinnews.org/report.asp?ReportID=46283.
164. United Nations Office on Drugs and Crime report, "Crime and Development in Africa," June 2005. Available online at: http://www.unodc.org/unodc/index.html.
165. Heather Deegan, "Elections in Africa – The Past Ten Years," Elections in Africa Briefing Paper No. 2, Royal Institute of International Affairs, April 2003, p. 4.
166. Joao Gomes Porto, "Coup D'Etat in São Tomé and Príncipe, *African Security Review,* 12(4), 2003, p. 33.
167. "US Funds Study for Airport Expansion and Deep-Water Port," *Vitrina* (Sao Tome news service, online at: http://www.cstome.net/vitrina), as reported by *United Nations Integrated Regional Information Network* (February 16, 2004).
168. Jean-Christophe Servant, "The New Gulf Oil States," *Le Monde Diplomatique,* January 8, 2003.
169. Edmund Daukoru, "Address on the Occasion of the Signing of the Production Sharing Contract (Psc) in Respect of Block 01 in the Nigeria- São Tomé and Príncipe Joint Development Zone," 1 February 2005.
170. "Amnesty for Sao Tome coup," *BBC News,* July 24, 2004. Online at: http://news.bbc.co.uk/2/hi/africa/3093331.stm
171. Joao Gomes Porto, "Coup D'Etat in São Tomé and Príncipe," 2003, p. 34.
172. Joao Gomes Porto, "Coup D'Etat in São Tomé and Príncipe," 2003, p. 34.
173. "Amnesty for Sao Tome coup," *BBC News,* July 24, 2004.
174. Bacher, Hans Ulrich and Olivier Cadot, "Oil and Chad's Northern Rebellion: Post hoc, ergo propter hoc?" European Rim Policy and Investment Council, July 2003, available at: http://www.erpic.org/perihelion/articles2003/july.htm.
175. Le Billon, 1999, p. 6.
176. Daniel Volman, "Oil, Arms, and Violence in Africa."
177. Stephen Ellis, "West Africa and its Oil," 135.

178. George B.N. Ayittey, *Africa in Chaos* (New York: St. Martin's Griffin, 1999), p. 21.

179. Heather Deegan, "Elections in Africa," 2.

180. George B.N. Ayittey, *Africa in Chaos*, p. 49.

181. *CIA World Factbook*

182. BBC Country Profile: Cameroon. Online at: http://news.bbc.co.uk/1/hi/world/africa/country_profiles/1042937.stm

183. United Nations Secretary General Kofi Annan in his statement on the adoption by the General Assembly of the United Nations Convention against Corruption.

184. Daniel L. Goldwyn, "Extracting Transparency," *Georgetown Journal of International Affairs,* Winter/Spring 2004, p. 6.

185. Richter and Tsalik.

186. United Nations Office on Drugs and Crime report, "Crime and Development in Africa," June 2005. Available online at: http://www.unodc.org/unodc/index.html

187. "Tracking Abacha's Stolen Billions." http://www.clickafrique.com/0700rpt/politics1707.asp, cited in United Nations Office on Drugs and Crime report, "Crime and Development in Africa," June 2005. Available online at: http://www.unodc.org/unodc/index.html

188. See, for example, Robert Klitgaard, "International Cooperation Against Corruption" *Finance & Development,* v35 n1 (March 1998) pp.3-7, as cited in Phil Williams and Doug Brooks, "Captured, Criminal, and Contested States: Organized Crime and Africa in the Twenty-First Century," *South African Journal of International Affairs,* 6(2), Winter 1999, pp. 86-96.

189. Rachel Flanary, "The State in Africa: Implications for Democratic Reform" *Crime, Law and Social Change* (Special Issue on Dealing with Corruption: The Next Steps edited by Alan Doig Vol. 29 Nos 2-3 (1998) pp. 179-196, as cited in Phil Williams and Doug Brooks, "Captured, Criminal, and Contested States: Organized Crime and Africa in the Twenty-First Century," *South African Journal of International Affairs,* 6(2), Winter 1999, pp. 86-96.

190. Congressional Research Service, "Nation's Hospitable to Organized Crime and Terrorism," Library of Congress, Federal Research Division, October, 2003

191. Heather Deegan, "Elections in Africa," 5.

192. United Nations Office on Drugs and Crime report, "Crime and Development in Africa," June 2005. Available online at: http://www.unodc.org/unodc/index.html

193. United Nations Office on Drugs and Crime report, June 2005.

194. United Nations Office on Drugs and Crime report, June 2005.

195. See Appendix A for a comparative data table of all the countries

196. New Partnership for Africa's Development (NEPAD). "A Summary of NEPAD Action Plans." Online at: http://www.nepad.org/2005/files/documents/2.pdf

197. Andrews.

198. "Constitutional change conference deadlocks over oil dispute," IRIN News.org, UN Office for the Coordination of Humanitarian Affairs, July 8 2005.

199. See their website at: http://www.transparency.org and the Global Corruption Report, at: http://www.globalcorruptionreport.org.

200. Susan Hawley, *Turning a Blind Eye: Corruption and the UK Export Credits Guarantee Department.* London: The Corner House, June 2003.

201. Michael Wiehen, as quoted in Susan Hawley, *Turning a Blind Eye: Corruption and the UK Export Credits Guarantee Department*. London: The Corner House, June 2003.

202. See their website, at: http://www.eitransparency.org

203. Dianna Games. *An Oil Giant Reforms,* 12.

204. See their website, at: http://www.eitransparency.org

205. Source: http://www.eitransparency.org/countryupdates/nigeriacountryupdate.htm

206. EIA Country Report, Angola, December 2004, available at http://www.eia.doe.gov/emeu/angola.html

207. Goldwyn and Morrison, CSIS Report on Gulf of Guinea.

208. Ngozi Okonjo-Iweala, "Anti-Corruption Reforms in Nigeria," paper presented to the Topical Seminar on Energy and Security in Africa (Abuja Nigeria, March 2005).

209. Princeton Lyman, "Nigeria's Economic Prospects," 2004.

210. Joseph Winter, "Obasanjo's Thankless Task."

211. Princeton Lyman, "Nigeria's Economic Prospects," 2004.

212. U.S. Department of State, Bureau of African Affairs, "Background Notes: Angola," June 2005. Online at http://www.state.gov

213. "Angola's Elusive Oil Riches," *New York Times,* June 15, 2004.

214. EIA Country Report, Angola, January 2005, p. 2.

215. John R. Brodman, Committee on Foreign Relations, 2004.

216. Daniel Mboungou Mayengue, "Gabon's President for Life" BBC Focus on Africa, January-March, 2003.

217. New Partnership for Africa's Development (NEPAD). "A Summary of NEPAD Action Plans." Online at: http://www.nepad.org/2005/files/documents/2.pdf

Chapter 3
A Region in Trouble

On May 20, 2005, the U.S. State Department issued a travel warning, advising citizens not to travel to Nigeria. The warning stated that "the lack of law and order in Nigeria poses considerable risks to travelers" and that "robberies by armed gangs have been reported on rural roads and within major cities."[1] Citizens—particularly those connected to the petroleum industry—were warned about kidnappings, and were told that "violent crime committed by ordinary criminals, as well as by persons in police and military uniforms, can occur throughout the country." Perhaps most disconcerting, the warning expressed "concern about the presence of groups and individuals linked to international terrorism" in the country, noting that "links were uncovered connecting Nigerians to al Qaeda in 2004" and that "senior al Qaeda leadership has expressed interest publicly in overthrowing the government of Nigeria."[2] Given the potential bright future for the region, as described in the previous chapter, such dire warnings should concern any observer.

West and Central Africa has long been one of the most conflict-ridden regions of the world. Since the end of the Cold War, African nations have seen a number of civil wars and increased ethnic violence, and have grappled with a variety of related security challenges, from refugees and poverty to corruption and the expanding HIV/AIDS pandemic. Conflicts in West and Central Africa typically encompass a cross-national dimension, as civil strife in one country tends to spill over into neighboring states. Porous borders throughout the region facilitate the trafficking of weapons and people, resulting in two different kinds of problems. First, the flow of weapons and people into a conflict region can prolong and intensify the fighting. Second, the flow of people away from a conflict region—in the form of refugees fleeing the fighting, as well as rebels seeking a safe haven from government security forces—creates a number of security challenges for neighboring countries, who would just as soon not have anything to do with the conflict. Further, the free flow of weapons out of a conflict region (as often happens when the violence has subsided) helps to fuel conflicts elsewhere. Border security is thus one of the most important security challenges in the Gulf of Guinea.

Within this context of porous borders and small arms proliferation, strategic resources like oil, gas, diamonds and important minerals can be seen as both a blessing and a potential curse. While global demand for such resources offers the potential for economic prosperity for average citizens throughout the region, conflicts over who will control these resources have led to considerable bloodshed over the past several decades. Indeed, the most troubling elements in the global security environment (non-state actors, international criminal syndicates, terrorist organizations) are especially dangerous in regions where oil revenues can purchase relatively unlimited power so easily. As Daniel Volman of the African Security Research Project has observed, "the possession of oil resources has unique consequences for national security and internal stability...oil production is capital intensive (and) requires the cooperation of central governments willing to protect these large foreign investments...it also can lead to political conflict and violence because it increases the stakes of political competition and encourages rival leaders and parties to resort to the use of force to gain control of the oil revenues."[3] With increasingly available (and lethal) paramilitary forces throughout the region, a state's professional military and police forces may not offer much hope for effectively countering the terrorist threat emerging in the Gulf of Guinea.

Despite attempts to enhance security throughout the region—particularly since September 11, 2001—conditions that make many countries in Africa desirable locations for terrorists still persist. These include a shortage of financial and technical resources, areas of instability and prolonged violence, corruption, weak judicial and financial regulatory systems, and porous borders and unregulated coastlines facilitating the movement of persons and illicit goods. This chapter will explore the most common security vulnerabilities of the region—a good majority of which are directly related to the long history of political instability in most West and Central African countries.

A History of Political Instability[4]

According to a recent report from the United Nations Office on Drugs and Crime, "Today, in 2005, it would be difficult to sum up the situation in West Africa in one paragraph, but it could fairly be said that democracy co-exists with a high degree of political violence in several countries of the region."[5] Indeed, West Africa has for many years been one of Africa's most politically volatile regions—35 out 72 successful coups in Africa between 1960 and 1990 occurred in this subregion.[6] In Nigeria and Côte d'Ivoire (Ivory Coast) internal communal violence has occurred during and after multiparty elections. The United Nations has poured billions of dollars and thousands of peacekeeping troops into West and Central Africa to try and curb the violence in some areas, and maintain a fragile stability in others. And yet, recent coup attempts in Equatorial Guinea, Sao Tome and Principe, and Nigeria illustrate a number of important concerns about Africa's new oil wealth.

In June 2002, a court jailed 68 people for up to 20 years for an alleged coup plot against Equatorial Guinea President Obiang Nguema. They included the main opposition leader Placido Mico Abogo. Amnesty International claimed that many of the defendants at the trial showed signs of torture.[7] Indeed, according to a report in *The Economist*, "many defendants turned up with broken arms and legs."[8] In March 2004, Zimbabwean police in the capitol city of Harare impounded a plane that flew in from South Africa with 64 alleged mercenaries aboard. The group said they were providing security for a mine in Democratic Republic of Congo, but a couple of days later an Equatorial Guinean minister announced that they had detained a group of 15 Armenians and South Africans, men who were believed to be the advance party for the group captured in Zimbabwe. The men were put on trial and received various sentences for plotting a coup in Equatorial Guinea. In EG, the mercenary group's leader—Nick du Toit, a South African—was sentenced to 34 years in jail. In Zimbabwe, the British leader of the mercenary group Executive Outcomes—Simon Mann—was sentenced to seven years for illegally trying buy weapons, a sentence that was reduced to four years on appeal. Others arrested with him were acquitted of any links to a suspected coup attempt after magistrates in Zimbabwe said prosecutors had failed to prove their case. One suspect, a German, died in prison in Equatorial Guinea after what Amnesty International claimed was torture. At the trial in Equatorial Guinea, du Toit told the court he was recruited by Simon Mann, and that they were trying to install an exiled opposition politician, Severo Moto. Subsequently, Moto was sentenced in absentia to a long prison term.[9]

In neighboring Sao Tome and Principe, an elaborate coup attempt was launched against the government of elected President Fradique de Menezes on July 16, 2003, while he was visiting Nigeria. A group of retired Sao Tomean mercenaries seized control of the twin-island state with the help of disgruntled officers in the country's small and poorly paid army. Denouncing rampant corruption in Menezes' government, the rebels declared a "junta of national salvation," saying the deposed leaders had no solution to the nation's problems and that they had acted in response to the "continuing social and economic decline of the country." A week later, however, the leaders of the coup were forced to capitulate, and Menezes returned home, accompanied by Nigerian President Olusegun Obasanjo.

Less than a year later, in April 2004, a plot to overthrow the Nigerian government was discovered and prevented. Four military officers, led by Major Hamza al-Mustapha (the former security chief of the late military dictator Sani Abacha) and a civilian were charged with planning to assassinate President Obasanjo. Most of the officers belonged to the Hausa tribe, one of the most powerful groupings in the Muslim-dominated north, which supported the opposition party during the 2003 elections in which Obasanjo won a second term.[10] According to the charges read in court, the group had been actively seeking to purchase a Stinger surface-to-air missile to be used in shooting down President Obasanjo's helicopter. One member of the group had already prepared a draft of a speech outlining the new regime that would replace Obasanjo's elected government.[11]

These recent coup attempts are but the latest in a long, troubling history of political instability throughout the region. A brief review of this history reveals a number of internal and external factors that play a role in the security challenges now faced by the nations of West Africa.

A Brief History of West Africa's Major Political Conflicts

For most Africans, the 1960s were the most important decade of the 20th century, as a wave of successful independence movements throughout the continent led to the establishment of most present-day African nations. In several of these, the transition from colony to nationhood was one of relative peace and optimism. The country of Gabon was granted its independence from France on August 1960, and in 1961 Leon Mba was elected president. A military coup overthrew President Mba's government in 1964, but French troops intervened and helped restore him to power. Upon his death in 1967, his vice president Albert Bernard Bongo succeeded him in the presidency. A single party system (until the 1990s) and President Bongo's popular management style helped ensure Gabon's relative stability throughout the next 35 years.

Similarly, its neighbors to the north and west—Cameroon and Equatorial Guinea—have enjoyed comparatively more peace and stability than several other countries in the Gulf of Guinea. In Cameroon, independence was formally achieved on January 1, 1960, and Ahmadou Ahidjo became its first president. The country was admitted to the United Nations in September of that year. A small, pro-Communist rebellion was suppressed by 1963, and President Ahidjo remained in office until 1982. Equatorial Guinea was granted independence from Spain on October 12, 1968, and Francisco Macias Nguema served as president for the next eleven years.

In contrast, the 1960s were a time of considerable turmoil for the northern giant of the region, Nigeria. The country became independent on October 1, 1960 mainly as a federation of three regions, corresponding roughly to the three main ethnic identities of the country—the Hausa, concentrated in the far north and neighboring country of Niger, the Yoruba of southwestern Nigeria, and the Igbo in the southeastern portion of the country. Under the constitution, each of the three regions retained a substantial measure of self-government, while the federal government was given exclusive powers in defense and security, foreign relations, and commercial and fiscal policies.

During the early 1960s, regional and ethnic tensions escalated between ethnic nationalities based largely on issues of representation. Prime Minister Tafawa Balewa, head of the Northern People's Congress (the largest of the three federated regions) routinely imprisoned leading opposition politicians, adding fuel to the already deteriorating political situation. Violence marred the Nigerian elections of 1964, and on January 15, 1966 a small group of army officers—mostly southeastern Igbos led by Major General Johnson Aguiyi-Ironsi—overthrew the government and assassinated Prime Minister Balewa and the premiers of the northern and western regions. The military government that assumed power was unable to quiet ethnic tensions or produce a federal constitution acceptable to all sections of the country. On July 29 of that year, northern Hausa-backed army officers staged another coup, killing Ironsi and replacing him with Lieutenant Colonel Yakubu Gowon. The coup was followed by a massacre of thousands of Igbo in the northern territories, who fled to their homelands in the southeast. As a result of these events, increasingly strong Igbo secessionist sentiment emerged.

In May 1967, Gowon's administration unveiled a plan to create a new 12-state structure for Nigeria. Among the most significant changes this reflected, the Eastern region would be divided into three states, two of them dominated by non-Igbo groups, ensuring the Igbo would not have access to the oil-rich Niger Delta region. The Igbo rejected these proposed constitutional revisions and insisted on full autonomy for the east. Finally, on May 27, 1967, Lieutenant Colonel Emeka Ojukwu—the military governor of the eastern region, who emerged as the leader of Igbo secessionist sentiment—declared the independence of the eastern region as the "Republic of Biafra," launching a violent civil war. Biafran forces crossed the Niger River, moving west in an effort to capture Lagos, the capital of Nigeria at the time. Gowon's military drove them back, imposed a naval blockade, and launched its own invasion of northern Biafra. Although France granted formal recognition to the independent Republic of Biafra, and provided military support to the rebels, the United Kingdom backed the Nigerian federal government and by January 1970 the Biafran revolt had been crushed and Nigerian forces declared victory in the civil war.

Other countries in the Gulf of Guinea faced similar forms of political turmoil. In the Republic of Congo, independence from France was granted independence on August 15, 1960 and the people chose Fulbert Youlou (a former Catholic priest) as their first president.[12] Youlou's three years in power were marked by ethnic tensions and political rivalries, and in August 1963 he was overthrown by groups affiliated with organized labor and opposition political parties. The Congolese military briefly took charge of the country and installed a civilian provisional government headed by Alphonse Massamba-Debat, whose administration was topped by a military coup in August 1968. Major Marien Ngouabi was chosen by the new National Revolutionary Council to be the new president. This Council was renamed the Congolese Labor Party later that year, and this party has held a tight grip on power ever since.

Meanwhile, countries neighboring those of the Gulf of Guinea also struggled with political coups and other forms of violence, some of which spilled over into other parts of the region. For example, in nearby Ghana, a group of senior army and police officers overthrew the government of Kwame Nkrumah in 1966, and banned his supporters from participating politics. A decade earlier, Ghana had (in 1957) become the first state in sub-Saharan to gain political independence from European colonial rule, and was initially held up as a model for other emerging independent countries to follow. Nkrumah, an ambitious leader with an ambitious socialist political agenda, spearheaded a number of development projects, including the widely-heralded Volta dam project, one of the world's largest and most successful hydroelectric projects. However, he also ruled with a heavy hand, reflected in the Deportation Act of 1957 (which made it legal for the government to expel all foreigners who were deemed a threat to the nation) and the Preventive Detention Act of 1958 (which allowed the government to detain persons for up to five years without trial). Despite a series of attempted assassinations and bomb attacks throughout the early 1960s (in which hundreds were killed or injured), Nkrumah developed a cult of personality (through the government-controlled newspapers) and amassed greater central control over every aspect of the government, declaring Ghana a one-party state in 1964.

The combination of a downward spiraling economic situation and increasingly dictatorial government policies led to increasing dissatisfaction with Nkrumah's administration, and on February 24, 1966 he was deposed in an almost bloodless coup. Over 500 of his supporters were imprisoned, and a variety of programs and projects were halted or reversed. Socialist organizations that Nkrumah had founded—including the Young Pioneers Movement, the Ghana Farmer's Cooperative Council, and Ghana Muslim Council, the Workers' Brigade, and the Kwame Nkrumah Ideological Institute—were disbanded, and new governmental agencies were established to address the country's economic troubles. However, in a surprisingly promising move, Ghana was peacefully returned to civilian control in just three and a half years. A Constituent Assembly was convened in early 1969 to draft a new constitution, which called for a parliamentary democracy. Elections were held later that year, and Kofi A. Busia was elected Prime Minister.

In the Democratic Republic of Congo, just north of Angola (the Gulf of Guinea's second largest oil producer), independence in 1960 was followed almost immediately by an army mutiny and a secessionist movement in the mineral-rich province of Katanga. A year later, its prime minister, Patrice Lumumba, was seized and killed by troops loyal to army chief Joseph Mobutu. In 1965 Mobutu seized power, later renaming the country Zaire and himself Mobutu Sese Seko.During his rule, he turned Zaire into a springboard for operations against Soviet-backed Angola and thereby ensured US backing. But he also made Zaire synonymous with corruption, and is believed by some western agencies to have amassed a personal fortune of close to $4 billion. Overall, while the 1960s began with a hopeful enthusiasm throughout much of the region, the decade closed with significantly less optimism for the future.

The 1970s witnessed the beginning of what became the continent's bloodiest and longest civil war. When Angola was granted its independence from Portugal on November 11, 1975, two opposing governments claimed to represent the new nation.[13] A civil war ensued, pitting the Marxist-oriented Popular Movement for the Liberation of Angola *(Movimento Popular de Libertação de Angola* or MPLA) against a coalition formed by the National Union for the Total Independence of Angola (*União Nacional para a Independência Total de Angola,* or UNITA) and the National Front for the Liberation of Angola (*Frente Nacional de Libertação de Angola,* or FNLA). Because of its Marxist agenda, MPLA received support from the U.S.S.R., including tanks and MIG-21 jet fighters, as well as training and operational support from 12,000-18,000 Cuban troops. Meanwhile, the U.S. and South Africa began supporting the generally pro-western FNLA-UNITA coalition, as part of the Cold War strategy of containing Soviet influence.

By early 1976, the MPLA had gained the upper hand, and its government—led by president Agostinho Neto—was gradually recognized by the international community. The defeated groups resorted to guerilla attacks, including bombings and sabotage against the strategically important Benguela railway. Meanwhile, in 1976 another opposition movement emerged in the oil-rich northern province of Cabinda. The MPLA government, with the assistance of Cuban troops, violently crushed this would-be separatist group. After Neto died in 1979, Angola's presidency was taken over by José Eduardo dos Santos, who has ruled the country ever since.

Meanwhile, the 1970s began with the final days of the Nigerian civil war, in which the Igbo had attempted to secede from Nigeria and form the Republic of Biafra. More than 2 million Nigerians died in the conflict, which formally ended on January 12, 1970 with a declaration of surrender over Biafran radio by Major General Philip Effiong. Nigerian President Yakubu Gowon announced he would remain in power for six more years to ensure a peaceful transition to democracy. However, in 1974 Gowon announced that the return to civilian rule would be postponed indefinitely. His timing was poor: High prices, chronic shortages, growing corruption, and the failure of the government to address several regional issues had already created a restless mood.

As a result, on July 29, 1975, Brigadier Murtala Ramat Muhammed overthrew Gowon in a bloodless coup. Muhammed moved quickly to address issues that Gowon had avoided. He replaced corrupt state governors, purged incompetent and corrupt members of the public services, and instigated a plan to move the national capital from industrial, coastal Lagos to neglected, interior Abuja.

Civilian rule, he declared, would be restored by 1979, and he began a five-stage process of transition. However, subsequent political and economic reforms made Muhammed extremely popular with many Nigerians, and on February 13, 1976, he was assassinated in a coup attempt, although his administration remained in power. His successor, Lieutenant General Olusegun Obasanjo, continued Muhammed's reforms, including the move toward civilian rule. Obasanjo also created seven new states to help redistribute wealth and began a massive reform of local government. In 1977 he convened a constitutional assembly, which recommended replacing the British-style parliamentary system with an American-style presidential system of separate executive and legislative branches. To ensure that candidates would appeal to ethnic groups beyond their own, the president and vice president were required to win at least 25 percent of the vote in at least two-thirds of the 19 states. The new constitution took effect in 1979. The restructured administration was called Nigeria's Second Republic. Obasanjo—who would later become a democratically elected president in 1999—won acclaim when he became Nigeria's first military leader to voluntarily surrender power to a civilian administration in 1979. Meanwhile, in nearby Ghana, a military coup was staged in 1972 by troops unhappy with cuts in military spending. Although at first popular, the military rulers were eventually overthrown in another coup, led by Flight Lieutenant Jerry John Rawlings, following a series of nationwide strikes by professionals and students. Rawlings, too, became a global celebrity by relinquishing power to an elected civilian in 1979.

The Republic of Chad, an oil-rich country located just north of Nigeria and Cameroon, also struggled during the transition from colony to independent nation, with a great deal of violence attributed to cultural tensions between the Arab-Muslim north and the predominantly black Christian south. In 1969, Muslim dissatisfaction with the first president, Ngarta Tombalbaye—a Christian southerner—developed into a guerrilla war. Even with the help of French combat forces, the government was never able to quell the insurgency, and Tombalbaye's rule became more irrational and brutal. This, combined with a severe drought, undermined his rule, and in 1975 President Tombalbaye was killed in a military coup led by another southerner, General Felix Malloum. Over the next three years, Malloum sought to diversify the ethnic representation in the government, mostly by including more northerners. He also appointed a northerner, Hissein Habré, as prime minister. However, Habré began to demand that more northerners be appointed to high government offices and that Arabic be used in place of French in broadcasting. Appealing for support among the large communities of Muslims and Arabs in N'Djamena, Habré raise a militia of northerners loyal to him, which then engaged in a series of battles against the national army in the capital city of N'Djamena in February 1979. President Malloum was replaced by a Libyan-backed northerner, Goukouki Oueddei, but the civil war among the 11 emergent factions was so widespread that it rendered the central government largely irrelevant. By mid-March 1979, more than 10,000 had died as a result of violence throughout the south.

Meanwhile, just south of Nigeria, in the Gulf of Guinea, another story of military intrigue and political turmoil was taking place in the tiny country of Equatorial Guinea. In 1972, President Francisco Macias Nguema (who had ruled the country since its indepdence in 1968) declared himself president for life. However, his increasingly repressive regime led an estimated 100,000 of the country's population to flee the country, and another 50,000 were reportedly executed. In 1979, his nephew—Teodoro Obiang Nguema Mbasogo, at the time a Lieutenant Colonel and a close advisor to the president—led a military coup which overthrew him. Shortly thereafter, Macias Nguema was tried and executed for a variety of corruption and human rights abuses.

Meanwhile, the political climate in the Republic of Congo went from bad to worse, with the assassination of President Ngouabi on March 18, 1977. Although the persons accused of shooting Ngouabi were tried and some of them executed, the motivation behind the assassination is still unclear.[14] A new Military Committee was named to head an interim government, with Colonel (later General) Joachim Yhomby-Opango as President. However, the next two years were filled with accusations of corruption, and Yhomby-Opango was removed from office on February 5, 1979 when Colonel Denis Sassou-Nguesso seized power in a military coup. Later that year, in the neighboring island nation of São Tomé and Príncipe, former Prime Minister Miguel Trovoada was arrested in October 1979 for involvement in an alleged plot against the government. Thus, the 1970s were a time of considerable instability throughout the entire Gulf of Guinea.

By 1980, many concerned observers of African politics began to feel fatigue after all the military coups and political turmoil, and it was hoped that the new decade would usher in a new, more peaceful decade. Unfortunately, that hope was short-lived. In December 1982, fuel storage tanks were blown up in the provincial capital of Huambo, Angola's second largest city. By the middle of the following year, the fighting in Angola's civil war reached a new fevered pitch, and on July 26, 1983 UNITA forces attacked a passenger train, killing nearly 50 people. Because of the Angolan government's sympathies for communist regimes, particularly the Soviet Union and Cuba, the U.S. under President Ronald Reagan continued support for UNITA. (The U.S. was, of course, also opposed to the involvement of Cuban troops in the Angolan conflict).

Meanwhile, at the opposite edge of the Gulf of Guinea, the people of Liberia awoke to their own political nightmare. On April 12, 1980, an unexpected and bloody coup led by Master-Sergeant Samuel K. Doe brought an end to the nine-year administration of President William Tolbert. The coup was uncharacteristically violent in a country which has enjoyed 133 years of relative political stability. Tolbert was shot in his bedroom, and his wife, Victoria, was arrested. A dusk-to-dawn curfew did not prevent a subsequent wave of looting, violence, and destruction of foreign-owned small businesses. In spite of international pleas for restraint, 13 high officials of the toppled regime were executed in front of television cameras on April 22. Only four of them, including President Tolbert's elder brother Frank, had been sentenced to death by an officers' tribunal. The nine others who were executed, including former Foreign Minister Cecil Dennis, Planning Minister David Neal, and Justice Minister Joseph Chesson, had been acquitted or sentenced only to life imprisonment. The United Nations, the Organization for African Unity (OAU), and the U.S. State Department all voiced displeasure at the executions, and these protests may well have saved the lives of the more than 80 other arrested members of the Tolbert government.

Nearby in Ghana, by 1981 the country was approaching famine and bankruptcy, and Jerry Rawlings again led a group of soldiers in a successful coup. However, between 1982 and 1987, Rawlings himself was the target of several coup attempts before his administration finally consolidated its control over the country's military and political organizations. Meanwhile, back in São Tomé and Príncipe, a coup attempt on March 8, 1988 by commandos allegedly allied with the exiled opposition group the São Tomé and Príncipe National Resistance Front, based in Gabon, was thwarted by security forces loyal to Marxist President Manuel Pinto da Costa. The commando group of about 40 crossed the Bight of Benin in small boats and were intercepted by security forces as they tried to seize police headquarters near the capital, São Tomé. At least two insurgents were killed.

In Chad, the 1980s began with some sign of hope that the widespread violence of the previous decade was over. Four separate conferences took place in the Nigerian cities of Kano and Lagos, during which Chad's neighbors attempted to establish a political framework acceptable to the warring factions. The final conference culminated in the Lagos Accord of August 21, 1979, which representatives of eleven Chadian factions signed. In November 1979, the National Union Transition Government (GUNT) was created with a mandate to govern for 18 months. Goukouni Oueddei, a northerner, was named President; Colonel Kamougue, a southerner, Vice President; and Habre, Minister of Defense. However, in January 1980, fighting broke out again between Goukouni's and Habre's forces. With assistance from Libya, Goukouni regained control of the capital and other urban centers by year's end. However, when Libya's forces withdrew to the Aozou Strip in northern Chad, this cleared the way for Habre and his forces to re-enter N'Djamena in June and lay claim once more to the presidency.

Not to be outdone by its neighbors, Nigeria experienced yet another military coup. In 1982 the world oil market collapsed, leaving Nigeria unable to pay its short-term debts, much less finance the projects to which it was committed. Eventually, the country was also unable to import essential goods. In January 1983, the government ordered the expulsion of all unskilled foreigners, claiming that immigrants who had overstayed their visas were heavily involved in crime and were taking jobs from Nigerians. In the elections of 1983, the ruling party claimed a decisive victory over several opposition parties, while observers cited widespread instances of fraud and intimidation. Finally, on New Year's Eve 1983, army officers led by Major General Muhammadu Buhari overthrew the Shagari government in a bloodless coup. Buhari's government enjoyed widespread public support for its condemnation of economic mismanagement, of government corruption, and of the rigged 1983 elections. This support waned, however, as the government adopted a rigid program of economic austerity and instituted repressive policies that included a sweeping campaign against "indiscipline," a prohibition against discussing the country's political future, and the detention of journalists and others critical of the government.

Buhari's support withered and in August 1985, Major General Ibrahim Babangida overthrew him to wide acclaim. Babangida rescinded several of Buhari's most unpopular decrees, initiated a public debate on the state of the economy, and eased controls over business. These actions set the stage for negotiations with the International Monetary Fund (IMF) for aid, a new round of austerity measures, and better relations with the country's creditors. For a time, Nigeria achieved a measure of economic recovery. Babangida maintained a firm grip on power, shuffling key officers from position to position to ensure they would not become too strong and forbidding political parties. Many Nigerians were disturbed by the general's favoring of northern elite interests, and Babangida faced and suppressed coup attempts in 1986 and 1990. Other tensions escalated, particularly religious strife between Christians and Muslims; several states, including Kaduna, Katsina, and Kano, had severe religious riots in the early 1990s.

In September 1990, two coup attempts in Gabon were uncovered and aborted. But in January 1992, Jean-Pierre Lemboumba Lepandou, head of President Omar Bongo's personal cabinet, was assassinated. In early February, students at the Omar Bongo University in the capital, Libreville, went on strike to underline demands for extensions of their scholarships and guarantees of jobs upon graduation. On February 3rd they burned down an auditorium, and the strike spread to a second university. The government announced that both universities would be closed until further notice. Teachers in Libreville also went on strike in February, calling for improved working conditions and better housing benefits. On February 22nd the government banned public gatherings, and it was announced that striking teachers would have their salaries cut at the end of the month. Strikes also hit the economic capital, Port-Gentil, where—at the instigation of the coalition of opposition parties known as the Coordination of the Democratic Opposition—most businesses shut down for the day on February 25th. Oil workers in Port-Gentil had already called a strike on February 20th. This led to a drop in production of about one-third of the normal output, with disruptions continuing until late May. Because oil represents 50% of the government's budget receipts, the work stoppage was a serious blow to Gabon's already struggling economy.

In neighboring Cameroon, decades of relative peace were disrupted in 1991 when newly legalized political parties and the promise of multiparty elections resulted in calls for the end of President Paul Biya's administration. In late January, police fired on antigovernment protestors in the northern town of Garoua, and by May large-scale demonstrations resulted in brutal suppression by military and police forces. By July, several organizations had been banned, hundreds of protestors arrested, and nearly 50 killed. After increasing protests and acts of organized political disobedience—the strongest of which occurred in the north and west of the country—President Biya agreed in 1993 to meet some of the demands of the opposition, and new political reforms were enacted. In 1997, opposition parties received significant minorities of a nationwide election, although Biya won a second seven-year term. Meanwhile, Nigerian troops invaded the petroleum-rich Bakassi Peninsula of Cameroon in early 1994, launching a border dispute that was officially resolved in 2002 by the International Court of Justice. However, Nigeria has yet to return the disputed territory, in accordance with the ICJ's ruling, and strong military tensions persist between the two neighbors.

Next door to both Gabon and Cameroon, political violence erupted yet again in the Republic of Congo. In 1992, Denis Sassou-Nguesso—who had held a tight reign on power since the military coup in 1979—allowed a multi-party presidential election to take place, which resulted in his defeat. For the next five years, tensions simmered between Sassou supporters and those of newly elected president Pascal Lissouba. When President Lissouba's government forces surrounded Sassou's compound in Brazzaville with armored vehicles on June 5, 1997 Sassou ordered his militia to resist. Thus began a 4-month conflict that destroyed or damaged much of the capitol city of Brazzaville. In early October, Angolan troops invaded Congo on the side of Sassou and, in mid-October, the Lissouba government fell. Soon thereafter, Sassou declared himself President again—a position he still holds today.

In Angola, the government and UNITA insurgents finally signed a peace agreement in March, 1991, leading to a cease-fire and multiparty elections under the watchful eyes of a UN peacekeeping force. However, when Jonas Savimbi—the leader of UNITA—lost the September 1992 elections to the incumbent, President dos Santos, he rejected the results of the election and ordered his troops to return to violence. By November 1992, government forces had expelled UNITA from the capital, but UNITA claimed control of nearly 75% of the countryside. In March 1993, UNITA's forces overtook the provincial capital of Huambo, Angola's second largest city, with a population of over 400,000. More than 12,000 people, mostly civilians, were estimated killed, and the city was destroyed. In November 1993, the U.S. and other countries formally ended their support for any of the warring factions in Angola's civil war, and the UN

Security Council imposed an oil and fuel embargo on UNITA.[15] However, the rebel group responded by simply exploiting a new source of revenue to supports its insurgency: diamonds. Between 1992 and 1998, UNITA obtained an estimated revenue of at least $3.72 billion from diamond sales.[16]

On November 20, 1994, UNITA leaders and the government signed a new peace agreement in Lusaka, Zambia. The Lusaka Protocol, as it became known, called for UNITA to disarm, demobilize and join a new coalition government, and arranged for a United Nations peacekeeping force (called the UN Angola Verification Mission) with 7,000 troops to provide security. After 16 years of war, the UN estimated that at least 500,000 people had been killed and 3.3 million of Angola's population of 10 million had been severely affected. Despite this new UN-mediated peace accord, Savimbi refused to go to Luanda, citing security concerns. Over the next 10 months, a series of recriminations and low-level skirmishes led to the resumption of outright hostilities between UNITA and the Angolan government.

On December 26, 1998 and January 2, 1999, two UN-chartered aircraft were shot down, killing 23 people; most observers claimed that UNITA was responsible. On January 17, 1999 UN Secretary General Kofi Annan reported to the Security Council that the 1994 peace agreement between the Angolan government and rebel forces had collapsed, and called upon the UN to terminate its peacekeeping mission, criticizing both Savimbi and the dos Santos administration for their lack of commitment to the peace process. The death of Jonas Savimbi in a gunfight with government forces in February 2002 finally raised the prospect of peace, and a formal ceasefire between the Angolan army and UNITA rebels was signed in April 2002. However, the government still faces trouble from the Front for the Liberation of the Cabinda Enclave (FLEC), a group of separatists in Angola's oil-rich northern province who demand more autonomy from the central government and a greater share of the country's oil revenue.

The West African region witnessed several other military coups and acts of political violence during the 1990s. In Côte d'Ivoire, president Henri Konan Bédié was overthrown in a December 1999 military coup led by General Robert Gueï, a former army chief of staff. Bédié's heavy-handed efforts to silence dissent and criticism had resulted in widespread dissatisfaction with his administration and the suspension of aid from the IMF, and thus the coup was accepted rather cordially by many in the country. In contrast, when (in May 1997) military officers overthrew the elected government of President Ahmad Tejan Kabbah in Sierra Leone, the coup met with high levels of opposition from civilians in Sierra Leone and was rejected by African and international organizations. After clinging to power for almost a year, the military junta agreed to return power to the civilian government by April 1998.

In Nigeria, the parade of coups and military rulers took a turn for the worst following the 1993 elections. Moshood Abiola, a wealthy Yoruba publisher, was widely believed to have won by a large majority, but the Hausa-supported military annulled the vote, and in November 1993 General Sani Abacha, the powerful secretary of defense, seized power. Among Abacha's first acts was the termination of all political activity. Abiola was later imprisoned after attempting to claim the presidency and died in prison in July 1998.

The Nigerian Labor Congress, which had already held a general strike to protest the annulled election of Abiola, organized another general strike to protest Abacha's coup. Political pressure groups such as the Campaign for Democracy also stepped up protests against Abacha. In May 1994 the government announced plans for political reform and held elections for local governments and delegates to yet another constitutional conference. In October 1995 Abacha lifted the ban on political activity, promised a transfer to civilian power in 1998, and later allowed five parties to operate. However, he continued his repression of dissidents, the most notorious instance of which was the hanging of Ken Saro-Wiwa and eight other activists in November 1995.

During the early 1990s, playwright and prominent environmental activist (and eventual Nobel prize nominee) Ken Saro-Wiwa led a series of protests the Western oil operations in the Niger Delta region of Nigeria, highlighting the fact that while his tribal lands were being destroyed, the revenues from these operations were not being used to improve public services (like electricity and water). He also founded a more radical youth movement, which reportedly engaged in sabotage against the Shell Petroleum Development Company of Nigeria (the Nigerian subsidiary of Royal Dutch/Shell, and the largest oil producer in the region). In his writings, Saro-Wiwa criticized corruption and condemned both Shell and British Petroleum.

Although Shell decided to cease operations in Ogoniland in 1993, the Nigerian government decided to arrest Saro-Wiwa and a number of his supporters in 1995. He continued writing letters from prison, some of which were published in newspapers like the *Mail and Guardian*, in which he wrote "The most important thing for me is that I've used my talents as a writer to enable the Ogoni people to confront their tormentors. I was not able to do it as a politician or a businessman. My writing did it . . . I'm mentally prepared for the worst, but hopeful for the best. I think I have the moral victory." Following a brief trial—at which he was accused of murdering government supporters—Saro-Wiwa was executed along with eight other Ogoni leaders, and his body was buried in an unmarked, common grave in the eastern city of Port Harcourt. The international condemnation that followed did little harm to the government, and the foreign oil companies continued their work with little disruption. Indeed, in November of 1995 Shell announced a new $3 billion investment in Nigeria just a week after the execution of the Ogoni leaders.[17]

The Abacha government imprisoned many people, among the most prominent being former President Olusegun Obasanjo and former vice president Shehu Musa Yar'Adua (who died in prison in December 1997), while other prominent Nigerians, including Nobel laureate Wole Soyinka, fled into exile. The execution and imprisonment of opponents and other violations of human rights intensified international pressure on Abacha and resulted in Nigeria's suspension from the British Commonwealth of Nations from 1995 to 1999. When Abacha died unexpectedly in 1998, the country began a rapid march toward civilian rule, and under the leadership of democratically-elected President Obasanjo has only recently begun to emerge from the tyranny and corruption of the past.

To the northeast of Nigeria, a new chapter in the history of political violence in Chad began when in April 1989, Idriss Deby—one of Habre's leading generals—defected from the government and formed his own militia, which launched a series of attacks on the national army. In December 1990, with Libyan assistance and no opposition from French troops stationed in Chad, Deby's forces successfully marched on N'Djamena. After 3 months of provisional government, Deby's Patriotic Salvation Movement (MPS) approved a national charter on February 28, 1991, with Deby as president. In the following 2 years, Deby faced at least two coup attempts. Throughout the 1990s, government forces clashed violently with several insurgent groups (including the Movement for Democracy and Development, the National Revival Committee for Peace and Democracy, the Chadian National Front, and the Western Armed Forces), particularly near Lake Chad and in southern regions of the country. Civilians have been killed in large numbers during these clashes, and—as mentioned in the previous chapter of this volume—the recent influx of oil revenues promises to prolong Chad's civil war and reduce the likelihood of a peaceful resolution.[18]

The new millennium has already seen more political violence in West Africa. Attempts to overthrow the governments in Equatorial Guinea, São Tomé and Príncipe, and Nigeria (described earlier in this chapter) have been seen within just the past few years. In the Democratic Republic of Congo, President Laurent Kabila was shot dead by one of his bodyguards in January, 2001. In Côte d'Ivoire, General Robert Gueï carried through on his promise of holding new elections in October 2000 (following the military coup he led in 1999 to overthrow the unpopular regime of Henri Bédié), but when early voting results indicated Gueï was likely to lose the election to opposition candidate Laurent Gbagbo, he dissolved the official election commission and declared himself the winner. Violent clashes and widespread protests eventually forces Gueï to step down, and Gbagbo declared himself the rightful winner. However, an attempted military coup in 2002 led to increased violence, which lasted throughout most of 2003 until a peace accord between the government and three ethnic-based rebel groups was reached. In April 2004, the United Nations sent a peacekeeping force of about 6,000 troops to help France—the country's former colonial power—and its contingent of 4,000 troops maintain security and enforce the peace accord. In November, 2004 Côte d'Ivoire' warplanes bombed French positions, killing eight soldiers and wounding 23 others. The French responded by destroying the government's planes while on the ground at Côte d'Ivoire's international airport at Abidjan. In response, thousands of pro-government youths, some armed with machetes, aces or chunks of wood, took to the streets of the country's commercial capital Abidjan looking for French targets.[19] Mobs set fire to a French school, and the United Nations Security Council called an emergency session to deal with the violence.

And in nearby Mauritania, President Maaouiya Ould Sid Ahmed Taya was nearly overthrown in a bloody coup attempt in June 2003. Authorities also disrupted two coup plots in August and September 2004. Ironically, President Taya had originally taken power a bloodless coup in December 1984, and although he was re-elected three times since, he angered many in his country—which is an Islamic republic—by his formal recognition of Israel and cooperation with the U.S.[20] Although the country is considered one of the poorest in North Africa, recent offshore oil discoveries offer a potentially bright future, and it is poised to become a significant oil producer in the first quarter of 2006.[21] Thus, perhaps it came as no surprise to some observers when, in early August 2005—while the president was out of the country, attending the funeral of Saudi Arabia's King Fahd—a group of rebel troops seized power in a bloodless coup d'etat. A communiqué was broadcast on state media, announcing that the "totalitarian regime" of President Taya had ended, and that a "Military Council for Justice and Democracy" would rule the country for a maximum of two years, following which it would organize free and fair elections.[22] Security chief Colonel Ely Ould Mohammed Vall was named as the new leader. Unlike previous coup attempts, this one was surprisingly calm and largely free of violence, but the international response was largely condemnation. UN Secretary General Kofi Annan said he rejected any attempt to change a government unconstitutionally,[23] a statement which the African Union endorsed, while Nigerian President Obasanjo said "the days of tolerating military governance in our sub-region or anywhere" were "long gone."[24] From this brief review of Africa's political history, observers have every right to be somewhat doubtful.

Summary

Why have so many coup attempts been organized in West Africa? As described earlier in this chapter, a critical factor that shapes the security landscape in West Africa is conflict over the control of mineral resources, which fuels war and undermines peace processes.[25] Conflicts in Equatorial Guinea, Nigeria and Angola have often involved groups who viewed their local oil industry as the spoils of war. For example, the nature of the violent conflict in Angola evolved from one focused on political and geo-strategic objectives of the Marxist-oriented MPLA, to a conflict driven by personal ambition, mutual suspicion and the prize of winning or retaining control of the state and the resources to which it gives access.[26] As described in previous chapters of this volume, large amounts of oil revenues in a non-transparent system invites corruption, in turn creating incentives to further limit transparency and accountability, and creating a climate of political instability and potential violence.

While each of West Africa's conflicts has its own story to tell, a comparative analysis reveals a number of common themes. To begin with, countries and entities outside the region have played an important role in fueling these conflicts. In some cases, former colonial rulers as well as the Cold War superpowers manipulated regional politics and organizations for their own parochial interests by establishing military bases, propping up autocratic regimes, and initiative policies that were in direct conflict with the political and economic development of West Africa.[27] Internal factors have also played an important role in prolonging or deepening the violent conflicts seen in West Africa. Corruption, interethnic rivalries, and religious ideologies have in some cases undermined the effectiveness of efforts to end the violence. As noted African scholar Ismail Rashid observed, "In some conflict-ridden countries, like Liberia and Sierra Leone, vital security institutions like the army . . . became predatory armed factions, just like the rebel insurgents that they were employed to fight."[28]

In sum, four decades of political instability frame our understanding of West Africa today. This history has left a legacy of mistrust and insecurity that influences contemporary politics throughout the region. It also explains in part why border security continues to be such a challenge throughout the region—when the security forces of a country are fighting internal struggles, there is naturally less attention to other security needs of the nation. One outcome of these porous borders is that conflicts in one West African country tend to impact the entire region. For example, the long civil wars in Angola (1975-2002), Sierra Leone (1991-2002) and Liberia (1989-1996) contributed to the migration of refugees and a rapid increase in the proliferation of arms throughout the region. In the case of Liberia, Charles Taylor (the country's former dictator, now in exile in Nigeria) had received financial support and weapons from Libya, Ivory Coast, and Burkina Faso for his rebel movement (the National Patriotic Front of Liberia) and subsequently for his government. Later, Taylor's alliance with the Revolutionary United Front (RUF) rebel group in Sierra Leone led to a flow of weapons that deepened the conflict in that country (and for which Taylor in return received access to the diamonds in the mining fields of Kono and Tongo under RUF's control).[29]

Weapons and refugees from these conflicts have thus saturated the region, creating a host of opportunities for criminal networks. Today, these networks are operating throughout West Africa, profiting from an enormous proliferation of small arms and light weapons, human trafficking, a healthy demand for illicit drugs, and a vibrant trade in diamonds and other commodities. Porous borders, underdevelopment, poverty, corruption and poor governance have combined with decades of political upheaval to create an environment uniquely hospitable to criminal networks.

Crime in West Africa

In large part because of the corruption described in the previous chapter, in which a small elite dominates all political and economic activities, African states are vulnerable to the rise of organized crime and the creation of symbiotic or collusive relationships between criminals and the political elite.[30] According to a recent report by the United Nations Office on Drugs and Crime (UNODC), "Over the last decade West Africa has taken its place as a key export zone for organized crime, represented most clearly by its use as a transit point for drug trafficking and as a source for fraudulent activity. . . . The future development of the region is threatened by high levels of organized crime, which erode trust in government and encourage corruption."[31]

The UNODC report also describes how Nigeria has become the West African center of an extensive transnational network of narcotics traffickers and money laundering.[32] The populace of Nigeria distrusts the police force, making citizens vulnerable to manipulation by criminals in urban centers such as Lagos, Enugu, Port Harcourt, Jos, Kano, and Kaduna.[33] For example, only 0.4% of stolen property is recovered. In part, this reflects a lack of capacity—but it also is a reflection of corruption among policemen who, when they do succeed in recovering stolen goods, tend to sell them to fences.[34] Countries with inefficient regulatory environments and high levels of corruption tend to have informal economies in excess of 40% of GDP. Large informal sectors are strongly associated with criminal activity—in the end, the grey market and the black market may be closely inter-related. And all this activity, which comprises the bulk of the economy in some instances, is untaxed.[35]

Criminal network activity in West Africa is dominated by the regional trade in weapons and drugs, although oil bunkering is becoming a significant problem for Nigeria. In December 2000, an interagency law enforcement working group in the U.S. government issued a report, International Crime Threat Assessment, that described the African climate for international organized crime and terrorism as follows: "Porous borders, ample routes for smuggling drugs, weapons, explosives, and other contraband, and corruptible police and security forces make sub-Saharan Africa an inviting operational environment for international criminals, drug traffickers, and terrorists."[36] Each of these activities pose important challenges for our understanding of the energy security environment in the region.

Small Arms and Light Weapons

The proliferation of small arms and light weapons is one of the greatest threats to national security and human security on the African continent. Small arms (conventionally, those that can be carried by an individual or on a small vehicle) are attractive in such a region because they are durable and the newest models offer high firepower at a relatively low price.[37] According to a recent report by the United Nations Security Council, West Africa has "about eight million illicit small arms in circulation . . . [and] more than half of these are being used to fuel insurgency and the destabilization of West Africa."[38] According to the Interpol sub-regional bureau for Southern Africa, at least four million of these weapons are unregulated.[39] Recognizing the severity of this challenge, the United Nations has become increasingly involved in trying to stem the flow of small arms and light weapons.[40]

In describing many parts of the developing world, Peter Singer of the Brookings Institution observed how "individuals and small groups can now easily purchase and wield relatively massive amounts of power."[41] Indeed, the number of small arms throughout Africa has been growing since the beginning of the continent's various struggles for independence. When hostilities ended, many of these weapons were left in the hands of civilians or in arms caches whose locations were forgotten or deliberately not identified so that they could be reused in any possible future conflict.[42] Proliferation of small arms and light weapons became a feature of the Cold War era, distributed both legally and illegally as part of superpower geopolitics. Their acquisition and use vastly increased during the 1990s, escalating and prolonging conflicts, and making them more deadly and entrenched.[43] For example, the regional arms trade reached its high water mark during the civil war in Angola, particularly following UNITA's election defeat in 1992.[44] Today, according to some observers, many nations of Africa are in the throes of "an internal arms race between the police, the military, presidential security forces, rebel groups, vigilantes, warlords, and criminal gangs."[45]

Throughout contemporary West Africa, small arms are the main weapons used in armed robberies, intra- and inter-communal feuds, local wars, armed insurrections, armed rebel activities and terrorism.[46] They are used to facilitate drug trafficking, smuggling and other such crimes. Small arms and light weapons are used to grossly violate human rights, to facilitate the practice of bad governance, to subvert constitutions, to carry out coup d'états and to create and maintain a general state of fear, insecurity and instability.[47] The ensuing culture of violence and lawlessness that is spawned by the use of these weapons hinders economic, political and social development and frustrates efforts to reconstruct societies afflicted by conflicts.[48]

Foreign arms brokers and their international arms smuggling networks prospered greatly from West Africa's—indeed, small arms and light weapons smuggled into conflict zones since the 1960s continue to play a role in sub-regional insurgencies and violent crimes throughout the region.[49] Brokers of small arms continue to reap significant profits because these weapons are in high demand among governments, militias and criminals; they are easy to transport and conceal; and arms controls are generally weak and seldom enforced.[50] Recent attempts to stem the flow of small arms have focused mainly on border security, with some success. For example, the Nigerian Customs Service reported that it had intercepted small arms and ammunition worth more than US$30 million at border posts in a six-month period in 2003. In a single haul in November 2003, it took in a consignment of 170,000 rounds of ammunition.[51]

However, the proliferation of small arms and light weapons has both external and internal dimensions. Reports from Ghana indicate that gunsmiths are now able to copy imported AK-47 assault rifles and locally produce weapons that may be used to arm the insurgent, militia and other groups threatening the stability of West Africa.[52] The implications of this include the fact that an individual Ghanaian gunsmith can travel to Nigeria or some other state without carrying any suspicious items, and help manufacture weapons locally. This means that border security guards looking for weapons are unable to stem the proliferation of small arms, because it is the knowledge (and not a weapon) that is being transported. In 2001, researchers estimated that 500 blacksmiths located in five regions of Ghana had the capacity to produce between 35,000 and 40,000 small arms annually. In 2003, a new study revealed that this was a huge underestimate: more than 2,500 gun-producing blacksmiths were identified in the Ashanti and Brong-Ahafo regions alone. Police in Ghana now estimate that nearly 30% of firearms seized in crimes are locally manufactured.[53]

In 2002, Nigeria's defense minister warned that the proliferation and illegal trafficking of small arms into that country was intensifying criminal activity in the country and raising the danger of violent clashes among Nigeria's several ethnic groups.[54] Such insecure environments make sustainable development impossible. Interstate conflict and internal insurgencies—fueled by the spread of small arms—destroy the physical and human resources needed for an economy to grow. Armed groups systematically block or damage transit routes, disrupt natural resource development or divert it for their own use, and attack key national industries as part of their combat strategy. Long-standing conflicts also divert human and economic resources away from agriculture, education, industry, and other constructive activities.[55] In sum, the continued proliferation of small arms and light weapons poses a vital threat to the long-term security of West Africa, an important challenge for U.S. policymakers to consider when formulating energy policy objectives in this region.

Drugs

According to a recent report by the United Nations Office on Drugs and Crime (UNODC), West Africa has come to play a significant role as a point of transshipment for cargos of heroin and cocaine that are produced in South Asia and South America, and destined for markets in Europe and North America.[56] Indeed, West African networks have taken over the cannabis, cocaine and heroin retail markets in several West European cities, and have strong market hubs in both producer countries (Brazil, Thailand, Pakistan, South Africa) and destination countries, including the U.S.[57] There is a small amount of trafficking within the region, but for the most part, drug consumption levels are not considered high in West Africa. Given higher profit markets outside the region, most of the drugs that enter West Africa are on their way somewhere else.[58] Much of the cocaine passes through the region via Cape Verde, Nigeria, Togo and Ghana, on its way to Spain, Portugal and the United Kingdom. Over the period 2000-2004, more than 1.4 tons of cocaine were seized en route to West Africa or from West Africa to Europe, not including two unusually large seizures of 2.29 and 7.5 tons.[59]

Every country in West Africa has the capacity to become a transit zone used by criminals of any nationality, but Nigeria has become a central hub of the drug trade.[60] Indeed, Southern Nigerian drug trafficking groups are perhaps the best known manifestation of West African organized crime. Of couriers intercepted with drugs transiting through West Africa, according to statistics compiled since 2000, 92% were West Africans and no less than 56% were Nigerians.[61] The UNODC report also describes an experiment at Amsterdam's Schiphol airport which involved screening passengers arriving from Aruba and the Dutch Antilles—a favorite drug-smuggling route used by some of the 1,200 couriers arrested at Schiphol in 2001. When Dutch customs officers noticed the increasing numbers of Nigerians using the route, they experimented by checking every single Nigerian arriving at Schiphol from Aruba or the Dutch Antilles for a period of 10 days, rather than operating the usual spot-checks only. They found that of 83 Nigerian passengers using the route over those 10 days, no fewer than 63 were carrying drugs.[62]

In recent years, Nigerian narcotics groups also have migrated into neighboring Benin, Chad, and Niger.[63] The spread of the drug trade is facilitated by the same security vulnerabilities that traffickers of small arms and light weapons find advantageous, such as porous borders, corruption, inadequate law enforcement, and an environment of extreme scarcity in which any means to make a profit is seen as better than none. This profit incentive is particularly salient when considering the security challenges of oil bunkering in the region.

Oil Bunkering

As noted in the previous chapter, it is estimated that by 2010 West Africa's main oil producers—Angola, Cameroon, Chad, Gabon, Equatorial Guinea, and Nigeria—will be exporting between 5 and 7 million barrels daily, earning roughly $51-62 billion.[64] With such huge sums of money at stake, it is obvious why criminal networks would take interest in the region's oil industry. The Gulf of Guinea is thus home to crime syndicates which have successfully stolen ever larger volumes of Nigerian crude oil since 2000. Senior Nigerian government sources have stated that as many as 300,000 barrels of oil may be exported from the country illegally every day, although this figure is regarded by some analysts as rather low. In any event, it suggests that illegal oil exports earn these criminals over a billion dollars per year and perhaps three or four times that figure.[65] According to a recent United Nations report, the smuggling of crude oil is estimated to account for as much as 35% of the Nigeria's oil exports, although estimates vary widely.[66]

Oil bunkering on this scale requires sophisticated organization, as well as the complicity of Nigerian officials up to a very high level. According to authorities, sophisticated gangs illegally tap crude oil from pipelines and the mangrove swamps and creeks of the Niger Delta, from where it is then loaded onto barges and other smaller vessels for transfer to sea-going tankers waiting offshore. It is then sold on the world market. Funds from the illegal trade have helped keep the Niger Delta awash with weapons in the hands of ethnically-based militia groups and criminal gangs. These frequently disrupt oil production activities and kidnap oilmen to press their demands for jobs and other local benefits.[67]

This activity flourishes amid the poverty and a sense of injustice in the Niger Delta region. As described earlier in this and the previous chapter, communities in this region have protested for years that while tribal lands are being destroyed by Western oil operations, the revenues from these operations were not being used to improve public services (like electricity and water). Since these communities feel that they derive no benefit from the oil trade, there is an obvious incentive for them to collaborate with criminal networks in the illegal export of oil. According to a recent study by Alex Vines, the Niger Delta region provided these networks "with an environment which has a pool of unemployed youth and armed ethnic militias who know the terrain well. They also face a corrupt or ineffective law enforcement effort, coupled [with] a weak judicial process. These networks also enjoy patronage from senior government officials and politicians, who use bunkering as a source for political campaigning."[68]

According to the United Nations Office on Drugs and Crime, the oil bunkering syndicates in the Gulf of Guinea are highly international, including not only West Africans, but also Moroccans, Venezuelans, Lebanese, French and Russians, for example. Oil bunkering is thus linked to wider patterns of organized crime, with cash, drugs and weapons all being traded in exchange for illegal oil.[69] There are two major oil theft networks operating in the Niger Delta region, with some extended activity reaching out to other nations in the Gulf of Guinea. In some instances, these networks have co-opted government officials and military personnel. For example, three Nigerian navy admirals were put on trial in 2004 for alleged involvement in the illegal oil trade. In January 2005, two of them—Rear Admirals Francis Agbiti and Samuel Kolawole—were court martialed for their negligence in allowing the arrested tanker *Africa Pride* to escape from navy custody in Lagos harbor in August 2004. A third defendant was found innocent of all charges. The *African Pride* had been intercepted on the high seas on October 8, 2003 near Royal Dutch Shell's Forcados oil export terminal, and was found to have taken on board 11,000 tons of crude oil without authorization. While in navy custody, the tanker's cargo of crude oil was illegally transferred to another ship. Two junior navy officers told the court-martial that they were paid to escort the *Africa Pride* from Lagos harbor to the high seas, where its cargo was transferred to a waiting ship and replaced by sea water. On August 10, the ship escaped—in part because no guard was on duty at the time.[70] Its 13-man Russian crew was arrested and is still awaiting trial in a Lagos court.[71]

Other Forms of Criminal Activity

Other means of illicit profit-making in West Africa comes in the form of money laundering and human trafficking. In their analysis of the former, Phil Williams and Doug Brooks note that in Nigeria, anti-money laundering laws passed in 1995 have had little impact: "enforcement has been uneven, producing few seizures and no convictions."[72] Their research concluded that "law enforcement agencies in many African countries do not have the specialized knowledge and expertise or the practical experience to maximize the traditional instruments used against organized crime even where these instruments are available through legislation." The problem, as a recent United Nations report has described, involves various elements of the regional economic environment. For example, throughout West Africa, almost all car purchases are of second-hand vehicles, often with few or no documents attached. This clearly offers possibilities for money-laundering through the motor trade.

The proceeds of crimes committed in Africa are also laundered abroad, most notably the monies stolen by a few notorious "kleptocrats" such as Mobutu Sese Seko and Sani Abacha. With the help of the German, Swiss and British Governments, Nigeria was able to recover US$240 million from the late Abacha's family in 2004. A report from the Commission of the European Communities estimates that stolen African assets held in foreign bank accounts are equivalent to more than half of the continent's external debt.[73] Further, the UN points an accusatory finger at "major international companies" who allow corrupt, wealthy elites to move their wealth to bank accounts outside Africa. "Some of the world's largest banks are known to have been complicit in such schemes, including the notorious Bank of Credit and Commerce International (BCCI), which had more branches in Africa than in any other continent, as well as some private banking operations."[74] As discussed in Chapter 1 of this volume, Riggs Bank in Washington, DC was recently the center of a corruption scandal involving Equatorial Guinea and its president, Obiang Nguema Mbasogo. Despite the fact that Obiang and his wife made cash deposits of nearly $13 million over a three-year period into their Riggs accounts, the bank never filed a single suspicious activity report to federal regulators as required by law.[75] At one point,

Equatorial Guinea's "oil account" at Riggs held $700 million.[76] According to the 2004 Congressional investigation into the Riggs scandal, millions of dollars moved through various accounts owned by Obiang's family and friends, and at least $35 million was moved offshore to countries with bank secrecy laws.[77] In short, leaders of several oil-rich countries have become incredibly wealthy, and have been able to move much of their wealth to safe havens offshore, while huge proportions of their countries' populations live below the poverty line. In fact, a World Bank report released in October 2004 indicated that up to 80 percent of revenues from Nigeria's oil industry accrue to only one percent of the general population.[78]

Because the poverty of the region has created a widespread state of desperation, trafficking in women from West Africa has also become a major transnational crime.[79] According to the United Nations, Nigeria is the center of a flourishing global trade in prostitutes.[80] Many of the girls or young women involved are from Edo State and Benin City because those individuals who pioneered the trade have kept it in the hands of networks of kin and associates, thus excluding outsiders. The main destinations are Europe—especially Italy—and the Middle East. Nigeria's international trade in prostitutes is believed by analysts to have grown in the 1990s as prospects for employment in Nigeria deteriorated. The organizers of the trade are often women, sometimes former prostitutes themselves, who have succeeded in making money and graduating to the status of madams, although they depend on men for forging travel documents and escorting the girls to their destination. The networks through which girls and young women are recruited are reported to be well organized and to be relatively solid and durable, rather than merely *ad hoc*. Many girls initiated into prostitution are obliged to undergo quasi-traditional religious rituals that bind them to secrecy, before being provided with forged papers and sent abroad, often via other West African countries. It is also reported that girls may be initiated into their new trade through rape and other violence.[81]

Beyond the sex trade, another form of human trafficking is also closely identified with the region. In March 2005, police found more than 60 children packed into a shipping container in Lagos; authorities believe they were meant to be sold as slaves or servants. The children, aged between five and 14, were in a container normally used for carrying fish. Child trafficking is an Africa-wide problem, with an estimated 200,000 children being shipped across West and Central Africa's borders each year.[82] As with other types of criminal activity discussed here, root causes include widespread poverty, porous borders, weak central governments and corruption.

Summary

In early June 2005, the growing menace posed by criminal activity in West Africa prompted Nigerian President Obasanjo to appeal personally to both President Bush and Prime Minister Blair for cooperation in curbing illicit oil sales, arms trafficking, and money laundering. There can be little doubt that contributing our resources and expertise and combating transnational crime would benefit the entire region. It would also be to the benefit of our own self interests. Indeed, as the Gulf of Guinea and West Africa become ever more important to the global supply of energy, U.S. foreign policy will have to take into account the need to address the security challenges posed by these criminal networks. The availability of weapons interacts with illegal oil bunkering, endemic corruption, high youth unemployment and social disintegration to produce a highly dangerous environment for any type of external investment. From separatist movements in Nigeria and Angola, to the criminal network activity described in this chapter, West Africa can indeed be viewed as a region in trouble.

Conclusion

Georgetown University Professor Chester Crocker argues that "in much of the transitional world . . . there is a footrace under way between legitimate governmental institutions and legal business enterprises, on the one hand, and criminal networks, often linked to warlords or political factions associated with security agencies, on the other . . . When state failure sets in, the balance of power shifts ominously against ordinary civilians and in favor of armed entities operating outside the law (or with tacit approval). It might appear that globalization would favor those societal actors most closely linked to international networks of commerce, banking, communications, and diplomacy. But that is only true if the legitimate networks are at least as efficient and well organized as those linking corrupt elites, warlords, and Mafiosi with the external facilitators who grease the wheels of criminal business enterprise."[83] Like other regions of the continent, West Africa suffers from chronic armed conflict, extremely high rates of poverty, porous border security, and governmental inefficiency and corruption. These conditions have permitted the growth of numerous armed insurgent groups, an extensive narcotics trafficking network centered in Nigeria; trafficking in women and children originating in many countries of the region; misallocation of natural resources such as timber, precious metals, and diamonds; and an enormous arms trafficking industry that is supplied from Eastern Europe and the former Soviet Union and regionally centered in Liberia. A strong driver of criminal conduct in West Africa is the region's rich supply of natural resources, which has attracted unscrupulous entrepreneurs from Europe and financed an array of criminal activity.[84] The wealth derived from these natural resources has also fueled corrupt, authoritarian regimes in several countries of the region, whose citizens some to view their national institutions as "prizes" to be won and exploited, rather than as forums for national government.[85] Criminal cartels routinely take advantage of governmental corruption throughout the continent, giving bribes to poorly paid officials and security forces in return for their turning a blind eye toward an illicit trade in drugs, weapons, and humans.

These security challenges underscore an environment that offers a host of potential opportunities for terrorist activity. Throughout the conflicts described above, various groups of insurgents, rebel factions, and government security forces have routinely used violence to terrorize local populations into submission and acquiescence. In some instances, attackers used systematic rape, or chopped off the limbs of innocent civilian noncombatants, for the main purpose of compelling some form of action on the behalf of their opponents. Such individuals can reasonably called both criminals and terrorists. While acts of terrorism in West Africa have been limited to local conflicts, the increasing importance of this region to the world's oil markets can transform such attacks into acts of global terrorism. With this in mind, the next chapter explores the terrorist threat to West Africa in greater detail.

Notes

1. U.S. Department of State, Bureau of Consular Affairs, "Travel Warning," May 20, 2005. Available online at http://www.state.gov

2. U.S. Department of State, "Travel Warning,"

3. Daniel Volman, "Oil, Arms, and Violence in Africa" (Washington, DC: African Security Research Project, February 2003). Available online at: http://www.prairienet.org/acas/military/oilandarms.pdf

4. Portions of this historical overview section have been drawn from various open sources, including the BBC and CNN websites, as well as from the *Encarta Encyclopedia* and other reference guides.

5. United Nations Office on Drugs and Crime, "Transnational Organized Crime in the West African Region," June 2005, 4.

6. Monica Juma and Aida Mengistu, "The Infrastructure of Peace in Africa: Assessing the Peacebuilding Capacity of African Institutions," A Report submitted by the Africa Program of the International Peace Academy to the Ford Foundation, September 2002, 9.

7. BBC News, Timeline of Key Events, Jan. 19, 2005, online at http://news.bbc.co.uk/1/hi/world/africa/country_profiles

8. *The Economist,* "What Oil Can Do to Tiny States," 23 January 2003.

9. BBC News, "Q&A: Equatorial Guinea 'Coup Plot'" 13 January 2005.

10. E. Blanche, "Africa's Teetering Giant," *Jane's Islamic Affairs Analyst,* 1 December 2004.

11. "Five Charged with Planning to Shoot Down Obasanjo's Helicopter," *IRIN News,* 22 October 22 2004.

12. This description of Congo is provided by the U.S. Department of State online country profile.

13. The following historical overview of Angola's political history is provided by several open source materials, including the BBC News Country Profile: Angola, available online at: http://news.bbc.co.uk/1/hi/world/africa/country_profiles/1063073.stm; the U.S. State Department's background notes (online at: http://www.state.gov/r/pa/ei/bgn); and the *CIA Factbook*, 2005.

14. More information on this event is available online at the *BBC News* website: http://news.bbc.co.uk

15. In 1993, Angola ranked seventh among U.S. oil suppliers, and in 1994 Chevron announced plans to invest $2.8 billion to expand oil production in the country. However, in May 1993, oil production had fallen to around 450,000 barrels/day (compared to 1992 level of 540,000/day); by 1994, it had had fallen to 350,000 barrels/day

16. A Rough Trade: The Role of Companies and Governments in the Angolan Conflict (London: Global Witness Ltd., 1998), as cited in Scott Pegg, "Globalization and Natural Resource Conflicts," *Naval War College Review* 61(4), (Autumn 2003), p. 88.

17. Scott Pegg, "Globalization and Natural Resource Conflicts," *Naval War College Review* 61(4), (Autumn 2003), p. 89.

18. Daniel Volman, Oil, Arms and Violence in Africa, African Security Research Project Washington, DC February 2003.

19. See "French troops destroy government aircraft after bomb strike kills French peacekeepers and American civilian." DefenseLink news, (Nov. 7, 2004). Online at: http://www.defencetalk.com/nes/publish/article_001996.shtml.

20. "Mauritania Officers 'seize power'," *BBC News*, August 4, 2005.

21. Arab Maghreb Union, report by the Energy Intelligence Agency, June 2005. Online at: http://www.eia.doe.gov/emeu/cabs/maghreb.html.

22. "Army seizes power to end 'totalitarian regime'," *IRIN News service*, August 3, 2005.

23. "Mauritanian Army Coup Condemned," *BBC News*, August 4, 2005.

24. "Mauritania Officers 'seize power'," *BBC News*, August 4, 2005.

25. Monica Juma and Aida Mengistu, "The Infrastructure of Peace in Africa: Assessing the Peacebuilding Capacity of African Institutions," A Report submitted by the Africa Program of the International Peace Academy to the Ford Foundation, September 2002, p. 11

26. Tony Hodges, *Angola from Afro-Stalinism to Petro-Diamond Capitalism.* Bloomington: Indiana University Press, 2001, p. 18.

27. Ismail Rashid, "West Africa's Post-Cold War Challenges" in *West Africa's Security Challenges: Building Peace in a Troubled Region,* edited by Adekeye Adebajo and Ismail Rashid (Boulder, CO: Lynne Reinner, 2004) p. 384.

28. Ismail Rashid, "West Africa's Post-Cold War Challenges," 384.

29. Comfort Ero and Angela Ndinga-Muvumba, 2004. "Small Arms and Light Weapons," in *West Africa's Security Challenges: Building Peace in a Troubled Region* edited by Adekeye Adebajo and Ismail Rashid (Boulder, CO: Lynn Reinner, 2004), p. 231.

30. For example, see Phil Williams and Doug Brooks, "Captured, Criminal, and Contested States: Organized Crime and Africa in the Twenty-First Century," *South African Journal of International Affairs,* 6(2), Winter 1999, pp. 86-96.

31. United Nations Office on Drugs and Crime, "Transnational Organized Crime in the West African Region," June 2005, p. 37.

32. Congressional Research Service, "Nation's Hospitable to Organized Crime and Terrorism," Library of Congress, Federal Research Division, October, 2003.

33. U.S. Department of State, *International Narcotics Control Strategy Report 2003*, X-43. Cited in Congressional Research Service, "Nation's Hospitable to Organized Crime and Terrorism," Library of Congress, Federal Research Division, October, 2003.

34. States in Crisis and General Insecurity "Does Africa need the Police?" *Le Monde Diplomatique* - English Edition - (August-September 1997), cited in Phil Williams and Doug Brooks, "Captured, Criminal, and Contested States: Organized Crime and Africa in the Twenty-First Century," *South African Journal of International Affairs,* 6(2), Winter 1999, pp. 86-96.

35. United Nations Office on Drugs and Crime report, "Crime and Development in Africa," June 2005. Available online at: http://www.unodc.org/unodc/index.html

36. U.S. Government, International Crime Threat Assessment (Washington, 2000), p. 34. http://clinton4.nara.gov

37. "Nigeria: Defence Minister Denounces Increased Number of Small Arms in Country," BBC report, 14 January 2002. http://www.clw.org/atop/newswire/nw011402.htm Cited in Congressional Research Service, "Nation's Hospitable to Organized Crime and Terrorism," Library of Congress, Federal Research Division, October, 2003.

38. United Nations Security Council, Press Release SC/7694, "Meeting on Threats to Peace and Security in West Africa," March 18, 2003. These include weapons acquired through both legal and illegal means. See http://www.undp.org/erd/archives/brochures/small.

39. Jane's Defence Network, 1999 "African Struggle over Smuggled Weapons," Jane's International Police Review, 1999.

40. For example, see the Program of Action to Prevent, Combat and Eradicate the Illicit Trade in Small Arms and Light Weapons in All its Aspects, described later in this volume. Also, see UN General Assembly resolutions 58/58 and A/59/181.

41. Peter W. Singer, "Corporate Warriors: The Rise of the Privatized Military Industry and its Ramifications for International Security," *International Security* (Winter 2001/2002), p. 196.

42. Jane's Intelligence Review, "African Struggle over Smuggled Weapons," November 23, 1999.

43. Monica Juma and Aida Mengistu, "The Infrastructure of Peace in Africa: Assessing the Peacebuilding Capacity of African Institutions," A Report submitted by the Africa Program of the International Peace Academy to the Ford Foundation, September 2002, p. 12. Also, for information on the impact of small arms and light weapons, visit the UN Development Program's Emergency Response Division website, at: http://www.undp.org/erd/small_arms.htm.

44. Charles Goredema, "Organized Crime and Terrorism: Observations from Southern Africa." Institute for Security Studies, *ISS Paper 101* (March 2005), p. 2.

45. Comfort Ero and Angela Ndinga-Muvumba, "Small Arms and Light Weapons," 223.

46. Foundation Document for the West Africa Action Network on Small Arms. Online at: http://www.iansa.org/regions/wafrica/waansa.htm

47. Foundation Document for the West Africa Action Network on Small Arms.

48. Monica Juma and Aida Mengistu, "The Infrastructure of Peace in Africa," 12. Also, for information on the impact of small arms and light weapons, visit the UN Development Program's Emergency Response Division website, at: http://www.undp.org/erd/small_arms.htm.

49. Comfort Ero and Angela Ndinga-Muvumba, "Small Arms and Light Weapons," 223.

50. Small Arms Working Group, "Small Arms and Brokers" briefing paper, International Action Network on Small Arms. Online at: http://www.iansa.org/documents/factsheets/small_arms_and_brokers.pdf

51. Lisa Misol, "Small Arms and Conflict in West Africa," Testimony before the US Congressional Human Rights Caucus, May 20, 2004; cited in the United Nations Office on Drugs and Crime report, "Crime and Development in Africa," June 2005. Available online at: http://www.unodc.org/unodc/index.html.

52. Emmanuel Kwesi Aning and Nicolas Florquin, "Ghana's Secret Arms Industry," *Jane's Intelligence Review*, December 1, 2004.

53. Emmanuel Kwesi Aning and Nicolas Florquin, "Ghana's Secret Arms Industry."

54. "Nigeria: Defence Minister Denounces Increased Number of Small Arms in Country," *BBC News*, 14 January 2002. http://www.clw.org/atop/newswire/nw011402.htm Cited in Congressional Research Service, "Nation's Hospitable to Organized Crime and Terrorism," Library of Congress, Federal Research Division, October, 2003.

55. Small Arms Working Group, "Small Arms and Development" briefing paper, International Action Network on Small Arms. Online at: http://www.iansa.org/documents/factsheets/small_arms_and_development.pdf

56. United Nations Office on Drugs and Crime (UNODC) report, "Crime and Development in Africa," June 2005. Available online at: http://www.unodc.org/unodc/index.html

57. UNODC, "Crime and Development in Africa."

58. UNODC, "Crime and Development in Africa."

59. United Nations Office on Drugs and Crime, "Transnational Organized Crime in the West African Region," June 2005, p. 21. Online at: http://www.unodc.org/pdf/transnational_crime_west-africa-05.pdf

60. UNODC, "Transnational Organized Crime in the West African Region," 21.

61. UNODC, "Transnational Organized Crime in the West African Region," 21.

62. UNODC, "Transnational Organized Crime in the West African Region," 21.

63. New Ambitions in the Fight Against Drugs," *Geopolitical Drug Newsletter* [Paris], October 2001. Online at: http://www.geodrugs.net/mini-lettres/AEGD6GB.pdf (cited in Congressional Research Service, "Nation's Hospitable to Organized Crime and Terrorism," Library of Congress, Federal Research Division, October, 2003).

64. Philippe de Pontent, "Sub-Saharan Africa Energy: Strategic Implications of Growing Competition for African Oil," Intellibridge report, June 30, 2004.

65. UNODC, "Transnational Organized Crime in the West African Region," 4.

66. UNODC, "Transnational Organized Crime in the West African Region," 4.

67. UN Office for the Coordination of Humanitarian Affairs, "Conviction of admirals confirms navy role in oil theft," UN Integrated Regional Information Network News, January 7, 2005. Online at http://www.irinnews.org

68. Alex Vines, "Light Weapons Proliferation in West Africa", paper presented at the United Nations Office on Drugs and Crime seminar, Dakar, Senegal, April 3, 2004. Cited in UNODC, "Transnational Organized Crime in the West African Region," 31.

69. UNODC, "Transnational Organized Crime in the West African Region," 31.

70. UN Office for the Coordination of Humanitarian Affairs, "Conviction of admirals confirms navy role in oil theft."

71. E. Blanche, "Africa's Teetering Giant," *Jane's Islamic Affairs Analyst,* December 1, 2004.

72. *International Narcotics Control Strategy Report 1998* (Washington" State Department, 1999), cited in Phil Williams and Doug Brooks, "Captured, Criminal, and Contested States: Organized Crime and Africa in the Twenty-First Century," *South African Journal of International Affairs,* 6(2), Winter 1999, pp. 86-96.

73. Commission of the European Communities, 'Communication from the Commission to the Council, The EUAfrica dialogue', accessed via: http://europa.eu.int/eur-lex/en/com/cnc/2003/com2003_0316en01.pdf, as quoted in the Commission on Africa, *Our Common Interest: Report of the Commission for Africa,* March 2005, p. 144.

74. UNODC, "Transnational Organized Crime in the West African Region," 31.

75. Terrence O'Hara and Kathleen Day, "Ex-Riggs Manager Won't Testify About Accounts," *Washington Post,* July 15 2004.

76. In May 2005, FBI agents arrested Simon Kareri, the former senior vice president at Riggs who was in charge of all the Equatorial Guinea accounts. He and his wife were arraigned in federal court on charges of fraud, conspiracy and money laundering, making them the first individuals held accountable for what has become known as the Riggs Bank money laundering scandal. Meanwhile, Riggs has closed all its Equatorial Guinea accounts (see the Written Statement of Riggs Bank N.A., to the Permanent Subcommittee on Investigations of the Committee on Governmental Affairs of the U.S. Senate, July 15, 2004).

77. Terrence O'Hara and Kathleen Day, "Ex-Riggs Manager Won't Testify About Accounts," *Washington Post,* July 15 2004.

78. International Energy Administration, "Nigeria," Country Analysis Report (April 2005), p. 5. Online at: (http://www.eia.doe.gov/emeu/cabs/nigeria.html.

79. Congressional Research Service (CRS), "Nation's Hospitable to Organized Crime and Terrorism," Library of Congress, Federal Research Division, October, 2003.

80. UNODC, "Crime and Development in Africa."

81. UNODC, "Crime and Development in Africa."

82. "Nigerian police find dozens of children packed in shipping container," Kuala Lumpur, *The Star,* March 7, 2005.

83. Chester A. Crocker, "Engaging Failed States," *Foreign Affairs* (September/October 2003), 36-37.

84. CRS, "Nation's Hospitable to Organized Crime and Terrorism."

85. CRS, "Nation's Hospitable to Organized Crime and Terrorism."

Chapter 4
The Emerging Terrorist Threat
to West and Central Africa

Marine Corps General James L. Jones, commander of the U.S. and NATO forces in Europe, recently commented that "the large, ungoverned spaces in Africa are very tempting" to terrorist organizations.[1] Indeed, recent intelligence reports have indicated that violent extremist groups are increasingly looking to sub-Saharan Africa as an attractive transit route for illegal materials and money laundering. According to a 2003 Congressional Research Service report, al Qaeda has already established at least tenuous links in parts of West Africa.[2] As former ambassador Princeton Lyman and J. Steven Morrison (2003) observed, "we have evidence that international terrorist networks are running interference in the civil wars of central and western Africa, dealing in precious gems and in arms trafficking in order to destabilize regimes there . . . so, our interests in the region are by necessity not purely humanitarian or commercial—we also must prevent developing states from becoming failed states, because of the implications this would have for the spread of global terrorist networks."[3] Indeed, according to Jonathon Schanzer, author of a recent book on Al Qaeda, "If you can't seal your borders and there are areas that no one's watching, it leaves the opportunity for exploitation."[4]

The *U.S. National Security Strategy* argues that "poverty, weak institutions and corruption can make states vulnerable to terrorist networks and drug cartels within their borders."[5] As described in the previous chapter, organized criminal cartels take advantage of a variety of security vulnerabilities throughout the Gulf of Guinea, including porous borders and weak border controls. The extensive land and sea boundaries of many African states are virtually unpatrolled. Many points of entry cannot be monitored by states with limited resources, resulting in opportunities for illegal immigration and organized criminals. Customs and immigration services throughout much of Africa are poorly developed, trained, equipped, and paid. As such, they are readily circumvented or intimated by the relatively sophisticated methods employed by drug dealers and others who can offer bribes and have access to speedboats and overwhelming firepower.[6] These and other regional security vulnerabilities can facilitate a host of activities for both criminal and terrorist networks—activities such as recruitment, fundraising, money laundering, weapons and drug trafficking, and training. As a result, issues of law enforcement, border patrols and military professionalism are becoming increasingly important concerns of U.S. policymakers as we look to increase our involvement in West and Central Africa's economic and political affairs as part of our long-term energy security strategy.

The "large, ungoverned spaces" that General Jones referred to have a number of common elements.[7] First, they are far away from population centers, which makes it harder for governments to gain human intelligence on the organization. Second, they are away from lines of communication, which constrains the operational capacity of government forces. Third, they are located near foreign borders, which facilitate escape to neighboring states when necessary. Fourth, these areas are typically within poor states, where security can readily be purchased, where corruption is widespread, and where impoverished, disenfranchised youth are easy targets for recruiters promising a better way of life. Finally, and perhaps most important, areas where the terrain is rugged and relatively inhospitable—whether from high, cavernous mountains as in Afghanistan, or from the dense vegetation cover found in much of Central and West Africa, southeast Asia, and Latin America—provide strategically useful staging grounds and transit routes for criminals and terrorists. As General Charles Wald, Deputy Commander of U.S. European Command, observed in 2004, "we can't allow areas like that to be ungoverned, to become havens for terrorists."[8]

Unfortunately, Africa is no stranger to global terrorism. Terrorist networks have already been established in the Horn of Africa and the eastern coastal states of Kenya and Tanzania.[9] In addition, failed or failing states in central and western Africa have already provided opportunity for al Qaeda and criminal networks possibly affiliated with it to profit from various underground financial and trade networks.[10] General Wald has been warning Congress for some time that al Qaeda affiliated groups are active in Mauritania, Mali, Chad and Niger.[11] U.S. security think tanks have also listed Nigeria—where the presence of radical Islam is growing—as being among nations that have al Qaeda cells.[12] Clearly, the socio-political environment in some sections of this region are primed for the formation of al Qaeda-friendly groups. For example, in September, 2004, a group of over 40 armed Muslim militants, wearing red bandanas and crying "Allahu Akbar" (God is Great), attacked two police stations in the Borno state of northeastern Nigeria.[13]

Meanwhile, economic globalization has brought an increasing presence of Western private interests throughout sub-Saharan Africa. From import-export companies to oil exploration to private security firms, the footprint of North American and European countries in Africa is significant and growing. For anti-western extremists, this trend offers an increasingly rich target environment. For example, in December 2001, the U.S. ambassador in Cameroon received a warning that al Qaeda planned to attack U.S. oil installations in Equatorial Guinea and Nigeria.[14] While politically-motivated attacks on oil pipelines have been common in Angola and Nigeria, other "soft targets" have recently been compelled to upgrade their security.

Al Qaeda demonstrated its ability to strike at U.S. interests in Africa with the 1998 bombings of the U.S. embassies in Kenya and Tanzania, killing 214 and wounding nearly 5,000. Since then, several attacks have taken place on the continent. In November 2002, a suicide bomber rammed a truck into an Israeli hotel in the Kenyan port city of Mombassa, killing 15 people, while another attacker fired two surface-to-air rockets at a commercial Israeli airliner, narrowly failing in their attempt to bring the aircraft down. In 2002, a gas tank bombing in Djerba, Tunisia killed 21 and injured more than 30 others. And in 2003, a series of suicide attacks carried out by the group Salafia Jihadia killed 33 and injured more than 100 others throughout Casablanca, Morocco.

Overall, the countries of sub-Saharan Africa are vulnerable to being used as venues for terrorist attacks, particularly because of weak governments, Western targets, porous borders and widespread corruption among border guards and other low-level officials susceptible to being bribed. Much of the world's concern about terrorist groups and movements are focused on North and East Africa, specifically from the Horn of Africa down the coast to Tanzania and across the entire Sahel region. However, all indications suggest that the global, borderless nature of terrorism will have an increasingly pervasive presence in other parts of Africa, including the Gulf of Guinea. Some observers question why al Qaeda (or more likely, an al Qaeda-inspired group) would want to orchestrate an attack in the Gulf, but an understanding of how important this region is becoming to the U.S., as described in the previous chapters, reveals the answer to such questions. Clearly, if Osama bin Laden and his followers are looking to counter U.S. influence and damage its economic and political institutions, one would expect that his transnational terrorist network would lend its support to local groups in the Gulf of Guinea. After all, this is what combatants in a global struggle for power and influence do regularly.

As described in a growing field of publications, most terrorist organizations act strategically. Terrorist attacks are meant to coerce state behavior, change policies, intimidate, or produce some other sort of action which the terrorists feel will help them achieve their strategic objectives.[15] International terrorists who want to cripple the global economy need not bother attacking countries where security is tight. They can inflict significant damage by choosing strategically valuable targets in countries that lack the will or the resources to police their own backyard.[16] Thus, an attack on any number of targets in the Gulf of Guinea region would be economically and politically disruptive. Appealing targets could include embassies and consulates of North American and Western European countries; hotels and housing complexes for Western visitors and oil workers; airports, shipping terminals, and more. From this perspective, the growing presence of Western multinational oil companies in Africa offers a proliferation of targets that terrorists might find attractive.

Contemporary Threats to Oil Infrastructure

Attacks on a country's oil infrastructure have already become common in several parts of the world, including Colombia and Iraq. In these and other countries, religious militants and secular insurgents all recognize the important relationship between oil and a state's regime. In fact, according to the World Bank project on "Economics of Civil Wars, Crime and Violence," the largest risk factor associated with civil conflict was found to be significant reliance on primary commodity exports like oil.[17] A country's oil infrastructure vulnerabilities include the following:[18]

- production facilities, such as petroleum fields, wells, platforms, and rigs;
- refineries and gas processing plants;
- transportation facilities, including pipelines and pumping stations, terminals and tank ships;
- oil and gas depots;
- administration buildings;
- distribution centers/petrol stations; and
- all personnel on or employed at these installations.

Of these, the blasting of oil pipelines is the most common form of attack, and has been the source of over 60% of disruptions to a country's oil infrastructure.[19] Attacks on oil pipelines are tactically easy, as there are long stretches of unguarded pipelines; since pipelines are relatively easy to repair, oil companies have often invested little in their protection.[20]

The global oil industry has been the victim of several direct terrorist attacks in recent years. Consider the following:

- Between 1986 and 1996, Colombian guerillas attacked pipelines and other oil industry infrastructure an estimated 985 times.[21]
- October, 2001 – Tamil Tiger separatists carried out a coordinated suicide attack on the *MV Silk Pride,* an oil tanker which was carrying more than 650 tons of diesel and kerosene to the port of Jaffna, in northern Sri Lanka. The attackers used five boats in the attack. One rammed the tanker, triggering an explosion on board, and three sailors died in the attack.[22]
- May 2002 – A cell phone was used to detonate an explosive device attached to a tanker truck in Israel's central fuel and gas depot north of Tel Aviv. The tanker was parked about 300 feet from a fuel storage tank in a densely populated residential area, but fortunately did not explode when the remote detonation occurred.[23]

- June 2002 – Several al-Qaeda operatives were arrested in Morocco, suspected of plotting raids on US and British tankers in the Strait of Gibraltar.[24]
- October 2002 – An explosive-laden boat slams into the French oil tanker *Limburg* in the port of Ash Shihr, off the coast of Yemen, splitting the vessel's hull. At the time of the blast, which killed one crew member and sent more than 90,000 barrels of Iranian crude oil pouring into the Gulf of Aden, the Limburg was picking up a pilot to guide it into the terminal.[25]
- March 2003 – A series of armed militia attacks on expatriate oil workers in Nigeria led to the temporary shutdown of that country's production.
- October, 2004 – Militants of the outlawed Kurdish Workers' Party (PKK) staged a series of bomb attacks on oil pipelines throughout southeastern Turkey.[26]
- April 2004 – Suicide bombers in three boats blew themselves up in and around the Basra terminal zone, a key hub of Iraq's oil production and distribution system and one of the most heavily guarded facilities of its kind in the world. On June 13, 2004, Iraqi Prime Minister Iyad Allawi admitted that saboteurs have attacked the country's 4,000 miles of pipelines 130 times in the last seven months, depriving the nation of $200 million in lost export earnings.[27]
- May 2004 – Gunmen killed six people in an attack on a Western oil company office in the Red Sea city of Yanbu.[28] Later this same month, residential compounds housing oil workers in Khobar, Saudi Arabia were attacked. The 16 people who were killed in the attack included an American, a Briton, and a 10-year old Egyptian boy whose father worked nearby. Al Qaeda claimed responsibility for the attack.[29]

As this brief sampling reveals, there is a growing nexus between terrorism and the oil industry worldwide, which is particularly dangerous for the emerging U.S. energy interests in the Gulf of Guinea. An overwhelming majority of international attacks over the last five years have not been against government or military targets, but have been against corporate interests.[30] Over half of all anti-U.S. attacks by international terrorists in 2002 were against business facilities, and although most of these were in Latin America it is logical to assume that increased commercial involvement in Africa (particularly in the oil extraction industry) will expose U.S. businesses to increased attacks there.[31] In truth, from Yemen to Angola there have already been a number of cases throughout the African continent involving the kidnapping of oil workers and their family members, explosions at oil pumping stations and pipelines, and export terminals. In many cases, these attacks were carried out by local groups motivated by financial gain (hostage-taking and extortion), though there is increasing concern that internationally-motivated terrorists will also take advantage of the continent's security vulnerabilities.

It is already understood that Al Qaeda is seeking to target the world's energy supply. In February, 2004, a message was posted to the al Qaeda-affiliated *al Qalah* (the Fortress) website[32] entitled "Map of Future al Qaeda Operations." It stated among other things that the terrorists would make it a priority to attack oil facilities in the Middle East. According to the posting, attacking the U.S. energy base in the Gulf would have three effects: Damaging the American economy; embarrassing the United States and emboldening other countries seeking to secure their own energy supplies; and forcing the U.S. to deploy further troops to the region to stabilize the situation. "The U.S. will reach a stage of madness after the targeting of its oil interests," the terrorists reason, "which will facilitate the creation of a new front and the drowning of the U.S. in a new quagmire that will be worse than the quagmires of Iraq and Afghanistan."[33] Later that year, in mid-December, Arab satellite channels aired an audiotape message by Osama bin Laden in which he called on his cohorts to take their holy war to the oil industry and to disrupt supplies to the U.S from the Persian Gulf. Two days later a follow-up statement by the Saudi branch of al Qaeda was published, calling on "all mujahideen . . . in the Arabian Peninsula" to target "the oil resources that do not serve the nation of Islam."[34]

According to James S. Robbins, a professor at the National Defense University and a counterterrorism expert, "The terrorists understand that they can influence oil markets through directed violence, and thus exploit a critical U.S. vulnerability."[35] Indeed, an act of terrorism against a major installation, such as an LNG liquefaction plant, a supertanker or an oil platform, could also create a spike in oil prices, raise global insurance rates, and damage production for some period. Even the fear of terrorism can disrupt the global economy. For example, in June 2005 the U.S. and U.K. missions in Lagos, Nigeria—which are just 100 meters apart from each other—received what was deemed a credible terrorist threat, and evacuated their compounds. Other consulates located along same road also closed, including those representing Germany, Italy and Russia.[36] This single event raised fears of economic insecurity in Africa's largest oil producer, and helped drive global oil prices to record highs—over $70 a barrel by mid-August. In addition to stationary targets like embassies and oil infrastructure, there is also a growing concern about the maritime dimension of the terrorist threat

Maritime Security and the Terrorist Threat

The shipping industry plays an integral role in the global oil transportation system—indeed, 60% of the world's oil is shipped by approximately 4,000 slow and cumbersome tankers. In order to transport oil from major producing countries to major consuming countries, these tankers must pass through geographic chokepoints, many of which are located in areas where violent groups with maritime capabilities are active. For example, the Bab al Mandab (a tiny waterway that runs between Eritrea, Djibouti and Yemen) was identified by the International Maritime Bureau (IMB) in 2003 as having one of the highest incidences of piracy beyond Indonesia and Bangladesh.[37] On the other side of the Arabian Peninsula, the Strait of Hormuz—which connects the Persian Gulf and the Arabian Sea—is only 1.5 miles wide at its narrowest point. Roughly 15 million barrels of oil are shipped through it daily. Between 1984 and 1987, when tankers were frequently attacked in the strait (a product of the Iran-Iraq war), shipping in the gulf dropped by 25%. In his 2003 State of the Union address, President George W. Bush revealed that U.S. forces had already prevented terrorist attacks on ships in this strategically-important region.

These vital shipping lanes—major points of vulnerability for the world economy—are so narrow at points that a single burning supertanker and its spreading oil slick could block the route for other vessels. Were terrorists to hijack a large bulk carrier or oil tanker, sail it into one of the chokepoints, and scuttle it to block the sea-lane, the consequences for the global economy would be severe: a spike in oil prices, an increase in the cost of shipping due to the need to use alternate routes, congestion in sea-lanes and ports, more expensive maritime insurance, and probable environmental disaster. According to U.S. Senator Bill Nelson, "sooner or later the terrorist is going to try to sink a tanker in the Strait of Hormuz, and when that occurs, and that free flow of oil out of the Persian Gulf ends, you're going to have another great energy crisis."[38] Worse yet would be several such attacks happening simultaneously in multiple locations worldwide.[39]

Thus, it should come as no surprise that there is clearly a strategic intent among terrorists to find and exploit vulnerabilities in maritime security. Shortly after the October 2002 attack on the French oil tanker *Limburg*, off the coast of Yemen, a communiqué issued by Al Qaeda's political bureau noted that "If a boat that didn't cost US$1,000 managed to devastate an oil tanker of that magnitude, imagine the extent of the danger that threatens the West's commercial lifeline, which is petroleum. . . . The operation of attacking the French tankers is not merely an attack against a tanker, but it is also an attack against international oil transport lines and all its various connotations."[40] Beyond attacking tankers in order to disrupt the global economy, the maritime shipping industry also offers targets for piracy. In the face of massive international efforts to freeze their finances, according to the analysis prepared by Anne Korin and Gal Luft, terrorist groups have come to view piracy as a potentially rich source of funding. In their recent *Foreign Affairs* article, Korin and Luft note that "the scourges of piracy and terrorism are increasingly intertwined: piracy on the high seas is becoming a key tactic of terrorist groups. Unlike the pirates of old, whose sole objective was quick commercial gain, many of today's pirates are maritime terrorists with an ideological bent and a broad political agenda. This nexus of piracy and terrorism is especially dangerous for energy markets: most of the world's oil and gas is shipped through the world's most piracy-infested waters."[41]

Overall, the number of pirate attacks worldwide has tripled in the past decade—putting piracy at its highest level in modern history.[42] Contrary to the stereotype, today's pirates are often trained fighters aboard speedboats equipped with satellite phones and global positioning systems and armed with automatic weapons, antitank missiles, and grenades.[43] According to statistics compiled by the IMB, both the frequency and the violence of acts of piracy have increased in recent years. In 2003, ship owners reported 445 attacks, in which 92 seafarers were killed or reported missing and 359 were assaulted and taken hostage. (Ships were hijacked in 19 of these cases and boarded in 311.) From 2002 to 2003, the number of those killed and taken hostage in attacks nearly doubled. Pirates have also increased their tactical sophistication, often surrounding a target ship with several boats and firing machine guns and antitank missiles to force it to stop.[44]

The concern over piracy is particularly strong in the Strait of Malacca, the 500-mile corridor separating Indonesia and Malaysia, where 42% of pirate attacks took place in 2003. According to Indonesia's state intelligence agency, detained senior members of Jemaah Islamiyah, the al Qaeda-linked Indonesian terrorist group, have admitted that the group has considered launching attacks on Malacca shipping.[45] In addition to piracy, some terrorist groups have apparently demonstrated an interest in providing their members with pilot training. For example, in March 2003, ten armed hijackers commandeered the chemical tanker *Dewi Madrim* off the coast of Sumatra, Indonesia. Armed with machine guns and machetes, they disabled the ship's radio, took the helm and steered the vessel, altering speed, for about an hour. Then they left in their speedboats, taking with them some cash, equipment, technical documents, and the captain and first officer, who are still missing.[46] For anyone familiar with the *9/11 Commission Report,* this event seems eerily reminiscent of the terrorists who took flight lessons in the United States in order to learn how to fly—but not necessarily land—passenger airliners.[47] It is thus relatively easy to speculate why terrorists would want to learn how to pilot an oil tanker.

The Maritime Terrorism Threat to the Gulf of Guinea

In 2004, the International Maritime Organization rated the Gulf of Guinea waters second in the world in piracy attacks, surpassed only by the Straits of Malacca.[48] Since 24 May 2005, four incidents of piracy have taken place in Nigeria's Bonny River alone.[49] There are 26 major ports in the Gulf of Guinea region, 6 of them in Nigeria, where billions of barrels of oil are loaded onto tankers each day. The need for U.S. assistance in protecting these ports is considerable. Even Angola—with the region's largest army and longest coastline—did not have a single naval patrol vessel in 2004 to protect its fishing grounds or burgeoning offshore oil industry.[50]

As a result, in early October 2004, leaders of 17 navies from West Africa, Europe and the U.S. met to discuss enhancing maritime security in the Gulf of Guinea. Participants from Africa included naval leaders from Angola, Benin, Cameroon, Equatorial Guinea, Gabon, Ghana, Nigeria, Congo, Sao Tome and Principe, and Togo. Other attendees at the meeting were from France, Italy, the Netherlands, Portugal, Spain, the United Kingdom and the United States. The conference featured discussions about combating piracy; the illegal trafficking of weapons, drugs and people; and the need to reduce maritime threats to economic development, such as those over national fishing rights and offshore oil production.[51] While this gathering did not result in a substantive change in the Gulf's maritime security vulnerabilities, at least it was recognized by all attendees that addressing these vulnerabilities requires a great deal of international cooperation.

On it's own, the U.S. is promoting several initiatives to bolster security in the region. The Gulf of Guinea Guard is a concept being promoted by members of the U.S. European Command (which has regional responsibility for Africa) to enhance the maritime capabilities of regional forces. It is designed to ensure adequate surveillance of littoral and deep-water maritime areas to detect, deter, and/or arrest illegal activities; disruption-free production of hydrocarbons in offshore facilities; and the protection of energy resources during storage and distribution.[52] The African Coastal Security Program is another initiative aimed at countering piracy and maritime security, prevent smuggling and protect offshore resources.[53] As part of this program, a large U.S Navy ship—the USS Emory S. Land—was deployed in February 2005 to the Gulf of Guinea to help West African navies become more effective in providing security in the oil-rich waters.[54] On board the vessel, which made stops in Ghana, Cameroon and Gabon during its six week tour, 1,400 U.S. sailors and Marines provided dozens of West African navy officers with maritime security training. And in June 2005, the U.S. Coast Guard Cutter "Bear" made a port call to Malabo, (among other Gulf of Guinea visits), the first U.S. ship visit to Equatorial Guinea in years.

In sum, there is growing recognition of the unique vulnerability to maritime terrorism that exists in the oil-rich Gulf of Guinea, and the U.S. and its allies are responding (although, as discussed later in this volume, the response to date has been rather haphazard and weak compared to the comprehensive approach that is needed). Nowhere is the maritime threat—or for that matter, the terrorist threat in general—more severe than in Nigeria, the continent's largest oil producer. As described earlier in this chapter, embassies and oil infrastructure have already become targets for terrorism and violence. In addition, as highlighted in the previous chapter, the level of criminal activity in several parts of the country—including smuggling and oil bunkering—presents enormous challenges for the Nigerian government. Recognizing this, the U.S. recently provided Nigeria's navy with 15 patrol boats, which are now being used to crack down on theft of crude oil in deep sea waters and in creeks of the Niger Delta.[55] A closer look at Nigeria's current social and political landscape reveals unique and troubling vulnerabilities to terrorism.

The Unique Case of Nigeria

The global terrorist threat to Nigeria is quite real: Osama bin Laden has previously cited Nigeria, home to about 60 million Muslims, as a candidate for "liberation" from western hegemony.[56] The country is already the scene of considerable political instability, in large part because of its history of corrupt, authoritarian governments willing to do anything to protect their control over the oil wealth (see chapters 2 and 3). In Nigeria, very little oil revenue is returned to the main oil producing Niger Delta region, which—after several decades of oil production—remains poorer than the Nigerian average. Human Rights Watch notes that the "anger at the inequities attributed to the oil economy has led increasing numbers of people from the communities in the oil regions to protest the exploitation of what they see as 'their' oil . . . without benefit to them or compensation for the damage done to their livelihoods."[57] In recent years, militant youth have frequently invaded oil pumping stations, demanding money for their villages. The oil companies mostly pay without question, regarding their demands as an unofficial community tax.[58] In March 2003, villagers blockaded an oil facility for four days in the region operated by the Anglo-Dutch company, Shell, and armed youths in the remote Nigerian oil-producing state of Bayelsa attacked an oil facility operated by Agip, an Italian-owned company.[59] In December 2004, villagers in the Delta region stormed and temporarily occupied three foreign-owned installations, two run by Shell and one operated by ChevronTexaco.[60]

Other forms of violence plague the region as well. Since 1999, several hundred oil workers and their families—many of them Westerners—have been kidnapped and held hostage.[61] In one such incident, on June 14, 2005, six employees of the oil services firm Bilfinger-Berger (a local contractor for Shell) were kidnapped in the Niger Delta region as they were traveling by boat to one of Shell's offshore operations. According to the Reuter's news agency, a group called the Iduwini National Movement for Peace and Development claimed responsibility. The group said it wants to put pressure on the Nigerian division of Shell, and that it was angry the firm had not delivered promised jobs and building projects.[62] Kidnapping has become so common that the oil multinationals move personnel by helicopter and rarely go into villages.[63]

In addition to kidnappings, the violence in this region has also resulted in the deaths of oil company employees and villagers. For example, in April 2004, gunmen attacked a boat carrying oil workers in the Niger Delta region, killing two Americans and three Nigerians. These workers had been sent to inspect

ChevronTexaco oil and gas facilities which had been abandoned by the company after the outbreak of violence in March 2003—installations which would normally have been producing 140,000 barrels of oil daily.[64] In September 2004, Nigeria deployed extra troops to the southeastern city of Port Harcourt to clamp down on escalating gang warfare in the country's most important oil center. The troops were rushed to the area following two shooting incidents in the city center that left 18 people dead. Those responsible for the violence are suspected to be members of rival armed gangs involved in "bunkering" oil—tapping large quantities of crude oil from pipelines, loading it into barges and selling it clandestinely to tankers waiting offshore.[65] In December 2004, thieves tapping an oil pipeline in Sanki-Ilado—a village lying in wetlands in the Apapa district east of Nigeria's commercial capital, Lagos—set it ablaze as they fled from police, causing an explosion that killed more than 20 people.[66]

These incidents are symbolic of the broader terrain of violence throughout the Niger Delta region, much of it a product of dissatisfaction with the distribution and control of its oil wealth. In addition to violence directed at the Nigerian government, rival ethnic groups in the region have also attacked each other, with several incidents occurring around Warri city and in Southeast Plateau State.[67] Since early 2003, mounting communal violence has resulted in dozens of deaths and the leveling of eight communities in and around the Warri petroleum complex—one of the largest in the entire Gulf of Guinea. The level of political violence prompted all the major oil companies to withdraw staff, to close down operations, and at one point to reduce output by over 750,000 barrels per day (almost half of Nigeria's output).[68]

It is important to note that these attacks have not only taken place at facilities on the Nigerian mainland, but have also targeted offshore oil rigs—formerly considered by observers as "safe" investments by oil companies who now find it almost impossible to work on the mainland and are increasingly looking to offshore operations to avoid extortion and damage to their property.[69] For example, in April and May of 2003, a large group of oil workers spent more than two weeks as hostages on four offshore Nigerian oil rigs. The hostage-takers, who claimed to have explosives, were from the Ijaw ethnic group, the largest of the 11 groups in the Niger delta.[70] The hostages included 35 Britons, 17 Americans and more than 150 Nigerian nationals.[71] One armed group of Ijaw in particular—the Niger Delta People's Volunteer Force—has been the source of increasing concern for the Nigerian government. The group is estimated to have about 2,000 armed members, and seeks "a restructuring" of Nigeria that would give the Ijaw ethnic group—the dominant tribe (roughly 8 million strong) in the oil producing Niger Delta—self-determination and greater control over local oil resources.[72] Since 2001, its leader, Mujahid Dokubo-Asari (known simply as Asari) has directed a damaging military and propaganda war against the state and federal governments and those he described as their agents, prompting the government to initiate several full-scale military operations against him.[73]

The Niger Delta People's Volunteer Force is an offshoot of the Ijaw Youths Council (IYC), which in November 1998 issued what become known as the "Kiama Declaration," demanding control of the oil resources from the Niger Delta by the people of the Niger Delta.[74] There was an immediate crackdown on the group by the military junta that then ruled Nigeria. When Asari became president of the IYC in 2001, he immediately changed the slogan of the organization to "Resource Control and Self Determination By Every Means Necessary," signaling his readiness to do battle with the Nigerian state. In 2004, operating from a hideout deep in the mangrove swamps of the Niger Delta, Asari warned oil companies to leave the region and threatened to blow up oil facilities in the region, causing the international price of crude to rise dramatically.[75] Full-scale violence was only averted that year when President Obasanjo agreed to a meeting with Asari, at which a disarmament and amnesty deal was reached.

While the Nigerian government has periodically engaged in negotiations with Asari and his group, there have also been several violent confrontations. On June 11, 2004, six people were killed when Nigerian troops raided an Ijaw village in the Niger Delta in search of weapons, and were subsequently engaged in a gun battle by armed militants.[76] In a separate incident—which did not involve Asari's group, but nonetheless served as a powerful motivator for him and his followers—Nigerian security forces killed up to ten unarmed Ugborodo protestors in February 2005 at the Escravos oil terminal. Members of the Ugborodo community had entered the facility following failed negotiations with Chevron-Texaco regarding employment issues.[77]

On September 20, 2005, authorities arrested Asari following a newspaper report that indicated he was preparing to renew his violent struggle. After his initial court appearance, Justice Minister Baya Ojo declared that Asari would be formally charged with unlawful assembly and treason, which carries the death penalty.[78] His lawyer, Uche Okoko, was also arrested and charged with similar offenses. The following morning, Asari's supporters stormed two oil flow stations owned by Chevron, and another owned by Shell. Alali Horsefall, the deputy leader of the Niger Delta People's Volunteer Force, declared "We will blow up everything. We will set fire to them."[79] Militants armed with machetes and assault rifles demonstrated in Port Harcout, hundreds of security reinforcements were sent to the delta region, and multinational oil companies asked their employees to stay away from work because of the deteriorating situation.[80] As of this writing, it is unclear how this situation will be resolved. But given recent history, it is likely that continued and escalating violence in Nigeria will again have a negative impact on the world's oil markets.

In sum, the Niger Delta region, (which is one of the wealthiest regions of the Gulf of Guinea in terms of oil reserves), is incredibly volatile and chaotic. Poverty, lawlessness, and extreme violence by armed gangs surrounds the West's vital energy extraction industry. Attempted government crackdowns have thus far failed to quell the unrest, and in some cases have exacerbated the problem by producing new recruits for armed groups like the Niger Delta People's Volunteer Force.

Militant Islam in Nigeria

In addition to these economic-related attacks in the Niger Delta, driven largely by groups seeking more control of oil reserves, the Nigerian government is struggling to deal with increasing violence based on ethnic tensions and religious ideology. During military rule, Nigeria was dominated by the largely Muslim, northern-based, Hausa-Fulani ethnic group who formed the bulk of the military's officer corps. Because of perceived marginalization and neglect of their communities, the mainly Christian Yoruba and Igbo ethnic groups of the south and east of the country became resentful of the Hausa. Today, this north-south ethnic divide still engenders suspicion towards the federal government—in some cases, a lack of faith in the government and police has even led to the growth of ethnic militias across the country.[81] Further, these political realities impact President Obasanjo's ability to do more for the Niger Delta. If he devotes too much attention to the mainly Christian south, where he gets most of his support, he risks being seen as a southern president. Most northern, Muslim dominated areas voted for the opposition in the last election, and alienating them further would risk worsening ethnic and religious tensions, and jeopardize the long-term commitment of successive governments to see through to completion the reforms Obasanjo has put in motion.[82]

In the north, the degree of suspicion of Nigeria's Islamic communities toward the government and the international community is already cause for particular concern. In the heavily Muslim state of Kano, for example, some Nigerian religious figures have preached that vaccinations against polio are actually part of a plot to sterilize Muslims, thus effectively barring the World Health Organization's efforts to eradicate polio worldwide.[83] Further, in 1999 shari'a law (Islamic law of a dogmatic and literalist sort) was adopted and implemented in 12 of the populous northern states, although clearly not all the inhabitants of these states are in favor of it.[84] As a result, the governments of Zamfara, Niger, Katsina, Sokoto, and other northern states have organized hisbah—so-called "religious police" (in reality, vigilantes) who are deployed for the purposes of enforcing shari'a codes.[85]

The rise of militant Islam in this part of the country has created an enormous challenge for Obasanjo's administration as well as for Nigeria's allies. On October 13, 2001, days after the commencement of the U.S. military campaign in Afghanistan, several hundred demonstrators gathered in Kano—the largest city in Nigeria's predominantly Muslim northern region—to protest the American action. The protesters carried banners criticizing the United States, and many reportedly displayed images of Osama bin Laden. The peaceful demonstration was immediately followed by rioting and street battles between Christians and Muslims, in which more than 100 people died. The international media reported these events as the most militant anti-American protest around the world since the beginning of hostilities in Afghanistan, and the violence was described as part of a rising tide of Islamic militancy and religious conflict in Nigeria.[86]

As Peter Lewis, a researcher at the Center for Strategic and International Studies, recently observed, "There is no doubt that religious polarization and the spread of fundamentalism pose major challenges to Nigeria's fledgling democracy . . . Conditions that foster radicalism—poverty, unemployment, social dislocation, cultural polarization, and a large pool of disaffected young men—are evident in abundance. Among Muslims, social grievances often find religious expression through fundamentalist appeals to piety, or through Islamist challenges to the political status quo. Both trends are evident in the country's political and religious landscape, and Islamist pressures may become a serious danger."[87] Militant Islamism has indeed become a significant force in Nigeria, and is already the source of growing unrest throughout other parts of West, North and East Africa as well. Throughout many parts of Africa, there are worries that Islamist extremists could find safe haven and that terrorist organizations would find opportunities for recruitment of militants to participate in religious insurgencies elsewhere. For example, in June 2005, the U.S. European Command revealed that about 25% of the nearly 400 fighters captured in Iraq had come from Africa.[88] Almost all of them have come from communities where militant Islam has taken root—communities where it is common to find greater loyalty to the concept of a global Muslim *umma* and caliphate than to the relatively young nation-states of which they are a part.[89]

Nigeria has one of the largest Muslim populations in the world, and the second largest on the African continent (after Egypt). While these northern Nigerian Muslim communities have usually been places of peaceful coexistence, recent years have seen a dramatic rise in violence. Since 1999, violence stemming from a combination of ethnic tensions and religious extremism has killed thousands. In one instance, religiously-based clashes in the northern city of Kaduna in November 2002 left over 200 people dead. The violence began when Muslim youths began protesting in opposition to the staging of the Miss World beauty pageant in Nigeria. On November 16, a newspaper article by a female fashion columnist, Isioma Daniel, suggested that the prophet Mohammed himself might have chosen a Miss World contestant for a bride. The deputy governor of the northern state of Zamfara responded by issuing a *fatwa* calling for Daniel's execution, and the ensuing riots between Muslims and Christians throughout the region forced the beauty pageant to relocate to London. In December 2003, a group of militants declared an Islamic state in Yobe, one of the northern states that embraced Sharia, although their movement was swiftly crushed by the military, with scores of people killed. In April, 2004 a group of Islamic fundamentalists were responsible for a series of violent confrontations in

Yobe state, terrorizing the local population until a significant military presence arrived to restore order. On May 18, 2004, President Olusegun Obasanjo declared a state of emergency in the central Nigerian state of Plateau after months of ferocious fighting between Christians and Muslims led hundreds dead. According to one source, fighting between rival Muslims and Christians in Plateau claimed 53,787 lives, one-third of them children, between 2001 and 2004.[90]

In October 2004, a brief but well-organized Islamic attack was led by members of Al-Sunna wa al-Jamma, a group that claims to be an African version of the Taliban (the Afghan fundamentalist militia that supported Osama bin Laden).[91] A 60-strong group of these Islamic fundamentalists ransacked the towns of Bama and Gwoza in the northern state of Borno, destroyed police stations and looted their armories before being chased by security forces to the hills and across the porous border into Cameroon.[92] Similar attacks have been reported throughout the northwest, and represent an alarming trend of religious extremism and its influence on local outbreaks of violence.[93] In fact, according to Stephen Ellis, a prominent observer of Africa affairs, there is apparently even support for Al Qaeda among the Muslim communities in northern Nigeria.[94] Overall, the large Muslim presence in this strategically important region, together with political instability and socio-economic decline, provide ideal breeding grounds for religious tensions and Islamic militancy. Thus, Nigerian authorities are increasingly concerned about the presence of preachers and financial support by Algerian, Libyan, Iranian and Pakistani Islamic groups which contribute to the spread of militant ideas.[95] Countering the influence of such groups is rapidly becoming a key element of U.S. counterterrorism policy, as will be discussed later in this volume.

In sum, Nigeria faces a terrorist threat on two fronts: in the north, from Muslim extremists bent on driving all Western "infidel" influences out of the region, and in the south, where a mix of separatists, criminal gangs and lawless thugs have been attacking the country's oil infrastructure as a means to extort or otherwise compel government and multinational behavior. In some parts of Nigeria a potent mix of communal tensions, radical Islamism, and anti-Americanism has produced a fertile breeding ground for militancy and threatens to tear the country apart.[96] Of further concern is that the combination of criminality, ethnic tensions and religious extremism could severely impact the oil-rich Niger Delta region. On that note, it is particularly troubling to some that Mujahid Dokubo-Asari, the leader of the Niger Delta People's Volunteer Force, converted to Islam in the 1990s. Similar combinations of ethnic tensions, poverty and increasing religious extremism are found throughout Africa, particularly in the countries that lie north of the Gulf of Guinea. For example, experts say Al Qaeda has already established a healthy presence in Mauritania (a country just a bit north of the Gulf of Guinea where, incidentally, oil has also recently been discovered), providing weapons training and ideological indoctrination. However, with the exception of certain northern regions of Nigeria, Islamic militancy has not yet evolved into the primary threat to the stability of most parts of West and Central Africa. Rather, the primary concerns for most terrorist analysts are related to the criminal activities in this region (as described in the previous chapter). As Princeton Lyman and Stephen Morrison argued in a recent *Foreign Affairs* article, "the terrorist threat in West Africa comes less from religion and politics than from lack of sovereign control and general debility."[97] As described throughout this volume, there is much the U.S. can and should do to help improve the governance and security challenges of this vital region of Africa so that international terrorist groups cannot take advantage of the currently prevailing conditions.

Conclusion

Overall, this analysis suggests that the oil-rich countries of the Gulf of Guinea are highly vulnerable to a terrorist attack. The incapacity of security forces throughout much of region to protect targets threatened by terrorism is in stark contrast with the great variety of such potential targets including embassies, the numerous agencies and projects of international development organizations, subsidiaries of American and European companies (including those related to the oil industry), and international tourist hotels.[98] According to Stefan Mair, deputy director of the German Institute for International and Security Affairs, "The U.S. embassies and offices of the development organizations already resemble 'wild west' forts of the 19th century. Oil and mining companies have resorted to protecting their property with private, paramilitary security services. Americans, Europeans and Africans who can afford to are increasingly withdrawing to heavily guarded and elaborately protected gated communities."[99] African countries, as with the rest of the developing world, lack the resources to effectively prevent or respond to acts of terrorism. Of course, the primary targets of such attacks might be an institution of (or private corporation headquartered in) the United States, Israel, or some other Western country, but as the 1998 embassy bombings in Kenya and Tanzania clearly demonstrated, many Africans will likely die in any major terrorist attack on Western targets in Africa.

   The militant Islamist dimension to terrorist violence in West Africa is particularly worrisome given the aforementioned interest expressed by al Qaeda in destabilizing the region and attacking its oil infrastructure. According to the Council on Foreign Relations, a non-profit think tank in the U.S., "any African nation with the combustible mix of a weak central government, widespread poverty, and an increasingly politicized Muslim population is at risk" of becoming a potential haven for terrorists.[100] The combination of weak central government and widespread poverty is already present throughout the Gulf of Guinea. Further, as the West increases its involvement with—and physical presence within—the countries of West and Central Africa, these countries run the risk of becoming new targets of the global terrorists who seek to attack the West wherever it can. For example, in Chad—where 52% of the population are Muslims—the newly discovered oil wealth and Western-built oil infrastructure offer several new and tempting targets for anti-American terrorists.

In the Gulf of Guinea, states are both potential victims and enablers of terrorism. This is largely why the U.S. is investing so much in building up the capabilities of these states, through initiatives like the Gulf of Guinea Guard and various military education and training programs. Because similar patterns of political repression, corruption and underdevelopment are common in the Persian Gulf, and because we have seen a rise in terrorist organizations operating in (and coming from) that region, a review of U.S. foreign policies in this region is warranted, and provided in the next chapter.

Notes

1. Esther Schrader, "U.S. Seeks Military Access in N. Africa," *New York Times*, 27 March 2004.

2. Congressional Research Service, "Nation's Hospitable to Organized Crime and Terrorism," Library of Congress, Federal Research Division (October, 2003).

3. Princeton N. Lyman and J. Stephen Morrison, "The Terrorist Threat in Africa," *Foreign Affairs* 83, no. 1 (January/February 2004): 75-86.

4. Quoted in Council on Foreign Relations, "Africa: Terror Havens," 30 December 2003. Online at http://www.cfr.org

5. White House. *National Security Strategy of the United States*, 2002.

6. Congressional Research Service, "Nation's Hospitable to Organized Crime and Terrorism," Library of Congress, Federal Research Division, October, 2003.

7. The following discussion is adapted from the research of Douglas Way, Chief Scientist at the Earth Satellite Corporation; specifically a presentation on using geospatial modeling to identify possible remote havens for terrorist and other illicit activity. For further information, see: http://65.61.22.59/geotech2003docs/ASPRS03.pdf.

8. Andrew Koch, No Safe Haven in Africa, *Jane's Intelligence Review*, November 9, 2004.

9. Princeton N. Lyman, "The Terrorist Threat in Africa," Testimony before the House Committee on International Relations, Subcommittee on Africa, April 1, 2004.

10. Princeton N. Lyman, "The Terrorist Threat in Africa," 2004.

11. Douglas Farah and Richard Shultz, "Al Qaeda's Growing Sanctuary," *Washington Post*, July 13, 2004. Also, see "Terrorism in Africa," Voice of America (editorial), April 7, 2004.

12. Associated Press. "U.S. Military Shows Interest in Africa." (Feb. 25, 2004). Available online at: http://www.military.com/NewsContent/0,13319,FL_Africa_022502,00.html

13. Elizabeth Blunt, "Nigeria's new breed of radical Islam," BBC News, Sept. 22, 2004. Online at: http://news.bbc.co.uk/1/hi/world/africa/3679960.stm; and BBC, "Nigeria police hunt 'Taleban'," BBC News, Sept. 22, 2004. Online at: http://news.bbc.co.uk/1/hi/world/africa/3679092.stm

14. Meredeth Turshen, "The Politics of Oil in Africa," *The Scholar and Feminist Online*, 2(2), Winter 2004.

15. For more on this, please see James Forest, editor, *Teaching Terror: Knowledge Transfer in the Terrorist World*, edited by James Forest (Boulder, CO: Rowman & Littlefield, 2006); *Homeland Security and Terrorism*, edited by Russell Howard, James Forest and Joanne Moore (New York: McGraw-Hill, 2005); *The Making of a Terrorist: Recruitment, Training and Root Causes*, edited by James Forest (Westport, CT: Praeger, 2005).

16. Anne Korin and Gal Luft, "Terrorism Goes to Sea," *Foreign Affairs* (November/December 2004).

17. Collier, June 2000, p. 6, referenced in Swanson, p. 13

18. The following list is from Brynjar Lia and Ashild Kjok, "Energy Supply as Terrorist Targets? Patterns of 'Petroleum Terrorism' 1968-1999," in *Oil in the Gulf: Obstacles to Democracy and Development*, edited by Daniel Heradstveit and Helge Hveem (London: Ashgate, 2004), p. 101.

19. Brynjar Lia and Ashild Kjok, p. 104.

20. For more on oil pipeline vulnerabilities and attacks, see "Pipeline sabotage is terrorist's weapon of choice," Institute for the Analysis of Global Security report on energy security at: http://www.iags.org/n0328051.htm

21. Alfredo Rangel Suarez, "Parasites and predators: Guerillas and the Insurrection Economy of Colombia," Journal of International Affairs (Spring, 2000), p. 589.

22. "Tamil Tigers claim tanker attack," BBC News, October 31, 2001. Online at: http://news.bbc.co.uk/1/hi/world/south_asia/1628218.stm.

23. "Israel depot bomb attack thwarted," BBC News, May 23, 2002. Online at: http://news.bbc.co.uk/1/hi/world/middle_east/2003806.stm.

24. Morocco 'Uncovers al Qaeda Plot," BBC News, 11 June 2002. Online at: http://news.bbc.co.uk/1/hi/world/africa/2037391.stm; and Chris Morris, "Terror fears spark ship escorts," BBC News, March 17, 2003. Online at: http://news.bbc.co.uk/2/hi/europe/2855769.stm.

25. "Yemen says tanker blast was terrorism," *BBC News*, October 16, 2002. Online at: http://news.bbc.co.uk/1/hi/world/middle_east/2334865.stm; and "Craft 'rammed' Yemen oil tanker," *BBC News*, October 6, 2002. Online at: http://news.bbc.co.uk/2/hi/middle_east/2303363.stm.

26. "PKK militants attack oil pipeline in south-eastern Turkey" *Alexander's Gas and Oil Connections* 9(22), November 11, 2004. Online at: http://www.gasandoil.com/goc/news/nte44561.htm.

27. John C.K. Daly, "The Threat to Iraqi Oil," *Terrorism Monitor* 2(12), June 17, 2004.

28. "Gunmen attack in Yanbu." Saudi Arabia-U.S. Relations Newsletter, May 1, 2004. Online at: http://www.saudi-us-relations.org/newsletter2004/saudi-relations-interest-05-01.html.

29. "Attack in Khobar," Saudi Arabia – U.S. Relations Newsletter, May 29, 2004. Online at: http://www.saudi-us-relations.org/newsletter2004/saudi-relations-interest-05-29.html.

30. U.S. Department of State. 2003. *Patterns of Global Terrorism, 2002.* Available online at: http://www.state.gov/s/ct/rls/pgtrpt/2002.

31. U.S. Department of State. 2003. *Patterns of Global Terrorism, 2002.*

32. al Qalah website: https://www.qal3ah.org/vb/index.php?

33. James S. Robbins, "No Blood for Oil," *National Review Online,* July 12, 2005. Online at: http://www.nationalreview.com/robbins/robbins200507120857.asp.

34. "Pipeline sabotage is terrorist's weapon of choice," Institute for the Analysis of Global Security report on energy security at: http://www.iags.org/n0328051.htm

35. James S. Robbins, "No Blood for Oil."

36. "U.S., U.K. Shut Missions in Nigeria," BBC News, June 17, 2005. Online at: http://news.bbc.co.uk/go/pr/fr/-/2/hi/africa/4103294.stm.

37. "Sentinel Worldview: West Africa" *Jane's Intelligence Review,* May 6, 2004.

38. Senator Bill Nelson (D-Florida), 6 December 2001, as cited in Gal Luft and Anne Korin, "Threats to Oil Transport," Institute for the Analysis of Global Security, December 2003. Available online at: http://www.iags.org/oiltransport.html.

39. Gal Luft and Anne Korin, "Threats to Oil Transport," Institute for the Analysis of Global Security, December 2003. Available online at: http://www.iags.org/oiltransport.html. Also, see Gal Luft and Anne Korin, "Terror's Next Target," *The Journal of International Security Affairs,* December 2003.

40. Michael Richardson, "Terror at Sea: The World's Lifelines are at Risk," *The Straits Times* (Singapore), 17 November 2003. Online at: http://www.stevequayle.com/News.alert/03_Terror/031117.terror.at.sea.html

41. Anne Korin and Gal Luft, "Terrorism Goes to Sea," *Foreign Affairs* (November/December 2004). Gal Luft is Executive Director of the Institute for the Analysis of Global Security (IAGS). Anne Korin is Director of Policy and Strategic Planning at IAGS and Editor of Energy Security.

42. Anne Korin and Gal Luft, "Terrorism Goes to Sea."

43. Anne Korin and Gal Luft, "Terrorism Goes to Sea."

44. Anne Korin and Gal Luft, "Terrorism Goes to Sea."

45. Anne Korin and Gal Luft, "Terrorism Goes to Sea."

46. Pirates Board Indonesian Tanker," *CBS News* (29 March 29). Online at: http://www.cbsnews.com/stories/2003/03/29/world/main546695.shtml; also, Michael Richardson, "Terror at Sea: The World's Lifelines are at Risk,"

47. National Commission on Terrorist Attacks Upon the United States. *Report of the National Commission on Terrorist Attacks Upon the United States* (the 9/11 Commission Report). Washington: Government Printing Office, 2004. Available online at http://www.gpoaccess.gov/911.

48. David L. Goldwyn and J. Stephen Morrison, *A Strategic Approach to Governance and Security in the Gulf of Guinea,* CSIS Report on Gulf of Guinea, July 2005.

49. Data compiled by the International Maritime Bureau is available online at: http://www.icc-ccs.org/main/index.php

50. "Sentinel Worldview: West Africa" *Jane's Intelligence Review,* May 6, 2004.

51. *American Forces Press Service,* "Maritime Security Conference Brings Navies Together" October 5, 2004.

52. Taken from presentations made at the Gulf of Guinea Maritime Security Conference, Naples, Italy, 3-5 October 2004.

53. "Sentinel Worldview: West Africa" *Jane's Intelligence Review,* May 6, 2004

54. "Us Helps West African Navies." *Voice of America News,* 1 February 2005.

55. "Nigeria Navy Buys 15 Patrol Boats To Fight Oil Smuggling," *Agence France Presse,* 3 January 2005. Available online at: http://www.defencetalk.com/news/publish/article_002034.shtml.

56. David Blair, "Terrorism Alert Closes Consulate in Nigeria," *Daily Telegraph* (UK), June 18, 2005.

57. Swanson, p. 19, citing Human Rights Watch, 1999, *The Price of Oil: CSR and Human Rights Violations in Nigeria's Oil Producing Communities*, Human Rights Watch. Online at http://www.hrw.org/reports/1999/nigeria/Nigew991-01.htm#P190_8265.

58. John Vidal, "Oil rig hostages are freed by strikers as mercenaries fly out," *The Guardian* (UK), May 3, 2003. Online at: http://www.guardian.co.uk/oil/story/0,11319,948743,00.html.

59. Anna Borzello, "Youths attack Nigeria oil plant," BBC News, April 21, 2004. Online at: http://news.bbc.co.uk/1/hi/world/africa/3647431.stm.

60. "Oil Workers kidnapped in Nigeria," *BBC News,* June 15, 2005.

61. Neal Adams, *Terrorism and Oil* (Tulsa, OK: PennWell Corporation), p.12

62. "Oil Workers kidnapped in Nigeria," *BBC News,* June 15, 2005.

63. John Vidal, "Oil rig hostages are freed by strikers as mercenaries fly out."

64. Glenn McKenzie, "Oil Workers Killed in Nigeria; Two from U.S." *Washington Post,* 25 April 2004, p. A21.

65. "Port Harcourt Gang Warfare Picks Up Pace," *UN Integrated Regional Information Network News,* 5 September 2004.

66. "Nigeria pipeline blaze kills 26," *BBC News,* 23 December 2004.

67. U.S. Department of State, Bureau of Consular Affairs, "Travel Warning," May 20, 2005. Available online at http://www.state.gov

68. Douglas *et al.*

69. John Vidal, "Oil rig hostages are freed by strikers as mercenaries fly out."

70. John Vidal, "Oil rig hostages are freed by strikers as mercenaries fly out."

71. John Vidal, "Oil rig hostages are freed by strikers as mercenaries fly out."

72. "Port Harcourt Gang Warfare Picks Up Pace," *UN Integrated Regional Information Network News.*

73. Ebimo Amungo, "Profile: Nigeria's oil militant," *BBC News,* 4 October 2004. Available online at: http://news.bbc.co.uk/go/pr/fr/-/1/hi/world/africa/3713664.stm.

74. Ebimo Amungo, "Profile: Nigeria's oil militant."

75. International Energy Administration, "Nigeria," Country Analysis Report (April 2005), p. 6 (http://www.eia.doe.gov/emeu/cabs/nigeria.html).

76. UN Office for the Coordination of Humanitarian Affairs, "Six Killed as Troops Raid Village for Arms," UN Integrated Regional Information Network News, June 14, 2004).

77. International Energy Administration, "Nigeria," Country Analysis Report (April 2005), p. 6 (http://www.eia.doe.gov/emeu/cabs/nigeria.html).

78. "Nigeria Militant Storms Oil Station," *BBC News,* 22 September 2005.

79. "Nigeria Militant Storms Oil Station," *BBC News,* 22 September 2005.

80. "Militants Shut Oil Facilities as Leader Appears in Court," *Irin News,* 22 September 2005.

81. Joseph Winter, "Obasanjo's Thankless Task," BBC News Analysis, October 7, 2004. Online at http://news.bbc.co.uk/hi/world/africa/3724520.stm.

82. Peter M. Lewis, "Islam, Protest, and Conflict in Nigeria," CSIS Africa Notes, 10 (December 2002). Washington, DC: Center for Strategic and International Studies. Online at: http://www.csis.org

83. Princeton N. Lyman, "The Terrorist Threat in Africa," 2004.

84. These states include Bauchi, Borno, Gombe, Jigawa, Kaduna, Kano, Katsina, Kebbi, Niger, Sokoto, Yobe, and Zamfara.

85. Peter M. Lewis, "Islam, Protest, and Conflict in Nigeria."

86. Peter M. Lewis, "Islam, Protest, and Conflict in Nigeria."

87. Peter M. Lewis, "Islam, Protest, and Conflict in Nigeria."

88. Eric Schmitt, "As Africans Join Iraqi Insurgency, U.S. Counters with Military Training in their Lands," *New York Times,* June 10, 2005; and Eric Schmitt, "U.S. and Allies Capture More Foreign Fighters" *New York Times,* 19 June, 2005.

89. "Faithful, but Not Fanatics," *The Economist,* June 28, 2003, as cited by Peter Chalk, 2004. "Islam in West Africa: The Case of Nigeria," in *The Muslim World After 9/11,* edited by Angel Rabasa, Cheryl Benard, et. al. Santa Monica: RAND, p. 414.

90. E. Blanche, "Africa's Teetering Giant," *Jane's Islamic Affairs Analyst,* 1 December, 2004.

91. Andrew Koch, No Safe Haven in Africa, *Jane's Intelligence Review,* November 9, 2004.

92. See Anthony Maliki, "Unwelcome in Borno: Talibans Muslim Fundamentalists from Niger, Chad, Cameroon Invade Borno State," in *Lagos Insider Weekly,* October 11, 2003, p. 32.

93. E. Blanche, "Africa's Teetering Giant."

94. Stephen Ellis (co-editor of African Affairs) in "Briefing: West Africa and its Oil," *African Affairs,* 102 (2003) p. 137.

95. Anelli Botha and Hussein Soloman, "Terrorism in Africa," University of Pretoria.

96. Princeton Lyman and J. Stephen Morrison, "The Terrorist Threat to West Africa," *Foreign Affairs,* January/February 2004, as cited in Council on Foreign Relations, "Africa: Terror Havens," December 30, 2003. Online at http://www.cfr.org

97. Princeton N. Lyman and J. Stephen Morrison, "The Terrorist Threat to West Africa," *Foreign Affairs,* January/February 2004, p. 83.

98. Stefan Mair, "Terrorism and Africa: On the danger of further attack in sub-Saharan Africa," *African Security Review,* 12(1) (2003), p. 109.

99. Stefan Mair, "Terrorism and Africa," 109.

100. Council on Foreign Relations, "Africa: Terror Havens," December 30, 2003. Online at http://www.cfr.org.

Chapter 5
A History of U.S. Foreign Policy in the Middle East and the Old Gulf

The Middle East is another uniquely troubled region of the world, and (like the Gulf of Guinea) also considerably well-endowed with natural resources. According to the U.S. Department of Energy, the share of world oil production accounted for by the major Persian Gulf producers will rise from 27% in 1990 to 36% in 2025.[1] Oil has provided huge revenues for the rulers of these countries, but neither political reform nor sufficient prosperity for the people.[2] Further, the huge revenues derived from energy resources has greatly reduced the incentives to develop diversified local economies throughout the region.

Access to large oil revenues channeled through the treasuries is a distinctive feature of the state in oil exporting countries of the Persian Gulf. Unlike the meritocratic, capitalist economies of the West—where governments collect taxes and use these revenues to fund public services like education, law enforcement, infrastructure maintenance and defense—these Persian Gulf states basically rely on oil revenues as their primary source of income, and redistribute this wealth (through systems of patronage) and provide services. Most economic activities outside the petroleum sector depend on government permits, contracts, support, and protection. Consequently, the Persian Gulf oil exporters have no significant market economy, but rather a protected concessionary and distributive economy that is directed by the government.[3]

Overall, in the Persian Gulf—much like many of the African countries described in the previous two chapters—the state uses industry for its political purpose. Indeed, according to Paul Michael Wihbey of the Washington-based Institute for Advanced Strategic and Political Studies, "Persian Gulf oil states have ignored the importance of economic development and diversification at the expense of rising social tension and instability."[4] As a result, political alienation is widespread and significant in the Persian Gulf, particularly in Bahrain and Saudi Arabia.[5] Gulf political systems are exclusive—the ruling families monopolize decision making—and, despite petitions and the formation of token national assemblies, many Gulf citizens correctly believe they have little or no influence on decision making.[6]

As discussed earlier in this book, the volatile mix of natural resource exploitation and political unrest is cause for concern. Further, just as it is in Nigeria and elsewhere, the oil infrastructure of these countries offers tempting targets for many groups bent on carrying out acts of political violence. Recent attacks on oil pipelines, stations, and other elements of the oil industry in Iraq and Saudi Arabia have had a noticeable impact on global energy markets; in Iraq, these attacks have been carried out despite (and to some extent, because of) the presence of U.S. troops—the world's most capable and well-equipped military forces. In Saudi Arabia, the National Guard, regular Saudi military forces, and Interior Ministry officers are tasked with protecting oilfields, pipelines (the country has around 10,000 miles), ports, refineries, and other oil facilities.[7] According to Nawaf Obaid, an advisor to the Saudi royal family, the regime spent $5.5 billion in 2003 on oil security.[8]

Saudi Arabia plays a critical role in global energy supply, particularly because it is the only country in the world with excess capacity in oil production. According to data compiled by the U.S. Department of Commerce, Saudi Arabia has 264.2 billion barrels of proven oil reserves (more than one-fourth of the world total) and up to 1 trillion barrels of ultimately recoverable oil. Saudi Arabia is the world's leading oil exporter and maintains production capacity of around 10-10.5 million barrels per day. Saudi Arabia maintains an excess production capacity of approximately two million barrels per day, a vital contribution to oil market stability in the event of unanticipated supply disruptions. Saudi Arabia is the most influential member of the Organization of Petroleum Exporting Countries (OPEC), and Saudi oil policy makers remain committed to being reliable suppliers and have renounced any interest in using an oil embargo as a "weapon" to influence U.S. foreign policy. Record oil revenues in 2003 have helped the Saudi Government close the year with a surplus of over $12 billion. Oil represents 90-95% of total Saudi export earnings, 75% of state revenues, and about 35-40% of GDP.[9]

For the past 60 years, the U.S. has provided the Saudi regime with considerable amounts of weaponry and technology in support of their oil security needs, for the simple reason that oil is a uniquely important resource for the United States' national security and economy growth. While U.S. petroleum imports have doubled since 1973, U.S. imports from Saudi Arabia have nearly quadrupled.[10] In 1943, President Franklin D. Roosevelt declared that "the defense of Saudi Arabia is vital to the defense of the United States,"[11] and this perspective has underscored our foreign policy decisions in the region ever since. As shown in Table 3.1, massive amounts have been spent throughout the region on U.S. defense weapons and technology, primarily in support of U.S. (and global) energy security interests. By some estimates, arms transfers to Saudi

Arabia and Persian Gulf states since 1990 have been valued at more than $100 billion.[12]

Table 5.1: U.S. Arms Licenses and Agreements
with Selected Persian Gulf Countries, 1990-2001 (in U.S. dollars)

Country	Total
Bahrain	$1,357,610,582
Kuwait	$5,200,164,699
Oman	$168,199,009
Qatar	$47,794,858
Saudi Arabia	$44,341,718,138
United Arab Emirates	$9,697,692,265

Source: Federation of American Scientists, U.S. Arms Transfer Database.

The importance of this oil-rich region to the U.S. cannot be overstated. Today, with 4.5% of the world's population, the U.S. consumes 26% of the world's oil[13]—over 20 million barrels per day.[14] Oil provides 40% of energy and 97% of transportation fuel in the U.S.[15] Oil is also critical to the U.S. military, since oil fuels nearly all weapons-delivery systems.[16] However, at present, the United States has only three percent of the world's proven oil reserves,[17] and thus currently imports more than half of the oil it consumes.[18] It is projected that U.S. oil consumption will rise by one-third over the next two decades, and that foreign oil will comprise two thirds of all oil consumed in the U.S. by 2020.[19]

Over 30% of the oil imported by the U.S. comes from the Persian Gulf, a region which contains 590 billion barrels of known reserves.[20] The combination of dependence on foreign oil and our national security needs has thus influenced foreign policy decisions in this region for decades, have has played a particularly important role in our relations with Iraq (with 113 billion barrels of proven oil reserves) and Iran (90 billion barrels). For example, in August 2002, Vice President Richard Cheney linked fears about Saddam Hussein's alleged possession of weapons of mass destruction to potential threats to America's access to Persian Gulf oil: "Armed with an arsenal of these weapons of terror, and seated atop 10 percent of the world's oil reserves, Saddam Hussein could then be expected . . . to take control of a great portion of the world's energy supplies."[21]

Perhaps unsurprisingly, a similar relationship between energy security and military intervention was a prominent part of President George H.W. Bush's announcement in 1990 that troops would be deployed to the Persian Gulf in order to liberate Kuwait from the clutches of Saddam Hussein: "The stakes are high. Iraq is already a rich and powerful country that possesses the world's second largest reserves of oil and over a million men under arms. It's the fourth largest military in the world. Our country now imports nearly half the oil it consumes and could face a major threat to its economic independence. Much of the world is even more dependent upon imported oil and is even more vulnerable to

Iraqi threats."[22] In both cases, U.S. military engagement with Iraq has been justified—at least in part—by the need to secure access to oil in the Persian Gulf.

The importance of oil to the U.S. and its allies has not gone unnoticed by the leaders of al Qaeda, who—according to industry expert Michael T. Klare—view attacks on Saudi Arabia's oil industry as the most effective way of undermining the regime's credibility and power, and thus are likely to initiate other strikes of this sort.[23] In fact, bin Laden explicitly endorsed such actions in a recent (December 2004) audiotaped message, calling on Muslim militants in the Middle East to "do your best to prevent them [i.e., the United States and its allies] from stealing oil. Focus your operations on it, especially in Iraq and the Gulf."[24]

The relationship between national security and energy security, centered for decades in the Persian Gulf, has recently become a topic of considerable scrutiny and debate. Historically, America's reliance on foreign oil supplies has led the United States to look the other way in its relationships with dictators and despots.[25] As Secretary of State Condoleeza Rice noted on a visit to the region in June 2005, "for 60 years, my country, the United States, pursued stability at the expense of democracy in this region here in the Middle East, and we achieved neither."[26] Indeed, rising Western dependence on Middle Eastern oil since the 1960s has not been matched by efforts to stabilize the region politically.[27] As a result, according to professor James Robbins of the National Defense University, "our dependence on energy from the Middle East has created a grave threat to our country, and because we are obligated to protect these energy sources, the threat will continue. Our military presence and occasional interventions to protect energy supplies cost billions of dollars and increases tensions in the region by giving the opponents of the United States targets to attack, and the means to substantiate their charges of "Western imperialism." The situation presents a paradox—we need to be there because of the threat to our energy supplies, but our presence incites our enemies to greater efforts against us."[28]

In January 2002, the Institute for Advanced Strategic and Political Studies organized a symposium entitled "African Oil: A Priority for U.S. National Security and African Development." Paul Michael Wihbey, a fellow of the Institute and a participant in this symposium, noted that if the United States is going to get more involved in the Gulf of Guinea, it "must not repeat the mistakes of the Persian Gulf."[29] Because we clearly concur with this perspective, this chapter addresses in detail some of the "mistakes" we should avoid in our emerging relationship with the countries of West Africa.

Cold War Policies and Energy Security in the Persian Gulf[30]

During the Cold War, U.S. foreign policies toward the countries of the Persian Gulf were primarily framed within the context of its bipolar struggle against the Soviet Union. The containment of communism provided an overarching strategic framework that clearly influenced many policy decisions between 1945 and 1991. Shortly after World War II, a veritable chess match developed between the Americans and the Soviets over who would have more influence in which countries. As one superpower would develop a strong relationship with an Asian, African, Latin American, or Middle East nation, the other superpower would counter with its own relationship-building efforts with other countries in the region. This almost amusing game played a particular role in defining both superpower's involvement in Iran, Saudi Arabia, Egypt and Iraq during the early part of the Cold War.

The initial diplomatic confrontation between the United States and the Soviet Union in the Gulf region came in 1946, when the Iranian government lodged a formal complaint with the UN Secretary Council that the Soviets were interfering in its internal affairs.[31] U.S. President Harry S. Truman responded by offering economic and political support to Tehran and warning the Soviets that he would consider the use of military force should they continue to occupy the territory they had seized in northern Iran. While the Soviets eventually backed down and withdrew their forces, the U.S. deepened its own involvement in Iran's affairs, and in 1953 orchestrated a regime change which replaced a popularly-elected government with an authoritarian one allied with the U.S.[32] In June, 1953 Iranian Premier Mohammed Mossadegh appeared to be seeking closer ties with Moscow when he requested a loan from them. Within the strategic framework of the Cold War, this naturally worried U.S. President Eisenhower, who authorized the CIA to do what it could to bring down Mossadegh's administration (although now there is considerable doubt about Mossadegh's supposed Soviet-friendliness). The coup that took place two months later brought Mohammed Reza Shah Pahlavi to power, and he remained a strong ally of the U.S. until he was overthrown by the country's Islamic Revolution in 1979.

American oil workers and military advisers were welcome in Iran, and the Shah became a major customer for U.S. arms and industrial goods.[33] By 1978, there were over 8,700 U.S. military technicians working in Iran, and thousands of other American specialists were working in the country's energy, transportation, and communications sectors.[34] Vast amounts of oil-generated revenue were spent on military modernization, the development of a domestic arms industry, highway construction, and other infrastructure improvements. Yet Iranians suffered from high inflation and the decline of traditional markets and enterprises.[35] In response to growing rumbles of discontent, much of it emanating from the country's influential Shiite clergy, the Shah clamped down on opposition movements and jailed many prominent dissidents. Before long, his notorious and widely feared domestic security organization, Savak (the Persian acronym for the National Intelligence and Security Organization) came to be seen by the masses as the principal expression of a tyrannical and discredited regime.[36] Anti-government sentiment coalesced in mass protests in 1978 and finally precipitated the departure of the Shah on January 16, 1979.[37]

Meanwhile, the U.S. also sought to develop a strong relationship with Saudi Arabia, largely because of their vast oil resources. According to energy security specialist Michael Klare, the history of U.S.-Saudi relations began in earnest during the early 1940s.[38] In February 1943, the Roosevelt administration extended Lend Lease assistance to Saudi Arabia, and American financial aid soon become a major source of income for the Saudi royal family.[39] To further cement U.S. ties with the kingdom, President Roosevelt met with King Abdul Aziz of Saudi Arabia aboard the *USS Quincy* on February 14, 1945 and established a tacit alliance between the two countries.[40] During the late 1940s, President Truman recognized that the U.S. domestic oil supply would not be sufficient to meet growing consumer, industrial or military demand. A diplomatic memorandum addressed to Under Secretary of State Dean Acheson in January 1945 outlined the U.S. foreign policy of seeking "a strong and independent Saudi Arabian Government" that would not be susceptible to "political penetration" and would allow U.S. access to its "vast oil resources."[41] The head of the ruling Saudi monarchy—Abdul Aziz bin Abdul Rahman al Saud (known to the West as Ibn Saud)—was willing to develop increased commercial and military linkages with the U.S. under the condition that the U.S. would guarantee his own security.[42] Ibn Saud's security concerns were primarily due to the fact that his Arab neighbors strongly disapproved of a strong U.S.-Saudi relationship, largely because of U.S. support for the state of Israel.

This marriage of convenience kept Soviet influence at bay—in fact, on several occasions Saudi Arabia's leaders publicly expressed their disapproval of communism, particularly because of its promotion of atheism and the political discrimination of Muslims in communist countries. Two events in particular also soured the relationship between Riyadh and Moscow. First, in 1946, the Iranian government's complaint to the UN Secretary Council about Soviet interference in its internal affairs led Ibn Saud to worry about the security of his own country. Second, between 1946 and 1948, the Soviet Union refused to allow its Muslim citizens to make the annual pilgrimage to Mecca. Together, these events helped secure a healthy pro-U.S. (and anti-Soviet) relationship that has lasted (and, for the most part, has kept oil prices stable) for the last half century. The Arabian-American Oil Company, or Aramco—invested huge sums in the development of Saudi Arabian oil fields after World War II, and the Department of Defense established a military base at Dhahran and helped modernize the Saudi armed forces.[43]

However, one event above any other threatened the long-term stability of the U.S.-Saudi relationship. In October 1973, Egyptian and Syrian forces coordinated a surprise attack on the state of Israel, but their forces began to suffer heavy losses once the Israeli forces were mobilized. In true Cold War fashion, the Soviets (who backed the Arabs), and the Americans (who backed the Israelis) exerted pressure on the two sides to accept a ceasefire, in order to ensure that the war did not escalate to an extent that would spark a military confrontation between the superpowers.[44] The Saudis, furious at the U.S. (and under pressure by its Arab neighbors) for its pro-Israeli stance, initiated an oil embargo which remained in place until the spring of 1974.[45] The Saudi embargo, coupled with reductions in production by several other Arab members of the Organization of Petroleum Exporting Countries, caused marked increases in the price of gasoline in the United States and Western Europe, contributing to economic downturns across the Western world.[46] Importantly, one middle east country that did sell oil to the United States despite the Saudi embargo was Iran, where the Shah held true to his alliance with the U.S. (which, after all, had brought him to power).

These two countries—Iran and Saudi Arabia—formed the backbone of what became known as the Surrogate Strategy.[47] This strategy was based on these two powerful countries protecting U.S. interests in the region. The policy required a moderate increase in U.S. involvement in the region, namely in the form of military training and U.S. weapons technology for Iran and Saudi Arabia, and strong diplomatic support for the Shah of Iran and the Saudi royal family.[48]

Next door in Iraq, Saddam Hussen was among the Baathist Party leaders who engineered a coup on July 17, 1958 that removed the regime of General Abdul Karin Qassem from power.[49] For the next decade, Hussein worked to consolidate power and eventually became president in 1979—the same year in which the Islamic Revolution in Iran, led by Shiite cleric Ayatollah Ruhollah Khomeini, resulted in a group of Iranian students storming the U.S. embassy in Tehran and taking U.S. diplomats hostage for 444 days. Clearly, the pro-U.S. Pahlavi regime had been replaced by one significantly opposed to U.S. interests. Meanwhile, a month later, the Soviets invaded Afghanistan, Iran's neighbor to the north. Within the context of Cold War strategy, U.S. President Jimmy Carter responded to these events in his 1980 State of the Union Address by declaring that "an attempt by any outside force to gain control of the Persian Gulf region will be regarded as an assault on the vital interests of the United States of America, and such an assault would be repelled by any means necessary, including military force."[50] This justification for U.S. military involvement in the region became known as the Carter Doctrine, and has been referenced on a number of occasions in the past two decades.

The outbreak of open war between Iraq and Iran allowed another strategic opportunity for U.S. involvement in the region, as it began supplying Saddam Hussein's regime with a variety of weapons and equipment. Not only did President Ronald Reagan's administration seek to counter the regional ambitions of the Soviets (who were also offering arms to the Iraqis), but there was also a real concern that, should Iran triumph, Khomeini's virulent anti-U.S. politics and orthodox interpretation of Islam would spread south towards Kuwait and Saudi Arabia—key states in the American energy security strategy.[51] In addition to supplying Iraq with conventional weaponry, Washington acquiesced when some of its Western European allies (most notably West Germany) assisted Saddam's regime in the development of chemical weapons, nor did it object publicly to Baghdad's subsequent use of those munitions against the Iranians.[52]

Overall, U.S. foreign policy towards the Persian Gulf between 1945 and 1991 was driven by a mix of anti-communism and energy security. The outcome of these policies has unfortunately not always been favorable. During the 1970s, nationalization of oil fields and transportation and production facilities by state governments in the Middle East caused significant fluctuations in the oil markets. This was coupled with the rise of domestic kleptocracy enforced by authoritarian regimes. A lack of democratization combined with the lack of infrastructure investments contributed to the rise of extreme Muslim fundamentalism in Iran (1978-79), further affecting oil production in the region. This decade also witnessed the birth of OPEC and a series of punitive oil embargoes. In the U.S., the resulting gas shortages, price hikes and rationing created a political firestorm costing more than a few politicians their jobs. And the decade ended on a very low point in terms of U.S. involvement in the Middle East, with the 444-day Iran hostage crisis symbolizing anti-American sentiment throughout the region.

During the 1980s, the Iran-Iraq war resulted in each country destroying each other's oil tankers in the Persian Gulf. When Kuwait began providing substantial loans to Iraq for the purpose of acquiring arms, Iran attacked Kuwaiti oil platforms and tankers—bringing the United States into the war as guardians of Persian Gulf oil shipping (under Operation Earnest Will, 1987-88).[53] Also during this volatile decade, the Saudi Arabian decision to flood the market with oil compelled OPEC to finally align prices at $32/barrel. The 1990s began with the Iraqi seizure of Kuwaiti oil fields (along with the rest of the country), using its American and Western European weaponry. The international community, led by the U.S., responded by sending the Iraqi army back home as quickly as they could scamper, although the oil fields they lit on fire along their escape route took considerably longer to put out and had a larger impact on oil market fluctuations than the conflict itself.

Rewards and Challenges Resulting from U.S. Cold War Policies

The Persian Gulf emerged from the Cold War rather grateful that the whole superpower bipolar struggle (in which they had often been used as pawns) was over. They also emerged, on the whole, more wealthy, prosperous and modern than they had been a half-century earlier. In the 1970s, the rapid influx of oil wealth led all the oil rich countries in the Persian Gulf to create extensive welfare systems, providing free health care, education and other services to all their citizens.[54] However, in the early 1980s the price of oil fell dramatically, leading to a reduction in revenues with which the government could provide these services.[55] Over time, rising expectations of continued government largesse (the main source of income in states like Saudi Arabia), coupled with a booming birthrate, have created the kind of socio-political environment that fosters unrest, even political violence. This unrest, in turn, has resulted in anger directed not only toward the wealthy, authoritarian regimes of these countries, but also toward their U.S. and Western European patrons.

Throughout the last half century, one could describe Americans as looking towards the Middle East with one hand on the gas pump and the other hand on the trigger. Worse yet, the U.S. has helped support a variety of autocratic and kleptocratic regimes, rather than promoting democratization, basic human rights, and the improvement of daily life for the average person in the region. Generations in the region have thus come to view the U.S. as caring much more about energy than about people, despite the nation's core democratic values and institutions. Recent surveys indicate that less than 15% of the population throughout this region holds a favorable view of the U.S.[56] Further, according to the 2005 Pew Research Center's Global Opinion Survey, 81% of respondents in the Middle East believe that U.S. policies caused the September 11th attacks.[57]

Generally speaking, a large majority of people in the Persian Gulf do not like the U.S., and many of them see America as a pariah, the source of society's ills throughout the region. Nowhere in the world have more U.S. flags been burned, U.S. leaders hung in effigy, U.S. citizens held hostage, and U.S. influence so pointedly cautioned against and resisted by religious and political leaders as in the Middle East. Some of this anti-U.S. sentiment is fueled by religious interpretations. Firebrand imams castigate the U.S. for its lack of morals, or condemn the U.S. for opposing the Islamic state of Iran (and by extension, its presumed opposition for the establishment of any other Islamic state). But recent studies have shed new light on the relationship between U.S. foreign policy and political violence against U.S. and allied targets. For example, as intelligence expert Paul Pillar (2005) has observed:

> The public words and actions of some terrorists provide the most obvious clues that perceptions of, and animosity toward, U.S. foreign policies can be roots of terrorism. The United States or its overseas interests has increasingly become, even prior to the attacks of September 2001, prime targets of international terrorist attacks. The leaders of terrorist groups regularly denounce U.S. policies ranging from military operations to diplomatic postures. And it has become a more frequently discussed issue in public debate within the United States whether America's own actions may anger those who might resort to terrorism, motivate those who do resort to it, and thereby increase the number of Americans who will become victims of future terrorist attacks.[58]

While animosity towards the U.S. is not entirely a new phenomenon, its violent product has only recently 'hit home' in the guise of attacks on U.S. and Western businesses, embassies, and people throughout the region. In Saudi Arabia, two major terrorist attacks in May 2004 raised specific concerns about the safety of Western oil workers and of Saudi oil facilities. In the first attack, on

May 1, a group of armed men killed six Westerners and a Saudi at the offices of ABB Lummus (a Houston-based subsidiary of ABB, the Swedish-Swiss engineering firm) in Yanbu. Following the attack, for which al Qaeda claimed responsibility, all 90 employees working on a joint Sabic/Exxon-Mobil refinery project in Yanbu chose to leave the country.[59] Four weeks later, on May 29, a terrorist attack at a residential compound in Khobar, near the oil center of Dhahran, killed 22 people—mainly foreign oil workers.[60] According to Jean-François Seznek of Columbia University, "The [May 29] attack was orchestrated to display that the royal family cannot maintain security in the heart of its own oil patch, and in that sense they succeeded."[61]

Violent opposition toward the Saudi regime—an indeed, toward regimes throughout the region—is fueled in part by the fact that after a half century of oil revenue transfers, the region remains largely underdeveloped. While the rulers of these countries enjoy incredible wealth and privilege, population growth throughout the Middle East over the last several decades has led to a large poor and restive population, leading to pressure on governments to expand education, medical care, and social services at breakneck speed.[62] As a result, regimes throughout the Middle East have found it increasingly difficult to satisfy the pressures that rapid population growth creates.[63] Meanwhile, emboldened by the nation's military prowess, energy security policies and free market ideals, U.S.-based oil companies have produced a legacy of optimistic oil extraction throughout this region, with little regard to how the local populations throughout the region might or might not benefit from the revenues related to such transactions.

For example, despite the enormous sums of money paid to Middle East countries for their oil, illiteracy rates are higher than the international average, and even higher than the average in developing countries.[64] At the turn of the century, Arab countries reported nearly 60 million illiterate adults, the majority of whom are women. Closely related, educational enrollment and attainment rates in the region are lower than in the less developed countries of East Asia and Latin America. The entire Arab world translates about 330 books annually, one fifth of the number that Greece alone translates.[65] Arab countries also have some of the lowest levels of funding for research and development in the world – a reflection of many leaders' unfortunate preference to spend oil revenues on arms and fast cars instead of improving and capitalizing on the human capital potential of their countries. Workforce productivity in the oil rich countries of the Middle East is barely half that of Argentina or Korea, and the situation is far worse in the oil-poor countries of the region (such as Djibouti, Jordan, Lebanon, and Yemen).[66]

Perhaps most importantly, political participation is less advanced in the Arab world than in other developing regions. In many countries in Latin America, Asia, and sub-Saharan Africa, freedom of association is less restricted, governments change through the ballot box, and people's groups have been encouraged to express themselves in various ways—trends foreign to much of the Middle East.[67] Although many Americans fought and died in the name of democracy and freedom for people in such faraway lands as Korea and Vietnam, the U.S. has been willing to sacrifice its human rights and development agenda in the Middle East in trade for a secure route to the oil fields of the region. For example, the annual U.S. State Department report on human rights violations is highly critical of Saudi Arabia's continued refusal to allow its citizens to elect a government. The same report notes that Egypt has implemented a variety of "emergency laws" that allow the government to jail—and even execute—citizens without proper judicial proceedings. The nation's energy security policies have even compelled the U.S. to prop up such unsavory authoritarian leaders as Saddam Hussein, when he was conveniently willing to battle the Iranian extremist influence and help prevent (or at least slow) the spread of radical Islam throughout the Persian Gulf.

Rather than compel authoritarian regimes to democratize, invest in schools and roads, allow for social and religious freedoms, develop connectivity to the global information highway, and so on, the U.S. has allowed its energy security interests to take precedence over all other foreign policy concerns. As Richter and Tsalik (2003) observed, "so intense is the need for oil that the U.S. often turns a blind eye to problems of governance, corruption, criminal activity, and humanitarian crises in those countries. The general populations of countries whose government leaders are corrupt, abuse human rights, or block any moves toward democracy equate U.S. inaction with complicity. This, in turn, undermines—rather than enhances—American energy security, since repressive regimes are prone to being violently overthrown by people who resent the U.S. for supporting their oppressors."[68]

In Saudi Arabia, for example, discrimination against the minority Shiite Muslims is widespread; they are systematically excluded from the Kingdom's already-limited political life, controlling no important government positions and having only nominal representation in the Consultative Council. More importantly, they are harassed by police and by ordinary Sunni Muslims, many of whom view the Shiites as apostates.[69] A lack of democracy and freedom is seen throughout the entire region, from Kuwait—where women were granted the right to vote in 2005, but (unlike the men of the country) must still abide by strict Islamic laws and conventions—to Djibouti (home to the U.S. Joint Task Force, Horn of Africa), where voters went to the polls in April 2005 in an election which President Ismail Omar Guelleh was sure to win: He was the only candidate.

Conclusion: Lessons Learned from U.S. Foreign Policies in the Persian Gulf

History has taught the West that the objective of Middle Eastern stability is important, but the need for stability should not be used to indefinitely postpone political and civil reform. By supporting corrupt and dictatorial regimes for immediate economic and strategic advantages, the West has actually prevented the kind of change necessary to stabilize these countries through representative government.[70] As U.S. intelligence expert Paul Pillar (2005) has observed, "Many Arabs feel stifled . . . by their own governments, which preside over unreformed economies and unresponsive political systems . . . [and] Washington is seen—and resented—as providing support to prop up the local oppressor."[71]

Overall, the backlash from the nation's foreign policy and energy security approaches in this region has led to greater insecurity for the U.S. Our continued support for undemocratic regimes, coupled with our willingness to do virtually anything to maintain open and reliable access to the oil resources of the Middle East, has produced increasing animosity throughout the region that will take years of hard work to reverse. The current administration appears to recognize this, as reflected in Secretary of State Rice's observation in June 2005, mentioned earlier in this chapter, that the U.S. has not been as strong about promoting democracy in the Middle East as we should have been.

From this analysis of the history of U.S.-Persian Gulf relations, the following lessons can be derived, which should inform our future policies toward the oil-rich countries of West Africa:

- Economically, regimes that focus on capital-intensive development of a single industry, rather than diversifying their economy, run afoul of fundamental economic principles, particularly in a globally interdependent environment.
- Regimes that remain in power not because of a popular mandate from the people they govern, but solely because of U.S. backing, are destined for trouble.
- When the main source of wealth in the country is the largesse of the ruling family, there is clearly a recipe for under-investment in economic diversification, meritocracy, innovation, creative/critical thinking, etc.
- Lack of transparency, rule of law, good governance—these problems which now plague the regimes of the Persian Gulf are directly related to the oil extraction industry

The history of U.S. foreign relations with the Persian Gulf was largely driven by the Cold War, bipolar struggle with the Soviet Union for regional influence. With China's growing reliance on oil imports (it is already the world's second largest consumer of oil),[72] coupled with its rapidly modernizing military and economy, will the U.S. default to similar competitive strategies and conflict, only this time with African players as the new pawns in the game? In the Persian Gulf, unequal distribution of opportunities for advancement coupled with political corruption and governmental incompetence has led to political unrest and a reservoir of recruits for groups such as al Qaeda. Can we avoid encouraging a similar fate for the oil-exporting countries of the Gulf of Guinea?

Clearly, problems arise when the pursuit of U.S. short-term interests conflicts with broader U.S. values. One could argue that much of the anti-American sentiment in the Middle East is in part caused by the perceived hypocrisy between American values and national economic interests. How can a nation that trumpets freedom and democracy above all else justify support for oppressive, authoritarian regimes simply to ensure the consistent extraction of strategic minerals, specifically oil and natural gas? Why is there so much instability in petroleum-rich regions where the U.S. engages with the underdeveloped world? These questions frame an important discussion for our country's burgeoning energy relationship with Africa.

Notes

1. U.S. Department of Energy, Energy Information Administration (DoE/EIA), *International Energy Outlook 2004* (Washington, D.C.: DoE/EIA, 2004), 213 (Table D1).

2. Oystein Noreng, "The Predicament of the Gulf Rentier State," in *Oil in the Gulf: Obstacles to Democracy and Development*, edited by Daniel Heradstveit and Helge Hveem (London: Ashgate, 2004), 10

3. Noreng, "The Predicament of the Gulf Rentier State," p. 11

4. Mike Crawley, "With Medeast Uncertainty, US turns to Africa for Oil," *Christian Science Monitor*, 23 May 2002.

5. Daniel L. Byman and Jerrold D. Green, *Political Violence and Stability in the States of the Northern Persian Gulf* (Santa Monica: RAND Corporation, 1999), xvii.

6. Byman and Green, *Political Violence and Stability*, xvii

7. U.S. Energy Information Administration, "World Energy 'Areas to Watch,'" August 2004, 6. Available online at: http://www.eia.doe.gov/emu/cabs/hot.html

8. U.S. Energy Information Administration, "World Energy 'Areas to Watch,'" August 2004, 6.

9. U.S. Department of Commerce, National Technical Information Service (NTIS), "Saudi Arabia Interim Country Commercial Guide, FY 2005." Available online at: http://strategis.ic.gc.ca/epic/internet/inimr-ri.nsf/en/gr126392e.html

10. Energy Information Agency, *Petroleum Imports by Country of Origin, 1960-2003. Annual Energy Review 2003*, Table 5.4.

11. Michael B. Stoff, *Oil, War and American Security* (New Haven: Yale University Press, 1980), referenced in Molly Farneth, "Powering Foreign Policy: The Role of Oil in Diplomacy and Conflict," Energy Security Initiative Report (New York: Physicians for Social Responsibility, October 2004), 6.

12. Michael Renner, "Fueling Conflict," in *PetroPolitics Briefing Book* (Washington, DC: Interhemispheric Resource Center/Institute for Policy Studies/SEEN, January 2004), 25, referenced in Molly Farneth, "Powering Foreign Policy," 10.

13. U.S. Energy Information Administration, May 2005. Available online at: http://www.eia.doe.gov/emu/cabs

14. U.S. Energy Information Administration, May 2005. Available online at: http://www.eia.doe.gov/emu/cabs

15. Molly Farneth, "Powering Foreign Policy," 1.

16. Molly Farneth, "Powering Foreign Policy," 1.

17. Amory B. Lovins, *Energy Security Facts: Details and Documentation* (Snowmass, CO: Rocky Mountain Institute, 2 June 2003), 2, referenced in Molly Farneth, "Powering Foreign Policy," 4.

18. Molly Farneth, "Powering Foreign Policy," 4.

19. Molly Farneth, "Powering Foreign Policy," 4.

20. U.S. Energy Information Administration, May 2002; American Petroleum Institute, 2003.

21. Richard Cheney, Speech to the Veterans of Foreign Wars 103rd National Convention, 26 August 2002, referenced in Molly Farneth, "Powering Foreign Policy," 7.

22. President George H.W. Bush, Address to the Nation Announcing the Deployment of United States Armed Forces to Saudi Arabia, 8 August 1990, referenced in Molly Farneth, "Powering Foreign Policy," 7

23. Michael T. Klare, "Fueling The Fires: The Oil Factor in Middle Eastern Terrorism," in *The Making of a Terrorist (Vol. III, Root Causes)*, edited by James JF Forest (Westport, CT: Praeger, 2005).

24. From an audiotape address released on Islamic websites on December 16, 2004, as transcribed by and posted at www.jihadunspun.com on December 24, 2004. For more on this, please see James S. Robbins, "No Blood for Oil," *National Review Online,* July 12, 2005. Online at: http://www.nationalreview.com/robbins/robbins200507120857.asp; and Thomas Quiggin, "Cutting the Cord: Economic Jihad, Canadian Oil and U.S. Homeland Security," in *Homeland Security: Protecting America's Targets* (vol. 3), edited by James J.F. Forest (Westport, CT: Praeger Security International, 2006).

25. Molly Farneth, "Powering Foreign Policy," 4.

26. "Signs of Life at State," *New York Times,* 4 July 2005.

27. Oystein Noreng, "The Predicament of the Gulf Rentier State," 10

28. James S. Robbins, "No Blood for Oil," *National Review Online,* 12 July 2005. Available online at: http://www.nationalreview.com/robbins/robbins200507120857.asp

29. Institute for Advanced Strategic and Political Studies, Oil Policy Initiative Group, *African Oil: A Priority for U.S. National Security and African Development* (July 2002) available online at: http://www.israeleconomy.org/strategic/africawhitepaper.pdf

30. Portions of the following historical section is drawn from a variety of open source material as well as from Robert J. Pauly, Jr., *U.S Foreign Policy and the Persian Gulf* (London: Ashgate Publishers), 23-33.

31. Pauly, Jr., *U.S Foreign Policy and the Persian Gulf,* 24.

32. Pauly, Jr., *U.S Foreign Policy and the Persian Gulf,* 25.

33. This paragraph adapted from Michael T. Klare, "Fueling The Fires: The Oil Factor in Middle Eastern Terrorism," in *The Making of a Terrorist (Vol. III, Root Causes)*, edited by James JF Forest (Westport, CT: Praeger).

34. For background, see Michael T. Klare, *American Arms Supermarket* (Austin: University of Texas Press, 1984), 114-23.

35. See ibid., pp. 121-26. See also Pollack, *The Persian Puzzle*, pp. 72-127; Yergin, *The Prize*, pp. 637-38, 644-46, 672-82.

36. On Savak, See Pollack, *The Persian Puzzle*, 74-75, 114-17.

37. For an account of these developments, see Pollack, *The Persian Puzzle*, 117-35.

38. See Michael T. Klare, "Fueling The Fires: The Oil Factor in Middle Eastern Terrorism," in *The Making of a Terrorist (Vol. III, Root Causes)*, edited by James JF Forest (Westport, CT: Praeger).

39. For background on these developments, see David S. Painter, *Oil and the American Century* (Baltimore: Johns Hopkins University Press, 1986), pp. 32-51; Stoff, *Oil, War, and American Security*, pp. 34-61.

40. For discussion of this encounter and its implications, see Michael T. Klare, *Blood and Oil: The Dangers and Consequences of America's Growing Petroleum Dependency* (New York: Metropolitan Books, 2004), 35-37; Aaron Dean Miller, *Search for Security* (Chapel Hill: University of North Carolina Press, 1980), 128-31; Yergin, *The Prize*, 403-5.

41. "The third American strategic interest in Saudi Arabia." Department of State paper covering U.S.-Saudi Relations, April 11, 1947. *State Department Files, 1956-1949*, vol. 12, 372.

42. Pauly, Jr., *U.S Foreign Policy and the Persian Gulf*, 24.

43 . See Klare, *Blood and Oil*, pp. 37-45; David E. Long, *The United States and Saudi Arabia* (Boulder, Colo.: Westview Press, 1985), pp. 33-50; Painter, *Oil and the American Century*, 96-127; Palmer, *Guardians of the Gulf*, pp. 40-84; referenced in Michael T. Klare, "Fueling The Fires: The Oil Factor in Middle Eastern Terrorism," in *The Making of a Terrorist (Vol. III, Root Causes)*, edited by James JF Forest (Westport, CT: Praeger).

44. Albert Hourani, *A History of the Arab Peoples* (Cambridge University Press, 1991), pp. 14-32, referenced in Pauly, p. 28.

45. Pauly, Jr., *U.S Foreign Policy and the Persian Gulf*, 28.

46. Pauly, Jr., *U.S Foreign Policy and the Persian Gulf*, 28.

47. Michael T. Klare, *Resource Wars: The New Landscape of Global Conflict* (New York: Henry Holt and Company, LLC, 2001), 60, referenced in Molly Farneth, "Powering Foreign Policy, 6.

48. Michael Renner, "Fueling Conflict," PetroPolitics Briefing Book, Washington, DC: Interhemispheric Resource Center/Institute for Policy Studies/SEEN (January 2004), p. 24, reference made in Molly Farneth, "Powering Foreign Policy, p. 6. As described earlier in this chapter, U.S. arms transfers to Saudi Arabia have been particularly significant of the last fifteen years, by some estimates exceeding $50 billion.

49. Pauly, Jr., *U.S Foreign Policy and the Persian Gulf*, 27.

50. James. E. Carter, "State of the Union Address" 23 January 1980, U.S. Department of State *Basic Documents* (Washington, DC. US Government Printing Office 1980). Reference made in Pauly, Jr., *U.S Foreign Policy and the Persian Gulf*, p. 28.

51. Murray Waas, "What Washington Gave Saddam for Christmas," in The Iraq War Reader: History, Documents, Opinions, ed. Micah L. Sifry and Christopher Cerf (New York: Simon and Schuster, 2003), 30-40, referenced in Pauly, 29.

52. Joost R. Hilterman, "The Men who Helped the Man to Gassed his Own People," in Iraq War Reader, 42-45, referenced in Pauly, 29.

53. For background on these events, see Palmer, *Guardians of the Gulf*, pp. 128-49. Referenced in Michael T. Klare, "Fueling The Fires: The Oil Factor in Middle Eastern Terrorism," in *The Making of a Terrorist (Vol. III, Root Causes),* edited by James JF Forest (Westport, CT: Praeger).

54. Byman and Green, *Political Violence and Stability,* 12.

55. Byman and Green, *Political Violence and Stability,* 12.

56. For example, (Pew Charitable Trusts, 2003; 2005); University of Jordan's Center for Strategic Studies, 2005.

57. Pew Charitable Trusts, 2005.

58. Paul Pillar, "Superpower Foreign Policies: A Source for Global Resentment," in *The Making of a Terrorist* (vol. 3), ed. J. Forest (Westport, CT: Praeger, 2005).

59. Neil MacFarquhar, "After Attack, Company's Staff Plans to Leave Saudi Arabia," *The New York Times,* May 3, 2004.

60. U.S. Energy Information Administration, "World Energy 'Areas to Watch,'" August 2004, p. 6. Online at: http://www.eia.doe.gov/emu/cabs/hot.html. See also, Neil · MacFarquhar, "Saudi Military Storms Complex to Free Hostages," *The New York Times,* May 31, 2004.

61. Quoted in Simon Romero, "Latest Terrorist Attack Increases Doubts About the Ability of Saudi Arabia to Pump More Oil," *The New York Times,* May 31, 2004.

62. Byman and Green, *Political Violence and Stability,* 12.

63. Byman and Green, *Political Violence and Stability,* 13.

64. United Nations Development Program (UNDP), *2002 Arab Human Development Report.* Available online at: http://www.undp.org/rbas/ahdr.

65. UNDP, *2002 Arab Human Development Report.*

66. UNDP, *2002 Arab Human Development Report.*

67. UNDP, *2002 Arab Human Development Report.*

68. Anthony Richter and Svetlana Tsalik, "Making Sure the Money Goes Where It's Supposed To," *New York Times* (December 4, 2003).

69. Byman and Green, *Political Violence and Stability,* 29.

70. Dominique Moisi, "Tragedy that Exposed a Groundswell of Hatred," *Financial Times* (London), September 24, 2001, referenced in Noreng, 10.

71. Paul Pillar, "Superpower Foreign Policies: A Source for Global Resentment," in *The Making of a Terrorist* (vol. 3), ed. J. Forest (Westport, CT: Praeger, 2005).

72. "Balanced Energy Supply-Demand Market for China in 2004," *People's Daily* (Beijing), 30 March 2004. Accessed at http://english.peopledaily.com.cn/200403/30/eng2/0040330_138924.shtml

Chapter 6
Contemporary U.S. Foreign Policies
in the New Gulf

On May 25, 2005, the *Associated Press* ran a story with the headline "U.S. outlines bigger effort to fight terrorism in Africa: Plan would pour $100 million each year into some of the least-policed areas."[1] The newspaper story describes our country's emerging counterterrorism efforts in Africa, giving special attention to the role of engaging U.S. special forces in countries such as Algeria, Chad, Mali, Mauritania, Morocco, Niger, Nigeria, Senegal and Tunisia. This exemplifies the global policy framework that the U.S. has pursued over the last several years; since the attacks of 9/11, the U.S. has focused an enormous amount of resources toward improving the security environment on every continent of the world, including Africa. Recent efforts include training and equipping the militaries of several Sahelian African nations, enabling them to contribute more effectively to the global fight against terrorist organizations. However, given the significantly increased focus on counterterrorism, one might get the impression that the U.S. concern for Africa is limited to security issues, which would be inaccurate. In fact, the U.S. has formulated an impressive array of policies targeting the immediate and long-term economic and developmental needs of the African continent, though many Americans know little (if anything) about them.

In fact, the U.S. is the world's largest provider of emergency humanitarian assistance to Africa. In 2004, the U.S. provided $3.2 billion in official development assistance to sub-Saharan Africa to help relieve poverty, provide humanitarian assistance, and spur economic growth.[2] In the volatile region of Darfur, Sudan—where the amount of refugees and violence has reached a state of crisis—the U.S. provided more than $638 million for humanitarian assistance between 2003 and 2005, along with an additional $150 million to support the African Union peace mission in the region. Over $600 million has been committed to the Africa Education Initiative (AEI), which supports training for teachers and administrators, scholarships, textbooks, and the construction of schools throughout the continent. The U.S. has committed even larger amounts of funding to combat deadly diseases like HIV and malaria. Overall, the U.S. is heavily engaged in helping Africa tackle many of its most challenging problems, although our emerging counterterrorism efforts seem to generate the most media attention.

Headlines such as the one cited above also inspire questions about how such a policy is formulated and implemented. Does the U.S. president arbitrarily decide to send our troops into parts of Africa on a counterterrorism training mission, or is Congress involved? What role (if any) do the Departments of Defense or State have in making such decisions? It is an unfortunate reality that the average American likely knows very little about the policymaking process in Washington, D.C. that is at the core of our country's efforts to grapple with the challenges in Africa described in the previous chapters of this volume. Thus, this chapter begins with a brief look at how foreign policies are made in the U.S. This will be followed by a brief overview of the strategic environment in which current U.S.-Africa policies are made and implemented, along with a description of organizations within the government that have primary responsibility for connecting these policies with practitioners.

The Policymaking Process in the U.S.

Political scientists occasionally describe a government's policymaking process as analogous to making sausage—a messy, complicated procedure performed by a wide variety of dubious actors, with blunt tools and questionable ingredients, in a perhaps less-than-perfect environment—something you really don't want to know too much about if you are to enjoy the final product. This description may reflect the realities of policymaking in many regards, but such a characterization masks important dimensions of the processes and outcomes that yield a greater understanding of the foreign policy arena. True, the "tools and ingredients" or "carrots and sticks" of policymaking are intricately nuanced, occasionally uncoordinated, and often bluntly applied. And the international environment is extremely complex, difficult to control, and rife with urgent crises that demand immediate attention. However, in general, U.S. policymakers tend to be extremely well educated and dedicated professionals, earnestly working to advance U.S. interests around the world. Nevertheless, the U.S. policymaking system is anything but simple, and it was designed to be that way for very good reasons.

In a democratically checked and balanced government, policymaking is inevitably going to be messy and complicated. The U.S. Constitution intentionally blueprinted our government system to be inefficient and cumbersome so that no tyrannical government could easily force its will on the U.S. population. Because foreign policy is often even more complicated than domestic policy, this "protection" extends to foreign populations as well. Yet there is obvious value to producing a focused, coherent, and well organized foreign policy that is efficiently and consistently administered. In the presidential leadership model, the

U.S. president establishes an agenda of policies and programs intended to move the country forward in a particular direction. The executive branch then works with the leadership of Congress to refine and gain approval of these policies, which then sets in motion an array of federal bureaucracies—and in some cases, private initiatives—that seek to achieve relevant policy objectives. Members of Congress will also put forward proposals which, if approved, can shape the policy environment.

Overall, despite the regular appearances of disorder and confusion, the U.S. foreign policymaking system is actually quite well structured. The next section of this chapter will outline the U.S.-Africa foreign policymaking strategy and hierarchy from the President through the Departments of Defense and State, and will list and briefly summarize the major policy agendas and programs at each level. The intention here is to give the reader a general sense of the policy environment in terms of vision, structure, and programs, and how the policymakers on the ground are connected to the broader ideas set out at the highest levels of government.

Overarching Policy: The National Security Strategy of the United States

U.S.-Africa policy development begins with the President's national vision, as described in the *National Security Strategy* (NSS) of the United States. The NSS lays out three overarching goals: political and economic freedom, peaceful relations with other states, and respect for human dignity.[3] To achieve these goals, the NSS is subdivided into eight major sections, each one describing broad imperatives for U.S. action: 1) champion aspirations for human dignity; 2) strengthen alliances to defeat global terrorism and work to prevent attacks against us and our friends; 3) work with others to defuse regional conflicts; 4) prevent our enemies from threatening us, our allies, and our friends, with weapons of mass destruction; 5) ignite a new era of global economic growth through free markets and free trade; 6) expand the circle of development by opening societies and building the infrastructure of democracy; 7) develop agendas for cooperative action with other main centers of global power; and 8) transform America's national security institutions to meet the challenges and opportunities of the twenty-first century.

Most of these imperatives apply directly to the general need for advancing security, democracy, and economic development agendas for Africa. In fact, Africa figures prominently and explicitly in the NSS:

> In Africa, promise and opportunity sit side by side with disease, war, and desperate poverty. This threatens both a core value of the United States—preserving human dignity—and our strategic priority—combating global terror. American interests and American principles, therefore, lead in the same direc-

tion: we will work with others for an African continent that lives in liberty, peace, and growing prosperity. Together with our European allies, we must help strengthen Africa's fragile states, help build indigenous capability to secure porous borders, and help build up the law enforcement and intelligence infrastructure to deny havens for terrorists.[4]

The emphasis on working together with other nations, as articulated in the NSS, is vital. According to a recent Africa Policy statement issued by the White House, the Bush administration recognizes that "Africa's great size and diversity requires a security strategy that focuses on bilateral engagement and builds coalitions of the willing."[5] This statement identifies "three interlocking strategies" to address the challenges faced by Africa: 1) Work with key anchor states in each sub-region—countries with major impact on their neighborhood, like South Africa, Nigeria, Kenya, and Ethiopia; 2) Engage allies, friends and international institutions in coordinating conflict mediation and successful peace operations; and 3) Support the African Union, sub-regional organizations and reforming states as a primary means of addressing transnational threats. These strategies combine with the NSS to provide a policy framework that informs a number of policies and programs specifically focused on Africa. Critical development initiatives include the African Growth and Opportunity Act; the Millennium Challenge Account; the Global Fund to Fight HIV, Malaria, and Tuberculosis (reinforced by the President's Emergency Fund for AIDS Relief); the Mother and Child HIV Prevention Initiative; and the World Bank's Heavily Indebted Poor Countries initiative. Each of these programs pursues laudable goals, yet each is pursued relatively independently, and without much regard for the dominating effects of regional energy policy.

The U.S. African Growth and Opportunity Act (AGOA), passed as part of the Trade and Development Act of 2000, provides beneficiary countries in sub-Saharan Africa with the most liberal access to the U.S. market that is available to any country with which we do not have a Free Trade Agreement. It reinforces African reform efforts, provides improved access to U.S. credit and technical expertise, and establishes a high-level dialogue on trade and investment in the form of a U.S.-Sub-Saharan Africa Trade and Economic Forum. By significantly opening U.S. markets to African goods—including chemicals, steel, footwear and clothing, fruit and other agricultural products, toys, wine, and oil—AGOA plays a vital role in meeting the economic development needs of the region. Conditions which African nations must meet in order to participate in AGOA include adopting neo-liberal policies, removing subsidies and price controls, and privatizing state assets. Specifically, the President may designate sub-Saharan African countries as eligible to receive the benefits of the Act if they are making progress in such areas as: establishment of market-based economies; development of political pluralism and the rule of law; elimination of barriers to U.S. trade and investment; protection of intellectual property; efforts to combat corruption; policies to reduce poverty, increase availability of health care and educational opportunities; protection of human rights and worker rights, and elimination of certain practices of child labor. The U.S. provides technical assistance seminars in Africa and the United States to explain the benefits of AGOA in order to ensure that African countries are able to take maximum advantage of its provisions.[6]

Once a country is designated as an eligible recipient of AGOA benefits, its indigenous farmers, manufacturers, and others have access to the world's biggest consumer. Since its initial launch in 2000, 37 countries have been declared eligible for AGOA: Angola, Benin, Botswana, Burkina Faso, Cameroon, Cape Verde, Chad, Republic of Congo, Democratic Republic of Congo, Djibouti, Ethiopia, Gabon, The Gambia, Ghana, Guinea, Guinea-Bissau, Kenya, Lesotho, Madagascar, Malawi, Mali, Mauritania, Mauritius, Mozambique, Namibia, Niger, Nigeria, Rwanda, Sao Tome and Principe, Senegal, Seychelles, Sierra Leone, South Africa, Swaziland, Tanzania, Uganda, and Zambia. Within each of these countries, AGOA is encouraging new and expanded industry. For example, Chandu EPZ Ltd—a Kenyan textile firm—now has contracts with JC Penny and Wal-Mart to produce tens of thousands of clothing units for the U.S. market. Caratex Botswana, another clothing maker with significant exports to the U.S., has grown from employing 500 in 2003 to around 1,300 people in 2005. With the launch of new business attire and jeans lines, the company anticipates that it will employ as many as 2,600 people. The U.S. is now importing tons of seafood from Senegal, woodcarvings from Tanzania, bird seed from Ethiopia, grapes from Namibia, handcrafted furniture from companies in Burkina Faso, Mali, Niger, Cameroon and Ghana, and clothing from countries throughout the continent.[7]

However, in reality, AGOA benefits are highly concentrated in a few countries and in the petroleum and mining sectors—in fact, U.S. imports from AGOA to date have been predominantly energy-related products. As described in chapters 1 and 2 of this volume, the U.S. is projected to import up to 25% of its oil from Africa by 2010. While originally set to expire in 2008, the U.S. Congress recently expanded and extended the application of AGOA to 2015— certainly a step in the right direction for long-term regional economic development. Continued diversification away from the energy sector, and progression towards truly free trade, would allow Africans to earn more every year than they currently receive in international aid, and the positive externalities of small-business-related income are tremendous.

Another U.S. initiative meant to reward good governance is the Millennium Challenge Account (MCA), where half the beneficiary countries are in Africa. In March 2002 in Monterrey, Mexico, President Bush called for a "new compact for global development," which links greater contributions from developed nations to greater responsibility from developing nations. He proposed a mechanism to implement this compact, in which development assistance would be provided to those countries that demonstrate a commitment to the rule of law, invest in human capital, and support free markets. With strong bipartisan support, the Millennium Challenge Corporation (MCC) was established on January 23, 2004 to administer the MCA. Congress provided nearly $1 billion in initial funding for FY04 and $1.5 billion for FY05. The President has requested $3 billion for FY06 and pledged to increase annual funding for the MCA to $5 billion in the future.[8]

The MCA promises to nearly double the amount of American aid for development in poor countries, while encouraging reforms that contribute to a healthier environment for economic growth and political stability. Candidates for the program are measured by 16 indicators, and often these measurements are provided not by the U.S. but by international agencies with particular expertise. For example, a private organization like Transparency International could rate the applicants on corruption; the World Bank Institute, on rule of law; Freedom House, on political rights; and the Heritage Foundation, on trade policy.[9] Under this approach, West African countries like Senegal and Ghana that respect civil liberties stand to benefit considerably. Participating countries would sign three-year contracts with the U.S., at the end of which the results of their investments and efforts in meeting MCA goals would be measured. However, while accountability plays a central role, the MCA program does not dictate to individual countries specifically how to spend the money given under the program, thereby giving them the leeway to institute projects best suited to their particular development needs. The MCA program clearly has potential linkages with the pursuit of transparency and accountability in the energy sector, and should be leveraged accordingly.

In addition to these bilateral initiatives, the U.S. also participates in several multilateral programs of interest, including two focused on relieving the enormous debt burdens of Africa's poorest nations. Indeed, debt relief is a critical component of an integrated economic development initiative for the continent. African countries struggle under the burden of huge debts, upwards of $300 billion, and must pay over $15 billion in debt servicing each year to rich country creditors and the World Bank and IMF, instead of spending that money on the health and education needs of their own people. As indicated in Table 6.1, external debt is a challenge faced by all the countries of the Gulf of Guinea.

The U.S. supports the existing debt relief framework, the Heavily Indebted Poor Countries Initiative (HIPC), which has currently approved partial debt relief for 23 African countries. Some observers argue that the program does not go far enough, and should offer complete debt cancellation to countries that can demonstrate "continued efforts toward macroeconomic adjustment and structural and social policy reforms—including higher spending on social sector programs like basic health and education"[10] as required by the IMF and World Bank.

Table 6.1: The Foreign Debt Problem in the Gulf of Guinea

	External Debt	% of Annual Budget Spent on Debt Payments
Angola	$10.45 billion (2004 est.)	7.7%
Cameroon	$8.46 billion (2004 est.)	3.9%
Chad	$1.1 billion (2000 est.)	1.5%
Congo	$5 billion (2000 est.)	0.8%
Equatorial Guinea	$248 million (2000 est.)	0.2%
Gabon	$3.804 billion (2004 est.)	8.3%
Sao Tome & Principe	$318 million (2002 est.)	12.1%
Nigeria	$30.55 billion (2004 est.)	3.4%

Sources: *2005 CIA Factbook*, and U.S. Department of State, Bureau of Africa Affairs.

Additionally, administration of HIPC must consider challenges and pitfalls unique to the new oil-rich countries in the Gulf of Guinea. This is especially poignant considering that, as highlighted in previous chapters of this volume, corruption and mismanagement of the original oil boom in Nigeria led to its enormous debt in the first place.

Recognizing the need for greater debt relief, the leaders of the world's most industrialized countries agreed at the July 2005 G-8 Summit[11] to an unprecedented $50 billion aid package for the developing world—the majority of it targeted toward the nations of Africa. These nations also agreed to cancel the multilateral debt of the 18 poorest countries of the world—14 of which are in Africa.[12]

U.S. interests in Africa also cover a range of issues beyond economic growth. For example, major health programs are intended not only to directly address the critical human capital component of economic development, but also to relieve suffering and improve the human condition. One such program, the International Mother and Child HIV Prevention Initiative, is a $500 million program aimed at relieving the suffering of women and children affected by HIV and intended to complement the Global Fund to Fight AIDS, Tuberculosis, and Malaria. Another, the President's Emergency Fund for AIDS Relief (PEPFAR), was introduced at the State of the Union Address in January of 2003 and is intended to commit $15 billion over 5 years to fight HIV/AIDS. The goals of this unprecedented effort include a special focus on 15 nations that account for more than 50 percent of the world's infections, where we will support treatment for 2 million people infected with HIV/AIDS, prevent 7 million new HIV infections, and support care for 10 million people infected and affected by HIV/AIDS.[13]

Despite initial budget delays, the programs are moving forward and are supervised by the President's Special Coordinator for International HIV/AIDS Assistance, who reports directly to the Secretary of State. According to the March 2005 report to Congress—a report that is prepared annually as mandated by Section 305 of P.L. 108-25, the United States Leadership Against HIV/AIDS, Tuberculosis, and Malaria Act of 2003—within the first eight months of the Emergency Plan, antiretroviral therapy treatment had been provided to 155,000 people, 152,000 of them in sub-Saharan Africa.[14] During the same time period, "1.2 million women benefited from services to prevent transmission of HIV from mother to child. We were also able to support care for more than 1.7 million people infected and affected by HIV/AIDS, including 630,200 orphans and vulnerable children."[15] These developments are promising, and observers can only hope that the U.S. can sustain the resources and political will to address this huge challenge over the long haul.

In addition to health initiatives, the U.S. is also investing in building the capacities of indigenous security forces in Africa and elsewhere. For example, in April 2004 the Bush administration announced the Global Peace Operations Initiative (GPOI), which provides $660 million over the next five years to train, equip and provide logistical support to forces of nations willing to participate in peace operations.[16] The primary goal of this initiative is to assist in the development of roughly 75,000 foreign troops who could be deployed on short notice and perform a wide range of peacekeeping activities throughout the world. As envisioned, the program will train 15 battalions (15,000 troops) per year, 10 of which will be in Africa. This focus on Africa builds on an ongoing State Department program that has provided training assistance to the region since the mid-1990s. But funding for that effort—the African Contingency Operations Training and Assistance (ACOTA) program—has stayed below $15 million in recent years. Another program, known as Enhanced International Peacekeeping Capacities (EIPC), and used to fund U.S. training for peace operations worldwide, has received even less money. Thus, the recent GPOI commitment to aiding the world's security forces reflects a much-needed recognition that strengthening international capacity and cooperation is essential for the U.S. to achieve its national security goals.

The goals of the GPOI were endorsed by G8[17] leaders at their June 2004 summit meeting at Sea Island, GA, adopting an "Action Plan on Expanding Global Capability for Peace Support Operations."[18] This was actually the third G8 Action Plan concerning peacekeeping in Africa. In June 2002, the G8 Summit at Kananaskis, Canada, adopted a broad Africa Action Plan that contained sections on conflict resolution and peace-building efforts. The more specific Joint Africa/G8 Plan to Enhance African Capabilities to Undertake Peace Support Operations was developed over the next year and presented at the June 2003 Summit at Evian-les-Baines, France.[19] In essence, the U.S. is clearly not alone in recognizing the need to provide bilateral training programs with African militaries. France and the United Kingdom have had a particularly significant presence in this area. Canada and several European Union countries played a key role in launching and supporting the Kofi Annan International Peacekeeping Training Center in Ghana, which opened in 2004. Overall, by training African peacekeepers and constabulary forces (or stability police), as well as providing equipment, transport, and logistical support, the U.S. and its allies are laying the groundwork for increased coordination with the UN, EU and AU, which will result in a much greater ability to achieve the goal of providing security throughout Africa.

In sum, the U.S. government has put forward an impressive array of programs and initiatives meant to address Africa's challenges and needs, from security to health to economic growth. The formulation and implementation of these policies involves several organizations within the government, each with its own strategic mission, history, culture, and resources. An understanding of this organizational diversity—and the ways in which each organization's efforts are (or are not) coordinated with each other—is an important component to truly understanding the issues addressed throughout this volume.

Organizations with Primary Responsibility for U.S.-Africa Policy

Of the many Executive Branch departments and agencies with interests in Africa, the organizations that are most directly involved with U.S.-Africa policy implementation are the Department of Defense (DoD), the Department of State (DoS), and the U.S. Agency for International Development (USAID). An examination of each one of these reveals the vital strengths they bring to an integrated strategy for addressing Africa's challenges.

The Department of Defense

The Department of Defense is directly involved in implementing the President's *National Security Strategy* all over the world. Organized into different Combatant Commands with specific regional responsibilities, the commands include Northern Command (NORTHCOM) for North America, Southern Command (SOUTHCOM) for South America and the Caribbean, Central Command (CENTCOM) for the Middle East and South West Asia, European Command (EUCOM) for Europe, and Pacific Command (PACOM) for the Far East and the Pacific. So where is the Africa Command? In fact, responsibility for Africa is divided between three different Combatant Commands. PACOM has responsibility for the Indian Ocean island nations like Madagascar, Mauritius, and the Comoros. CENTCOM has responsibility for the Horn of Africa, which includes Egypt, Ethiopia, Eritrea, Djibouti, Somalia, Kenya, Sudan, and the Seychelles. And EUCOM has responsibility for the remaining majority of African countries, including all the Gulf of Guinea states.[20]

This geographical division of responsibility for Africa into three different Combatant Commands can sometimes cause difficulties with coordination of policy concerning transnational issues. Take the Darfur crisis for example. The major conflict is in Sudan (CENTCOM responsibility) but the bulk of the refugees and humanitarian relief work is in Chad (EUCOM responsibility). Therefore planning to deal with this crisis incurs an additional set of coordination requirements that would not be necessary if there existed an independent Africa Command. There have been quite a few articles in military professional journals that argue for the creation of such a Combatant Command, but resource constraints, institutional inertia, turf wars, and ongoing mission priorities will probably rule this out for some time. However, our analysis indicates that an independent Africa Command would be a vital component in an integrated strategy for addressing the continent's economic and security challenges, especially as Africa's relevance to the U.S. increases on multiple fronts.

The existing Combatant Command headquarters—responsible for oversight and implementation of the nation's defense policies—are rather distantly removed from the African states themselves. CENTCOM is based out of Florida, with a significant forward presence in the Middle East; EUCOM is based out of Germany; and PACOM is based out of Hawaii. However, to support the Combatant Command headquarters, the Department of Defense deploys military specialists directly into various African countries to serve in Defense Attaché Offices (DAOs) or in Offices of Defense Cooperation (ODCs). Defense Attaché Offices are based out of U.S. Embassies and are the primary interface between the U.S. Department of Defense and the host nation's Ministry of Defense. Bilateral coordination and information exchange take place through these diplomatic conduits along military, political, economic, and social lines. The Defense Attaché is the primary advisor to the U.S. Ambassador on national security and defense issues, and is critical for understanding host nation defense capabilities and security challenges. Offices of Defense Cooperation are also co-located with U.S. Embassies and are responsible to oversee a variety of direct military-to-military engagement programs. The ODC chief is primarily responsible for training and equipping host nation militaries in accordance with U.S. policy goals, and supervising funding for humanitarian assistance programs, educational exchanges, and other bilateral arrangements.

The DAOs and ODCs are usually led by specially trained, regionally-focused officers from across the armed services, but there are some program shortfalls worth mentioning, specifically personnel and training. Most DAOs and ODCs are understaffed and overstretched, making it extremely difficult to engage effectively and consistently across the broad spectrum of policy implementation opportunities. Many DAOs are required to take on the ODC responsibilities in addition to their own, because ODCs have not been established in some embassies. Further, numerous countries have neither DAOs nor ODCs, and must be engaged from distant offices in regional hubs. This further limits the time an "expert" can spend in a country and inhibits accurate local assessments and consistent military engagement. Among the Gulf of Guinea states, Nigeria has both a DAO and an ODC; Cameroon, Chad, Gabon, Congo and Angola have only DAOs; and Equatorial Guinea and Sao Tome and Principe, have neither, meaning that other DAOs in the region must include them in their areas of responsibility. Put simply, our physical presence in the Gulf of Guinea does not yet match the importance given by recent policies toward the region.

Officers serving in these positions range in expertise, but are always committed to the goals of the U.S. defense policies toward Africa. The Department of the Army has established a comprehensive training program for its Foreign Area Officers (FAOs) that includes a graduate degree in appropriate regional studies, language training, and a year of regional immersion. After this three- to four-year training period (depending on the difficulty of the language), officers are assigned to positions in their region or to relevant Combatant Command headquarters, where they will work as Attachés, ODC Chiefs, or analysts for the rest of their careers. Unfortunately, there are wide discrepancies in the training and assignment programs between the different military services, and subsequently the skill sets of individual officers may vary tremendously.

The Department of Defense policy strategy in Africa starts broadly at the top and hierarchically works its way down to local implementation by the DAOs and ODCs in the field. The Department of Defense produces several major policy documents to support the President's vision as laid out in the National Security Strategy, three of which have considerable salience for this discussion. To begin with, the *National Defense Strategy* (NDS) "outlines an active, layered approach to the defense of the nation and its interests. It seeks to create conditions conducive to respect for the sovereignty of nations and a secure international order favorable to freedom, democracy, and economic opportunity."[21] The NDS translates the President's broad NSS objectives into four more narrowly focused strategic defense objectives: 1) secure the U.S. from direct attack; 2) secure strategic access and retain global freedom of action; 3) strengthen alliances and partnerships; and 4) establish favorable security conditions. In an impressively concise 20-page document, the NDS explains how the DoD will accomplish its objectives and offers implementation guidelines to structure strategic planning and decision-making.

Complementing this, the *National Military Strategy* (NMS) "is guided by the President's *National Security Strategy* and serves to implement the Secretary of Defense's *National Defense Strategy* [by providing] focus for military activi-

ties [and] by defining a set of interrelated military objectives from which the
Service Chiefs and combatant commanders identify desired capabilities and
against which [the Chairman, Joint Chiefs of Staff] CJCS assesses risk."[22] This
document translates strategic defense objectives into more tangible military
training and readiness priorities. And finally, the Department of Defense *Security Cooperation Guidance* outlines four goals for all U.S. military interactions
with foreign partners: 1) build relationships that promote specific U.S. security
interests; 2) develop allied and friendly capabilities for self-defense and coalition operations; 3) provide U.S. forces with peacetime and contingency access
and en-route infrastructure; and 4) improve information exchange and intelligence sharing to harmonize views on security challenges.[23] These goals are
meant to shape the U.S.' international security relationships in order to support
the President's vision as stated in the *National Security Strategy.*

Within the Department of Defense, the U.S.-Africa policy hierarchy continues downward through each service. For example, the *Army International Activities Plan* (AIAP) is a policy document that provides the Army-specific implementation plan for the Department of Defense's *Security Cooperation
Guidance* (SCG). The AIAP seeks to aid in the integration, synchronization, and
coordination of Army international activities so that they support the goals of the
SCG, the *National Defense Strategy,* and ultimately the President's *National
Security Strategy.* The AIAP comprehensively describes every single international military engagement program, lists the partner countries to which each
applies, identifies the legal authority and action agency for each, and demon-
strates the linkages between each program and specific Army strategic objectives and capability requirements, as well as overarching defense policy goals.

The AIAP does a good job of prioritizing programs and partner countries,
but much of this is classified. An example of a specific AIAP goal that is clearly
linked to the President's NSS is "promote effective civilian control of the military, and democratic values and institutions in countries key to regional security." In conjunction with the detailed program list and clear engagement priorities, this goal serves to guide resource allocation decisions to effectively marry
up the most constructive policy tool with the most appropriate partner country.
Several of the most important AIAP programs are focused on providing assistance to African nations. For example, as mentioned earlier, the African Contingency Operations Training Assistance (ACOTA) seeks to improve the capability
of African nations to respond rapidly to resolve sub-regional issues. ACOTA-
trained forces enhance African military capabilities to respond to crises in the
region.

Other AIAP programs that provide assistance to African militaries have a
more global focus. Many of these programs stem from a core policy goal of enhancing the military capabilities of allies and friendly nations. Security Assistance Programs sponsored by the DoD include Foreign Military Sales—
(authorized by the Foreign Assistance Act of 1961, as amended, and the Arms

Export Control Act (AECA), as amended)—which is generally defined as the government-to-government sale of services, training, and materiel, as identified on a letter of offer and acceptance, to a foreign country or international organization on a reimbursable basis. Foreign Military Financing Grants (authorized by Congress) enable foreign governments to purchase U.S. defense articles, services and training, and may also be used to enhance peacekeeping capabilities, for nonproliferation, anti-terrorism, or demining programs.

The International Military Education and Training (IMET) program is a key component of U.S. security assistance that provides training on a grant basis to students from allied and friendly nations. The program exposes students to the U.S. professional military establishment and the American way of life, including amongst other things, U.S. regard for democratic values, respect for individual and human rights, and belief in the rule of law. Students are also exposed to U.S. military procedures and the manner in which our military functions under civilian control. The overall objective of the program is to further the goal of regional stability through effective, mutually beneficial military-to-military relations which culminate in increased understanding and defense cooperation between the United States and foreign countries. Funding is appropriated from the international activities budget of the Department of State. The Expanded International Military Education & Training (EIMET) Program is a part of the overall IMET Program, but is different in that it trains military and civilian officials, including civilian personnel from non-defense ministries and personnel from the country's legislative branch who are involved in military matters. Training varies from managing and administering military establishments and budgets, to promoting civilian control of the military, and to creating and maintaining effective military justice systems and military codes of conduct, in accordance with internationally recognized human rights.

IMET and EIMET are complemented by an array of other education-related initiatives. For example, the Army War College International Fellows Program provides opportunities for senior military from allied and friendly countries to study, research, and write on subjects of significance and the security interests of their own and allied nations. The Command and General Staff College International Officer Program provides opportunities for selected foreign officers to participate with their U.S. counterparts in the Command and General Staff Officer Course and the School of Advanced Military Studies. In another initiative, called the Joint Combined Exchange Program, U.S. Special Forces work with host nation forces to improve basic soldier skills, promote military professionalism, and reinforce the principle of a military that is responsive to a democratically elected, civilian government. The Regional Defense Counterterrorism Fellowship Program (CTFP or "CT Fellowship") provides education and training on how to detect, monitor, and interdict or disrupt the activities of terrorist networks ranging from weapons trafficking and terrorist related financing to actual operational planning by terror groups. These programs help establish mutual understanding and good working relationships between U.S. and foreign officers, including many from throughout Africa. They also complement the overarching DoD Informational Program, which seeks to promote an understanding of U.S. society, institutions, and ideals and the way in which these elements reflect U.S. commitment to basic principles of internationally recognized human rights.

Another program that promotes mutual understanding is the Military Personnel Exchange Program (MPEP). The explicit objective of this program is to develop closer relationships between the U.S. Army and foreign military services by exchanging officers and senior NCOs of similar qualifications and grades. Exchange personnel achieve this objective by sharing experiences, professional knowledge and doctrine. The program's aims also include: fostering an understanding of and appreciation for the policies and doctrines of each country's armed services; and promoting mutual confidence, understanding and respect. A similar initiative, the Reciprocal Unit Exchange Program, consists of small unit exchanges with foreign armies on a formal, temporary, and reciprocal basis. Typically, these exchanges are for a specific period of time and normally coincide with selected training events. The two units involved—units of the same type within the same type of larger unit—attend the training event in the respective foreign country and then return to their parent unit. Unfortunately, neither of these exchange programs are regularly exercised in Africa.

The U.S. National Guard Bureau State Partnership Program (SPP) specifically ties a state's National Guard and reserve components to a host nation, and is beginning to be considered for more African countries. These and other programs complement annual multinational exercises—military maneuvers or simulated wartime operations between two or more forces, or agencies of two or more allies or friends, involving planning, preparation, and execution of military operations for the purpose of training and evaluation—in providing assistance to our allies and fostering better understanding of U.S. policy.

The U.S. also sponsors a number of Humanitarian and Civic Assistance (HCA) programs, which seek to foster goodwill toward the U.S. in general—and specifically the U.S. military—by providing a tangible, long-lasting service. Army units deployed for training, exercises and operations perform HCA as an exercise add-on. Assistance is limited to medical, dental, pediatric and veterinary care to rural populations; construction of rudimentary surface transportation systems; well drilling and construction of basic sanitation facilities; and rudimentary construction/repair of public facilities (hospitals, schools, orphanages). These types of programs enhance civil-military cooperation and relationships, and demonstrate American humanitarian concern. These objectives are also achieved through the DoD's Medical Outreach programs, like MEDFLAG, which provide medical training, exchanges of medical information and techniques with host nation medical personnel, and medical humanitarian and civic assistance visits to rural areas in places such as Morocco, Rwanda, Cameroon, and Gabon.

In sum, the Department of Defense manages an impressive global array of security assistance programs and initiatives. Regionally, each Combatant Command takes steps to synchronize its security policies with all those of the hierarchies above. The Office of the Secretary of Defense (OSD) prioritizes regional objectives in its Contingency Planning Guidance (CPG), and the Chairman of the Joint Chiefs of Staff publishes the Joint Strategic Capabilities Plan (JSCP). From these and the documents explained above, the regional Combatant Commanders produce Theater Engagement Plans. European Command (EUCOM), which has the majority of the responsibility for U.S.-Africa military policy, maintains a EUCOM *Theater Engagement Plan* (TEP) but also publishes specific *Country Campaign Plans* (CCP) for an even narrower focus. Some relevant example programs from EUCOM's regional strategy for Africa include the Gulf of Guinea Commission and the Gulf of Guinea Guard concepts.

With EUCOM's facilitation, the Gulf of Guinea Commission was officially created in July of 2001 and includes Nigeria, Cameroon, Gabon, Equatorial Guinea, Sao Tome and Principe, Congo-Brazzaville, Democratic Republic of Congo, and Angola. The commission aims to: provide a framework for consultations among the members in order to enhance cooperation and development; prevent, manage, and resolve conflicts resulting from delimitation of maritime borders; and promote close consultation in the exploitation of energy resources in the region. The Gulf of Guinea Guard is a concept being promoted by EUCOM to enhance the maritime capabilities of regional forces and is designed to ensure: adequate surveillance of littoral and deep-water maritime areas to detect, deter, and/or arrest illegal activities; disruption-free production of hydrocarbons in off-shore facilities; protection of energy resources during storage and distribution.[24]

At the individual country level, the Department of Defense requires ODCs or DAOs to prepare a *Combined Education and Training Program Plan* that lists specific U.S. program objectives for that country. This document is directly linked to EUCOM's corresponding Country Campaign Plan, general Theater Engagement Plan, and the overall AIAP. The Department of Defense representative in the U.S. Embassy is required to explain the host country objectives, which are developed in tandem with the host nation's Ministry of Defense leadership, and provide an evaluation of the prior year's program successes and failures. The document includes all the minute administrative and financial details of DoD operations in the host country—past, present, and proposed.

Finally, the Combined Education and Training Program Plan tracks additional training programs available to the host country, including relevant programs outside DoD, such as: the Counterterrorism Fellowship Program (CTFP); African Contingency Operations Training and Assistance (ACOTA); Aviation Leadership Program (ALP); Bilateral or Regional Cooperation Programs; Com-

batant Command Initiatives; Disaster Response and Humanitarian Assistance
(HA); Enhanced International Peacekeeping Capabilities (EIPC); exchanges
(training or PME); International Narcotics Control and Law Enforcement (IN-
CLE); Joint Combined Exchange Training (JCET); Mine Action programs; Africa Center for Strategic Studies Programs (ACSS); Counter Drug Training Support (CDTS); U.S. Military/Naval/ Air Force/Coast Guard Academy Foreign
Cadet Program; and the State Partnership Program (SPP).

Of these, one of the most recent and perhaps ambitious ventures is the Africa Center for Strategic Studies (ACSS). Currently located at the National Defense University in Washington, D.C., ACSS "designs, develops, and conducts
programs in pursuit of the strategic objectives of the Department of Defense.
The mission of the ACSS is to support the efforts of the Department of Defense
and other U.S. agencies to promote democracy and assist African nations in improving their security by promoting good governance, security sector professionalism, and democratic civil-military relations."[25] Combining an academic
approach (through research projects and seminars) with practical policy objectives and recommendations, ACSS seeks "to promote the development of long-
term, mutually beneficial security relations between the United States and African countries." The staff and faculty of ACSS focus primarily on security studies, civil military relations, counterterrorism, conflict prevention and management, and defense economics. By their own account, ACSS "does not make, nor
does it seek to advocate U.S. policy," but rather, seeks "to increase understanding, to explain the facts, and to shed light on U.S. actions and interests on and
towards the African continent," and "to reflect the concerns and interests [of
African]...participants and relay those views and concerns back to policymakers
in the U.S. government."[26]

In truth, ACSS does provide a critical interface and an open policy discussion environment between a wide variety of U.S. and African stakeholders. Recent seminars hosted by ACSS include a March 2005 topical seminar, held in
Abuja, Nigeria, entitled "Energy and Security in Africa: Meeting the Challenge
in Petroleum Producing States." Participants included defense, finance, energy,
and foreign office representatives from numerous African countries, private energy company delegates, and representatives from a broad array of international
civil society organizations and NGOs. An executive summary of seminar highlights was subsequently forwarded to high-level U.S. policymakers in the interagency, and a comprehensive program highlights paper was published for even
wider dissemination. ACSS has sponsored many other similar conferences to
study and discuss ways to tackle the challenges of small arms proliferation,
counter-terrorism issues, and other relevant security topics. Participants gain a
better understanding of U.S. policy toward their countries and forge professional
relationships with each other, which can help them respond more effectively to
the security challenges they face at home.

In sum, the Department of Defense has institutionalized a diverse and detailed policy implementation hierarchy to assist in the effective execution of U.S.-Africa policy. Of course, astute observers may rightly question whether this system is always used correctly or not, and whether the policies formulated are appropriate or being implemented effectively. These are issues that will be explored later in this volume. Nevertheless, the policy system within the Department of Defense can be considered quite sound and meticulous.

Department of State

The Department of State is arguably the most important actor for transforming the President's foreign policy vision into reality on the ground. However, it is also institutionally and culturally less formally structured than the Department of Defense. The popular paper "Defense is from Mars, State is from Venus"[27] is somewhat of a parody, yet the generalizations hold relatively true. In this paper, the two organizational cultures are described as alien to each other as life forms from two competing planets, the warriors from Mars and the diplomats from Venus. The "Martians" (Department of Defense) have very short hair, stand up straight, and are sometimes found in odd clothing—white, green, and blue suits. They wear decorations with symbolic meanings that only they understand and appreciate. They speak an odd language filled with cryptic words and expressions—for example, "force-multiplier," "template the battlefield," and "bogey."

Meanwhile, the Venutians (Department of State) typically demonstrate an aptitude for making small talk in a seemingly endless round of official cocktail parties and ceremonies. Their normal style of dress is a dark three-piece suit or business clothes that do not stand out in a crowd, and they are frequently spotted overseas in Embassies and at "official events" where they represent the United States. Venutians are more conversant on international issues than domestic ones, and tend to speak a somewhat foreign variant of English, using acronyms and unusual words like "consul," "demarche" and "cable traffic." While it is easy to find humor in such characterizations of the differences between the two organizational cultures, there is nonetheless more than a grain of truth to them—a difference that is clearly seen in the types of policies embraced by each organization. Naturally, Department of Defense initiatives focus on security assistance and the military levers of national power, while Department of State programs are more concerned with the diplomatic realm.

Another significant difference between the two organizations is that while the DoD manages a system for developing Foreign Area Officers and Defense Attachés who specialize in a particular region for their entire careers, Department of State Foreign Service Officers (FSOs) do not specialize in a region, but rather in a particular field of service. For example, an FSO can be a political specialist, an economic specialist, or a consular specialist, (among other fields). Their training programs and assignments generally reflect this specialty, but are not focused on any particular region of the world. The advantage of this system is that "economic" FSOs can be utilized anywhere in the world and apply their broad economics knowledge and experience to further the goals of their assigned U.S. Mission. The disadvantage is that over the course of a career, FSOs may be assigned to a wide variety of international locations without ever developing extensive depth in one region or another.

Under the leadership of Secretary of State Colin Powell (and perhaps because of his extensive military background), the Department of State (DoS) and the U.S. Agency for International Development (USAID) jointly prepared these organizations' first ever joint strategic plan. *Security, Democracy, Prosperity: Strategic Plan, Fiscal Years 2004-2009—Aligning Diplomacy and Development Assistance*[28] clearly lays out the U.S.' foreign policy and development assistance priorities. The mission statement of this important document explains that the aims of DoS and USAID "are clear...[and] anchored in the President's *National Security Strategy* and its three underlying and interdependent components— diplomacy, development, and defense." The primary aims of the *Strategic Plan* are: 1) to build and maintain strong bilateral and multilateral relationships; 2) to protect the U.S. and its allies against the transnational dangers and enduring threats arising from tyranny, poverty, and disease; and 3) to combine diplomatic skills and development assistance to foster a more democratic and prosperous world integrated into the global economy.

The *Strategic Plan* also articulates four strategic objectives: 1) achieve peace and security; 2) advance sustainable development and global interests; 3) promote international understanding; and 4) strengthen diplomatic and program capabilities. These objectives are then subdivided into 12 corresponding strategic goals and numerous performance goals that can be used to evaluate the organizations' efficacy. Well-organized and clearly explained, the *Strategic Plan* is an excellent blueprint to guide U.S. foreign policy, and generally complements the Department of Defense's policies described earlier.

The organizational unit within Department of State that has primary responsibility for U.S. foreign policy toward Africa is the Bureau of African Affairs. While the Bureau of African Affairs does not have an official guidance document that follows from the *Strategic Plan* or the *National Security Strategy*, the State Department has adopted six goals that guide policy efforts toward Africa:[29]

- Increase democracy, good governance, and respect for the rule of law;
- Expand United States trade and investment with Africa to spur economic development and improve the well-being of Africans;
- Conserve Africa's environment because people and the institutions they create to govern themselves cannot prosper when the air is unfit to breathe, water is unavailable and forests and farmlands have become barren;
- Combat the spread of HIV/AIDS and other infectious diseases that threaten to cost Africa a generation of its most productive citizens;
- Reinforce African support in the Global War on Terrorism; and

– Promote regional stability by ending Africa's wars. Doing so is an absolute necessity if the other five policies are to succeed.

These goals inform budgetary decisions and personnel assignments in the Bureau of African Affairs,[30] which are then translated into specific programs and initiatives managed by the Department of State. These include security initiatives like the Anti-Terrorism Assistance (ATA) program, the African Coastal Security Program, the Pan Sahel Initiative (PSI), (which grew into a more rounded program, the Trans-Saharan Counter Terrorism Initiative (TSCTI), the East Africa Counterterrorism Initiative (EACTI), and various programs to support peacekeeping operations throughout Africa. In addition, the Bureau of African Affairs is involved in Foreign Military Financing (FMF), International Military Education Training (IMET), and African Contingency Operations Training Assistance (ACOTA) programs, which are jointly coordinated between the Departments of State and Defense, and described earlier in this chapter.

The Department of State's Anti-Terrorism Assistance (ATA) Program was initiated in 1983 as a means of providing specialized training and equipment to nations facing terrorist threats.[31] Authorization for the program stems from the Foreign Assistance Act (FAA) of 1961, as amended, which governs how the U.S. provides training services and equipment to other countries. Specifically, the ATA program provides training and equipment related to bomb detection and disposal, management of hostage situations, VIP protection, senior leadership crisis management exercises, physical security, and other matters relating to the detection, deterrence, and prevention of acts of terrorism, the resolution of terrorist incidents, and the apprehension of those involved in such acts.[32] Section 572 of the FAA mandates that the ATA program's activities be designed to achieve three objectives: 1) To enhance friendly countries' anti-terrorism skills; 2) To strengthen the United States' ties with friendly governments "by offering concrete assistance in this area of great mutual concern;" and 3) "To increase respect for human rights by sharing with foreign civil authorities modern, humane, and effective anti-terrorism techniques." The ATA program is implemented by the Department of State's Bureau of Diplomatic Security, which works closely with the Department's Regional Security Officers (RSOs) in each embassy.[33] However, section 573(b) of the FAA also requires that the Assistant Secretary of State for Democracy, Human Rights and Labor be consulted when choosing countries that will receive ATA assistance, and when determining the nature of the assistance to be provided—an important dimension of the program which relates to this volume's focus on governance and democratization in the Gulf of Guinea. More on this topic is provided in chapter 10.

Another important initiative is the African Coastal Security (ACS) Program, launched in 1985 as part of the U.S.-sponsored African Civic Action Program, which sought to strengthen regional cooperation in search and rescue, pollution control, and training operations. This program was designed in particular to help

West African states patrol and defend their Exclusive Economic Zones (EEZ) against treaty violations, illegal fishing, and smuggling.[34] By 1995, funding for ACS had dried up, and the program lay dormant until April 2003, then the Bush administration announced plans to re-launch the program. The newly invigorated program will provide naval vessels, radar and communications equipment, coastguard training and coordination in order to improve the capability of African governments to combat piracy, terrorism, trafficking in narcotics, trafficking in persons and immigrant smuggling, and general smuggling. The program will also build the capacity of these countries to respond effectively to possible threats of violence to offshore drilling rigs and other kinds of operations. Given the growing maritime threat to the Gulf of Guinea, as described in chapter 4 of this volume, the need for the African Coastal Security (ACS) Program is clear and urgent.

Another security-related program is the Pan Sahel Initiative (PSI), which was launched by the Department of State in October 2002 as a War on Terrorism-related effort to assist Mali, Niger, Chad, and Mauritania in detecting and responding to suspicious movement of people and goods across and within their borders through training, equipment and cooperation.[35] The Sahel is a stretch of land from east to west Africa, containing nine of the world's poorest countries (Burkina Faso, Cape Verde, Chad, Gambia, Guinea-Bissau, Mali, Mauritania, Niger and Senegal) and approximately 47 million inhabitants. The primary goal of the PSI was to provide training and equipment in order to enhance the border security capabilities of these countries, and encourage better regional cooperation and coordination in combating arms smuggling, drug trafficking, and the movement of trans-national terrorists.[36] As part of this initiative, teams from the 1st Battalion, 10th Special Forces Group (Airborne) were sent in March 2004, to Mali and Mauritania to provide training on mobility, communications, land navigation, and small unit tactics.

Despite its successes, the Pan Sahel Initiative was constrained from its inception by limited funding and a limited focus. However, the program was subsequently replaced by the more ambitious Trans-Saharan Counterterrorism Initiative (TSCTI), which is funded at about $100 million a year for five years, and was officially launched in June 2005 with Exercise Flintlock. Similar to the PSI, U.S. special operations forces will train their counterparts in seven Saharan countries, teaching military tactics critical in enhancing regional security and stability.[37] At the same time, they will encourage the participating nations to work collaboratively toward confronting regional issues. However, unlike the program it replaces, the Trans Saharan Counterterrorism Initiative will introduce a more comprehensive approach to regional security. The Defense Department will continue to focus on military operations, expanding its scope from the company to the battalion level. But other U.S. government agencies also will become active players in the program. The U.S. Agency for International Development, for example, will address educational initiatives; the State Department, airport security; and the Department of Treasury, efforts to tighten up money-handling controls in the region. While providing an interagency approach to the region, the United States will continue efforts to convince participating nations to think regionally about their mutual security concerns.[38]

A similar security assistance program, the East Africa Counterterrorism Initiative (EACTI), provides $100 million dollars to increase the regional counterterrorism capacities of Kenya, Ethiopia, Djibouti, Uganda, Tanzania, and Eritrea. Formally announced in June 2003, EACTI seeks to reduce the scope and capacity of terrorists to act in the region by focusing on such critical areas as military training for border and coastal security; immigration and customs; airport/seaport security; police and law enforcement training; terrorist tracking databases; disruption of terrorist financing; regional information sharing and cooperation; and community outreach through education, assistance and public information.[39] The EACTI also includes a strong public diplomacy and outreach component, and provides training assistance for senior-level decision-makers and legislators who are involved in drafting legislation on terrorist financing and money laundering.[40]

In addition to these initiatives, the Department of State also manages several programs to support peacekeeping operations throughout Africa. For example, the African Crisis Response Initiative (ACRI) was launched by the Clinton administration in the mid-1990s to provide training assistance to enhance indigenous peacekeeping capabilities throughout the continent. After training about 9,000 troops from eight countries, ACRI was replaced by the African Contingency Operations Training and Assistance (ACOTA) program under the Bush administration. ACOTA seeks to redress ACRI shortfalls by emphasizing more training sustainability, uniquely tailored and country-specific programs, and more robust peace-enforcement capabilities.[41] ACOTA has been recently subsumed into the much broader Global Peace Operations Initiative (GPOI), which provides $660 million over the next five years to train, equip and provide logistical support to forces in nations willing to participate in peace operations.[42] As described earlier in this chapter, GPOI will assist in the development of roughly 75,000 foreign troops (50,000 of them in Africa) who could be deployed on short notice and perform a wide range of peacekeeping activities throughout the world.

Beyond the TSCTI, ACOTA, GPOI, and other security assistant programs, the U.S. has consistently provided support for an array of UN peacekeeping operations and training initiatives. Africa's role in these operations has risen dramatically in the past ten years. According to research conducted by the Henry L. Stimson Center, the contribution of African troops to UN peacekeeping missions has risen from 13% in 1994 to 35% in 2004 (Table 6.2).

Chapter 6

Table 6.2: Africa's Presence in UN Peacekeeping Missions

	1994		2004	
African Peacekeepers	10,205	13%	21,255	35%
Non-African Peacekeepers	67,906	87%	39,476	65%
Total UN Peacekeepers	78,111	100%	60,731	100%

Source: The Henry L. Stimson Center, 2004.[43]

One reason for this increase is that the number of operations and peace-keepers in Africa has grown dramatically in the last five years. In 2004, the UN led 16 peace operations, and seven of them are in Africa: Burundi, Cote d'Ivoire, Liberia, Ethiopia-Eritrea, Democratic Republic of Congo, Sierra Leone, and the Western Sahara. These African missions accounted for over 80% of *all* UN peacekeepers deployed worldwide that year.[44] Given the dramatically worsening events in the Darfur region of Sudan, as well as the challenges of violent non-state actors operating elsewhere in Africa—including the Lords Resistance Army, which is carrying out a vicious campaign of banditry and terrorism in both Uganda and the Sudan—there will likely be a need for an even greater peacekeeping presence on the continent.

In recognition of this, the U.S. has also offered its support to the recently announced Africa Union Standby Force (ASF). The ASF is a multinational force empowered to intervene in serious conflicts around the continent. With an eventual capacity of 20,000 peacekeepers, ASF troops will deploy under the auspices of the AU to intervene in border wars and internal conflicts.[45] A model for the ASF comes in part from the United Nation's Multinational Standby High Readiness Brigade (SHIRBRIG), headquartered near Copenhagen, Denmark.[46] Although little direct coordination has taken place between these two organizations, it is certainly feasible—indeed, even recommended—given the time it will take before the African Union can truly offer this capability to their members without outside assistance.

The U.S. has also supported the establishment of the Kofi Annan International Peacekeeping Training Center (KAIPTC). The idea of the KAIPTC was first conceived by Ghana in 1997, and was originally intended to provide training for the country's substantial force contributions to Peace Support Operations (PSO) worldwide.[47] However, the first few years of existence were hampered by a severe lack of funding. In 2002, the German government and then the United Kingdom led other nations—including the U.S.—in a drive to meet the Center's funding needs, and KAIPTC ran its first course in June 2003. A course on disarmament, demobilization and reintegration was run in November of that year, in coordination with the Pearson Peacekeeping Center of Canada, and KAIPTC launched its first full annual training and education cycle in March 2004. (More on this is provided in subsequent chapters.) Through these and other initiatives, the U.S. Department of State is clearly engaged in meeting the security assistance objectives described in the administration's overall strategic guidance.

At the implementation end of the foreign policy spectrum, individual Country Teams in each U.S. Embassy—under the guidance of the U.S. Ambassador—link the policies of the Departments of State and Defense and any other department or agency (like USAID) that is present in that particular country. The Country Team is usually comprised of the Ambassador, the Deputy Chief of Mission, the chiefs of the Political, Economic, Consular, and Public Affairs sections, the Defense Attaché, and other agency representatives. The document used to provide strategic guidance to individual Country Teams is the *Mission Performance Plan* (MPP). Prepared annually, MPPs comprehensively outline specific goals, objectives, and performance indicators to focus and evaluate the Embassy's programs in a given country. These goals are directly linked back to the *Strategic Plan* and ultimately, to the President's *National Security Strategy*. However, each Ambassador has considerable flexibility and responsibility to place emphasis on programs and priorities that he or she deems most important for U.S. policy and most relevant to the specific target country. For example, in Equatorial Guinea the U.S. Mission aims to improve adherence to democratic practices and respect for human rights along with the rule of law; encourage continued strides in fighting corruption and increasing political stability; support stronger civil societies and more transparent electoral processes; and promote broad-based economic growth. In sum, the policy initiatives and personnel of the U.S. Department of State generally complement those of the DoD in achieving coordination of the *National Security Strategy's* goals related to global defense and diplomacy.

U.S. Agency for International Development (USAID)

The *National Security Strategy* places international development in line with defense and diplomacy as the third pillar of U.S. national security, because poverty fueled by lack of economic opportunity is one of the root causes of violence today.[48] The lead proponent of this pillar is the U.S. Agency for International Development (USAID), which promotes peace and stability by fostering economic growth, protecting human health, providing emergency humanitarian assistance, and enhancing democracy in developing countries. Through its field offices in sub-Saharan Africa, Asia and the Near East, Latin America and the Caribbean, and Europe and Eurasia, USAID is actively engaged in over 100 developing countries. The types of assistance USAID provides include technical assistance and capacity building, training and scholarships, food aid and disaster relief, infrastructure construction, small-enterprise loans, budget support, enterprise funds, and credit guarantees.[49]

Like the Department of State, foreign assistance provided by USAID is governed by a number of federal laws and regulations, including the Foreign

Assistance Act of 1961; the Federal Grant and Cooperative Agreement Act of
1977; the Government Performance and Results Act of 1993; and the Federal
Acquisition Streamlining Act of 1994. Overall, much of the regulatory and
statutory framework in which USAID conducts its work is outside its direct control. These laws and regulations also govern the implementation instruments
USAID relies upon to accomplish its goals, such as: subcontracts to local organizations in developing countries; transfers to other federal agencies; contributions to international organizations such as the United Nations; implementation letters with host country governments; university partnerships; and public-
private alliances, known as Global Development Alliances, that deal with international development challenges. As of 2005, USAID has working relationships,
through contracts and grant agreements, with more than 3,500 companies and
over 300 U.S.-based private voluntary organizations. Also, to provide technical
assistance regarding opportunities at USAID, the Agency's Center for Faith-
Based and Community Initiatives meets regularly with faith-based and community organizations and has developed an email list of approximately 1,200 members.[50]

In addition to the federal legal framework, USAID policy development and
implementation is guided by a principles-oriented strategy adopted by the
agency. According to a recent USAID guidebook, "nine principles guide U.S.
development and reconstruction assistance (Figure 6.1). The principles are fundamental to the success of assistance as an instrument of U.S. foreign policy and
national security. They are not a checklist, but rather a summary of the characteristics of assistance that achieves development objectives, including economic
growth, democracy and governance, and social transition."[51]

Based upon these principles, USAID has identified a set of goals and requirements which guide the prioritization and distribution of U.S. foreign assistance. To begin with, a priority is given to "fragile" states, where there is a limited willingness or ability of the local government to provide basic security and
services to significant portions of its population, often leading to questions of
governmental legitimacy. In these countries, where violent conflict is a reality or
at great risk, the primary goals of USAID are to achieve a basic level of stability, mitigate the impact of existing conflicts (to include addressing governance
effectiveness and legitimacy issues), and move from a "state of crisis" to a "vulnerable status" where developmental progress is possible.

Figure 6.1: Principles of Development and Reconstruction Assistance.

1. **Ownership:** Build on the leadership, participation, and commitment of a country and its people.
2. **Capacity Building:** Strengthen local institutions, transfer technical skills, and promote appropriate policies.
3. **Sustainability:** Design programs to ensure their impact endures.
4. **Selectivity:** Allocate resources based on need, local commitment, and foreign policy interests.
5. **Assessment:** Conduct careful research, adapt best practices, and design for local conditions.
6. **Results:** Focus resources to achieve clearly defined, measurable, strategically focused objectives.
7. **Partnership:** Collaborate closely with governments, communities, donors, NGOs, the private sector, international organizations, and universities.
8. **Flexibility:** Adjust to changing conditions, take advantage of opportunities, and maximize efficiency.
9. **Accountability:** Design accountability and transparency into systems and build effective checks and balances to guard against corruption.

Source: *USAID Primer: What We Do and How We Do It* (Washington, DC: USAID, March 2005), available online at: http://www.usaid.gov

Specifically, the agency recognizes the need to enhance stability and address sources of stress and conflict in political, economic, and social spheres; improve security and provide an environment that enhances personal safety and establishes conditions under which serious outbreaks of generalized violence are averted; encourage reforms related to conditions driving fragility and that increase the likelihood of long-term stability; and develop the capacity of institutions fundamental to lasting recovery and transformational development.[52]

A second category of countries, "Transformational Development States," also receive significant amounts of U.S. foreign aid. These include mostly low income countries, with correspondingly low social indicators, but where the government has demonstrated a strong sustained commitment to development progress, as indicated by policy performance and sound proposals for using Millennium Challenge Account (MCA) funding. Here, USAID will support government efforts to strengthen policies and institutions that represent sound public investments and are likely to achieve economic, political, and social progress. For those low income countries which are not yet MCA-eligible, but whose governments are considered reasonably stable and capable of managing internal conflict, USAID will provide assistance with improving basic education and health, promoting good governance and the rule of law, and encouraging economic freedom and growth (including agriculture, trade, and improved business climates) in order for the government to eventually gain access to MCA funding. For middle income countries, USAID will promote eventual graduation from developmental foreign aid—but not necessarily from aid for special concerns and global issues, like combating terrorism—while strengthening U.S. trade and security relationships. Finally, USAID assistance is prioritized by the importance and urgency of a particular foreign policy concern (like a high rate of HIV/AIDS) that motivates assistance, as well as the willingness of the local government to cooperate with the U.S. in addressing this foreign policy concern.[53]

Based upon the development principles and strategic guidance described here, USAID has developed a broad range of foreign assistance policies and programs that address the needs of Africa.[54] Some of the most recent and prominent of these include HIV/AIDS prevention programs, the Africa Education Initiative, the Initiative to End Hunger in Africa, and the Trade for African Development and Enterprise program. Since 1987, USAID has initiated HIV/AIDS prevention programs in 32 countries, and is recognized in the developing world as a technical leader in the design and development of these programs. Over 850,000 people have been reached with USAID HIV prevention education, and 40,000 people have been trained to support HIV/AIDS programs in their own countries. In his 2003 State of the Union Address, President Bush announced the Emergency Plan for AIDS Relief (PEPFAR), a five-year, $15 billion initiative to turn the tide in the global effort to combat the HIV/AIDS pandemic. PEPFAR builds on the Global Fund to Fight AIDS, Tuberculosis, and Malaria, established in 2002 by independent public-private partnerships to fight three of the world's most devastating diseases. The United States, through USAID and the Department of Health and Human Services, is the largest contributor to the Global Fund and has pledged $500 million to date.

The Africa Education Initiative (AEI), announced by President Bush in June 2002, seeks to increase access to quality basic educational opportunities in Africa.[55] Specifically, AEI activities help improve primary education by providing teacher training, textbooks and other learning materials, support for community involvement, and scholarships to girls. AEI also seeks to address the impact of HIV/AIDS on schooling and the education system. This initiative is managed by the USAID in conjunction with the Department of State (as described earlier). As of 2004, according to a USAID report, the program has awarded nearly 17,500 scholarships to girls in seven countries, while over 130,000 new and existing teachers in 12 countries have acquired new skills. Primary school children in Senegal and Guinea have received 770,000 new textbooks, and over 925,000 African primary school children have improved learning environments.[56]

The Initiative to End Hunger in Africa (IEHA), announced by President Bush in August 2002, seeks to reduce hunger in Africa by half by 2015, in keeping with the UN Development Goals of the Millennium Declaration.[57] IEHA's key principles include building regional dynamism, synergies, and spillovers; building alliances and broad-based political and financial commitment among public and private development partners in Africa and elsewhere; and focusing investments on core activities designed to eliminate hunger in Africa. IEHA's investments are concentrated in 1) science and technology, 2) agricultural trade and marketing systems, 3) human and institutional capacity, 4) producer organizations, 5) protecting the vulnerable, and 6) environmental management. In FY 2004, IEHA supported efforts in six countries and from three regional platforms. With the FY 2004 expansion of the program to three additional countries, IEHA's reach was extended to cover Ghana, Kenya, Mali, Mozambique, Uganda, and Zambia, as well as the three regional missions that support multi-country efforts in East, West, and Southern Africa.[58]

The Trade for African Development and Enterprise (TRADE) initiative, announced by President Bush in October 2001, seeks to strengthen the ability of African companies and businesses to expand regional and international trade, improves the enabling environment for business and trade, and helps countries mainstream trade into their development agendas.[59] TRADE enables African countries to take advantage of increased trade opportunities with the United States provided by the African Growth and Opportunity Act (AGOA) and the recently passed AGOA Acceleration Act of 2004. TRADE works with host-country governments and private sector partners, primarily through three regional trade hubs located in Botswana, Ghana, and Kenya. Similar USAID programs in Africa are focused more specifically on environmental and economic education. For example, in Equatorial Guinea and the Democratic Republic of the Congo, the Central African Regional Program for the Environment/Congo Basin Forest Partnership helps local organizations develop programs to ensure that the next generation of African conservationists has access to high-quality academic and technical information to reduce dependence on external sources of technical expertise. In Senegal, the Digital Freedom Initiative (DFI) has enabled dozens of Senegalese small and medium-sized enterprises launch and successfully manage cybercafe operations.[60]

Overall, USAID works in close partnership with private voluntary organizations, indigenous groups, universities, American businesses, international organizations, other governments, trade and professional associations, faith-based organizations, and other U.S. government agencies to achieve a comprehensive and ambitious development agenda. However, it is likely that USAID is most well-known throughout the world for its ability to respond to man-made and natural disasters. Indeed, from earthquakes, volcanoes, hurricanes and tsunamis to civil wars and other forms of political conflict, USAID has built an impressive reputation for its disaster relief efforts. As the U.S. government agency charged with providing humanitarian relief on behalf of the American people, USAID provides both short- and long-term humanitarian assistance. USAID's key humanitarian assistance approaches include providing experts on the ground immediately after a disaster hits to assess damage and needs; providing immediate relief to victims of natural disasters; helping communities devastated by natural disasters and conflict rebuild by supporting projects in community infrastructure and services, as well as economic and agricultural reactivation (including employment and skills training); and developing local capacities in disaster planning and preparedness (including development of early warning systems).

In sum, the policies and personnel of USAID provide considerable leadership and depth to the *National Security Strategy's* objectives in the area of global development. While many of its activities are implemented jointly with the Department of State and other agencies of the U.S. government, USAID has earned a deservedly positive reputation for its efforts throughout the last several decades. However, as described in chapter 11, there is clearly room for improvement in the area of agency and policy coordination.

Other Major Players in the U.S.-Africa Policy Arena

Several other U.S. agencies and organizations are directly involved in projects and initiatives throughout the African continent. For example, the Departments of Energy and Commerce, the Millennium Challenge Corporation (MCC), the Overseas Private Investment Corporation (OPIC), the U.S. Trade and Development Agency (USTDA), and the Export-Import Bank of the United States all have broad international agendas, but due to the developmental nature of their programs, direct a significant amount of effort and resources toward Africa.

Throughout the last decade, the Departments of Energy and Commerce have supported U.S. oil interests with official trade missions and ministerials throughout the Gulf of Guinea. In doing so, these agencies help foster positive relationships between U.S.-based multinational corporations and the leaders of African nations. The Millennium Challenge Corporation (MCC) administers the Millennium Challenge Account (MCA), described earlier in this chapter. The Overseas Private Investment Corporation (OPIC) is a self-sustaining U.S. government development agency whose mission is "to mobilize and facilitate the participation of United States' private capital and skills in the economic and social development of less developed countries and areas, and countries in transition from non-market to market economies."[61] To accomplish this, OPIC encourages investment by providing political risk insurance to help U.S. companies manage risk; providing financing through direct loans and loan guarantees; and by leveraging private capital through OPIC-supported funds. These are all critical needs for economic development, and OPIC support for Africa has increased from investments amounting to $90 million in 2001 to about $1 billion in 2003.

The U.S. Trade and Development Agency (USTDA) is a small, independent federal agency that seeks to advance economic development and U.S. commercial interests in developing and middle-income countries. The USTDA delivers its program commitments through overseas grants, contracts with U.S. firms, and the use of trust funds at several multilateral development bank groups. Programs are designed to "help countries establish a favorable trading environment and a modern infrastructure that promotes sustainable economic development."

In Africa, major projects focus on trade capacity and security, energy projects, and air and sea port infrastructure development.[62] And the Export-Import Bank of the United States[63] provides protection against overseas political and commercial risk, and gives U.S. exporters the ability to offer competitive financing to their international buyers through export credit insurance and loan guarantees. These programs are especially important for Africa because they encourage much needed direct U.S. investment in potentially unstable, underdeveloped countries, and they serve as a means of lowering the cost of critical investment capital for African businesses and entrepreneurs.

Conclusion

In sum, the U.S. foreign policy continuum (from the highest national, strategic level to the lowest country-specific implementation level) involves a broad range of organizations, in theory striving to achieve common goals within an overarching national strategic framework. Three primary categories of activity in the U.S.-Africa policy arena—defense, diplomacy and development—are led, respectively, by the Departments of Defense and State and USAID. Within each of these, the formulation and implementation of U.S.-Africa policy is clearly organized and reasonably consistent. At the Country Team level, there is even coordination between the departments via the Ambassador's relationship with the Defense Attaché and other agency representatives within a specific country. However, a number of critical discrepancies remain in the overall consistency and focus of U.S. foreign policy programs in Africa. Why this happens, and how it may be overcome, will be discussed in more detail in Chapter 11 of this volume.

The intent of this discussion has been to provide readers with a general idea of the types of programs already in place, and how the policy implementers on the ground are connected to the policymakers at the highest levels of government. Specifically, this chapter has provided a cursory overview of the foreign policy strategy and hierarchy that affects ongoing U.S.-Africa policymaking, because it is important to understand this basic structure when contemplating our government's strengths and weaknesses in achieving effective policy outcomes.[64] The remaining chapters of this volume will examine the policymaking realities from the African perspective, discuss the re-establishment of U.S. policy priorities, and develop a policy framework that may help fortify U.S.-Africa policymaking in the long run, specifically regarding energy security and national security issues in the Gulf of Guinea.

Notes

1. Edward Harris, "U.S. outlines bigger effort to fight terrorism in Africa: Plan would pour $100 million each year into some of the least-policed areas," *Associated Press*, 25 May 2005.
2. "Key U.S. Government Assistance Programs for Africa," Fact Sheet, U.S. State Department Bureau of Public Affairs, Washington, DC, July 11, 2005.
3. Available at http://www.whitehouse.gov/nsc/nss.pdf
4. *National Security Strategy of the United States*, p. 10-11.
5. See White House, Africa Policy, online at: http://www.whitehouse.gov/infocus/africa
6. For more on this initiative, please see http://www.agoa.gov and http://www.agoa.info.
7. For more on this initiative, please see http://www.agoa.gov and http://www.agoa.info.
8. For more on this, see http://www.mca.gov/about_us/overview/index.shtml
9. Marquis, Christopher. "New System Begins Rerouting U.S. Aid for Poor Countries." *The New York Times* (Feb. 22, 2004).
10. IMF Fact Sheet available at http://www.imf.org/external/np/exr/facts/hipc.htm Accessed 10 April 2004.
11. The "G-8" is the nickname for the group of eight major industrialized nations: Canada, France, Germany, Italy, Japan, Russia, the U.K., and the U.S.
12. The debt relief agreement was approved by the IMF and the World Bank in September 2005. However, it is important to note that while this agreement focuses on multilateral debt, it does not address the bilateral debt. In many African countries, particularly Nigeria, the majority of debt is actually bilateral.
13. *Engendering Bold Leadership: The President's Emergency Plan for AIDS Relief*, First Annual Report to Congress (March 2005), p. 5. Available online at: http://www.state.gov/documents/organization/43885.pdf.
14. *Engendering Bold Leadership*, p. 5-6.
15. *Engendering Bold Leadership*, p. 5-6.
16. This discussion paraphrases Bradley Graham, "Bush Plans Aid to Build Foreign Peace Forces," *Washington Post*, 19 April 2004. Also, see Nina M. Serafino. *The Global Peace Operations Initiative: Background and Issues for Congress* February 16, 2005. Available online at: http://www.fas.org/sgp/crs/misc/RL32773.pdf
17. G8 refers to the "Group of 8" major industrialized democracies: Canada, France, Germany, Italy, Japan, Russia, the United Kingdom and the United States. G8 heads of state, plus representatives from the European Union, meet at annual summits.
18. Available online at http://www.g8usa.gov/d_061004c.htm
19. These documents are available online at http://www.g8.gc.ca/2002Kananaskis/kananaskis/afraction-en.pdf and http://www.g8.gc.ca/AFRIQUE-01june-en.asp.
20. EUCOM has responsibility for a total of 91 countries in Europe and Africa.
21. The National Defense Strategy of the United States of America—March 2005 can be found at http://www.globalsecurity.org/military/library/policy/dod/nds-usa_mar2005.htm

22. The National Military Strategy of the United States of America—March 2005 can be found at
http://www.globalsecurity.org/military/library/policy/dod/d20050318nms.pdf.

23. Department of Defense Security Cooperation Guidance available at the Security Cooperation and Education Center website: http://scetc.tecom.usmc.mil.

24. Taken from presentations made at the Gulf of Guinea Maritime Security Conference, Naples, Italy, 3-5 October 2004.

25. Find out more at http://www.africacenter.org

26. Find out more at http://www.africacenter.org

27. Available at
http://www.au.af.mil/au/awc/awcgate/ndu/dod_from_mars_state_from_venus.doc

28. Available at http://www.state.gov/s/d/rm/rls/dosstrat/2004.

29. See Phillip Carter III (Deputy Director of the Office of East African Affairs), "U.S.-Africa Relations at the Beginning of the 21st Century," Remarks to the Africa Summit at the University of Miami, Miami, Florida, 21 February 2004. Available online at: http://www.state.gov/p/af/rls/rm/29993.htm.

30. For example, see William M. Bellamy (Principal Deputy Assistant Secretary for African Affairs), "Budget Priorities for Sub-Saharan Africa," Testimony Before the Senate Foreign Relations Committee, Washington, DC, 2 April 2003. Available online at: http://www.state.gov/p/af/rls/rm/20249.htm.

31. See Anti-Terrorism Assistance Program, online at http://ciponline.org/facts/ata.htm.

32. Karl Wycoff (Associate Coordinator, State Department Office of the Coordinator for Counterterrorism), "Fighting Terrorism in Africa," Testimony to the House International Relations Committee Subcommittee on Africa, Washington, DC, 1 April 2004.

33. Karl Wycoff (Associate Coordinator, State Department Office of the Coordinator for Counterterrorism), "Fighting Terrorism in Africa," Testimony to the House International Relations Committee Subcommittee on Africa, Washington, DC, 1 April 2004.

34. See "African Coastal Security (ACS) Program" available online at: http://www.globalsecurity.org/military/ops/acsp.htm.

35. U.S. Department of State, "Pan Sahel Initiative," Office of Counterterrorism, Washington, DC, 7 November 2002.

36. Ambassador Cofer Black (Coordinator for Counterterrorism), "The Prevention and Combating of Terrorism in Africa," (Remarks at the Second Intergovernmental High-Level Meeting on the Prevention and Combating of Terrorism in Africa), Algiers, Algeria, 13 October 2004.

37. The Trans-Sahara region spans ten African and Maghreb countries and is an area of acute vulnerability due to vast expanses of desert and porous borders. With a long history of being a center through which arms and other illicit trade flow, it is becoming increasingly important as terrorists now seek to use these routes for logistical support, recruiting grounds, and safe haven. The U.S. Government has indications that extremist groups with experience in Afghanistan and Iraq are operating in the Sahel region.

38. Global Security.Org, "Trans-Saharan Counterterrorism Initiative (TSCTI)" description. Available online at: http://www.globalsecurity.org/military/ops/tscti.htm

39. See Phillip Carter III (Deputy Director of the Office of East African Affairs), "U.S.-Africa Relations at the Beginning of the 21st Century," Remarks to the Africa Summit at the University of Miami, Miami, Florida, 21 February 2004. Available online at: http://www.state.gov/p/af/rls/rm/29993.htm and J. Cofer Black (Coordinator, Office of

the Coordinator for Counterterrorism, Department of State), Testimony to the Foreign Operations Subcommittee Hearing on Foreign Assistance and International Terrorism, April 21, 2004. Online at:
http://appropriations.senate.gov/hearmarkups/record.cfm?id=220649
    40. U.S. Department of State, Patterns of Global Terrorism, 2003. Released by the Office of the Coordinator for Counterterrorism, 29 April 2004. Available online at:
http://www.state.gov/s/ct/rls/pgtrpt/2003/31578.htm
    41. For a good discussion on ACOTA, see Russell J. Handy, "Africa Contingency Operations Training Assistance: developing training partnerships for the future of Africa" in *Air and Space Power Journal*, Fall 2003.
    42. This discussion paraphrases Bradley Graham, "Bush Plans Aid to Build Foreign Peace Forces," *Washington Post*, 19 April 2004. Also, see Nina M. Serafino. *The Global Peace Operations Initiative: Background and Issues for Congress*, February 16, 2005. Available online at: http://www.fas.org/sgp/crs/misc/RL32773.pdf
    43. Victoria K. Holt (Senior Associate, The Henry L. Stimson Center), "Peacekeeping in Africa: Challenges and Opportunities" Testimony to the Subcommittee on Africa, House Committee on International Relations, U.S. House of Representatives, 8 October 2004. Data cited are courtesy of UN Department of Peacekeeping Operations and UN Information Center (Washington, DC).
    44. Victoria K. Holt "Peacekeeping in Africa: Challenges and Opportunities."
    45. Theo Neethling, "Shaping the African Standby Force," *Military Review*, May-June 2005, 68.
    46. Theo Neethling, "Shaping the African Standby Force," 69.
    47. See "Brief on the Kofi Annan International Peacekeeping Training Centre (KAIPTC)," available online at: http://www.kaiptc.org/kaiptc/abkaiptc.htm.
    48. Online at: http://www.usaid.gov/about_usaid/presidential_initiative.
    49. *USAID Primer: What We Do and How We Do It* (Washington, DC: USAID, March 2005), available online at: http://www.usaid.gov.
    50. *USAID Primer*, 22. Additional information about how USAID implements its activities through contracting mechanisms can be found on USAID's website: http://www.usaid.gov/business.
    51. *USAID Primer*, 10.
    52. *USAID Primer*, 4.
    53. *USAID Primer*, 4.
    54. USAID policies can be found at http://www.usaid.gov/policy and at http://www.dec.org.
    55. *Status of Presidential Initiatives FY 2004*, USAID Bureau for Policy and Program Coordination, April 2005, 4.
    56. *Status of Presidential Initiatives FY 2004*, 4.
    57. *Status of Presidential Initiatives FY 2004*, 20.
    58. *Status of Presidential Initiatives FY 2004*, 20.
    59. *Status of Presidential Initiatives FY 2004*, 22.
    60. *Status of Presidential Initiatives FY 2004*.
    61. Find out more at www.opic.gov.
    62. Find out more at www.ustda.gov.
    63. Find out more at www.exim.gov.
    64. As with any research and analysis project, there is inevitably more that can be explored about context, socio-political history, and so forth than space allows. For readers

seeking additional analysis on the issues addressed in the first half of this volume, we recommend Michael J. Siler, *Strategic Security Issues in Sub-Saharan Africa: A Comprehensive Annotated Bibliography* (Westport, CT: Praeger, 2004); George B. N. Ayittey, *Africa in Chaos* (New York: St. Martin's Press, 1999); Jane Boulden (ed.), *Dealing with Conflict in Africa: The United Nations and Regional Organizations* (New York: Palgrave MacMillan, 2003); Graham Harrison, *The World Bank and Africa: The Construction of Governance States* (London: Routledge, 2004); and Albert Tevoedjre, *Winning the War Against Humiliation: The Report of the Independent Commission on Africa and the Challenges of the Third Millennium* (Paris: United Nations Development Program, 2002). Also, more information on U.S.-Africa policy is available on the websites of the agencies and organizations discussed in this chapter. These websites are listed in the bibliography provided at the end of this volume.

Chapter 7
A New Framework for 21st Century U.S.-Africa Policies

As described in the previous chapter, the overarching themes from the President's *National Security Strategy* that weave their way down through the policy implementation strategies of the Departments of State and Defense include noble and lofty goals like democratization and good governance, economic development, regional stability, and mitigation of major health and environmental crises. While there are very few people who would argue against any of these positive policy themes in general, there are certainly diverging perspectives on how to most effectively implement policy. For that matter, there are several macro-level debates that need to be addressed up front: Why should the U.S. care? Who should be responsible for enacting and sustaining transformational policy initiatives? What are the policy priorities and how should the U.S. approach them? This chapter will attempt to broadly answer these questions and will introduce a model of a U.S.-Africa policy framework that we believe will be useful for planning and implementing coherent and effective policy in the future.

Why Should the U.S. Care?

First, a question which some readers may ask is why the U.S. should care about Africa—or more explicitly, why should U.S. taxpayers prioritize the development issues of Africans over domestic concerns of their own? In a harsh Hobbesian reality, poor, sick people in Burkina Faso really have no impact whatsoever on U.S. citizens living in Kansas. Of course, in an idealistic world where U.S. foreign policy was driven by moral values and Christian ethics alone, there would be no question that the plight of hundreds of millions of suffering human beings would be an absolute priority. Unfortunately for humanity, foreign policy around the world is driven directly by national interests, which is logical, if somewhat unfair. If that were not the case, the collective West could have quite easily and cheaply averted such tragedies as, for example, the Rwandan genocide in 1994.

In the post-9/11 security environment, the argument that the U.S. needs to alleviate oppression and poverty in developing countries because otherwise these conditions proliferate "breeding grounds for terrorists" has become ubiquitous in foreign policy circles and mainstream media discussions. (This theme is addressed in chapter 4 of this volume). Yet there are plenty of poor people in the world (2 billion people live on less than $2 a day—roughly a third of humanity) that have no intention of becoming terrorists at all. In fact, most poor people spend nearly all of their energy just trying to eke out a living and provide meagerly for their families, one day at a time. Granted, political oppression and gross economic inequalities combined with poverty, desperation, and radical ideology and leadership certainly are the ingredients for instability and violence. However, beyond these stark realities, there are additional reasons why the U.S. needs to engage with Africa more comprehensively.

For example, a plausible argument can be made that in an increasingly connected world, the threats of infectious disease, illegal immigrants, and violent crime that frequently plague developing nations will soon be knocking on the U.S.' doorstep. Immigration issues clearly top political and security agendas in the U.S. and Europe, and it seems as if there is a new foreign health threat fended off every few months—from mad cow disease to the Asian avian flu to the West Nile virus. Globalization of trade and commerce is already a reality, and with that come all the negative externalities of massive human migrations as well. However, these concerns are not new, and have historically not been enough to motivate significant long-term engagement with developing countries to an extent that makes them better developed places from which emigrants, disease, and crime would not flow prolifically.

So, perhaps energy security—as discussed at length earlier in this volume— provides a more important national interest to justify our increased attention to Africa. Previous chapters of this volume have illuminated how the avid pursuit of energy resources in foreign lands via military and economic domination has historically produced deep instabilities and strong international resentment. However, because of the inevitable and non-negotiable short- and medium-term fossil fuel demands of the U.S. economy,[1] energy security plays a prominent role in the current administration's *National Security Strategy*:

> Enhance energy security. We will strengthen our own energy security and the shared prosperity of the global economy by working with our allies, trading partners, and energy producers to expand the sources and types of energy supplied, especially in the Western Hemisphere, Africa, Central Asia, and the Caspian region. We will also continue to work with our partners to develop cleaner and more energy efficient technologies.[2]

In essence, energy resources, more specifically enormous oil and natural gas deposits, are a very practical and real reason why the U.S. should care about Africa. As described in chapter 1 of this volume, oil is necessary for transportation, militaries, heating, and so forth. The U.S. consumes about a quarter of the world's oil production, and imports over half of what it consumes. Securing access to oil is clearly a vital national interest for the U.S., as it meets two basic criteria: the first criterion is that the United States has committed or is likely to commit significant public-sector resources to advance or protect it; the second is that it is a major foreign policy end in itself, not simply a contributor to a larger objective.[3] In sum, energy security has a special place in any president's policy agenda. However, the absolutely critical details are in *how* energy security is actually obtained.

Energy security and national security are intertwined, particularly when considering the multiple state and non-state actors who can wreak considerable havoc on the U.S. economy based solely on the nation's significant dependence on foreign oil. Drawing on lessons learned from the last half century of oil extraction activity in the Middle East, this analysis suggests a policy framework is needed for developing new energy relationships in the Gulf of Guinea that will complement—rather than conflict with—the nation's security agenda. Effective U.S.-Africa policy requires a coherent, integrated approach to ensure that the nation's energy and national security goals are successfully pursued in tandem. For example, after the attack on the USS Cole, we helped Yemen strengthen its port security and coast guard. Will we wait to help the nations of Africa do the same until after terrorist attacks have occurred in this region, or will we be more proactive in our policy initiatives? The remaining sections of this chapter will provide a rationale for greater policy coordination and integration, and a framework through which transformational policy initiatives can better meet the needs of both the U.S. and the states of the Gulf of Guinea.

Sharing Responsibility for Enacting and Sustaining Transformational Policy Initiatives

At the broadest level, there is a debate over the general assessment of responsibility and capability for transforming and stabilizing the developing world. In one camp, there are those who argue that the developed world, the United Nations (UN), and the international financial institutions (IFIs) like the World Bank, International Monetary Fund (IMF), and World Trade Organization (WTO) are the only players who have enough clout, wisdom, experience, and funding to really make a difference. Supporters of this argument point out that weak local institutions lack the capacity to implement real transformational policies, and that there is a dearth of qualified local technocrats with the knowledge to oversee complicated initiatives. Others explain that decades of local mismanagement and corruption have only led to huge external debts, gross inequalities, excessive waste of resources, and a continuation of the vicious cycle of poverty. And finally, in underdeveloped countries where leadership and governance is good, and policies are generally sound, the lack of financial resources is the major obstacle to transformational policy implementation. Therefore, this "externalist" camp concludes that it is up to competent, wealthy outsiders to come in to jump-start and supervise the critical policy reforms necessary to make real progress.

In the other camp are those who argue that all these external organizations actually make things worse for developing countries. Critics claim that the IFIs don't really understand the unique political, social, economic, and cultural factors in each country, and that subsequently their policy recommendations are unrealistic, ineffective, and unattainable. Others maintain that the Western-centric states merely use the IFIs as tools for pursuing their own political and economic interests, usually at the expense of citizens in the underdeveloped states. Therefore, this "internalist" camp concludes that external players should be ignored as much as possible and that transformational policy solutions must be home-grown and locally initiated. The reality of this debate is, of course, somewhere in the middle.

Based on extensive field research, and significant time spent working and living in Africa, a few basic assumptions can be proposed regarding how this general debate applies to the Gulf of Guinea states. First, and this may sound obvious, but neither externalists nor internalists can fundamentally change political, social, economic, and cultural institutions overnight. Local governments could implement stark transformational policy reforms, but most are unlikely to do so. And even if they did, the corresponding lag between policy reform and real societal transformation would take at least a generation. The governments of Cameroon, Chad, Equatorial Guinea, Gabon, Congo, and Angola are clearly more concerned about preserving systemic stability than implementing radical reforms. The government of Nigeria is at least trying to implement transformational policy initiatives, but real momentum is extremely difficult to achieve amidst a tremendously complex quagmire of internal obstacles.

Second, there cannot be any significant political and economic transformation amidst a rampant culture of corruption. For years, the development community diplomatically talked around the issues of good governance and corruption as fundamental barriers to progress. In the mid-1990s, supported by objective reporting from Transparency International, the World Bank under James Wolfensohn began to directly address the importance of these issues. The Gulf of Guinea is particularly rife with corruption, as the recent Transparency International rankings indicate (Table 7.1).

Table 7.1: Transparency International's Corruption Rankings, 2004

Country	TI Ranking, 2004 CPI*
Angola	133
Cameroon	129
Chad	142
Congo	114
Equatorial Guinea	n/a
Gabon	74
Sao Tome & Principe	n/a
Nigeria	144

Source: Transparency International *Corruption Perceptions Index* (CPI), 2004. Higher scores (out of 145 total) indicate higher levels of corruption. "n/a" indicates Transparency International does not have enough data to include these countries in their 2004 ranking. For more, please see: http://www.transparency.org.

Further, as highlighted in previous chapters of this volume, countries with large amounts oil have shown a tendency for governmental corruption and political violence. As a result, many external players in the Gulf of Guinea are including anti-corruption conditions and good governance requirements as part of any policy and assistance packages. Today, the most vocal proponents for transforming Africa policy are calling for dramatic increases in financial assistance as the key to meeting the Millennium Development Goals, while also recognizing this important dimension of transparency.

For example, the Africa Commission (led by British Prime Minister Tony Blair) called for $25 billion per year in aid for the next 20 years.[4] However, the Commission also recognized that this aid must not be allowed to fuel the kinds of corruption, violence, and mismanagement identified in earlier chapters of this volume. "Ensuring the money is well-spent will depend on two factors. First, good governance in Africa must continue to advance. But, second, donors must significantly improve the quality of aid and how it is delivered: that means more grants, more predictable and untied aid, and donor processes that are less burdensome on the already stretched administrations of African countries. It must also be better harmonized with the aid of other donors and better in line with the priorities, procedures and systems of African governments. Above all, it must be given in ways that make governments answerable primarily to their own people."

Recent attention has also been given to how the U.S. supports global development. According to the Organization for Economic Cooperation and Development (OECD), the U.S. provided $16.3 billion in development assistance in 2003—roughly 0.15% of the $11 trillion gross national income that year.[5] As world-renowned economist Jeffrey Sachs recently observed, "only a small proportion of this assistance is directed at transformational development, and only a small part of that actually transforms the economies of developing countries."[6] In fact, of the $4.7 billion the U.S. gave to sub-Saharan Africa in 2003, only $118 million was targeted for "U.S. in-country operations and direct support for programs run by African governments and communities—just 18 cents for each of the nearly 650 million people" of this continent. After explaining how development aid is just as fundamental as military spending to U.S. national security,[7] Sachs offers four steps to turn what can be perceived as a "crisis in international development" into "an opportunity for the U.S. to reassert its moral and political authority as a world leader." First, he argues, our political leaders must educate the American public on the need for more developmental aid. Second, the U.S. should significantly increase its contribution to global development. Third, we should ensure that this money is spent through a number of reliable channels, including intergovernmental and nongovernmental organizations. And fourth, Congress and the White House "should overhaul the structure of U.S. developmental assistance programs to enable development to play the strategic role required for national security."

Clearly, as reflected in previous chapters of this volume, we endorse the recommendations of the Africa Commission, Sachs, and others who call for greater amounts of debt relief and direct financial assistance for Africa. Unfortunately, in our assessment, these efforts are unlikely to produce real reform in the Gulf of Guinea, even if the aid is controlled by "reliable channels" before it reaches the average African in need. The level of endemic corruption in this subregion is so completely overwhelming that it must be addressed *a priori* via both internal and external mechanisms.

Overall, in response to the general question of who bears responsibility for enacting and sustaining transformational policy initiatives, our answer is "everybody." Neither internal nor external players can succeed on their own. In other words, neither the industrialized West (through its government representatives and its multinational oil companies) nor the African state leaders can, on their own, effectively tackle the complex challenges faced by any developing nation in today's interdependent, globalized economic system. Ideally, external resources can be leveraged effectively to support genuine internally driven policy initiatives (a primary goal of the Millennium Challenge Account, described in the previous chapter). From this perspective, the U.S. can and should pursue its energy needs in the Gulf of Guinea, while gradually and consistently applying pressure for transformational policy initiatives to come from within the states themselves.

Priorities of a 21st Century Policy Framework

In considering U.S.-Africa policy, it is imperative to establish a set of priorities that addresses both the U.S.' national energy and security interests as well as the interests of the Gulf of Guinea states themselves. As discussed in previous chapters of this volume, the U.S.' immediate energy and security interests are best pursued by approaching policy from a long-term perspective. The same is true for the security and development policies of each Gulf of Guinea state. By acknowledging these critical overlapping interests and common priorities, we can develop a sound policy foundation from which to work together.

From this perspective, a strong argument can be made that general policy priorities need to be human security, economic development, and democratization – in that order. The concept of "human security" examines both the national and the global concerns of human security, and gives special attention to the security of people rather than political entities. In 1994, the United Nations Development Program (UNDP) argued in its annual *Human Development Report* that security should not focus exclusively on nations and territory, but also on individuals. The report suggests that in order to achieve the objectives of global peace and prosperity, people everywhere must be secure in their homes, their jobs, their streets, their communities and their environment. Thus, human security must be seen as a universal concern, relevant to all nations rich and poor, north and south. The report also highlights the interdependent nature of many common threats to an individual's security, including drugs, crime, pollution, corruption, unemployment and governmental oppression. In this and later documents, the UNDP has argued that the many dimensions of human security can only be tackled through a comprehensive and integrated development agenda. Given the complex challenges throughout Africa, as identified in this volume, we are convinced that any effort to transform the socio-political landscape of the Gulf of Guinea must integrate security, economic development, and democratization.

Security is an absolute prerequisite for both economic development and democratization. The U.S. and other Western countries have pursued various policies over the past 40 years that have focused to some degree on promoting democratic change and economic development. However, the concepts of democracy and macroeconomic reform mean nothing to people who lack basic physical security, health security, food security, etc.; and who are barely earning enough to get by day to day. The idea of human security as understood from the perspective of Africans surely compels us to rethink energy security and national security as narrowly defined concepts from the U.S. perspective, and this is critical for establishing sound policy foundations and realistic policy goals.

Economic development is the second priority after human security, and is arguably more important to most citizens of underdeveloped countries than is democracy. Much has been written about the interrelationship between economic development and democracy, and some of this will be addressed in subsequent chapters. For now, we submit that most African stakeholders will not truly take ownership of externally driven efforts aimed at democratization until they feel genuine progress with regards to economic development.

Democratization is the third priority upon which U.S.-Africa policy must be based. As discussed in previous chapters of this volume, there can be no long-term energy security in states that are not politically stable. Democracy, adapted to local culture and unique national factors, is what will guarantee this stability by institutionalizing peaceful mechanisms for political compromise and thereby strengthening the relationship between the society and the state.

These three general policy priorities form the *essential foundations* of U.S.-Africa policy, and must be considered as part of every major policy initiative. Without regard for the fundamentals of human security, economic development, and democratization, in that order, U.S. policy will not be realistic or relevant to the stakeholders on the ground in Africa.

Brilliant policymaking is useless without effective implementation, and in fact, it is in this stage that most "good ideas" go wrong. Somewhere in between government offices in Washington, D.C. and policymakers on the ground in Africa, there are large omissions and missed coordination points that render much of the well-intended U.S.-Africa policy rather feckless. To assist in getting this part right, we propose the following policy *implementation requirements*: interagency coordination, public-private partnerships, and multilateral cooperation.

Interagency coordination refers to the tremendous potential increase in effectiveness of U.S.-Africa policy achievable if all government actors are playing from the same sheet of music. Conversely, if U.S. agencies are attempting to make progress on political, economic, social, or security problems without thorough coordination with each other, many inefficiencies will be introduced. Unnecessary redundancy, duplication of effort, glaring needs and resource gaps, and destructive interference from working at cross-purposes are all results of poor coordination. The remaining chapters of this book will provide examples of failed interagency coordination, and will make recommendations on how to improve.

Public-private partnerships are critical for successful and sustainable solutions to economic and security problems. The private sector is the real engine of economic growth, and some security, development, and even democracy issues have strong private sector support because of clear, direct financial incentives. Other issues are more prone to be dominated solely by government attention because they are considered a "public good" or because they frankly apply most obviously to stakeholders without many financial resources. However, our analysis suggests that long-term solutions to economic and security problems must be addressed coherently by both private and public institutions working together with a common purpose.

Multilateral cooperation is an absolute requirement for any effective foreign policy agenda. There are so many international stakeholders that play a role in economic, security, and governance challenges, and that offer prospective solutions, it is foolish not to work together more closely when policy goals align. Unfortunately, for political reasons, too many practical opportunities for synergy are completely missed. Closely coordinated, mutually supporting multilateral approaches can be extremely effective in achieving a desired policy outcome. And when policy goals are at odds between significant international actors, it is essential to address these discrepancies head-on and up-front in order to avoid unnecessary confrontation, misunderstanding, and collateral damage to local third-party constituents.

Finally, with these essential foundations and implementation requirements in mind, policymakers must remain focused on the long-term considerations of U.S. policy in Africa. All levels of policy planning and implementation need to understand the linkages between the essential foundations and the desired security end states. All stakeholders need to realize the synergy achievable by effectively synchronized and thoroughly coordinated policy implementation practices. And overall, national leadership and key department and agency leadership needs to be consistent and harmonized in focusing all efforts to achieve the *desired policy outcomes* in two interdependent arenas: long-term energy security and national security.

Figure 7.1 provides a visual representation of how the elements of our integrated policy framework come together to help achieve these desired outcomes. Application of this integrated framework to the policymaking process may encourage thoughtful questions and more critical analysis so that pursuit of short-term energy security does not lead to long-term negative impacts on U.S. national security.

One method of initially evaluating the merits of this U.S.-Africa policy framework is to compare it with the policy framework of others. Recently, Senator Chuck Hagel (R-NE), Chairman of the Senate Foreign Relations Subcommittee on International Economic Policy, Export and Trade Promotion, published an article in Foreign Affairs in which he laid out seven "Principles of a Republican Foreign Policy."[8] Paraphrased, these are: 1) the U.S. must remain committed to leadership in the global economy; 2) U.S. foreign policy cannot ignore global energy security; 3) U.S. long-term security interests are connected to alliances, coalitions, and international institutions—as extensions of our power, not constraints; 4) the U.S. must continue to support democratic and economic reform; 5) increased importance of Western Hemisphere to U.S. foreign policy; 6) the U.S. must work with allies to combat poverty and spread of disease worldwide; and 7) the importance of strong and imaginative public diplomacy. Hagel's policy framework aligns well with the model presented in this chapter, and thus is worthy of consideration by this republican administration. For example, our primary focus is on energy security in the Gulf of Guinea (Hagel's second principle), incorporating economic development (principles 4 and 6), with a special focus on the role of multinational cooperation (principle 3) and public diplomacy (principle 7). Thus, a quick evaluation indicates that the model provided in this volume may indeed be a useful fit for the current policy environment.

Figure 7.1: U.S.-Africa Policy Framework

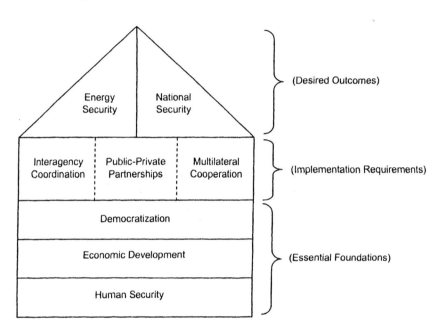

Leading Transformational U.S.-Africa Policy for the 21st Century

All three of the policy implementation requirements above are directly linked to good national leadership, both U.S. and African. Without this leadership, brilliant policy recommendations are useless. In the U.S., all too often, consistent, effective Africa policy is at the bottom of the agenda due to competing priorities, immediate crisis management, and general disinterest and ignorance by domestic constituents. Operating on two, four, and six-year election cycles tends to increase the importance of short-term policy results, often at the expense of long-term impacts or sustainability. As a plethora of government agencies and private sector actors pursue their agendas relatively independently, much potential coordination is overlooked. And unfortunately, partially due to the U.S.' position as the world's leading global power, many multilateral relationships are affected by grand strategy politics rather than by more practical policy synchronization opportunities.

In Africa (as described in chapters 2 and 3 of this volume), historically kleptocratic governments use their positions of power to serve their immediate selfish interests, and not the long term needs of their populations. Government institutions are often ineffective and corrupt, and private sector players are weak or embedded within shady government relationships. Too many African leaders have been willing to accept dubious contracts with the highest international bidders based on kickbacks and bribes, and without regard for their effectiveness in terms of development priorities. And in general, the leadership of African regional organizations has been hesitant to act firmly or speak forcefully about egregious abuses by national leaders.

However, recent events in Africa may reflect a turning of the tide. In 2003, a group of former and present African leaders convened a series of meetings in which they debated how to confront what Robert Rotberg calls "the continent's pathology of poor leadership."[9] These meetings culminated in the establishment of the African Leadership Council, the goals of which include promoting new standards of good governance and advising international organizations, individual countries, and donor agencies on how to improve leadership. Among its early initiatives, the council issued a Code of African Leadership which specifies that leaders should "offer a coherent vision of individual growth and national advancement with justice and dignity," adhere to the letter of the law (especially term limits), encourage dissent and disagreement, respect human rights and civil liberties, strengthen the rule of law, promote policies that eradicate poverty, and improve the well-being of their citizens, ensure a strong code of ethics, refuse to use their offices for personal gain, oppose corruption, and bolster personal freedoms.[10] These "commandments" reflect the leadership experiences of the council's membership, which is chaired by former President Sir Ketumile Masire of Botswana and includes former Nigerian head of state General Yakubu Gowon, Vice President Moody Awori of Kenya, former Prime Minister Hage Geingob of Namibia, and a dozen other present and former prime ministers and cabinet ministers from a range of countries. According to Rotberg, all of them "are regarded throughout Africa as men of unusual personal probity and esteem and as accomplished proponents of good governance."[11]

Based on their experiences, the council has also proposed a series of courses to train current and future political leaders how to best provide their citizens with security, commerce, social and health services, education and "a sense of belonging to a national enterprise."[12] Through seminars on constitutionalism, the rule of law, ethics, accountability, good fiscal management, coalition building, and the fundamentals of micro- and macro-economics, the council seeks to become "a vanguard for fundamental reform on the continent."[13] While the U.S. and other western countries have offered their support and assistance to this organization, it clearly represents the belief (held by many of the continent's inhabitants) that Africa's problems require African solutions.

In a similarly promising development, the African Union established a Commissioner responsible for democracy, human rights and good governance,[14] and recently launched the African Peer Review Mechanism—an initiative meant to promote good governance—as well as a Peace and Security Council, aimed at the prevention, management and resolution of conflict in the continent.[15] The African Peer Review Mechanism (APRM) is a voluntary mechanism open to all member states of the African Union.[16] To join, a country must willingly submit to (and facilitate) periodic peer reviews, and adhere to established parameters for good governance in both political and economic dimensions. On November 3, 2002, twelve countries signed an agreement of intent in Abuja to participate in the APRM: South Africa, Algeria, Angola, the Democratic Republic of Congo, Egypt, Ethiopia, Ghana, Mali, Mauritius, Mozambique, Nigeria and Rwanda. Eighteen months after a country becomes a member of the APRM process it must submit to an initial review, followed by mandatory reviews which take place between three and five years thereafter as part of a consultative, not a punitive, process.

The 15-member Peace and Security Council, headquartered in Addis Ababa, Ethiopia, is legally empowered to intervene in any African Union member country that experiences genocide, crimes against humanity, an undemocratic change of government or an uprising by rebel forces.[17] In March 2004, the AU's executive council elected the first states to serve on the Peace and Security Council.[18] Five countries, one per region—Central, East, North, Southern, and West Africa—were elected to serve for a three-year term, with 10 others to serve for a term of two years thereafter. Gabon, Ethiopia, Algeria, South Africa and Nigeria were elected for the first three-year term, while Cameroon and Congo (Central Africa), Kenya and Sudan (East Africa), Libya (North Africa), Lesotho and Mozambique (Southern Africa), and Ghana, Senegal and Togo (West Africa) were elected to serve the subsequent two-year term.[19] The council will have a standby reaction force and an early warning system, and—according to its initial chairman, Nigerian President Olusegun Obasanjo—will target rebel groups seeking regime change as well as rogue governments that undermined human rights and the rule of law.[20] Clearly, these and other much-needed regional initiatives offer hope that the U.S.' increasing investment in Africa's future will be complemented by an increased African commitment to capitalizing on this investment for the benefit of the continent's future, instead of contributing once more to the history of kleptocracy and corruption described earlier in this volume.

Good leadership, both American and African, is critical to successful long-term energy and security policy. Effective leadership can create an inclusive dialogue with all stakeholders in order to understand the true root causes of a problem set. High quality leaders help define an issue in such a manner that constituents understand the short and long-term costs and benefits of policy solutions. The leaders themselves comprehend the implications and techniques of applying various elements of national power and can orchestrate government efforts accordingly. Good leaders establish a clear vision for policy outcomes and ensure that strategic guidance and regulatory frameworks keep public agencies and private corporations synchronized in pursuit of a common good. And internationally, outstanding leaders use personal relationships, negotiations, compromise and diplomacy to ensure that major international stakeholders are working together to effectively grapple with common problems efficiently. Although very difficult to measure objectively, it is this leadership that will make or break U.S.-Africa policy efforts in the Gulf of Guinea.

Conclusion

Thus far, this volume has focused largely on current and historical issues of energy security and national security policy. Previous chapters have explored the political history of the Gulf of Guinea, drawing attention to a number of security challenges, including corruption, poor governance, criminal activity, border and infrastructure vulnerabilities, and increasing religious fundamentalism in some areas. We have also analyzed the historical experience of U.S. foreign policy relationships with the oil-rich countries in the Persian Gulf, drawing lessons that can be applied to future energy security policy initiatives in the Gulf of Guinea. For example, we have identified a variety of politicizing factors that lead individuals to become actively opposed to their regimes and to the presence of Western oil extraction firms. As the historical record shows, U.S. support for regimes that are not taking adequate care of all their citizens contributes to anger toward these regimes as well as toward the U.S. Thus, as we increase our involvement in the affairs of western and central African nations, we must be careful to avoid contributing to triggering factors that can quickly transform oppressive governments, opposition groups, or individual anger into more active violence and increased long-term instability.

We now turn our attention toward a vision of Africa many years from now. Building on the previous chapter's overview of the U.S. foreign policymaking establishment, the discussion provided in this chapter has offered a framework through which our nation can contribute to a better future for the Gulf of Guinea, a future of peace, prosperity and security. As observed earlier in this discussion, security is the fundamental cornerstone upon which all other policy framework elements must be built. Thus, the following chapter explores the topic of security in greater detail.

Notes

1. See Chapter 1 for a discussion on the merits and realities of energy conservation and alternative energy sources in the long run versus the short and medium terms.

2. *National Security Strategy of the United States,* 19-20.

3. Dan Henk, "U.S. National Interests in Sub-Saharan Africa," *Parameters* (Winter 1997-98), 95-96.

4. Commission for Africa, *Our Common Interest: Report of the Commission for Africa* (London, March 2005), 14.

5. OECD defines official development assistance as the sum of grants and sub-market rate loans made to developing countries to promote economic development and welfare. Cited in Jeffrey D. Sachs, "The Development Challenge, *Foreign Affairs* 84, no. 2 (March/April 2005), 79.

6. Jeffrey D. Sachs, "The Development Challenge," *Foreign Affairs* 84, no. 2 (March/April 2005), 80.

7. Jeffrey Sachs, "The Development Challenge," 86.

8. Chuck Hagel, "A Republican Foreign Policy," *Foreign Affairs,* July-Aug 2004.

9. Robert I. Rotberg, "Strengthening African Leadership: There is Another Way," *Foreign Affairs,* 83, no. 4, p. 16.

10. Available online at:
http://bcsia.ksg.harvard.edu/publication.cfm?ctype=event_reports&item_id=126.

11. Robert Rotberg, "Strengthening African Leadership," 18.

12. Robert Rotberg, "Strengthening African Leadership," 17.

13. Robert Rotberg, "Strengthening African Leadership," 17.

14. See the recommendations from the 2nd Implementation Committee held in Addis Ababa, 27th March 2002 where strong support was expressed for the establishment of a portfolio within the Commission of the African Union of a Commissioner responsible for democracy, human rights and good governance. Available online at:
www.telecom.net.et/~ena/archivenglish/MARCH2002/85630.2703.htm. This was subsequently approved in Durban during the inaugural summit establishing the African Union.

15. Jagdish Bhagwati and Ibrahim Gambari, "Political will, not just aid, can lift Africa out of despair," *Financial Times,* July 5, 2005.

16. Jackie Cillers, "NEPAD's Peer Review Mechanism," Institute for Security Studies, Occasional Paper No. 64 (November 2002). Available online at:
http://www.iss.co.za/Pubs/Papers/64/Paper64.html.

17. Matome Sebelebele, "Africa's Peace, Security Body," *BuaNews* (International Marketing Council of South Africa), 27 May 2004. Available online at:
http://www.southafrica.info/ess_info/sa_glance/constitution/au-peacesecurity.htm.

18. See the initial protocol and other Council documents at the Africa Union website:
http://www.africa-union.org/organs/orgThe_Peace_%20and_Security_Council.htm

19. Matome Sebelebele, "Africa's Peace, Security Body," *BuaNews* (International Marketing Council of South Africa), 27 May 2004. Available online at:
http://www.southafrica.info/ess_info/sa_glance/constitution/au-peacesecurity.htm

20. See the initial protocol and other Council documents at the Africa Union website:
http://www.africa-union.org/organs/orgThe_Peace_%20and_Security_Council.htm.

Chapter 8

Addressing the Security Challenges of the Gulf of Guinea

Security in general is an absolute baseline requirement for people to live normal lives and to pursue their goals in a stable environment. Security is essential for the steady expansion of human capital, for public confidence in a system of government, and to attract the private capital investments needed for economic growth. The Gulf of Guinea states must have the motivation and capability to provide adequate security for their citizens, businesses, and individual governments in order for democratization and economic development to take hold. And yet, as described in previous chapters of this volume, the region is currently plagued with rampant insecurity, which U.S.-Africa policy must address head on.

Thus far, a basic premise of this volume has been the need to enhance U.S. energy security—initially defined, from the U.S. perspective, to mean securing energy production platforms, energy transport facilities, and all accompanying infrastructure, in order to guarantee U.S. access to required energy resources. However, our commitment to tackling the Gulf of Guinea's challenges must also incorporate an understanding of human security, regional security, and internal security. Human security is a term that acknowledges the individual level of security. If people are insecure, then that insecurity can quickly spread throughout a state, the region, and the globe. In other words, human security is really a bottom-up approach towards national and international security.[1] The United Nations recognized this approach in a 1994 report:

> The concept of security has far too long been interpreted narrowly: as security of territory from external aggression, or as protection of national interests in foreign policy or as global security from the threat of nuclear holocaust. It has been related to nation-states more than people. . . . Forgotten were the legitimate concerns of ordinary people who sought security in their daily lives. For many of them, security symbolized protection from the threat of disease, hunger, unemployment, crime [or terrorism], social conflict, political repression

195

and environmental hazards. With the dark shadows of the Cold War receding, one can see that many conflicts are within nations rather than between nations.[2]

Human insecurities are derived from those threats that target the survival of human beings and which states cannot, will not, or are unable to deter or prevent. Such threats include disease, famine, poverty, political oppression, lack of housing, etc. The European Union's *A Human Security Doctrine for Europe* further defines human security as:

> individual freedom from basic insecurities . . . genocide, widespread or systematic torture, inhuman and degrading treatment, disappearances, slavery, and crimes against humanity and grave violations of the laws of war as defined in the Statute of the International Criminal Court (ICC).[3]

These insecurities, in one form or another, have always been present in the developing world. They cross state borders, affect the physical environment, put enormous pressure on political systems and societies—especially those within a region of weak states—and (as described in previous chapters of this volume) present vulnerabilities for criminal and terrorist organizations to exploit.[4]

Regional security refers to the mitigation of inter-state conflict and intra-state conflict with causes and/or effects that spill over the borders of one state into another. Regional security also concerns uncontrolled movement of goods and persons across porous national borders, which—as previous chapters have emphasized—is a critical problem throughout western and central Africa. And internal security refers strictly to limiting intra-state conflict and criminal violence within a particular state. While energy security is intricately linked to all other categories of security, and is thus addressed throughout this volume, it is also important to recognize that human security, regional security and internal security represent different root problems and different effects on local populations and U.S. interests; therefore, each one requires independent analysis and unique policy solutions.

This chapter begins with a review of internal security challenges and responses in the Gulf of Guinea, including those that spill over into the broader category of regional security. The discussion will also focus on assessing regional security capabilities and providing policy recommendations that may be used to deal with the major challenges faced by regional security organizations. Human security, as the broadest and most all-encompassing category, will be addressed in more detail through the discussions of economic development and democratization provided in the next two chapters of the volume.

Ultimately, U.S. interests are best served when countries are internally secure, regions are stable, and military forces throughout the world are willing and able to contribute effective capabilities to national, regional and international operations.[5] Unfortunately, to date most of the U.S.' security cooperation relationships in Africa have been focused on crisis response, rather than driven by a serious, long-term strategy. The under-resourced counter-terrorism institutions of poor African states make them vulnerable candidates for terrorist attacks, recruitment, fundraising and money laundering. Until now, state security institutions have largely been geared toward suppressing domestic threats, ethnic unrest or separatist insurgencies rather than transnational Islamist extremist threats.[6] Without dramatic improvements in African security infrastructure, training, and equipment, we are convinced that the U.S. cannot effectively achieve its long-term energy security and national security goals.

Internal Security

From the perspective of most Gulf of Guinea governments and populations, the most pressing security issues are internal and not regional. A history of authoritarian regimes, corruption, ethnic conflict and struggle over local resources like oil, gas and diamonds has created a political environment within most of these countries where citizens come to view their national institutions as "prizes" to be won and exploited, rather than as forums for national government.[7] The extensive land and sea boundaries of many African states are virtually unpatrolled, while customs and immigration services throughout much of Africa are poorly developed, trained, equipped, and paid. Organized criminal cartels take advantage of a variety of security vulnerabilities throughout the Gulf of Guinea, including porous borders, weak border controls and governmental corruption, giving bribes to poorly paid officials and security forces in return for their turning a blind eye toward an illicit trade in drugs, weapons, and humans. These same security vulnerabilities also offer opportunities for terrorist networks, as described in Chapter 4 of this volume.

Despite recent efforts, the internal security situation in West and Central Africa remains relatively grim. Robert Kaplan (2000) noted that "as small-scale violence multiplies at home and abroad, state armies will continue to shrink, being gradually replaced by a booming private security business….and by urban mafias….who may be better equipped than municipal police forces to grant physical protection to local inhabitants."[8] For the U.S., the current inability of most African security forces to adequately protect economic and political targets of terrorism is most troubling in the context of the Global War on Terrorism.[9] At the very least, oil companies working in the Gulf of Guinea would certainly appreciate a more robust security environment within which to operate. For Africans themselves, the current internal security crises directly undermine basic human security, inhibit economic development, and render democratization efforts ineffective and relatively unimportant. Nowhere is this more obvious than in the oil-rich Niger Delta.

The biggest threats to security in Nigeria are the criminal oil cartels operating in the Niger Delta who are leading the sub-region along a chaotic, lawless path not unlike Colombia. Roughly half of Nigeria's Army battalions were recently deployed internally for "policing" missions, but the military is not properly configured or trained to be police. There are many well-armed private militias in the sub-region who are actively supporting local politicians and are directly involved in violent crime and illegal oil bunkering. Reasonable estimates indicate that in the Niger Delta alone there are close to 20,000 (non-government) men under arms, and that at least 150,000 barrels of oil are being stolen every day. This criminal activity provides $3-$4 billion per year in illegal oil revenue that funds continued theft, violence and instability. In fact, members of Mujahid Dokubu-Asari's private militia (one of Nigeria's more notorious local warlords, described in chapter 4) actually triumphed over the Nigerian Army in a 2004 battle. At the time of this writing, Asari's Niger Delta People's Volunteer Force (NDPVF) continue to attack and seize western oil production facilities, and threaten to disrupt production for the foreseeable future. U.S.-Africa policy must help Nigeria tackle this difficult internal security problem head-on or it is likely to be repeated in other similarly unstable locations throughout the Gulf of Guinea.

The Role of the Military

The key security institutions within African states include the military, the gendarmes (in all Francophone countries), the national police forces, and the legal institutions that support the rule of law. Historically, African militaries have been deployed within their own borders to suppress violent insurrections and maintain political stability far more often than they have been deployed externally to fend off foreign threats. In this chapter, we broadly argue for a redefining of the roles and responsibilities of African militaries, and for an augmentation of internal policing capabilities. Professional militaries should be reorganized and trained to assist almost uniquely in the maintenance of regional security.

Throughout the world, one of the key challenges to creating a professional military is in the area of leadership selection. Unfortunately, in many Gulf of Guinea militaries, leaders are chosen based on political loyalty, ethnic or family ties, or outright bribery. An established, and often corrupt hierarchy perceives many of the best and brightest young officers as threats, and few of them are rewarded for thinking outside the box and making recommendations for systemic improvements. Real institutional change must come from the top, and if African presidents were to get serious about transparency, diversity, and professionalism within their officer corps, the states themselves would benefit tremendously.

Often the best trained and equipped, Presidential Guard units ironically reflect a lot of what is wrong with Gulf of Guinea military institutions in this regard. Chosen precisely because of their political and clan loyalties, these officers are often the most tactically competent, technically proficient, and best-educated men in the military. However, their functional missions and extreme political loyalties may actually prohibit the democratic process and the associated potential leadership transition. In other words, until even the most proficient military units are truly professionalized, their immediate tactical abilities with respect to establishing internal security are counterproductive to much larger systemic and institutional problems. African militaries must be loyal first to the state as an apolitical institution, and not to any particular individual or political group. This is a huge challenge given the current political conditions in Cameroon, Chad, Equatorial Guinea, Gabon, Congo, and Angola in particular, (and clearly elsewhere in Africa outside the Gulf of Guinea). As explained later in this chapter, this absence of military professionalism and political neutrality must be addressed directly by U.S.-Africa policymakers, and should be one of the highest priorities for all specific military engagement mechanisms.

However, it is our belief that the military should not be the dominant security provider in African states, and that there is in fact a need for comprehensive security sector reform, of which the armed forces are only a small part. Professional African militaries are essential for addressing regional security issues, but the most important component for human, internal, and energy security is an effective body of law enforced by competent civilian police, a fair and impartial judiciary, and an equitable penal system. Effective police forces must be established to enable internal security, which, in conjunction with economic development and democratization, will lead to improved human security. Both approaches—military and law enforcement—are absolutely necessary if the U.S. wants to guarantee its long-term energy security.

The Role of Law Enforcement

Professional and capable internal security forces are the most important component for providing fundamental security and stability in Gulf of Guinea states. However, current standing armies are not designed or trained to fill this critical role effectively, and most national police forces are hopelessly corrupt and ineffective. For example, the Centre for Law Enforcement Education in Nigeria (CLEEN, an NGO) estimates that policemen at checkpoints resort to shooting in one of twenty instances where motorists refuse to pay bribes demanded.[10] The Nigerian national police garner very little trust from the population, partially because many police see their job as a moneymaking opportunity and not as a security provision platform for society. (Most junior police make about $68 per month, and rationalize improprieties as additional "earned income".) In January 2005 the Inspector General (IG) of the national police force, Tafa Balogun, quit his post following corruption allegations and was subsequently brought to court to face counts of stealing public funds worth more than $98 million. Police reforms in Nigeria are underway under the new IG, Sunday Ehindero, who changed the police motto from "Operation Fire for Fire" to "Serving with Integrity and Honor" and is putting considerable effort into instilling the principles of "democratic policing" and a zero-tolerance policy on corruption—but this will take considerable time. In the interim, many western oil companies have been driven by the political violence in the Niger Delta region to hire private security forces and to pay local police forces supplemental income for extra and better help. However, it would clearly be more desirable in the long run (and probably less expensive) if the Nigerian government could provide adequate public security.[11]

Nigeria is not the only Gulf of Guinea state that needs dramatic internal security reform—in fact, they all do. Across the board there are real problems with lack of capacity in local coast guard and law enforcement institutions. In Equatorial Guinea, for example, U.S. energy companies do not trust ill-disciplined local forces and are understandably concerned about the lack of a credible response to any breakdown of law and order on a large scale, actions by a potentially aggressive neighbor, or a terrorist attack.[12] With huge energy revenue streams at stake, and no armed security out on oil platforms or tankers,[13] U.S. oil companies are very vulnerable to attack. Regarding the Chad-Cameroon pipeline, there is no comprehensive, coordinated government security provision to protect this important national revenue stream—which is perhaps indicative of underlying regional energy security problems. Instead, the energy conglomerate spends approximately $5-10 million a year on private pipeline and facility security provided by COTCO (a private company with about 400 unarmed guards[14]) and there is almost no coordination between COTCO and state security forces, or even between the gendarmes and police themselves in different provinces within Cameroon. Clearly, both private African citizens and U.S. energy companies would benefit from the construction of a genuine public security capacity, built up professionally and for the long term.

Effective policing is critical to establishing and maintaining internal security, but there is often inadequate capacity of national police forces to perform effectively. Ineffective policing creates an environment where militaries are frequently used to suppress instability, often with blatant human rights violations. Consequently, many civilians resort to arming themselves for their own security (especially in ethnic minority sub-groups) because they do not perceive that they are protected by state security organizations. This mentality, combined with the proliferation and availability of small arms, creates real problems of burgeoning instability in Gulf of Guinea states.

Improved law enforcement consists of much more than just training police forces. In fact there are numerous institutional mechanisms and capabilities that must be appropriately addressed in order to produce real increased internal security in an unstable country. For example, the relatively successful, (and perhaps regionally appropriate), UK plan for establishment of law and order in Sierra Leone used the following interim criteria:[15]

1) Body of applicable law agreed
2) Effective judiciary established
3) Detention rules agreed
4) Detention review procedure in place
5) Appeal procedure in place
6) Forces equipped and trained for law enforcement in place
7) Detention facility established
8) International police force established
9) Joint policing procedures in place
10) Local police academy opened
11) Local police force established
12) Handover of law and order to police force

Although Sierra Leone is an extreme case, these planning criteria demonstrate the complexity of tasks needed to truly change a law enforcement system and the requirement for a diverse collection of training, expertise, and resources. Internal security is intrinsically linked to economic development, democracy, and long-term energy security, and should be planned for and committed to accordingly.

There are many critical issues regarding the priorities and methods of law enforcement reform, (varying tremendously from country to country), and this section will only touch on a few of them very briefly and generally. U.S.-Africa policymakers need to delve deeper into this topic and employ subject matter experts to assist in the formulation of a broad and coherent policy strategy. Our analysis indicates that the U.S. must do much more in terms of training and supporting professional national police forces, and that this is actually even more important to long-term stability and development—and by extension, energy security—than is military engagement.

Some of the internal insecurity and law enforcement problems in the Gulf of Guinea stem from the institutional challenges of endemic corruption, poor institutional design, and lack of training and resources. Some of the programs discussed below, which are intended to influence the professionalism and institutional culture of the armed forces, may be analogously applied to law enforcement institutions as well. In particular, continued professional and educational exchanges and the development of objective oversight institutions may be useful for targeting corruption. (Dealing with endemic, institutionalized corruption will be addressed in more detail in subsequent chapters.)

Our analysis suggests that the decentralization of national police forces is directly linked to democratization and devolution of central power in "federal" systems like Nigeria, and would pay enormous dividends in terms of local policing effectiveness, trust, and credibility. Every Gulf of Guinea state has a national police force, and all of them are tightly and centrally controlled from the top.

This may be effective in small countries like Equatorial Guinea and São Tomé and Príncipe, but in larger more diverse ones like ones like Nigeria, Cameroon, Congo, and Angola, it is not. In semi-authoritarian regimes like Cameroon, Gabon, Congo, and Angola, the national police simply become another instrument of single political party control and "big man" domination. Sure, police forces need to be standardized to some extent at the national level, but daily coordination, decision-making, and execution need to be more in touch with the local realities of diverse and far flung provinces or states.

The Role of Private Security Firms

Throughout the oil-rich countries of West and Central Africa, the security gap created by insufficient military and police forces is being filled by the private sector. Today, a huge transnational industry provides a variety of guarding, escort, intelligence, training and other services to energy companies operating in the Gulf of Guinea.[16] Private security firms often recruit individuals with former military or police experience, who come to be seen in some communities as being more professional and trustworthy than national security forces. In some cases, governments have even contracted with these private security firms, recognizing that the specialized capacities they offer (often including advanced equipment and training) far exceed what their own forces can provide. Market mechanisms help good/reputable security firms gain these contracts, which in turn contributes to the establishment and oversight of professional security norms and standards in the private security industry. For example, private security agents working for Shell are trained in human rights requirements and are clearly briefed on restrictions on the use of violence.

There are, however, several drawbacks and risks involved with private security firms. For example, these firms generally exist not for the pursuit of a public good but for private benefit, and thus have no real stake in the big picture of Africa's long-term development. Security is a state function, and private security should only be used to fill gaps temporarily. These firms are often expensive, and their members can be difficult to control, particularly because there is no real accountability to the citizens of the communities in which they operate. Further, when the citizens of a country view private sector security firms as more competent than national forces, this can lead to an erosion in the government's commitment to developing their own public law enforcement capabilities.

Despite these and other shortcomings, the security challenges in the Gulf of Guinea are such that it is clearly impossible to get rid of private security firms in the foreseeable future. Thus, the countries of the region must try and mitigate associated risks as best they can. Energy companies' long-term interests in the Gulf may encourage these private firms to form strong, mutually-beneficial partnerships with government law enforcement agencies. This potential for public-private cooperation can be realized most effectively by ensuring that security contracts are written so that private firms are linked to larger security goals—otherwise, their immediate security tasks/procedures may undermine the broader national security efforts. In essence, there must be a clear distinction between private and public security roles and responsibilities.

Private security firms can be a valuable addition to the security picture when properly constrained and focused. Specific examples include providing physical security, where they can be very supportive of maritime and port security goals. In a post-conflict society, demobilized soldiers are easy recruits for private security needs (although doing so requires a solid regulatory framework within which private security firms can operate so as to mitigate associated risks), and some private firms have also benefited from recruiting/paying locals to provide surveillance to enhance environmental security. In Nigeria, a division of labor between the public and private sector is attempting to improve the security situation in the Delta region. Here, the Army and Navy (complemented by national and mobile police forces) secures most critical energy infrastructure elements, and official sub-regional paramilitaries guard important facilities onshore, while international private security firms are hired by oil majors to secure offshore platforms. Locals are hired for surveillance of long stretches of pipeline, and bonuses are awarded for incident-free sectors.

Overall, private security firms have an important presence throughout the Gulf of Guinea, and should thus be utilized appropriately. However, our analysis also indicates that this region does not need more private security companies—rather, it is clearly in these countries' interests to properly train and equip their national security forces instead. To do so will require a lasting commitment from partner nations like the U.S.

The Role of Partner Nations

Although U.S. political and economic involvement in certain parts of Africa was certainly significant during the Cold War, the two countries with the greatest historical commitment to addressing Africa's internal security challenges are France and the U.K. The U.S. is clearly a newcomer to Africa when compared to these two former colonial powers, both of which have exerted significant military influence in the region since at least the 19th century. Today, however, all three nations play an important role in African security affairs.

Compared to any other external military, France has by far the most dominant permanent presence in Africa. On the continent itself, there are permanent French garrisons in Senegal, Côte d'Ivoire, Gabon, and Djibouti, and ongoing operational missions in Côte d'Ivoire, Chad, and the Central African Republic. In most cases, there are between 1,000 and 3,000 French troops in each country, while in Côte d'Ivoire there are over 6,000 at the time of this writing. There are also fifteen military training schools in Africa sponsored by France and open to students from all over the region (see Table 8.1). Each French military school offers a variety of courses relating to its specific subject area, and is staffed by French and host nation military officials.

Table 8.1: French military training schools in Africa as of 2005.

Type of School	Location
Center for Judicial Police	Porto-Novo, Benin
Center for Post-Conflict De-mining and Cleanup	Ouidah, Benin
Center for Naval Instruction	Attécoubé, Côte d'Ivoire
Military Staff College	Koulikoro, Mali
School of Military Administration	Koulikoro, Mali
Peacekeeping School	Koulikoro, Mali*
Infantry School	Senegal
Officer Formation School	Senegal
Center for Mobile Gendarmes	Ouakam, Senegal
School of Military Health Service	Lomé, Togo
Military Technical Training School	Ouagadougou, Burkina Faso
Aviation Training Center	Garoua, Cameroon
Center for Maintaining Law and Order (Gendarmes)	Awae, Cameroon
Military Staff College	Libreville, Gabon
School of Military Health Service	Niamey, Niger

* Expected to move to Bamako, Mali in 2006

In addition to these French-sponsored schools, there are French advisors permanently placed in many other national military schools across Francophone Africa. The French government also provides financial support and a resident officer to the Kofi Annan International Peacekeeping Training Center (KAIPTC) to facilitate its International Peace Support Operations Course (IPSO).[17] And finally, there is a French military engagement program, RE-CAMP, (Reinforcing the Capacity to Maintain the Peace in Africa), that is designed especially to train and equip African militaries for peacekeeping missions. All of this makes France a very important partner for the U.S., especially at the intersection of national security and energy security policy in the Gulf of Guinea.

The U.K. is considerably less militarily involved in Africa than France, and the only current major U.K. troop commitment is in Sierra Leone.[18] However, this mission provides an excellent example to U.S.-Africa policymakers of a focused, sustained, and relatively successful post-conflict development approach. Unlike the U.S. "band-aid" slapped on Liberia's crises, the U.K. has pledged real commitment to security sector reform in Sierra Leone. Officially the mission was expected to last about ten years, but unofficially, those directly involved expect it to go on for much longer—until the job is done. The intensive and robust U.K. approach will likely help Sierra Leone weather the continued sub-regional instability spilling over from Guinea and Côte d'Ivoire, whereas Liberia may not be so fortunate.

Comprehensive security sector reform begins with a realistic threat reassessment within each country, and this should be fairly supported by external stakeholders. Many African militaries are products of the colonial period, designed either in the model of their former colonial masters, or forged by years of armed struggle against them. The colonial period is over, and for the most part, national independence struggles are a thing of the past. It is time to reevaluate the African military paradigm, and then to restructure and reprioritize accordingly. Strong external influences can be helpful or harmful in security sector reform. What can be truly detrimental are security policy recommendations that promote primarily the interests of the external players themselves. Whether designed to create markets for military equipment, to prop up corrupt but cooperative leadership, or to strictly secure raw materials for export, some external recommendations can be counterproductive to real long-term security. What is needed is assistance with an honest appraisal of security requirements from the perspective of the host nation, and professional recommendations on how to achieve corresponding goals. The policy framework outlined in Chapter 7 may be helpful for informing security sector reform necessities, processes, and implications.

Improving the U.S. Response to Africa's Internal Security Challenges

From the analysis provided here, it is clear that partner countries like the U.S. can have the most impact on Africa's security challenges in two areas: professionalizing local military forces and enhancing law enforcement capabilities.

Professionalizing Africa's Militaries

In most African states, subjectively controlled[19] militaries are more often used to quell internal violence and crush internal opposition than to carry out national defense against an external threat. This is not the basis for sound civil-military relations and indicates a lack of sound African institutions needed to address the rule of law. Samuel Huntington's classic *The Soldier and the State* highlights the importance of maximizing professionalism of a military, creating a politically sterile or neutral officer corps, and making the military a tool of the state as a whole, not of any particular subset of the population. This was great advice in 1957, and it was great advice at its 15th printing in 2000. This argument logically points to two major security needs the U.S. should address directly: 1) the need for fundamental reform of the role and mindset of African militaries; and 2) the need for capable domestic police forces to provide internal security.

Competent, professional, and well-run armed forces under democratic civilian leadership can play an important role in addressing the threats of civil war and large-scale humanitarian crises, as well as the needs of counterinsurgency and anti-terrorism campaigns.[20] As described in chapter 6, the International Military Education and Training (IMET) program (created in 1976) is a financing arrangement through which the U.S. pays for the professional training and education of foreign military students and officers, as well as a fairly limited number of civilian support personnel. One of the more subtle, but powerful advantages of IMET is that participants are immersed in the professional U.S. military culture and establish close personal relationships that may prove to be useful professional contacts in the future. While IMET training takes place primarily within the continental U.S., Joint Combined Exchange Training (JCET) initiatives involve the deployment of Special Operations Forces to train military units in other countries. Both programs foster collegial international relations and enhance the military capabilities of African nations allied with the U.S. However, this analysis suggests the need to look differently at military engagement as a tool for shaping a country's future, not a reward for results or simply a crisis response. Thus, changes in the scope and objectives of the IMET and JCET programs are warranted.

A truly professional military will not commit atrocities, but will instead institutionalize constraints on power under democratic civilian leadership. Correspondingly, IMET programs need to refocus away from simply transferring tactical and technical expertise, instead centering on military professionalism and democracy-support programs. Fundamental reform of African militaries starts with training the officer and NCO leadership, as well as the ministries of defense, on the proper role of the military in a civil society. Selfless core values of public service and a sense of true professionalism need to be engendered over the long term, and the U.S. should allocate significant resources to building solid civil-military relationships to prevent future conflicts and to guarantee cooperation in tough times. Skeptics will argue that the last thing Africa needs is more military training and funding, and that only "well-behaved" militaries should be rewarded with U.S. support through IMET and other programs. However, this misses the critical point that the military can be a powerful agent of change in a society, especially where other institutions tend to be grossly underdeveloped. The very professional U.S. military has historically played a leading role in racial and gender integration, and currently serves as one of the great social equalizers in American society.

True institutional character change must come from within, but external providers certainly can help it along tremendously in terms of resources and expertise. IMET programs must be sustained with partner nations over the long run, so that continuity and consistency can have the desired effect. (Since it is usually treated as a reward, and not a shaping mechanism, IMET programs bounce all over the world to reflect political favor with the latest set of "allies".) The U.S. has not sustained IMET in Africa anywhere except maybe Botswana and Senegal, and they are significantly more stable and democratic than other comparable nations. Training needs to be sustained long enough, and for a large enough quantity of people, so that it achieves a "critical mass"—enough to really make an impact (numbers of people, rising to all levels). Individuals tossed back into a "sea of corruption" will make no impact on their respective institutions.

There are many problems with military "professionalization" programs, one of which is that the countries that need them most probably don't want them. Entrenched leadership at the highest levels may be threatened by these ideas, and others, who are not far-sighted, may not find such training useful when compared to more immediately operational tactical training. Sometimes these programs are considered "soft," and their effectiveness may not be objectively measurable in the short term, thereby discouraging both potential external partners and African participants who must make tough resource allocation decisions. However, it is highly likely that in the long run, this somewhat intangible component of military professionalism is one of the most critical to achieving real progress in terms of security at all levels.

The easiest way for the U.S. to really make an impact in this arena is if select African presidents were to endorse the notion that a professional military is indeed a necessary component of a healthy civil-military relationship and critical for sustainable security. At a president's request, the U.S. could engage directly with defense restructuring initiatives, training in the professional military ethic, and establishment of military schools where both technical competencies and philosophical paradigms could be inculcated. Some African governments might even be willing to pay for this training through the U.S. military or a respectable associated civilian contractor, like MPRI. This is a potentially financially viable option for small, newly oil-rich countries like Equatorial Guinea and São Tome and Principe.

In addition to potential support from an enlightened president, there are many senior Gulf of Guinea officers still on active duty who have personally benefited from IMET programs in the past. A lot of them still hold the U.S. military in high esteem, and would be very happy to reengage more directly and on a grander scale, for the benefit of their beloved, but broken institutions. The real challenge arises when neither presidents nor senior military officers are particularly interested in professionalization programs, or are even outright opposed to them. Even in this worst-case scenario, there are still good options for U.S.-Africa policy to pursue the same intentions, albeit less directly.

First, official U.S. engagement with African militaries of questionable background must be allowed by domestic U.S. lawmakers. If well-intended legislators (or their staffers) prohibit military engagement with unprofessional African militaries on the grounds of historic human rights violations or inadherence to democratic principles, this self-defeating logic limits U.S. options inappropriately. This would be like a hospital refusing the sickest patients any treatment until they had cured themselves to a more reasonable level. For example, IMET is a wonderful tool for fundamentally altering the outlook, philosophy, and competencies of foreign militaries. It is an essential shaping component of U.S.-Africa engagement, and should not be treated as simply a reward for good behavior. Rather, IMET programs should be dramatically stepped up and military exchanges with Gulf of Guinea states should be increased across the board.

In addition to an expansion of IMET efforts, there are a number of other options that can be used to influence reluctant states to improve the professionalism of their militaries. The Office of Defense Cooperation (ODC) within each country has authority over a number of programs that can be used directly or indirectly to do just this. (See Chapter 6 of this volume for a description of these programs.) The bottom line is that U.S. policymakers must recognize the important contribution of these programs—not just to their stated technical assistance goals—but also to their potential for impacting institutional culture. For their part, the U.S. military actors who actually engage directly with their African counterparts must consciously incorporate specific components of the professional military ethic into all their training and activities.

For a good illustration of security sector reform planning from the ground up, the U.S. would do well to observe the U.K.'s efforts in Sierra Leone, as mentioned previously. This is a great example of a long-term commitment to professionalizing a completely broken institution, backed up with financial resources, trainers, and an acknowledgement of the long time required to do so.

In addition to improving the professionalism of African militaries, demilitarization should be another clear component of U.S.-Africa policy. In some Gulf of Guinea countries, Angola and Chad for example, demilitarization has become an obvious and stated national goal. After decades of civil war and internal instability, the governments of Chad and Angola recognize that their enormous militaries must be downsized and restructured. Funding, particularly from growing oil revenues, should be reallocated to more constructive national development projects, and national threats should be reassessed. With borders on unstable regions like Sudan (Darfur in particular) and the DRC, the new focus should probably be on containment of regional instability and peacekeeping operations.

In fact, most Gulf of Guinea states would benefit from a reassessment of external security threats and corresponding national military roles. Assuming that armies should generally not be deployed to suppress internal dissent, significant military restructuring and funding reallocation should be possible across the board. More professional militaries are better suited for the regional cooperation and interoperability necessary to deal with the problems of regional insecurity. Demobilization, disarmament, and reintegration (DDR) programs are an essential component for both rebel militias and bloated state militaries. If coupled with effective economic development and governance programs, DDR can contribute to security at all levels. The U.S. can and should apply significant resources to assist Gulf of Guinea states accordingly.

Another critical element of military professionalism is the need for the establishment of effective oversight institutions, in particular for command and finance. The egregious levels of corruption of senior military commanders in many Gulf of Guinea states are truly staggering. Leaders with access to professional revenue streams usually use their positions for blatant personal gain, with clear detrimental effects on the equipment, soldiers, and training of their subordinate units. Not only do a majority of witnesses turn a blind eye, but many are openly awaiting their turn at the trough. Nowhere is institutionalized corruption more endemic than in Central Africa, and its pervasiveness and damaging effects cannot be overstated. Therefore, specific institutions with clear mandates to root out embezzlement and outright theft must be established in conjunction with training mechanisms designed to implement professional military ethics.

One way for the U.S. to have a significant impact on professional military ethics and the requisite supporting institutions is to support the establishment or improvement of institutionalized training centers and courses in the Gulf of Guinea, and in Africa in general. This is especially true for military academies and staff colleges. By contributing significant resources, the U.S. can insist on having a say in the content, direction, and environment that will influence future generations of military officers and leaders in the region.

There are several approaches that should be considered, and probably advanced simultaneously. Bilateral engagement with individual states is an excellent way to bolster or create national military academies for specific regional partners. For example, with a mature military player like Nigeria, military academy exchange programs may allow African students or American faculty to assist the flow of professional military ideas and methods into Nigeria. With smaller states like Equatorial Guinea or STP, the U.S. could actually be instrumental in helping establish a military academy from the ground up, perhaps along the modified West Point model used in Afghanistan.

Another way to have a similar impact is to reinforce existing French and African staff colleges and training programs by incorporating U.S. military faculty and specifically focused education components. France is currently the only external power to wield significant military influence in the Gulf of Guinea region. Yet despite the historically strong French-African relationships in Central Africa, our recent experience indicates that most Francophone countries are eager to reach out to the U.S. military for professional training and exchanges. For example, Cameroon is establishing a War College, with French assistance, that will target lieutenant colonels from all services of the armed forces, and will be open to officers from around the sub-region. The U.S. could be an important partner in this process, and may therefore be able to exert critical influence over senior military leaders and their professional management techniques. This could also be replicated in Gabon if the U.S. wanted to reinforce the French-sponsored Staff College in Libreville. Of course, U.S.-French cooperation is an important prerequisite for this approach to be effective, and will be discussed in more detail in Chapter 11.

Improving Law Enforcement Capabilities

Like professional militaries, professional police forces must also be composed of diverse and competent individuals who are chosen on merit, trained rigorously, and properly equipped. The current low level of U.S. engagement in this arena in the Gulf of Guinea is appalling. For example, Nigeria is one of Africa's biggest narcotics transit points, (especially for drugs destined for Europe and the U.S.), and has tremendous law enforcement challenges and problems, (as discussed earlier). Yet the U.S. International Narcotics and Law Enforcement Office is only authorized a single position in the U.S. Embassy in Nigeria, and even that was not filled at the time of this writing. Nigeria has approximately 300,000 police (compared to about 80,000 military) and it is extremely important for policymakers to increase U.S. training and influence in this critical realm.

Regarding the important question of how to approach improved law enforcement training in Gulf of Guinea states, it is useful to examine the U.S.-sponsored International Law Enforcement Academy (ILEA) in Gaborone, Botswana as a role model.[21] ILEA Gaborone is run by a conglomerate of U.S. law enforcement agencies that work together to support interagency policy goals.[22] Spearheaded by the Department of Homeland Security's Federal Law Enforcement Training Center (FLETC), the integrated headquarters includes representatives from the Departments of Treasury, Justice, State, and other federal agencies, but interestingly, there is almost no Department of Defense involvement at all.[23] To date, ILEA has implemented training programs with eleven SADC countries and five IGAD countries, and is considering expanding to include several ECOWAS states as well. ILEA is legally restricted from using funds to train military units, so programs focus on national police forces and gendarmes that do not fall under the Ministry of Defense. (Unfortunately, almost all gendarmes in the Gulf of Guinea fall underneath the direction of Ministries of Defense.) Training programs include courses and conferences on topics such as the following: combating transnational terrorism; criminal investigations; international banking and money laundering; personnel and facility security; small arms trafficking; trafficking in persons; and others. ILEA also hosts law enforcement executive development programs aimed at mid-level security managers.

Because of its immediate relevancy to internal security issues in the Gulf of Guinea, ILEA should be dramatically expanded to include police officers from all constituent states, and should also be allowed to incorporate all gendarmes, regardless of ministerial affiliation. ILEA should also actively seek partnerships with some of the existing regional gendarmes training centers sponsored by France, (i.e. in Senegal and Cameroon), to help promote professional law enforcement ethics in key leaders. Again, there are great potential benefits to working more closely with France in pursuit of U.S. energy and security interests in the region. And finally, because of the common interests in security and counter-terrorism, ILEA and the Department of Defense should work more closely together in terms of Gulf of Guinea policy strategy and implementation. (More on the potential synergy and necessary policy coordination and multilateral cooperation required of these ideas in Chapter 11.)

One of the biggest constraints to policy implementation is always budgetary—i.e. who is going to pay for these good ideas? Given the overlapping constituencies that will benefit from improved African law enforcement institutions, there are some creative ways to approach this matter. Oil companies used to normally just pay ransoms when their executives were kidnapped or their oilrigs were taken over, but now they usually pay up front for better security, as the former got too common and expensive. Corporations regularly pay top dollar for private security firms or will arrange for direct payments to national police forces to ensure protection of human and physical capital assets. This is indicative of a broken system, and clearly most African entrepreneurs and citizens cannot afford such luxuries. Besides direct U.S. training and funding for professional, capable national police forces, perhaps business-government partnerships could be used to leverage resources and common interests. (More on this in Chapter 11.) Oil companies are invested for the long haul and certainly need security to guarantee stable profit margins. Since U.S. and host governments also value domestic security, some portion of the costs could be subsidized through the provision of advisors, training teams, police academies, equipment, or other resources. (There will be no shortage of qualified U.S. police training contractors after the work in Iraq is complete.)

The endemic insecurity within Gulf of Guinea states impedes domestic economic and political development and leads to the type of long-term instability directly contrary to U.S. energy and national security interests. Increased sensory and monitoring technology on energy extraction platforms, along with harsher penalties for offenders caught in acts of destruction, are well-intended responses to the situation, but they are destined to prove inadequate in the long run. An integrated approach that guarantees stakeholders effective participation in the benefits derived from an oil industry adequately protected by indigenous security forces is needed. Such an approach will require both a professional military force and competent civil law enforcement agencies. However, for the most pressing domestic security concerns, law enforcement capabilities are much more critically needed than military ones. Efficient, non-corrupt, objective and competent police forces should be an absolute priority for U.S. energy and security policy.

In sum, the internal security challenges faced by states in the Gulf of Guinea are many and complex. For many countries, these challenges are beyond the scope of their national forces—indeed, their militaries are often untrained, rampantly corrupt, and ineffective at providing security, while their navies exist in name alone, completely incapable of securing offshore energy production. France and the U.K. have contributed historically to helping their former colonies address these challenges, but there is still much that must be done. As the U.S. pursuit of its energy security goals leads to increasing involvement in this region, there are important steps we should take to improve the security environment. However, simply securing oil production and transport facilities is not enough. External partners (both countries and private firms) could improve the technological capacity of host nations for security (including maritime security) by providing training, equipment and overall engagement in addressing local development challenges. Local regional military cooperation and security agreements between energy producing states (not with extra-regional players) can also be very effective. Indeed, despite the preponderance of internal security challenges, many of the issues relating to energy security are clearly regional in nature. Thus, the next section of this chapter will discuss regional stakeholders and their approaches to dealing with security accordingly.

Regional Security

As described in Chapter 3, conflicts in West and Central Africa can encompass a cross-national dimension, as civil strife in one country tends to spill over into neighboring states. Porous borders throughout the region facilitate the trafficking of weapons and people, resulting in two different kinds of problems. First, the flow of weapons and people into a conflict region can prolong and intensify the fighting. Second, the flow of people away from a conflict region—in the form of refugees fleeing the fighting, as well as rebels seeking a safe haven from government security forces—creates a number of security challenges for neighboring countries, who would just as soon not have anything to do with the conflict. Further, the free flow of weapons out of a conflict region (as often happens when the violence has subsided) helps to fuel conflicts elsewhere.

Fortunately for the Gulf of Guinea states, however, they do not suffer from the same kind of regional insecurity issues as Sierra Leone, Liberia, Guinea, and Côte d'Ivoire in West Africa; the DRC, Rwanda, and Burundi in Central Africa; or Ethiopia, Eritrea, Sudan, Uganda, and Somalia in the Horn of Africa. The major regional insecurity issues for the Gulf of Guinea include the unresolved Bakassi peninsula dispute between Nigeria and Cameroon;[24] some cross-border banditry by armed criminal groups from Chad and the Central African Republic; and a few incompletely resolved maritime territorial disputes such as that between Gabon and Equatorial Guinea. These issues are not related to civil wars and ethnic strife to the extent that they are in other parts of West and Central Africa and the Horn of Africa, however, they are directly related to energy security concerns. The unresolved Bakassi Penninsula issue and other smaller maritime territorial disputes are significant because they involve competing claims to areas rich in energy resources; and the issue of cross-border bandits may potentially threaten the security of the Chad-Cameroon oil pipeline.

Maritime security is the most pressing regional security issue for the Gulf of Guinea states from the perspective of U.S.-Africa policymakers, as indicated by the enormous recent number of conferences, articles, political discussions, and potential policy initiatives, etc. Yet securing offshore oil facilities, maritime transport, and supporting coastal infrastructure is only a band-aid and not a solution.[25] This volume argues that the guarantee of real long-term energy security requires much more than this, but there are some important mutual benefits of improved maritime security in the Gulf of Guinea: enhanced control over strategic coastal resources (oil and gas) and fisheries would provide better protection from both domestic and foreign opportunists; improved surveillance and interdiction capacity could deter terrorists and illegal activities such as arms smuggling and drug trafficking; and increased regional cooperation and information sharing may deter anti-democratic elements, enhance environmental protection, and increase overall regional stability.

Principal Contributors to Regional Security in Africa

The key players in developing African regional security mechanisms are the United Nations, the African Union, sub-regional organizations, and a variety of major external partners. We will examine each of these briefly in turn as part of the broader African security context before focusing on the Gulf of Guinea states specifically.

The United Nations Department of Peace Keeping Operations (UNDPKO) has been very busy in Africa, where approximately 80% of its global peacekeepers are posted. As Table 8.2 illustrates, there are eight ongoing peacekeeping operations in Africa, as of June 2005.[26]

Since the UN has no permanent standing military, ready brigade, or quick reaction force, it relies on voluntary troop donations from member states. Traditionally, the major troop-contributing countries are Bangladesh, Pakistan, Nigeria, India, Ethiopia, Ghana, Nepal, South Africa, Uruguay, Jordan, Morocco, and Senegal. These contributions are driven both by national security interests and, to be brutally honest, by purely economic incentives. The UN pays all military observers a fixed salary of approximately $4,000 per month, regardless of country of origin. The UN pays troop-contributing countries about $1,000 per month for each peacekeeping soldier; but each government then decides how much to actually pay their soldiers. Relatively speaking, this is a lot of money for the countries listed above, and it does not all go to the soldiers themselves. For example, a Ghanaian private normally gets paid about $135 per month, and about $600 per month during peacekeeping operations. The Ghanaian government keeps the additional $400 per month difference, or about 40%.

Table 8.2: UN Peacekeeping Operations in Africa

Name	Location	Date Established	Military Strength	Annual Budget ($US millions)
MINURSO	Western Sahara	Apr 1991	226	44
UNAMSIL	Sierra Leone	Oct 1999	3,371	292
MONUC	Dem. Rep. Congo	Nov 1999	15,901	958
UNMEE	Ethiopia & Eritrea	Jul 2000	3,329	205
UNMIL	Liberia	Sep 2003	14,820	822
UNOCI	Côte d'Ivoire	Apr 2004	6,038	378
ONUB	Burundi	Jun 2004	5,363	330
UNMIS	Sudan	Mar 2005	10,000*	280
		Totals	**59,048**	**$3.3 billion**

Note: These figures represent only military peacekeepers and do not include the approximately 13,000 civilian police and other UN, international, and local civilian employees working with peacekeeping missions in Africa.
* Indicates the authorized strength, although the actual strength at time of writing was only 432.

And although military observers are paid on a higher, separate scale, directly by the UN, some countries require them to pay a fair portion of that salary back into government coffers. Clearly, this is quite a moneymaking venture for poor militaries from underdeveloped countries.

Despite their recent proliferation in Africa, there are many who doubt the efficacy of UN peacekeeping operations after the debacles in Rwanda and Sierra Leone, and very questionable effectiveness in Liberia and the Democratic Republic of the Congo. There are many challenges facing the UN's Department of Peacekeeping Operations (UNDPKO), and a few of them are worth mentioning here. To categorize broadly, the UNDPKO's major challenges are in resources, planning, training, and information.[27]

Without a well-trained, deployable military capability of its own, the UN faces an enormous challenge of mobilizing necessary resources when confronting a regional conflict. In addition to the problem of soliciting troop contributions from member states, the UN must also request logistical support, transportation, specialized capabilities, and often, additional funds. Even when willing member states are forthcoming with contributions, it is often difficult to get the right type and number of units and equipment to match the specific mission needs. This problem is exacerbated by the problem of timely generation and deployment of donated headquarters and troops, and amplified in a crisis because there exists no strategic reserve capability. It is often even more problematical to ask for and receive reinforcements when the mission is not going well.

Because of the highly political nature of Security Council resolutions, and the subsequent blurring of the strategic, operational, and tactical levels of peace support operations, the UNDPKO does not take a very coherent, mission-focused approach to planning. Often, the actual mission commander has not yet even been identified during initial planning, and therefore cannot play an active role in preparing for the mission. National training varies tremendously from country to country, and historically there has been no standardized pre-deployment training for volunteered units. Though UNDPKO is gradually changing this by instituting pre-deployment training for headquarters elements, there are still no standard operating procedures (SOPs) for units assigned to the UN.

Some of the major information challenges are inter-mission cooperation and information management and intelligence. Because of the diverse composition of UN peacekeeping forces, there is often little cohesion between different national headquarters within the same mission.[28] There are also real coordination and cooperation problems between UN agencies working in the same region, and there are only weak mechanisms to pass on "lessons learned" to subsequent missions. In fact, the now-famous Brahimi Report specifically pointed out the lack of an effective institutional capacity to learn from previous mistakes. The UN has no organic intelligence collection or analysis assets at all, and there are many political obstacles towards overcoming this shortfall. Many countries do not want to share their national intelligence capabilities with the UN, for security reasons, and many do not trust the UN to develop assets of its own. Finally, the UN has a difficult time managing expectations for many of its missions because local stakeholders expect far too much from the deployment of very limited forces.

As the Brahimi report astutely confirmed, "No amount of good intentions can substitute for the fundamental ability to project credible force." Given the overwhelming challenges above, and its dubious track record, perhaps the United Nations is not the best institution to guarantee regional security in Africa. To move one level closer to the regional security issues, we should now briefly examine the African Union.

The African Union (AU) engages with regional security issues primarily through its Peace and Security Council and its plans for an African Standby Force (ASF). The multinational Peace and Security Council is legally empowered to intervene in any AU member country that experiences genocide, crimes against humanity, an undemocratic change of government or an uprising by rebel forces.[29] As mentioned in chapter 6, the ASF is projected to consist of five standby regional peacekeeping brigades based on the major existing sub-regional organizations: ECOWAS, CEEAC, SADC, IGAD, and the Maghreb Union. The AU's approach is meant to overcome some of the difficulties faced by the UN, due to its lack of an organic military component, but there are still many challenges ahead. The constituencies of these five regional organizations are listed in Table 8.3.

Table 8.3: Regional Organizations for African Security

Organization	Member States
Economic Community of West African States (ECOWAS or CEDEAO)	Burkina Faso, Benin, Cape Verde, Côte d'Ivoire, Gambia, Ghana, Guinea, Guinea-Bissau, Liberia, Mali, Niger, Nigeria, Senegal, Sierra Leone, Togo (15 states)
Economic Community of Central African States (ECCAS or CEEAC)	Angola, Burundi, Cameroon, Chad, Central African Republic, Congo-Brazzaville, Democratic Republic of Congo, Equatorial Guinea, Gabon, Rwanda, São Tome and Principe (11 states)
Southern African Development Community (SADC)	Angola, Botswana, Democratic Republic of Congo, Lesotho, Malawi, Mauritius, Mozambique, Namibia, Seychelles, South Africa, Swaziland, Tanzania, Zambia, Zimbabwe (14 states)
Inter-Governmental Authority on Development (IGAD)	Djibouti, Eritrea, Ethiopia, Kenya, Somalia, Sudan, Uganda (7 states)
Maghreb Union	Algeria, Libya, Mauritania, Morocco, Tunisia (5 states)

The Economic Community of West African States (ECOWAS or CEDEAO by its French acronym) is arguably the strongest and most experienced regional organization in Africa in militarily terms. (ECOMOG is the military operations group of ECOWAS and has more than eight years of peacekeeping experience in Liberia and Sierra Leone.) The U.S. Department of State provided $9 million to ECOWAS in 2004 to help pay for peacekeeping operations in West Africa, and Congress requested $45 million to strengthen ECOWAS in 2005. ECOWAS is evidently furthest ahead in preparation to be ready as an AU ASF brigade.

The Economic Community of Central African States (ECCAS or CEEAC by its better known French acronym) is arguably the weakest regional organization in Africa, both militarily and economically. Due to the tremendous current security challenges within member states, (DRC, CAR, Congo, Burundi, and Rwanda for example), CEEAC is quite far behind ECOWAS in terms of meeting AU ASF ready-brigade expectations. However, CEEAC is taking small steps in the right direction, has managed to pull off a regional brigade maneuver training exercise, and is preparing for a second one at the time of this writing.[30]

The Southern African Development Community (SADC) is easily the strongest regional organization in Africa economically, and historically has a solid record of professional militaries. The regional powerhouse, South Africa, has taken a strong political lead on many African security issues, but is relatively inexperienced in peacekeeping operations. The South African National Defense Force (SANDF) has been undergoing a painful transformation process since the end of apartheid in 1994, and is balancing difficult trade-offs between representativeness and experience, especially in the officer corps. Nevertheless, SADC is probably the second most prepared AU ASF brigade, after ECOWAS.

The Inter-Governmental Authority on Development (IGAD) is comprised of quite competent and experienced militaries from Kenya, Ethiopia, and Uganda, but is wracked by its own regional security problems with Sudan, northern Uganda, and what is left of Somalia. However, the core military capabilities for a solid AU ASF brigade are certainly present.

In North Africa, the regional security apparatus is particularly weak, and the AU regional brigade may be formed around the Arab Maghreb Union plus Egypt. Part of the problem is that Morocco, a major peacekeeping player, removed itself from the AU after political differences over the status of Western Sahara. Also, Libya, under Kaddafi, has always seen itself as something of a continental leader—not recognized as such by the other states. For political reasons, the Maghreb Union has not made much progress in preparing to be an AU ASF brigade, though it has a lot of competent national military capability in its constituent member states.

A complicating factor for potential U.S. regional security approaches to the Gulf of Guinea is the challenge of national memberships and troop commitments to existing security institutions and AU ASF brigades. For example, the Gulf of Guinea states are mostly members of CEEAC, but Nigeria is the lead power of ECOWAS and Angola is a member of both CEEAC and SADC. Based on our research in preparing this volume, we conclude that it is not prudent to create yet another regional security organization based on Gulf of Guinea energy producers, but rather that U.S.-Africa policymakers should do their best to reinforce and strengthen existing sub-regional organizations of the AU.

Skeptics will point out that historically the AU's predecessor, the Organization for African Unity (OAU), was pretty inept at resolving regional security issues and unwilling to get involved in internal ones. Nonetheless, we believe that the AU is really quite a significant improvement on the old OAU, and is certainly the best hope from the perspectives of Africans themselves. However, the relatively new AU does not thus far have much institutional experience in peacekeeping missions. It has organized unarmed military observers (MILOBS) missions to Burundi and the Comoros, initiated political mediation missions in Côte d'Ivoire and Somalia, and is attempting to do both of these things to support the peace process in Sudan. The AU has not had any genuine successes up till now, but has not embarked on any bona fide peacekeeping missions yet either. Sudan's Darfur crisis may be the AU's first real test, but it is an extremely difficult situation and the AU organization is still in its infancy.

In sum, there are many regional security challenges in the Gulf of Guinea, and several organizations are involved in addressing them. From our analysis, there is much the U.S. can do to bolster these efforts.

Improving the U.S. Response to Africa's Regional Security Challenges

As noted earlier, U.S. involvement in addressing Africa's security challenges is relatively recent compared to France and the UK. During the 1990s, the Clinton administration initiated the African Crisis Response Initiative (ACRI) to bolster Africa's indigenous peacekeeping capabilities. ACRI trained and equipped more than 6,000 troops from seven African states between 1997 and 2000. Several of these ACRI-trained forces helped implement United Nations' peacekeeping operations in the region. The program ended in 2002, and was replaced by the African Contingency Operations Training and Assistance (ACOTA) program.

As a successor to the ACRI, ACOTA emphasizes a more robust Chapter Seven[31] approach that allows UN-mandated forces to more aggressively implement peacekeeping operations.[32] In 2004, ACOTA trained and helped equip approximately 9,000 African soldiers in nine battalions for emergency use as peacekeepers for ECOWAS and AU missions. Ongoing and upcoming training missions include Mozambique, Senegal, Botswana, Nigeria, and a few potential others. Unfortunately, due to other priorities, U.S. funding for African peacekeeping in general shrank from $41 million in 2002 to $30 million in 2003.[33] However, this financial commitment has shifted again with the introduction of the Global Peace Operations Initiative (GPOI).

As part of the G8 Africa Action Plan announced in June 2004, GPOI pledges $660 million over 5 years in order to train 75,000 peacekeepers around the world, but with an emphasis on Africa. The plan calls for 15 battalions to be trained per year, with 10 of those trained in Africa, and 5 trained in Europe or the U.S.. GPOI will train African peacekeepers and constabulary forces (or stability police), and will provide necessary equipment, transport, and logistical support. The plan calls for increased coordination with the UN, EU, and AU, and an improvement in regional training centers. The U.S. has also offered support for an Italian initiative, the Center of Excellence for Stability Police Units (COESPU), collocated with the European Gendarme Force Headquarters in Vicenza, Italy. More on these and other security assistance initiatives is provided in Chapter 6 of this volume.

The U.S. has also turned its attention to supporting the efforts of regional organizations like the African Union, although there are considerable difficulties to be overcome before the AU can truly affect the security challenges faced by its members. By briefly examining some of the AU's problems and failings,[34] U.S.-Africa policymakers may be able to discern effective ways to provide much needed support to this important organization.

1) *Institutional and conceptual*—many supporters of the AU have idealistic perceptions of African unity, and tend to ignore the reality of strong sub-regionalism and centrifugal external influences.

2) *Financial*—the lack of resources, equipment, and logistics hampers the AU's potential effectiveness (for example, most quality training is currently paid for and supported by foreigners).

3) *Organizational and structural*—the many diverse histories, backgrounds, training, and standard operating procedures (SOPs) of the constituent members create internal problems that often erode the strength of the overarching AU superstructure.

4) *Military capabilities*—the brigades of regional peacekeeping forces must be harmonized, trained together, and properly equipped and supported; but they are not.

5) *General*—many AU countries are still mistrustful of each other, and there is tension between the reality of good ideas versus their implementation in contentious political climates.

In addition to strong and public support for the African Union and its sub-regional security organizations, (ECOWAS, SADC, CEEAC, etc.), there are other regional and sub-regional security cooperation efforts with multinational sponsors that U.S.-Africa policymakers should consider supporting. For example, the Kofi Annan International Peacekeeping Training Centre (KAIPTC), collocated with the Ghana Armed Forces Staff College in Accra, Ghana is envisioned to become the premier peacekeeping training center in Africa, but could benefit from much more direct U.S. engagement.

Officially opened in 2004, the KAIPTC was originally a Ghanaian idea whose initial phases of construction were funded by Germany and the United Kingdom. The U.K. has picked up subsequent construction costs and has paid for research on "best practices" and curriculum development, but other primary sponsors include the Netherlands, Italy, France, other European states, and Canada, (through its Pearson Peacekeeping Center). However, at the time of this writing, there has not been much financial support yet from the U.S.. Though the KAIPTC has a regional (ECOWAS) focus and genuine local ownership, it will never be self-funded, and needs continuous strong external donor support (funding, resources, personnel, etc.), otherwise it would surely fail. Foreign permanent staff includes officers from the U.K., Germany, and France in full-time positions, and one U.S. officer assigned part-time from EUCOM. Because the U.K. is by far the biggest contributor of funds and training staff, most course content is quite U.K.-centric. There is nothing wrong with a strong UK lead for an institution like this, but the U.S. is missing a great opportunity to engage with and transform African military leaders by not being more directly involved.

The KAIPTC's vision is "to develop into a world class education, training, and research facility, embracing all aspects of peace operations"[35] and it focuses primarily on train-the-trainer courses for African military and security officers and civilian diplomats. A fantastic medium for exchanging ideas and making contacts with professionals from around the continent, KAIPTC brings together key leaders from all across Africa, and has great linkages to international civil society and institutions.[36] It has tremendous modern teaching facilities, (especially by most African military standards), and has a Conflict Prevention Management and Resolution Department (CPMRD) which is the research engine for "best practices" for the whole spectrum of Peace Support Operations (PSOs). KAIPTC offers an election-monitoring course with a civilian focus, and a disarmament, demobilization and reintegration (DDR) course, along with several others. The International Peace Support Operations (IPSO) course is its flagship course, and usually includes about 90 students from more than 25 African countries—a real mix of military, gendarmes, police, and ministry of foreign affairs civilians. The objective of the IPSO course is to study and understand the principles, procedures, and techniques involved in the planning, coordination and conduct of UN and other Peace Support Operations. Because of the clear parallels between the KAIPTC mission and the policy goals of U.S. programs like the African Contingency Operations Training and Assistance (ACOTA) program and the Global Peace Operations Initiative (GPOI), there are numerous synergy and coordination opportunities to which U.S.-Africa policymakers should be more attentive.

In addition to the KAIPTC, there are other similar institutions outside the region worth mentioning. South Africa is creating a peacekeeping training center in tandem with the Scandinavian sponsored NGO ACCORD (African Centre for the Constructive Resolution of Disputes). This international partnership is currently launching an Institute for Peace and Reconciliation outside Johannesburg, resourced primarily with foreign funds and staffed by international and SANDF (South African National Defense Force) officers. There is also an already established Kenyan Peace Support Training Centre (PSTC) located at the Kenyan Staff College in Karen, Kenya. Courses are sponsored by the UK and other international donors, and attract students from the Horn of Africa, and East, Central, and Southern Africa in particular.

Each of these important training centers has the opportunity to shape the future capabilities and professionalism of the leadership of the AU's ASF brigades. While the KAIPTC is predominantly focused on ECOWAS, the other two institutions center on SADC and IGAD respectively. CEEAC, which includes most Gulf of Guinea states, is noticeably missing such a regional training center. U.S.-Africa policymakers should therefore consider either sponsoring more Gulf of Guinea security professionals as students attending courses at established PSO training centers, or perhaps working with France, the AU, and CEEAC to create a similar regional center of their own.

In addition to bilateral security assistance, the U.S. could simultaneously take a more multilateral and regional approach to pushing the agenda of professional military ethics through robust support for regional training centers, like the KAIPTC, and by giving more direct developmental assistance to the African Union's ASF brigades. Rather than trying to create new regional security alliances, it is best for the U.S. to use existing institutions and support the AU's progressive but embryonic concept for regional peacekeeping brigades. Again, by taking a dominant role in the formation and training of such units, the U.S. can exert influence in the doctrine and professionalism of participating militaries. This method engages militaries at the broadest useful level and produces a remarkable set of positive externalities.

The empowerment and coordination of regional organizations is probably the most important contribution U.S.-Africa policy can make towards dealing with regional security issues. Regional organizations should be the primary agents of Peace Support Operations (PSOs) in general, and strong U.S. support can affect their philosophy as well as their competence in the field.

There are, however, a few concerns about using regional organizations to address regional security issues in their own backyards. Due to potential historical involvement in a conflict, there are legitimate questions of impartiality. And there are perceptions that individual national agendas may not coincide with an evenhanded and objective approach to regional conflict resolution. For example, in Sierra Leone the UN replaced most of the ECOWAS forces when it finally came into Sierra Leone for peacekeeping duties. The UN troops were multinational and were brought in from outside the region to replace the Nigerian-dominated ECOWAS forces, in part because local stakeholders did not consider the Nigerians to be fair or impartial. Admittedly, in this case the peacekeepers traded off regional knowledge and expertise for political legitimacy.

However, in general, the benefits of regional solutions for regional problems far outweigh the challenges. As a counter-example, when the UN sent international peacekeepers into Liberia, the decision was made to take a task-sharing approach with the Nigerian-led ECOWAS forces, rather than replacing them. This was in part due to the acknowledged local experience and capabilities of the regional troops. Another major advantage of using regional forces is the clear alignment of incentives. Whereas many UN troop contributors arguably donate peacekeepers for almost purely economic reasons, regional states have an additional set of national security incentives that may drive their motivation. For example, not only do Indian and Pakistani troops have no real historical knowledge or experience of operations in the DRC, but they have no real national stake in the outcome of the MONUC mission.[37] In contrast, a CEEAC brigade, if properly trained and organized, would have a vested interest in maintaining regional security in Central Africa.

In more general U.S.-Africa policy terms, there are numerous advantages to the pursuit of broad regional empowerment. Improved military professionalism will help with operational capabilities for PSOs, and will contribute directly to improved regional security—the necessary baseline requirement for development. Increased regional cooperation may also encourage improved regional coordination along economic lines and could further economic development via increased trade. In this vein, it is critical for regional organizations to be institutionally strong and effective in order to assist states in overcoming the multiplicity of problems caused by historically imposed artificial national borders. And finally, improved regional synchronization can put positive pressure on democratic norms, rule of law, institutional development, human rights standards, and environmental standards within member states. Increased interaction and coordination requirements can encourage countries to "bring each other up" based on their various strengths and relative levels of development.

When pursuing regional solutions for regional problems, U.S.-Africa policy must remain realistic and cannot expect too much, too fast. For this reason, it is important to reinforce existing institutions and encourage ongoing developments. Using the African Union as a baseline, and strongly supporting its security and development programs in conjunction with other international contributors, is far more effective than trying to create something new.

As discussed in earlier chapters, the Gulf of Guinea Commission was officially created in July of 2001 and includes Nigeria, Cameroon, Gabon, Equatorial Guinea, Sao Tome and Principe, Congo-Brazzaville, Democratic Republic of Congo, and Angola. The commission aims to provide a framework for consultations among the members in order to enhance cooperation and development; prevent, manage, and resolve conflicts resulting from delimitation of maritime borders; and promote close consultation in the exploitation of energy resources in the region. The Gulf of Guinea Guard is a concept being promoted by EUCOM to enhance the maritime capabilities of regional forces and is designed to ensure: adequate surveillance of littoral and deep-water maritime areas to detect, deter, and/or arrest illegal activities; disruption-free production of hydrocarbons in off-shore facilities; and protection of energy resources during storage and distribution.[38]

The idea of a distinctive commission to facilitate cooperation and discussion about unique energy security issues is sound, but the proposal for the Gulf of Guinea Guard is unfortunately unrealistic and impractical. Members of the Gulf of Guinea Commission come from ECOWAS, CEEAC, and SADC, and these existing regional organizations will remain primordial in terms of currency unions, trading blocs, and security arrangements. The U.S. cannot unilaterally and externally expect to achieve a higher level of regional coordination and cooperation outside these organizations.

Unfortunately, the Gulf of Guinea Guard concept will not work as currently proposed, for a variety of reasons. First, it does not address the priority security interests of the African states themselves. Rather, it addresses the U.S.' priority security interests in the region. Therefore, the idea may move forward only if the U.S. pushes hard and pays for its development almost entirely. The African constituents understand that the U.S. perceives energy security in the Gulf of Guinea to be very important, and will allow EUCOM to move forward at its own expense. Free equipment and training will be welcomed, but local ownership and resource contribution is a long way off.

Second, it doesn't synchronize with the AU's regional ASF brigade concept—something that ECOWAS, CEEAC, and SADC members perceive as an organic African initiative that is correctly aimed at their priority regional security issues. These three regional organizations have begun wholeheartedly organizing, preparing, and committing their limited resources to make these regional brigades work. The ASF brigades and the Gulf of Guinea Guard concept address totally different problem sets, and this is important to recognize.

Third, most Gulf of Guinea states do not have the capacity in terms of resources and training to execute maritime security at the high level proposed. This means that they lack the ships, aircraft, and surveillance and communication technology, in addition to the appropriately trained military personnel required to execute.

Fourth, and most importantly, the member states do not yet have the political will or confidence in each other to make this new regional organization truly functionally capable. In fact, rather than regional maritime cooperation, there is currently direct maritime competition and potential conflict between most prospective members. Consider, for example, the territorial water disputes between Equatorial Guinea and Nigeria, Equatorial Guinea and Gabon, and the ongoing Bakassi issue between Nigeria and Cameroon. Although on the surface these disputes seem to have been resolved through compromise or international court rulings, underneath there exist real tensions and mistrust. The Bakassi issue alone is a showstopper for genuine Gulf of Guinea security cooperation. And because most Gulf of Guinea states do not yet really trust their neighbors, they will not share regional security information in any real way.

And finally, although Nigeria is apparently quite willing to take on the lead for Gulf of Guinea security cooperation, this enthusiasm is ironically detrimental to the concept at large. This is because most of the other member states do not really trust Nigeria's intentions, nor do they want Nigeria to be the spearhead and dominant partner of any regional maritime organization.

As an illustrative example of the lack of regional trust and cooperation, take for instance the International Maritime Office (IMO) of the UN. For years, IMO has been trying to get the Gulf of Guinea states to work together to develop regional search and rescue (SAR) capabilities as a safety net for maritime operations. Yet although the resource requirements are not that difficult, and the cooperation does not require sharing of sensitive information, (as the Gulf of Guinea Guard would), the political will and mutual trust does not exist to turn this good idea into a functioning operational concept.

In sum, we recommend pursuing regional solutions for dealing with regional problems wherever practicable. For regional security threats, as perceived by the African states themselves, the U.S. should strongly reinforce and significantly add to the AU's up and coming regional ASF brigades. A robust professionalization component would be a very worthwhile investment here. For energy security issues that are important to individual African governments, (but perhaps even more so to U.S. companies and consumers), the U.S. should pursue bilateral approaches to improving maritime security. In doing so, the U.S. can work around some of the region's inherent political challenges and can simultaneously emphasize military restructuring and professionalism.

Conclusion

As demonstrated in this chapter, there is much the U.S. can do to strengthen the security environment in the Gulf of Guinea. Internal threats faced by these nations include criminals, mercenaries and war profiteers who take advantage of weak governments, porous borders, widespread poverty and a history of corruption. They also face problems within the security institutions themselves, where there is urgent need for law enforcement training, professionalism, and equipment. For the oil-rich countries of this region, special training is needed for the complicated array of security requirements essential to safeguarding energy resources, production facilities, and transport infrastructure. While national governments should take primary fiscal responsibility for their own security, most are relatively incapable due to the poor status of equipment and training, and current debt burdens inhibit the capability of most African nations to pay the high costs of new security equipment.

The situation calls for new public/private security ventures, involving all stakeholders who have a vested interest in protecting the energy infrastructures of this region. Through a more coordinated approach to security assistance and development, the U.S. can build the capacity of these states to effectively tackle their security challenges, creating a more hospitable environment not only for U.S. interests but for all the region's citizens. Private corporate involvement is vital: if oil companies do not establish good relations with local communities in energy source areas, perceptions of inequality and exploitation will continue to create instability and may lead to terrorism. Security training and execution should be conducted by a combination of military, law enforcement, and private security companies that are well supervised and coordinated by national governments. Beyond training military and police forces, U.S. contributions could include intelligence and surveillance to counter smugglers, bandits, oil thieves, and terrorists. In fact, U.S.-donated buoy tenders are already reducing oil bunkering in the Niger delta.

Beyond an individual country's challenges, there are also a number of regional threats to security that require cooperation between countries. These include transnational criminal and terrorist organizations, the cross-border flow of weapons and drugs, piracy and other maritime security challenges. International maritime security is a global public good, and the costs for it should be covered by all those who both benefit and have the means—including the U.S. and its allies. In tackling these and other regional security challenges, we should support the network of multinational organizations that Africans have established for themselves. The African Union should take the lead on overall continental security improvement, while regional organizations like ECOWAS and ECCAS should take the lead in their respective regions.

Overall, true security of a country's energy infrastructure can only be realized when it is seen as beneficial to (and a responsibility of) everyone. Algeria provides a good case in point. Here, despite years of terrible internal violence, the gas pipelines and other potential terrorist targets have seldom been attacked because—unlike Nigeria—there is a widespread perception throughout the population that the country as a whole derives benefits from the energy resource industry. Building this perception—and by extension, confidence in the government—should be a key component in the U.S. National Security Strategy.

Conflict prevention is always better and usually cheaper than any conflict resolution option. The best conflict prevention is to intervene in weak states before they fail, by promoting security, economic development, and democratization. Security (in all its forms) is an absolute prerequisite for economic development and democratization, not least because stakeholders need institutionalized means to solve political differences without violence. Efforts to prevent governmental corruption and develop a country's infrastructure are sure to fail unless a secure operating environment is provided by a professional military and police force. Indeed, internal security plays a critical role in economic growth. At the most fundamental level, development assistance is futile if businesses and households are constantly at risk of seeing their goods appropriated by armed groups. In a lawless environment, neither production nor trade can proceed.[39] At a macro level, insecurity translates into states that may directly or indirectly enable transnational terrorist threats to emerge. The U.S. should implement security programs in tandem with economic development programs, as both are absolutely essential to long term stability.

In conclusion, the reformation of African militaries and police forces can help lead the way for real societal transformation in the Gulf of Guinea. In the longer term, the U.S. cannot and should not focus its energy security efforts on simply protecting oil pipelines and extractive industries in sub-Saharan Africa. Rather, the focus should be on ensuring that the local populations of Nigeria, Angola and other countries have it in their best interests to protect these pipelines themselves. This can only be done by empowering these populations to reap the benefits of their natural resources and facilitating a secure environment in which to pursue the individual opportunities of economic and political freedom.

Notes

1. For more on this, please see Madelfia A. Abb and Cindy R. Jebb, "Human Security and Good Governance: A Living Systems Approach to Understanding and Combating Terrorism," in *The Making of a Terrorist: Recruitment, Training and Root Causes*, edited by James JF Forest, (Westport, CT: Praeger, 2005).

2. United Nations Development Program (UNDP) Report, 1994, 3, 22-23 as quoted by Liotta, 4-5.

3. A Human Security Doctrine for Europe, The Barcelona Report of the Study Group on Europe's Security Capabilities, 15 September, 2004, 9.

4. Madelfia A. Abb and Cindy R. Jebb, "Human Security and Good Governance: A Living Systems Approach to Understanding and Combating Terrorism," in *The Making of a Terrorist: Recruitment, Training and Root Causes*, edited by James JF Forest, (Westport, CT: Praeger, 2005).

5. *Army International Activities Plan,* 13 August 2004, p. 6.

6. Stevenson, Jonathan. Africa's Growing Strategic Resonance. *Survival,* vol. 45, no. 4 (Winter, 2003), 157.

7. Congressional Research Service, "Nation's Hospitable to Organized Crime and Terrorism," Library of Congress, Federal Research Division, October, 2003.

8. Robert D. Kaplan, *The Coming Anarchy.* New York: Random House, 2000, 49.

9. For more on this, please see chapter 4.

10. *IRIN News Service,* 24 May 2005.

11. Andrews.

12. From an energy and security briefing given by multiple major U.S. energy firms in Malabo, Equatorial Guinea, 4 May 2005.

13. Most Gulf of Guinea states do not allow private security guards to carry firearms.

14. From a briefing by a senior COTCO representative, Yaoundé, Cameroon, 5 May 2005.

15. Taken from a lecture on post-conflict reconstruction given by LTC Rupert Robson (UK) at the KAIPTC on 20 June 2005.

16. For more on this industry, please see P.W. Singer, *Corporate Warriors: The Rise of the Privatized Military Industry* (Cornell University Press, 2003).

17. More on this is provided in Chapter 6.

18. There is also very strong UK financial and staff support to the KAIPTC, and the UK shares directing responsibility with the Kenyan staff at the Kenyan Peace Support Training Centre (PSTC).

19. Samuel Huntington articulates the distinction between subjective and objective control of militaries in his classic *The Soldier and the State: The Theory and Politics of Civil-Military Relations* (Cambridge: Harvard University Press, 1957). In particular, Chapter 4 of the book examines the political power of a nation's military (its capacity to control other people), as derived from both formal authority and informal influence (affiliations, resources, interpenetration, and prestige). Huntington describes *subjective* control as involving institutions and legal instruments which constrain the military's political power, while *objective* civilian control over the military is derived from a high degree of professionalism, autonomy, and political neutrality, leading to a military that is politically neutral and whose leadership is clearly limited to military issues. For more on this, please see Chapter 10.

20. James Jay Carafano and Nile Gardiner, "U.S. Military Assistance for Africa: A Better Solution," Heritage Foundation Backgrounder #1697, available at http://www.heritage.org/Research/Africa/bg1697.cfm

21. Many of these details were taken from a personal interview with Seymour Jones, the Director of ILEA, Gaborone in Gaborone, Botswana on 18 February 2005.

22. There are currently three ILEA locations globally: one in Budapest, Hungary focused on Eastern Europe and headed by the FBI; one in Bangkok, Thailand focused on Southeast Asia and headed by the DEA; and this one in Gaborone, Botswana focused on Sub-Saharan Africa and headed by DHS.

23. Part of this may be due to historical legislative constraints on DoD's role in the arena of law enforcement. However, given the contemporary international security environment, restrictive legislation should be rewritten to foster greater cooperation and coordination between all relevant stakeholders.

24. Despite the 2004 ICJ ruling, the Bakassi issue remains de facto unresolved at the time of writing, and is still a source of sub-regional insecurity and occasional international violence.

25. For a good, broad discussion of this topic, see "Terrorism Goes to Sea", *Foreign Affairs*, Nov-Dec 2004.

26. Figures provided by the UN. Updates available at http://www.un.org/Depts/dpko/dpko/index.asp

27. Some of these are taken from lectures by Mr. Mitonga Zongwe and COL Seymour, UNDPKO, Office of Operations, given on 21 June 2005 at the Kofi Annan International Peacekeeping Training Centre, Accra, Ghana.

28. Because of these information and coordination problems, UNDPKO is trying to deploy coherent units with their own HQs, like the Indian and Pakistani Brigades currently deployed to the DRC.

29. For more on this, please see the Africa Union website, at: http://www.africa-union.org

30. The Bar-el-Ghazel maneuver training exercise is planned to take place in Chad in the late fall of 2005.

31. Use of force to maintain international peace and security under Chapter Six of the United Nations Charter has been interpreted to be authorized in a strictly defensive posture. Chapter Seven specifically authorizes the use of force in an offensive posture in order to maintain or restore international peace and security.

32. More on ACOTA is available on the U.S. State Department website, at http://usinfo.state.gov

33. J. Stevenson, p. 166.

34. Some of these were taken from a lecture by Dr. Kumi Ansah-Koi, Department of Political Science, University of Ghana, given at the KAIPTC, 28 June 2005.

35. Find out much more at http://www.kaiptc.org

36. For example, KAIPTC has strong partnerships with King's College (UK) and the Pearson Peacekeeping Center (Canada).

37. This is not to say that the Indian and Pakistani peacekeepers are not courageous, motivated, or effective - only to point out systemic institutional misalignments of incentives.

38. Taken from presentations made at the Gulf of Guinea Maritime Security Conference, Naples, Italy, 3-5 October 2004.

39. James Dobbins, et. al. *America's Role in Nation Building: From Germany to Iraq.* Santa Monica: RAND, 2003.

Chapter 9
Facilitating Economic Development

As a region, sub-Saharan Africa is the most consistently poor and underdeveloped part of the world. The chronic level of poverty, despair, insecurity and hopelessness is truly alarming, especially as the developed world leaps ahead in terms of social and technological progress. In modern history, sub-Saharan Africa has continued to fall behind the rest of the world as measured by the United Nation's Human Development Index (HDI), but why is this? Why has this one region been such an economic development disaster, especially since it is so blessed with an abundance of natural resources?

In 2004, the CEO of the U.S. Overseas Private Investment Corporation (OPIC) wrote that "the absence of development in most of these countries is most often due to political instability, inappropriate macroeconomic policies, corruption, the absence of secure property laws, and the lack of a market-oriented regulatory environment that discourage both foreign and domestic private investment."[1] This is a particularly concise and powerful statement; but there are volumes of economic, political, social and anthropological accounts that attempt to explain the gross relative inequality in the world today through a variety of factors. Two of the most recent, and well written, are *The Wealth and Poverty of Nations* by David Landes and *Guns, Germs, and Steel* by Jared Diamond. As a good introduction to development studies, these two books outline in detail a couple of broad sets of opposing arguments that elucidate the complicated factors that have contributed to modern international disparity. Diamond primarily uses natural factors such as geography, climate, indigenous plant and animal species, disease, and resources to explain the historical evolution of regional inequalities.[2] His argument puts the emphasis on geographic location as the main determinant of development. Landes, however, puts more responsibility directly on the shoulders of the people themselves, regardless of geographic location. He uses culture as the primary independent variable to explain regional inequalities. For example, Landes trumpets the Protestant work ethic as one of the driving forces behind the success of the developed world, and Arab male

229

chauvinism as one of the detractors from Middle Eastern development.[3] In reality, the truth lies somewhere in between these two points of view, and both arguments have relevancy to the Gulf of Guinea.

Another way to analyze the chronic underdevelopment of sub-Saharan Africa, and thereby seek corresponding policy solutions, is to utilize the general "internalist" and "externalist" perspectives in tandem. The externalist argument looks outside Africa for an explanation for its poor state of affairs. The most radical arguments state that the West in general, and Europeans in particular, imposed foreign institutions on Africa that were doomed to failure. Basil Davidson succinctly expresses this argument in *The Black Man's Burden: Africa and the Curse of the Nation State.*[4] Externalists also argue that the legacies of the slave trade and colonially imposed artificial state boundaries, combined with Western neocolonialist practices since independence, as well as the impacts of U.S. and Soviet Cold War policies, have continued to exacerbate the political, economic, and social development problems in Africa. The policy implication of this logic is that it is the moral and financial responsibility of the West to directly address Africa's development woes.

The internalist argument puts the blame more squarely on Africans themselves, in particular, poor leadership and governance since independence. George Ayittey outlines this view quite clearly in *Africa in Chaos*. Internalists argue that authoritarian regimes and military dictatorships, prebendalist economic mismanagement and statist development strategies, and outright theft by kleptocratic governments are more accurately to blame for Africa's problems.[5] The implications here are that development solutions and initiative must come from within the African states themselves. Of course, in reality, the best explanations of inequality in Africa engage a combination of externalist and internalist reasoning to enlighten policymakers seeking potential solutions to development problems.

This chapter is not meant to be a comprehensive analysis of sub-Saharan Africa's economic development challenges, nor is it a template for economic development strategy and policy in general. There are plenty of well-researched reports that lay out prospective economic development solutions in quite a bit of detail. Instead, this broad introduction is simply intended to frame the discussion before focusing more explicitly on the role of U.S. policy regarding economic development in the Gulf of Guinea as it relates directly to energy security and national security.

The Links Between Energy Security, National Security and Economic Development

Extensive development of the African energy sector must be accompanied by a commitment to sustainable economic development at local and regional levels. History has demonstrated that primary product economies, especially those based on oil, too often result in precarious economic and political volatility. The U.S. may try to satisfy its energy interests by continuing to extract offshore oil from collapsing and chaotic states, but this would ignore the recent experiences of Chevron Nigeria, Ltd, which has been involved in several seizures of its off-shore oil-drilling rigs by impoverished Nigerian youths—in one case (April, 2002) even holding 43 hostages for several days. On shore, the Niger Delta is plagued with violence as gangs compete for "bunkering" stolen oil. Violent deaths average about 1,000 per year, putting the Niger Delta on par with Co-lombia and Chechnya.[6] In the long run, it clearly makes more sense for the U.S. to ensure that its oil extraction efforts are seen as beneficial to improving the quality of life of local populations. It must be in the people's best interests to support and facilitate U.S. energy interests, not oppose them.

There are obvious and immediate threats to energy extraction directly due to economic underdevelopment. For example, poor people who tap into onshore pipelines to steal oil, or who seize offshore oil platforms and workers as bargain-ing chips, are motivated by immediate cash incentives. Although there are wealthy organized criminal cartels and local warlords behind a lot of this activ-ity, the actual perpetrators are usually unemployed young men seeking personal enrichment in the absence of a steady job. For many young men, the gun has become the last resort of employment.[7]

Huge inequalities in the Gulf of Guinea countries are also a cause of violent crime and an omen of future instability. Though many corrupt government offi-cials in oil producing states have enormous illegitimate revenue streams and swollen secret bank accounts, very few average citizens currently see the bene-fits of their country's natural resource endowments. Historically, this has been blatantly obvious in Nigeria, Cameroon, Gabon, Congo, and Angola for quite some time. This gross injustice directly affects U.S. national security, especially when many U.S. energy companies are perceived as being the benefactors of a state's oil wealth at the expense of the local population. Never mind the fact that the local governments themselves are far more to blame for the inequalities; the large U.S. multinationals are still media favorites and easy targets for culpabil-ity.

As an illustration of how local inequality threatens the U.S., consider Douala, the economic capital of Cameroon, where oil and business wealth exist side by side with dire urban poverty. While businessmen and government minis-ters park their Mercedes sedans to dine at the upscale Meridien Hotel (where the average room charge is over $200 a night), street children wash in gutters and young men earn less than $2 a day for pulling heavily laden carts around the city barefoot. In the last few years, there have even been well-documented outbreaks of cholera in Douala due to the open sewers and lack of access to clean water. This disease is usually characteristic of refugee camps in desolate, war-torn ar-eas, not of economic capitals in potentially wealthy countries. While the gov-ernment fails to deliver adequate social services, local mosques are in fact very responsive to the poor, and often provide critical emergency relief to the neediest people. There are a few of these mosques in which the imams are suspected of preaching somewhat extremist messages and are likely funded by external fundamentalist sponsors. In exceedingly poor neighborhoods, these conditions are very plausibly breeding the kind of radicalism and anti-western resentment that directly threaten U.S. interests at home and abroad.

If African national oil wealth can be more equitably distributed and better used for the economic development and social welfare of the people, there is likely to be less resentment of the energy extractors and less interference with the process itself. Visible gains in economic development would also engender more legitimate support for African governments themselves. For this to work properly, it would require transparent accountability of energy revenues, tangible economic benefits to average citizens, and an openly democratic and responsive process for making resource allocation decisions. After security, economic development is the most basic need, and a prerequisite for real stability. Of course, there are many other complicating factors involved, but simply put, the people who "own" the national rights to an energy resource must have an incentive to see it developed in order to support, and not detract from, the process.

In addition to facilitating secure and reliable access to energy resources now and in the immediate future, there are several other reasons why it is in the U.S.' interests to promote economic development in the Gulf of Guinea. Some of the guiding principles of the *National Security Strategy* are to champion aspirations for human dignity; to work with others to defuse regional conflicts; to ignite a new era of global economic growth through free markets and free trade; and to expand the circle of development by opening societies and building the infrastructure of democracy. Each of these is relevant to the Gulf of Guinea and is directly related to economic development.

Human dignity is a complicated concept, and this volume does not intend to entertain philosophical quandaries nor explore theoretical economic principles such as maximizing individual utility functions. However, in the most basic sense, human dignity is directly related to human security, the ability to earn an honest living, individual rights and freedoms, and the just application of the rule of law. The latter two concepts will be addressed in the next chapter, on democracy. Human security involves the freedoms from fear, from hunger, from want, etc. As discussed briefly in the previous chapter, the concept of human security encompasses the guarantee of individual freedom from basic insecurities as well as genocide, widespread or systematic torture, inhuman and degrading treatment, disappearances, slavery, crimes against humanity, and grave violations of the laws of war as defined in the Statute of the International Criminal Court (ICC).[8] As two scholars—Madelfia Abb and Cindy Jebb—have observed, "These insecurities, in one form or another, have always been present in the developing world. They cross state borders, affect the physical environment, put enormous pressure on political systems and societies—especially those within a region of weak states—and present vulnerabilities for criminal and terrorist organizations to exploit."[9]

Human security is directly linked to economic development. The continued failure of a state's government to address the economic development challenges that restrict an individual's ability to put food on the table for his family undermines trust in the political system. If people feel that they cannot trust the political system, then they will turn their allegiance elsewhere—they may identify with a tribe that straddles a state border, a religious sect, or other such group. People without food, or without a livelihood, thus view leaving the polity as a viable alternative, leading to refugee flows or internally displaced people which put pressure on domestic political systems and neighboring political systems, as well as offering vulnerabilities for terrorists to exploit.[10] In the Gulf of Guinea states, where unemployment often exceeds 50%, the economic development dimension of human security—including the ability to earn a living—is particularly important.

The chronic deficiency of quality schools, roads, power supply, health facilities, and economic opportunities is a notorious component of the "vicious cycle" of poverty, corruption, instability, and poor governance that plagues Africa. Even if managed appropriately, in most states oil revenues alone cannot solve these challenges.[11] To begin with, the oil sector employs relatively few Africans; fewer still are needed once the oil rigs and pipelines are up and running. Economic development policy must comprehensively address value-added employment and educational opportunities, improved social safety nets and healthcare, and a myriad of infrastructure improvements that could serve to attract private investment—the real engine of growth for an economy.[12]

Economic underdevelopment is clearly associated with internal and regional conflicts in sub-Saharan Africa. This appears to be the case even more so in underdeveloped states that have significant natural resource wealth.[13] Particularly relevant to the Gulf of Guinea, there are various hypotheses about linkages between energy resources and conflict in poor countries. First, energy resources do not necessarily cause conflict, but can exacerbate divisions between groups vying for political power and control over revenue streams. This is especially true when energy revenues are the single dominant source of foreign income—which, as highlighted in Chapter 2, is typical of virtually every Gulf of Guinea state. Secondly, political movements often end up being overshadowed by violent criminal networks when control of valuable resources is involved. This is apparently the case in the Niger Delta. If economies were more broadly diversified, and legitimate employment levels approached full employment, this level of heightened economic development would arguably contribute significantly to decreased levels of conflict—one of the U.S.' stated goals. This is yet another reason why the U.S. should care about economic development in the Gulf of Guinea.

The concepts of global economic growth, open markets, and free trade not only support the U.S. economy, but could also contribute to the reduction of dependency of poor African economies. We wholeheartedly support the "trade not aid" argument, and believe that African economic self-sufficiency not only reduces the U.S. aid burden, but contributes immensely to long-term regional stability. Currently, sub-Saharan Africa attracts only 0.7% of global foreign direct investment (FDI) flows,[14] but this is changing with increased investment in the energy sector in the Gulf of Guinea. High oil prices and increased production present a historically unique chance for these states to really develop in the next twenty to thirty years. Under good leadership, and within the right policy framework, economic development in the Gulf of Guinea could experience a "big push" before energy sources change in the long term. Petroleum earnings are relatively critical income sources for development due to their dominant role in gross domestic product (GDP) composition and strong foreign exchange potential. Additionally, domestic energy production, especially from natural gas, can be directly used for local electrification projects. As Africa has experienced a rapid increase in both population and urbanization, power provision is an essential prerequisite for sustained economic growth. As globalization continues to connect the world's markets, and electronic information flows make it difficult to be truly isolated from international events, it is in both U.S. and African interests to directly harness the Gulf of Guinea's tremendous energy potential for regional economic development.

Finally, we are convinced that economic development is a prerequisite condition for truly opening societies and building the infrastructure of democracy—another stated U.S. national security principle. Economic development is at least a complement, if not a precursor, to real democratization. Using the comparative method of research, one can find many cases where economic development has led democratization (most of the "Asian Tigers" for example), but arguably, not as many where real democracy has come first. The reality is that in most Gulf of Guinea states, average citizens are currently far more immediately concerned with finding a job and putting food on their table than they are with their political rights and freedoms. Distribution of wealth is also an important aspect, as economic development which benefits a very few is not likely to bring about the kinds of change needed for long-term energy security and national security. Sustainable economic growth, and public investments for improving the quality of life, can give a populace the appropriate incentives and abilities to take ownership of their own nation's challenges. Economic development may be an evolutionary process, but there is certainly room for "great leaps forward," especially given the enormous potential of the energy sector in the Gulf of Guinea.

Policy Analysis and Recommendations

Given the internalist versus externalist debate articulated earlier in this chapter, what can the U.S. really do to most effectively assist with economic development in sub-Saharan Africa? Previous chapters of this volume have already explored an array of existing development programs and their proponents, from international initiatives (like those of the IMF and World Bank, as well as the G-8 commitment to providing debt relief to 18 of the world's poorest countries), to regional initiatives (including the New Partnership for African Development and other efforts of the African Union, ECOWAS and SADC), to U.S. bilateral initiatives (such as the Millennium Challenge Account, the U.S. African Growth and Opportunity Act, and a flurry of USAID programs). Indeed, it is quite possible for an ordinary researcher to get lost amid this teeming jungle of efforts to tackle Africa's development challenges. While U.S. support for these and other efforts is driven by an overall concern for improving the lives of all Africans, coordination at the policy development and agency implementation levels is not always what is should be. More on this is provided in Chapter 11. For now, though, it is important to emphasize the core, fundamental objectives of economic development policies which are most likely to benefit all countries in the Gulf of Guinea. From our analysis, we believe there are a small number of very big, obvious steps that would most certainly have a positive impact: qualified debt relief, as is currently being undertaken by the G-8; an elimination of agricultural subsidies, to level the trading field and allow African farmers to fairly capitalize on their comparative advantages; economic diversification, away from primary product monocultures; assistance with development of African industry, so that value-added processing can be applied to primary sector commodities before export; and assistance with the development of human capital through greatly improved education systems.

These broad, sweeping recommendations require serious political commitment and financial investment from the U.S. and other external contributors, but they also require obligations and assurances from African governments themselves. As the CEO of OPIC accurately pointed out, "the political will for establishing a good investment climate has to come from the country itself, and cannot be externally imposed without considerable difficulty."[15] This suggests that neither externalist nor internalist development strategies will be very effective on their own, and must be complementary, coordinated, and mutually supported.

To help focus the discussion down from the rather unhelpfully broad economic development policy recommendations above, it may be useful to briefly examine a more specific energy-related economic development strategy. The following "key pillars of an effective energy strategy" come from discussions between a host of internal and external stakeholders at the 2005 Energy and Security Conference in Abuja, Nigeria, sponsored by the Africa Center for Strategic Studies (ACSS):

1) Consistent emphasis on the welfare of the individual—i.e., work to eliminate injustices, disadvantaged groups, marginalized groups, and inequity;
2) A stable macroeconomic environment—i.e., fiscal and monetary policies to make oil money use efficient and equitable;
3) Full disclosure of oil revenues and contracts—i.e., government transparency to counter corruption;
4) Zero tolerance for corruption, with publicized prosecution and punishment, while recognizing that this requires strong leadership;
5) Reinvestment of oil money for economic diversification and job creation—i.e., not just spent on immediate needs or wasteful extravagances;
6) Protection of energy infrastructure, transportation networks, and personnel from criminals, activists, and transnational extremists;
7) Improvements in law enforcement at all levels, with better information sharing between countries;
8) Environmental protection;
9) Health sector investment, because those most affected by rampant disease epidemics are the economically active population, resulting in severely reduced productivity, stunted economic growth prospects, and shockingly high youth dependency ratios; and
10) Basic education and vocational training initiatives, which need to be approached with the same determination and funding as President Bush's proposed $15 billion PEPFAR program.

Almost all of these "pillars" are directly related to economic development, and most of them are clearly the primary responsibility of African governments. We submit that most of the major obstacles to economic development, as it relates to the energy sector, are internal, not external or transnational. However, recognizing that as an external influence, the U.S. still has an important role to play in economic development strategy, it is necessary to illuminate the best places for U.S.-Africa policy to concentrate. In general, there are three areas where the U.S. can and should make the biggest impact on economic development with regards to energy security and national security: growth of the African private sector; energy revenue stream management; and anti-corruption reforms.

Of course, explicit policy implementation must be country-specific, but this chapter will deal with recommendations applicable to all states in the Gulf of Guinea. One way to subsequently refine a development strategy may be to divide the states into different groups based on the size and maturity of their energy sectors: new energy producers (e.g. Equatorial Guinea, São Tome and Principe, Chad), strong energy producers (e.g. Angola, Nigeria), and waning energy producers (e.g. Gabon, Congo, Cameroon). Based on the unique characteristics of each states' economic, political, social, and cultural characteristics, the three major U.S. focus areas must be individually tailored to apply most effectively.

The Important Role of the Private Sector

The private sector is the real engine of economic growth, but is grossly underdeveloped and unfortunately encumbered by government bureaucracy and corruption in most Gulf of Guinea states. The history of extractive colonialism, followed by post-independence authoritarian regimes that subscribed to economic models varying from African socialism to Afro-Marxist ideologies, set the stage for this condition. However, with the enormous growth in recent years of capitalist investment in the energy sector, the time is right for the U.S. to put even more emphasis on private sector-led economic growth across the board.

As the World Bank summed up, "Most effective approaches to development will be led by the private sector, but with effective government to provide the governance framework, facilitation or provision of physical infrastructure, human capital investments, and social cohesion necessary for growth and poverty reduction. The fundamental challenge in stimulating economic growth is to create the right economic incentives that will encourage local economic actors to build capital and to manage it effectively."[16]

From the perspective of entrepreneurs and businessmen, the reality on the ground in the Gulf of Guinea is that the biggest impediments to economic development are the lack of effective basic infrastructure, (i.e., reliable electricity, water, roads), corruption, lack of access to capital, and lack of security. Provision of adequate internal security by increasingly professional law enforcement was discussed in the previous chapter. And corruption, which is absolutely the single biggest impediment to development in Central Africa, will be addressed at the end of this chapter and in the next. Subsequently, our analysis indicates that public funds for development are best spent on immediately providing critical infrastructure requirements, and not on subsidizing prospective business ventures or grandiose state-sponsored development schemes. Private funds should be the lifeblood of business investments, because the market is more likely to back successful, competitive ideas and projects. If the requisite network of power and transport were available, then creative and industrious African entrepreneurs would be empowered to accelerate local economic development and would rapidly hasten the establishment of a stabilizing middle class.

Individual entrepreneurs are the driving force behind innovation and wealth creation in a capitalist system, but they are not the only necessary element. Carl Schramm's "Four Sector Model"[17] clearly explains how each of the following components plays a critical role in setting the conditions for real economic growth: 1) high-impact entrepreneurs, 2) large mature firms, 3) the government, and 4) universities. Schramm argues that individuals with entrepreneurial skills offer new ideas and energy, but cannot do much for economic growth on their own: rather, the funds and groundwork to turn these ideas into reality requires both large, established firms and a government committed to fostering new business and innovation. Finally, he notes, universities can serve as incubators for research, creative thinking and innovation.[18] Unfortunately, in the Gulf of Guinea states, there are real problems with all these components. Private entrepreneurs are not empowered; most large firms are inefficient parastatals or are owned by extractive foreigners; government bureaucracy and corruption impedes economic growth; and most local universities are not competitive with their western counterparts. And regrettably, but understandably, too many of the best and brightest African students trained at western universities are choosing to seek employment in the West, rather than returning home to make a difference.

This analytical approach gives U.S.-Africa policymakers some excellent pressure points upon which to focus limited resources. The U.S. can directly assist African business entrepreneurs by taking a variety of measures to address their biggest impediments. The U.S. can push and assist with industry privatization schemes, and can take steps to encourage more U.S. foreign direct investment (FDI) by leveraging OPIC and Export-Import Bank "investment encouragement and protection tools". The U.S. can apply even stronger pressure for institutionalized corruption reform programs, and can provide some of the necessary training and technical support. And finally, the U.S. can help strengthen African universities, and can create U.S. university scholarship incentives for young African leaders to return to their countries—specifically educated and prepared to tackle their most urgent problems. Each of these general policy strategies will strengthen Africa's private sector to lead the charge in economic development. And each of these approaches can be implemented in the energy sector to begin with, expanding outwards from there.

One caveat is necessary at this juncture. Although the private sector should be empowered to innovate and create wealth in the Gulf of Guinea economies, it should not be held primarily responsible for social development more broadly. In other words, oil companies do not need to be like USAID, they just need to be transparent and accountable. It is the responsibility of honest, democratic African governments to utilize their tax revenues for improving social welfare, and the U.S. must push them to do so accordingly.

Energy Revenue Stream Management and Planning Ideas

True empowerment of the African private sector is absolutely necessary for successful economic development, yet there are some major governmental reforms that are essential as well. Significant economic and infrastructure development cannot take place in a climate of rampant political corruption and mismanagement of oil revenues. Postponing the discussion of political corruption for a bit longer, this next section will address the more specific role the U.S. can play with regards to energy revenue stream management and planning.

Again, there is a direct correlation between this component of African economic development and U.S. interests in national security and energy security. This was recently summed up quite well by Ambassador Ahmedou Ould-Adallah, the United Nations Special Representative for West Africa:

> Strong security implies strong legitimacy. Indeed, given the relationship between poor governance, endemic conflict, state collapse and rising criminality, it appears that one of the most effective ways to combat and prevent rising criminality in the Gulf of Guinea is to also assist this region in its efforts to institutionalize transparent and accountable governance. Issues like accountable management of national resources (oil, diamonds, timber, etc.) and equity in the distribution of national revenue must be part of the security equation. If these political measures are not taken, the new boost in resource extraction in the sub-region, notably oil, could only stimulate internal conflict on power-sharing and resource distribution and fuel political violence and economic delinquency.[19]

In the Gulf of Guinea states there is a publicly recognized general failure to use oil wealth for the development and benefit of local populations, but there are almost no immediate incentives for the governing oil elite to change the system. Blatant theft of oil wealth is a major factor leading to economic exclusion, and may be combated with increased transparency in the energy sector. Yet, though transparency is essential for accountability, it must also be coupled with government expenditures that directly benefit the population. These are broad internal challenges that must be addressed directly by African governments, but may certainly be overcome more easily with appropriate external assistance.

Case studies of other energy producing states demonstrate the importance of strong institutions to handle oil money.[20] There are a variety of options for revenue stream management, and each different model has its advantages and disadvantages. Oil companies can be nationalized and publicly managed, like in Venezuela, which allows revenues to flow directly into government coffers. However, these systems are often subject to mismanagement, inefficiency, and politicization. Arguably, governments of the Gulf of Guinea states are currently too corrupt to use this system effectively for real economic development. If a state oil sector is rapidly privatized, as was the case in Russia, there may be a tendency for a handful of insider oligarchs to receive the lion's share of revenues. Although probably more efficient than state-run oil companies, a privately dominated energy sector requires a strong national tax system to glean revenues for the public good. Unfortunately, most of the Gulf of Guinea states currently have weak, ineffective, and corrupt tax regimes. Yet another model distributes oil revenues directly to the people in the form of an annual payment, as in Alaska and Alberta. This is a wonderfully direct and democratic method for giving constituents great incentives to promote security of the energy sector, and it allows energy funds to contribute directly to local economic development. However, given the realities in the Gulf of Guinea states, this model is impossibly optimistic. Most of these African governments barely have a handle on administrative demographics and population registries, and again, the bloated bureaucracies and corrupt institutions are currently incapable of executing this model effectively. Another possibility, and certainly not the only other option, is the creation of a national oil fund with legal and constitutional constraints on spending, like in Norway and Chad. This model is probably the most practicable for our case study countries, and is one with which the U.S. can assist in implementation and enforcement. One of the risks is that the kind of unchecked, semi-authoritarian governments that characterize most of the Gulf of Guinea might simply change the legal frameworks to suit themselves, at the expense of true economic development for constituents.

Of course, oil revenue stream management models must be suited to an individual state's characteristics, taking into account each one's unique institutions, political culture, and socio-economic realities. No model will precisely fit all of the Gulf of Guinea states, but there are surely some constants. Most importantly, each national model must be transparent to the population, administratively feasible, and contain some objective oversight mechanism to counter corruption. These are the key elements that U.S.-Africa policy can and should attempt to influence most directly.

By examining new and reforming African oil revenue management models, U.S. policymakers may find the best methods to assist with the necessary transformation of the currently operating systems in Gulf of Guinea. In Cameroon, for example, the *Société National de Hydrocarbons* (SNH) is partially responsible for objective oversight of the national petroleum sector.[21] Previously maintained secretly by the President's office, ostensibly for reasons of national security, Cameroon's oil revenues have been published "openly" since 1995, in part due to World Bank insistence. Since 1999, Cameroon has established new petroleum and gas codes, backed by a presidential implementation decree, and has publicly pledged support for the Extractive Industries Transparency Initiative (EITI). There are noticeably some young, western-educated professionals at SNH who are trying to do the right things and run the energy business clearly. SNH is occasionally touted as a "model" for other countries in the sub-region, some of which have solicited advice on energy sector reform, specifically Gabon, Congo, and the DRC.

However, in reality, SNH is still a very confidential organization, and there is very little public knowledge about how oil revenues are actually spent. The bright reformers at SNH have been working on new contract models to try and garner better profits for Cameroon. This could mean more popular benefits in terms of economic development; however, SNH only negotiates the contracts with the major oil firms, and is not in charge of implementing the contracts or overseeing the collection and expenditure of revenues. That is the unique responsibility of the Ministry of Mines and the Office of the President, neither of which are particularly transparent or accountable.

Regarding a case like Cameroon, the U.S. can and should explicitly make oil revenue stream transparency and accountability more of a priority. In order to assist the willing internal actors with systemic changes for the benefit of the population, focused technical assistance, relevant professional and educational exchanges, political pressure, public diplomacy, and other diplomatic and economic incentives could be very effective. In fact, for each Gulf of Guinea state, the U.S. should apply a highly prioritized, openly publicized, individually tailored program of assistance and pressure to help shape the transformation of energy sector revenues. Appropriately managed and distributed, these enormous petroleum revenues stand ready to fundamentally alter the state of economic development in the sub-region.

Another illuminating example, which U.S.-Africa policymakers should examine more closely, is the case of ExxonMobil (or Esso) in Chad. As described in Chapter 2, Chad recently tapped into major oil deposits in the Doba oil fields, but because of Chad's landlocked status, the cost of getting this oil to port was prohibitively expensive for the government and the multinational oil companies. The World Bank agreed to help finance this enormous investment as part of a consortium that included the governments of Chad and Cameroon as well as the private oil companies—but there were conditions. The World Bank insisted on such things as a revenue oversight board that is both impartial and internationally monitored; strict transparency of revenue streams; stringent limits on spending of oil wealth with prioritization for economic and social development projects; and a guaranteed reserved income for the production region itself. Many of these stipulations were no doubt a result of observing problems in other parts of oil-producing Africa, and appear really quite ideal.

In addition to progressive revenue stream management and oversight, the Chad example includes many illustrations of how to give the local population incentives to support an enormous energy sector development project. Esso-Chad incorporated training programs for production operations for Chadian nationals, thereby increasing local human capital and providing employment. In conjunction with the German Council for Sustainable Development (*Deutsche Gesellschaft für Technische Zusammenarbeit*, or GTZ, the German equivalent of USAID), the energy consortium embarked on a consultative process for local compensation and development projects aimed specifically at bringing poor Chadians "on board." Furthermore, Chadian subcontractors have benefited from the acquisition of food, water, construction, and manpower supply contracts. Finally, the consortium very effectively publicized the 5% of oil profits earmarked for the production region itself, and immediately began applying the revenues to visible infrastructure development projects, like roads.

Despite the appearances of a real "success story" in Chad, there are some factors that policymakers must consider if attempting to replicate this model elsewhere in the Gulf of Guinea. Arguably, the implementing circumstances in Chad were unique and unrepeatable in that major energy companies do not usually need financial assistance with their oil exploration and development projects, as they did in landlocked, politically fragile Chad. Therefore, there is little potential leverage to force African governments and private energy concerns into compliance with objective monitoring, transparency, and accountability standards by withholding U.S. or international funds. Without a hard economic bargaining chip, it is extremely difficult to convince African governments to submit to externally imposed revenue constraints when they have no immediate political incentive to do so either. There are also some serious concerns with the genuine effectiveness of Chad's revenue oversight institutions due to apparent loopholes in the legal safeguards and subtle nuances in the governing regulations and enforcement mechanisms.[22]

Notwithstanding these shortcomings, the lessons of the "Chad model" are apparent, and the underlying principles are sound. Oil wealth must be perceived to be spent on development priorities for the people of each country, as this is absolutely critical for stability and security in the energy sector. Of course, the best form of perception is transparent reality, and the oversight institutions and legal framework used in Chad could be modified to correct for ambiguities and then specifically adapted to apply effectively to various individual states. The ability to affect oil revenue stream management models to mobilize economic development opportunities is one of the main reasons why the U.S. should capitalize on its prevailing involvement in the energy sector in the Gulf of Guinea.

In conjunction with applying pressure to establish accountability and oversight of oil revenue management, the U.S. should assist more directly with mitigating macroeconomic consequences of oil-based economies. For example, exchange rate stabilization may be a problem for African energy producers due to "Dutch disease" effects of oil revenues.[23] Better central bank control and discipline is also needed to assuage volatility exacerbated by oil price fluctuations; and hard currency reserves are necessary for shock stabilization, but are usually completely lacking in the Gulf of Guinea states. Extravagant government consumption with oil wealth too often replaces necessary investment and savings, which increases instability and does nothing to ameliorate long-term development problems. And governments need to invest energy revenues in competitive, productive investments that will pay off and provide a buffer in times of financial crisis, not just on social projects. Additionally, investment in human capital is essential so that African countries can one day move away from technological dependence on the developed world.

The U.S. can assist African governments in overcoming some of these key macroeconomic challenges through technical advice, professional and educational exchange programs, and public support of internal reformers. Wherever possible, U.S.-Africa policymakers should support ongoing local initiatives that are showing signs of success. For example, Nigeria's President Obasanjo has assembled an economic "dream team" of western-educated and internationally experienced economists and public administrators who are aggressively fighting corruption and pursuing economic development. These young technocrats have put together the Nigerian Economic Empowerment and Development Strategy (NEEDS)—which, although only about one year old at the time of writing, seems to be a pretty good program, broadly on track and quite successful with monetary reform.[24] There are also some promising indicators within Nigeria at the sub-national level. For example, Ondo State's official development strategy is extremely well written and full of concrete examples of effective and specific policy recommendations designed to promote local economic security.[25] U.S. policymakers (and other external "experts" like the World Bank) would do well to recognize the strengths of indigenous development ideas, and should provide strong support to their implementation, specifically by targeting the corruption and weak institutions that prevent their realization.

Anti-Corruption Requirements and Instruments

Corruption is arguably the biggest impediment to economic development in the Gulf of Guinea, and absolutely plagues the energy sector.[26] For years, Transparency International has ranked Nigeria, Cameroon, and Equatorial Guinea among the world's most corrupt countries, and Human Rights Watch has alleged that more than $4 billion dollars of oil revenues disappeared from Angolan government coffers between 1997-2002.[27] In addition to theft of oil revenues, typical corruption includes: government officials embezzling funds directly from public coffers and taking kickbacks from tendered contracts; businessmen grossly inflating contracts and failing to deliver services or products; individual police and security officials extorting bribes from citizens; and average people paying illegal "sweeteners" for preferential treatment on a daily basis. Unfortunately, in Central Africa, dishonesty and fraud are both expected and accepted on a daily basis, and many officials and functionaries will not perform their duties without a bit of "dash" (additional cash payment). Yet clearly, corruption negatively affects the judicious use of national resources and government revenues, discourages foreign and domestic investment, prevents advancement of the most qualified people, and exacerbates conditions of poverty and insecurity.

Such rampant corruption is a complex, insidious problem that is institutional and cultural, internal and external. David Landes or George Ayittey might surmise that endemic corruption is primarily an internal, cultural variable that can only be addressed by fundamental societal changes driven by motivated and powerful internal actors. Our analysis suggests that this is absolutely true, and that genuine counter-corruption reform can only truly begin with positive leadership by example from the presidents on down. Unfortunately, many of the ruling elite and vested interests in Gulf of Guinea governments are corrupt themselves, and have been for so long that this is virtually impossible. Usually, sporadic official anti-corruption efforts are aimed at mid-level management or low-level street perpetrators, and appear to be more for demonstration than effect. In many cases, there can be no real high-level "house cleaning" without a complete change of government.

As for the externalist, institutional arguments for corruption, Jared Diamond or Basil Davidson might point to factors beyond the control of Africans themselves, like the history of African state formation or the prevailing conditions of the international market. We agree that part of the problem of government corruption in the Gulf of Guinea is attributable to the weak concept of national identity caused by the artificial, colonially imposed state boundaries, and the historically extractive role of government institutions. Because people do not feel much responsibility to the state, and instead focus their allegiance only on their own particular ethnic group or local community, they do not feel compelled to judiciously exercise responsibility of public resources. Rather, they see an obvious opportunity to take advantage of their turn at the helm of one of the state's wealth-producing apparatuses, and make no qualms about helping themselves to their share. This problem is exacerbated by the lack of a strong, independent private commercial sector within which enterprising individuals could get ahead fairly and legally. Additionally, and despite the changes in regulations as a consequence of the Global War on Terrorism, there are international banking secrecy laws that still allow corrupt African leaders to stash away millions of dollars of stolen energy revenues with no consequences whatsoever.[28]

Due to the multifaceted and destructive nature of corruption in the Gulf of Guinea, we submit that U.S.-Africa policymakers must think hard for creative and effective ways to significantly promote transparency and accountability at the internal, cultural level as well as the external and institutional level. The benefits from success with such efforts would be comprehensive and could include extensive potential improvements in governance, economic development, and security.

Despite its current reputation for corruption, and its historical legacy of mismanagement and extraction by government elites, U.S.-Africa policymakers should consider Nigeria as a great case to scrutinize for potentially successful anti-corruption reforms that may be replicable and supportable in other Gulf of Guinea countries. President Obasanjo's "dream team" has recently embarked on a full-scale assault on both public and private sector corruption as part of an overall economic reform agenda, with far and high-reaching effects. They are trying to refocus government on providing basic services; trying to create an environment for the private sector to lead economic growth; and have initiated NEEDS, a very tough economic reform program, imposed by themselves—not by the IMF. The Nigerian government also signed up for a series of international programs such as the G8 transparency compact and EITI, under which they have initiated contracts for independent auditors to examine their national energy revenue streams.

Nigeria's reformers have initiated a series of internal programs that, if prosecuted fully, will have terrific impacts on anti-corruption efforts. The new "Due Process" mechanism is aimed at government contracting, which is a huge source of corruption. Senior officials estimated that as little as 14% of each government contract dollar allocated for capital projects actually went to pay for work completed. However, the new Due Process Office is committed and has moved forward by streamlining contracts processing and adding significant contract transparency to the system. Because approximately 40% of Nigerian oil revenues go unaccounted for, and there is a lot of "missing" government money in general, President Obasanjo also established an Independent Corrupt Practices Commission (ICPC) and an Economic and Financial Crimes Commission (EFCC)—both of which have had real effects at high levels.

Under the progressive and determined Finance Minister, Ms. Okonjo-Iweala, the Nigerian government began to save energy revenue windfall, attributable to the surge in oil prices, as hard currency reserves. It also began a policy of public disclosure of government budgets at all levels, including the previous five years. The government budget allocations at the national, state, and sub-state levels are now published openly and regularly in newspapers, thereby directly informing the public on the allocation of their resources and causing some fine conversations about accountability at all levels of government. Of course, there are some real challenges encountered by obstructions from rent-seeking, vested interests opposed to such transparency, but some of the more progressive thinkers in the government are trying to lock these reforms in legislation so that they endure after the current administration.

A few other Gulf of Guinea states also have indigenous counter-corruption organizations that are in their infancy and may be more likely to succeed with U.S. support. For example, in July 2005 Cameroon announced the creation of a new national finance investigation agency (*Agence Nationale d'Investigation des Finances,* or ANIF), apparently modeled roughly along the lines of Nigeria's EFCC. Only time will tell if ANIF will be an effective tool for accountability, or if it will be just another front for heavily vested elite interests. In Angola, the Coalition of Reconciliation, Transparency and Citizenship (RTC), is an example of a civil society group trying to reduce corruption, increase transparency, and institute more mechanisms of accountability. RTC's "Free Angola" campaign has published startling research about bribery at the grass roots level, is committed to monitoring government activities to ensure that it lives up to its social promises made in the 2004 budget, and is pressuring the government to prepare a national plan to combat corruption.[29]

Although complex and difficult, U.S.-Africa policymakers must engage more directly in the battle against corruption throughout the Gulf of Guinea. The struggle will take a long time to produce systemic results, but is absolutely essential to any long term U.S. energy and security interests in the sub-region. The key question is therefore how best to help?

For external factors, the U.S. should push for more transparency in international (secret) banking and continue to hold U.S. corporations to high standards of accountability through mechanisms like the Foreign Corrupt Practices Act and the stringent public disclosure requirements for publicly traded companies. For private companies and other foreign countries that earn tremendous profits through unscrupulous relations with wealthy African leaders, it is a bit more difficult. However, increased transparency in international markets and financial institutions can assist in tracking capital flight and subsequent investment from dishonest elites. This influential facet of corruption has considerable consequences on the energy sector and security environment in the Gulf of Guinea, and must be pursued more aggressively.

For internal factors, the U.S. should recognize the value of education and exchange programs for key African leaders and officials, but should not fall into the trap of giving U.S. solutions. It is far more effective to equip intelligent Africans with the best tools to find and implement their own policy solutions, as evidenced by Nigeria's "dream team" and their ongoing reform efforts. Fundamentally, to address endemic corruption from an external vantage point, the U.S. must do all it can to assist with the development of internal, African institutions, legislation, and processes that shore up security, economic development, and democracy in a transparent and accountable environment.

One organization that may offer a good model of how to do this is the U.S.' International Trade Administration (ITA). The ITA has a "Good Governance Program" that aims to advance the rule of law for international business in order to increase market access and ensure a level playing field for U.S. companies in emerging markets. It does this by actively promoting transparency through business ethics and anti-corruption, accountability in corporate governance, fairness in commercial dispute resolution, and protection of intellectual property rights.[30] The ITA's "Six-Phase Business Ethics Program" outlines concrete steps designed to increase transparent and ethical business and government practices in a given country. These six steps are: 1) raise awareness; 2) develop basic guidelines for codes of business conduct; 3) business ethics training; 4) business ethics manual and other resources; 5) private-public sector cooperation; and 6) sustainable initiatives.

If well coordinated and adapted to individual national characteristics, U.S.-Africa policymakers might be able to apply some of the ITA's approach more systematically across multiple organizations at various levels of government around the Gulf of Guinea. The U.S. could encourage the creation of an institutional ethics watchdog apparatus for government employees and use of government funds. The U.S. could support a reward-for-reporting system, or a free anonymous phone number for corruption tips. There are many good ideas for anti-corruption reform, but the efforts must be supported at the highest levels of the target countries in order for them to be effective.

Conclusion

As described in Chapter 7, human security and economic development are part of the essential foundations upon which energy security and national security are built. In addition to qualified debt relief, elimination of western agricultural subsidies, and the development of human capital and strong education systems, the private sector has an enormous role to play in African economic development. An augmented private sector can empower entrepreneurs and lead to economic diversification, enabling Africans to free themselves from dependency and pull themselves out of poverty. For the private sector growth engines to function properly, motivated individuals need adequate security, infrastructure and capital. Additionally, economic development will not be achievable in the Gulf of Guinea unless the glaring problem of corruption is tackled head-on by the U.S., and more importantly, by the African governments themselves. In the Gulf of Guinea states, corruption is intrinsically linked and anathema to both economic development and good governance. A critical component of anti-corruption and development initiatives is the reform of energy revenue stream management processes and institutions. Insecurity, poverty, political instability and inadequate governance currently threaten the tremendous potential benefits of the energy sector. An integrated, long-term approach is thus needed to address key issues and to ensure long-term stability in support of U.S. energy security goals.

In turn, human security and economic development can only be truly institutionalized through good governance—loosely defined as encompassing quality democratic institutions, a supportive political culture, and trustworthy, effective leaders. As discussed in previous chapters of this volume, there can be no long-term energy security in states that are not politically stable. Democracy, adapted to local culture and unique national factors, is what will guarantee this stability by institutionalizing peaceful mechanisms for political compromise and thereby strengthening the relationship between the society and the state. As explained in the following chapter, the current lack of democratic institutions and culture in the Gulf of Guinea poses a serious threat to our nation's long-term energy security and national security interests.

Notes

1. *Private Sector Investment in Development*, Peter Watson, Chairman, President, and CEO of the Overseas Private Investment Corporation (OPIC), Aspen Institute, 31 July 2004, 4.

2. Jared Diamond, *Guns, Germs, and Steel: The Fates of Human Societies* (New York: W.W. Norton and Company, Inc., 1999).

3. David Landes, *The Wealth and Poverty of Nations: Why Some are Rich and Some So Poor* (New York: W.W. Norton and Company, Inc., 1999).

4. Basil Davidson, *The Black Man's Burden: Africa and the Curse of the Nation State*, Three Rivers Press, New York, NY, 1992.

5. George Ayittey *Africa in Chaos: A Comparative History* (New York: St. Martin's Press, 1999).

6. From the UN's Integrated Regional Information Network (IRIN) Africa Briefing, 31 August 2004.

7. Emphasized by Ghana's Minister of Defense, in an address to students at KAIPTC's IPSO course, 13 June 2005, Accra, Ghana.

8. A Human Security Doctrine for Europe, The Barcelona Report of the Study Group on Europe's Security Capabilities, 15 September, 2004, 9.

9. Madelfia A. Abb and Cindy R. Jebb, "Human Security and Good Governance: A Living Systems Approach to Understanding and Combating Terrorism," in *The Making of a Terrorist: Recruitment, Training and Root Causes*, edited by James JF Forest, (Westport, CT: Praeger, 2005).

10. Madelfia A. Abb and Cindy R. Jebb, "Human Security and Good Governance."

11. Equatorial Guinea with its tiny population and huge oil revenues, (the "Kuwait of Africa"), may be an exception in the short run.

12. See *"A Ten-Year Strategy for Increasing Capital Flows to Africa" produced by the Commission on Capital Flows to Africa in June 2003.* Available at The Corporate Council on Africa homepage at: http://www.africacncl.org. Members of The Corporate Council on Africa account for roughly 85% of all FDI in sub-Saharan Africa according to the U.S. Department of Commerce.

13. Diamonds in Liberia and Sierra Leone; oil in Nigeria, Sudan, Congo-Brazzaville; and a variey of mineral wealth in Angola and the DRC for example.

14. Witney W. Schneidman, "The Commission on Capital Flows to Africa," *The Africa Journal* (Aug/Sep 2003), 11.

15. Peter Watson, *Private Sector Investment in Development*, 8.

16. *The Role and Effectiveness of Development Assistance: Lessons from World Bank Experience*, World Bank research paper, available online at http://econ.worldbank.org.

17. Carl Schramm, "Building Entrepreneurial Economies," *Foreign Affairs* Jul/Aug 2004, 104.

18. Carl Schramm, "Building Entrepreneurial Economies," 107-110.

19. Ambassador Ahmedou Ould-Adallah, United Nations Special Representative for West Africa, remarks made at the Gulf of Guinea Maritime Security Conference, 4 October 2004, Naples, Italy.

20. For examples of case studies, "resource curse" statistics, and a good revenue stream management discussion, see "Saving Iraq From Its Oil", *Foreign Affairs*, July/August 2004.

21. Author interviewed an SNH official and chose to allow him anonymity, but readers can find out more at http://www.snh.cm.

22. For an excellent study of Chad's oil revenue model, see Ian Gary and Nikki Reisch, *Chad's Oil: Miracle or Mirage?- Following the Money in Africa's Newest Petro-State*, Catholic Relief Services and Bank Information Center, February 2005.

23. See chapters 1 and 2 of this volume for a general description of Dutch Disease and its effects.

24. More on NEEDS, and its state-level counterpart (dubbed "SEEDS" for State Economic Empowerment Development Strategies) is provided in Chapter 2.

25. Author received a printed copy of the official Ondo State development strategy during a personal interview with Ondo's Secretary of State, Dr. Olusegun Mimiko, Ondo, Nigeria, 29 January, 2005.

26. Please see Chapter 2 for more on this, including individual country examples.

27. Full report available online at: www.hrw.org/reports/2004/angola0104/index.htm.

28. Please see Chapters 2 and 3 for a discussion on the billions that have been looted by country leaders in the Gulf of Guinea.

29. *IRIN News Service,* 30 March 2005

30. Find out more at http://www.ita.doc.gov/goodgovernance.

Chapter 10
Democratization and Leadership
for Good Governance

*Bad governance is the major reason for conflicts and underdevelop-
ment in Africa today.*[1]

From the research and analysis provided thus far in this volume, it should be
clear that democracy in the Gulf of Guinea is important to achieving U.S. energy
security and national security objectives. At the grand strategic level, poor governance in developing countries is the most significant threat to U.S. national
security and energy security interests in the world today. This may seem to be an
incredible claim given the current vast array of security threats from non-state
actors, international terrorist groups, rogue states, "loose nukes," etc. However,
we are convinced that it is the lack of effective governments and stable societies
that are in fact a root cause of these other known threats. Indeed, if angry, disen-
chanted citizens had open, effective government institutions within which they
could address grievances and resolve disputes, they would be far less likely to
turn to violence. If governments had transparent, accountable mechanisms to
connect their policies to the informed desires and aspirations of their constituents, they would be far more stable. And stable governments supported by educated citizens are far more likely to successfully mitigate internal problems and
peacefully address external issues that affect U.S. energy and security concerns
worldwide.

The bottom line is that true liberal democracies are the most stable, peaceful, cooperative form of government, and are the least likely to threaten U.S.
national security and energy security interests. This is not a call to export the
U.S. system of government to the rest of the underdeveloped world—that would
be foolish and impossible. Rather, this chapter argues that assisting with the
development of indigenously-tailored liberal democracy in poor, violent, unstable regions is not just a nice thing to do—it is inextricably linked to our own
security and quality of life. The important point for the Gulf of Guinea is that
unconditionally supporting non-democratic regimes for the sake of access to
energy reserves is simply not in the U.S.' best interests in the long run. Rather, it

251

is vital that U.S.-Africa policymakers work to foster African national cultures of ownership and pride in good governance, democracy, the rule of law, civil rights and liberties, etc.—so much so, that citizens and governments alike work peacefully together to prevent the emergence of threats that may affect national security and energy security.

Before launching into a more detailed discussion of what the U.S. can and should do to tackle the problem of poor governance in the Gulf of Guinea, it is useful to examine democracy in a broader sense. In reality, what is democracy? This word is used a lot today but it is difficult to pin down a precise meaning. If people assume that democracy means the sudden appearance of a job for everyone, food on every table, and a car in every garage, they will be gravely disappointed. Democracy can be described as a product or as a process. As a product, democracy can be envisioned as an idyllic end state, where every major decision is consultative or taken by popularly elected officials, and there are guarantees of basic human rights and freedoms for every citizen. Democracy can also be thought of as a process—a process of improving participatory mechanisms and institutionalizing human rights, gradually incorporating more and more of society. Our analysis indicates that it is more useful to think of democracy as a process, and it is important to recognize that it takes considerable time to develop. However, we also recognize that democracy is a natural progression of an informed humanity.

What defines a democracy? In a gross oversimplification, one could draw a long horizontal line, to represent a spectrum or continuum of governance. At one extreme end are purely authoritarian regimes, at the other, true liberal democracies. North Korea and Sweden may be good examples of states that approximate these diverse paradigms, authoritarian and liberal democratic respectively. Authoritarian regimes are relatively easy to identify, but what defines a liberal democracy? It is commonly accepted that requirements include the rule of law, institutionalized checks and balances on power, a fair and impartial judiciary, and guarantees of human rights, individual freedoms, and freedom of the media. In essence, a liberal democracy exhibits the kinds of healthy political institutions and culture that are absent under authoritarian regimes. Of course, most states in the world today are at neither the authoritarian nor liberal democratic ends of this spectrum, but rather, somewhere in between. And in the last 20 years, the world has seen a general trend of states moving in the direction of the liberal democracy end of the continuum, with some notable exceptions regressing back towards authoritarianism—perhaps states like Myanmar, Belarus, or Zimbabwe.

A more useful mark along this spectrum is that which denotes the beginning of democracy—the bare minimum requirement to even be considered a democracy at all. This is called an "electoral democracy," and most developing nations are struggling along with the democratic process somewhere here around this point on the spectrum. Some have clearly passed this point, while others are still attempting to reach it. So what defines an electoral democracy? The commonly accepted minimum requirement is that of "free and fair" elections; yet this term is always controversial. For this discussion, take "free" to mean universal suffrage, and "fair" to mean that there is a realistic possibility of opposition victory. There are many infamous cases of one-party states or dominant-figure regimes where elections are held symbolically, and the incumbent is guaranteed victory. But that's not fair, and that's not an electoral democracy. A good African example of a newly emerged electoral democracy might be Kenya, where President Kibaki of the opposition managed to defeat an incumbent party and a young Kenyatta. Besides perhaps São Tome and Principe, it is questionable whether any of the Gulf of Guinea states have actually even achieved the threshold of electoral democracy, despite the presence of elections. And certainly, none of them even come close yet to being liberal democracies.

Again, most of the developing world is struggling along somewhere around the electoral democracy mark, but as mentioned earlier, it takes significant time to democratize. It is instructive to examine a basic U.S. timeline to illustrate this point more clearly, while keeping in mind that most African nations are about 45 years old. The U.S. declared independence in 1776, but the constitution was not written until 1789, and this was only after the second attempt at forming a national government. It took 89 years after independence, in 1865, for the U.S. to officially abolish slavery. It was not until 1920, a full 144 years after independence, that the U.S. guaranteed women the right to vote—finally obtaining an environment of "free" elections. Further, it took 178 years after independence, before (in 1954) the U.S. legally enforced integration of public schools in the south. It was not until the 1970s, almost 200 years after independence, that the U.S. moved to a universal direct primary to choose candidates for a presidential election. (Nigeria is already trying to do this.) Before then, political parties usually chose their own candidates behind closed doors, rather undemocratically. And finally, there is the case of the 2000 election in the U.S., after which many constituents filed lawsuits claiming that due to a variety of reasons, the election was not "fair" at all. Of course, the comparison between the U.S. and the (on average) 45 year-old democratic experiences of Africa is a bit contrived, and we are not implying in this volume that African states will take hundreds of years to develop truly democratic systems. However, the point remains that major systemic institutional and cultural changes in governance do take a great deal of time to emerge and stabilize.

One of the complications for African states and the rest of the developing world is that these countries are not just struggling with democratization, but with the parallel challenge of economic development as well. What is the nature of this relationship between democracy and economic development? Is one a prerequisite for the other? If so, which one comes first? Or do they have to occur simultaneously? Many scholars will argue that democracy is a precondition for economic development, but there are a few examples to the contrary.

In 1960, Singapore, South Korea, and Zaire (now Democratic Republic of the Congo), were equally poor, as measured in terms of GDP per capita. Today, 45 years later, Singapore and South Korea are developed nations with high income and high standards of living, but the Congo is even poorer than it was in 1960. Was it democracy that led the fantastic growth of these "Asian tigers?" No. It was manufacturing-led export growth and investment rigidly enforced by very undemocratic "chaebols" in South Korea, and by the infamous authoritarian premier Lee Kuan Yew of Singapore. Economic development came first; democratization began later.

Consider also the cases of two giants, China and Russia. In 1989, both states embarked on ambitious reform programs. Russia opted to liberalize its economy and democratize at the same time; China chose to focus on liberalizing the economy without democratizing. Fifteen years later, the Russian economy is in shambles with many of the valuable production sectors in the hands of oligarchs, while China's economy has experienced phenomenal growth, averaging over 9% per year for the last several years. Many outsiders have accused President Putin of cracking down on democracy recently in an attempt to regain control of the state and promote economic development, while in China, the state still censors the internet access of its citizens and makes no qualms about being undemocratic, despite tremendous economic transformation.

So what is the true relationship between economic development and democracy? One can argue this conundrum both ways effectively, but consider this paradox: sometimes the democratic process can impede critical decisions and far-reaching policies that can bring rapid economic development, and yet, without the democratic process there exist no checks and balances to ensure that development is for the people, not the elite. Unfortunately, there exist far too few "benevolent dictators," like Lee Kuan Yew, and in Africa the world has seen time and time again confirmation of that old axiom, "power corrupts, and absolute power corrupts absolutely." It is for these reasons that the U.S.-Africa policy framework introduced in Chapter 7 places security and economic development as more fundamental priorities than democracy; yet there is no doubt that good governance in Africa will require democratization.

Much has been said over the past several decades about the challenges and misadventures of democratization on the African continent. Nonetheless, the energy and security needs of the U.S. compel a renewed and sustained commitment to promoting the political institutions and norms of a healthy democracy. Internal stability has its roots in effective and legitimate governments. In defining governmental legitimacy, the democratization and development literature is rich with prerequisites such as the establishment of a well-developed civil society, crosscutting social and economic cleavages, transparent and accountable governance, protection of individual and minority rights, and sustainable economic growth. In the long run, it is in the best interests of U.S. national security and energy security to have a reliable supply of oil from a variety of international partners that are internally stable. Governmental legitimacy in the Gulf of Guinea is thus vital to the U.S. energy security agenda—clearly, adding more unstable regimes to the pool of oil suppliers will not give the U.S. reliable energy or security.[2]

Realities of Democracy in the Gulf of Guinea

Democracy and freedom in Africa are noble and lofty goals that can only be achieved through decades of consistency and commitment by actors on all sides. As Kaplan has observed, "Democracy emerges only as a capstone to other social and economic achievements,"[3] but must remain as a beacon for policymakers and implementers alike. Based on our research, we strongly believe that the U.S. can effectively assist with the democratization process in the Gulf of Guinea, but policymakers must realistically take into account some of the most difficult obstacles. Some of the current challenges are based on the historical evolution of African political institutions, and some of them are linked directly to current cultural realities and popular misgivings from the modern African perspective.

In order for U.S.-Africa policymakers to make a significant impact on good governance, it is important that they consider how the historical process of state formation has affected Africa's current governance challenges. Here again, the comparative method of examining another region for parallel lessons may be informative. The idea of the stable nation-state in Western Europe is directly related to the process of democratization; yet in fact, the European nation-state is the product of hundreds of years of bloody civil wars and inter-state fighting. For over three hundred years, Catholics killed Protestants and vice versa; Germanic tribes and Italian city-states fought each other mercilessly; and England, France, Germany and others were repeatedly at war with each other. Out of this cauldron of violence and struggle for national identity and political control emerged the modern nation-state, which is the strong basis for European liberal democracies today.

Africa did not have this same process of state formation at all. In fact, African states were artificially created by outside powers at the Berlin conference near the end of the 19th century, and did not benefit from the turbulent—but arguably unifying—"natural" state formation process experienced in Europe and elsewhere. Is it any wonder that today the issues of democratization and economic development are further complicated by pervasive questions of state legitimacy and national identity?

At independence, a generation of African leaders basing their legitimacy on anti-colonial civic nationalism inherited the apparatus of relatively effective authoritarian colonial states. In most cases, the new regimes started with Western parliamentary and legal institutions, but soon adopted one-party state models. Within a few years, military coups and inter-ethnic conflicts had become features of many African political systems. By the 1970s, almost all African polities could be categorized as "weak authoritarian states" lacking in both legitimacy and effectiveness.

During the Cold War, U.S. national security policy in sub-Saharan Africa consisted of little more than supporting regimes that were supposedly anticommunist, regardless of how undemocratic or how oppressive they might have been. As long as a government allowed U.S. access and influence, and denied the same to the U.S.S.R., they would receive American financial and military support. This blatant contradiction between U.S. interests and values propped up infamous autocrats and dictators and often led to horrific civil wars. The continent of Africa was like a playing field upon which the two superpowers competed in an international game of power and strategy, woefully ignoring the long-term effects on local political and economic development. Unfortunately, this occurred during most of independent Africa's formative years, and the negative effects are still felt today.

Social scientists have proposed various models to describe post-colonial African political systems. Neopatrimonialism, sultanism, tribalism, clientelism, prebendalism, and public sphere dualism adapt models of traditional or feudal politics to the modern African setting or offer explanations based on theories of ethnic nationalism. Some analysts have emphasized the dysfunctional nature of African politics using concepts like predatory elite, vampire state, and kleptocracy. Using a historical perspective, one could argue that modern African political systems have resulted from colonialism's abortion of Africa's organic political development, combined with the clash between traditional cultural values, rapid modernization, corrupt leadership, and continued external interference. In any case, the political institutions in the Gulf of Guinea states are in drastic need of improvement, and the U.S. is now uniquely poised to contribute productively to their transformation.

In addition to appreciating a historical perspective, U.S.-Africa policymakers must also consider current cultural realities in the Gulf of Guinea that impede the democratization process. In most of the countries, the government is all too often perceived to be a vehicle for enrichment and not a calling to public service. Many elected, appointed, and civil service officials simply use their positions for private gain and do little to nothing for public benefit. Corruption is rampant and nepotism is the norm. Of course, this outrages many private citizens, but many more still clamor, compete, and often attempt to bribe their way into a position of governmental authority so that they too can steal their share. This erodes public confidence in government institutions and completely undermines the concept of a representative democracy. As discussed in the previous chapter, corporatist government interests also plague the private business sector by stifling the capitalist innovation and competition required for real economic development.

For average citizens, the concept of democracy is vague, elusive, and altogether not that important. Most people are far more concerned with the immediately personal issues of security and economic development, and are extremely skeptical of the benefits of their supposedly "democratic" systems. In the absence of major economic improvements, many constituents perceive elections as the only "dividend" of democracy, and become cynical because in the Gulf of Guinea, most of those are neither truly free nor fair. There is a glaring need for a much better media campaign to explain to populations the potential benefits of liberal democratic systems, and to temper their expectations of elections and the beginnings of democratic transformation. Further, many governments still have much to do in the area of providing civil liberties to their people. For example, Freedom House lists Cameroon, Equatorial Guinea, Republic of the Congo, and Angola as strongly "Not Free," and Gabon and Nigeria as only "Partly Free."[4]

It is fair to say that many Africans consider democracy a luxury, not a necessity, and that people do not see the long-term effects of how it may increase security and economic development. Often thinking of more immediate effects—how will this help me now?—citizens resent the expenses of their "democratic" systems. Democracy is not cheap for a developing country when considering the costs of campaigns, elections, public institutions, etc., and many would rather see the money spent elsewhere.[5] This is especially true in Gulf of Guinea countries where public funds are often used to support only the campaigns of incumbents, and many constituents do not perceive any real connection between an election and legitimate popular consent.

Other obstacles to democratization in the Gulf of Guinea include the generally weak concept of citizenship and the impediments posed by vested political interests. These two factors are related because people do not feel strong responsibilities to the system, partially due to a lack of national identity, and partially due to the glaring endemic corruption within the majority of government institutions. The minority elite are probably the biggest challenge to political reform efforts because they control the majority of the national administrative and financial power, and stand to lose the most with real democratization.

Given the tremendous local obstructions discussed above, we are convinced that American policymakers are often too idealistic, and that transforming the Gulf of Guinea states into true liberal democracies may take generations. However, based on broad U.S. values and specific energy and security interests, U.S.-Africa policymakers must continue to try to push these states beyond the basic threshold of electoral democracies. Despite the time and fundamental cultural changes required to see this policy goal through to completion, in the long run it is essential for U.S. interests to do so. The next section of this chapter will explore some of the most effective ways to specifically impact democratization in the Gulf of Guinea.

What Can the U.S. Do to Improve Governance?

As with economic development policy, real change in African governance must come from within the states themselves. An external player can only facilitate and encourage internal stakeholders who have the drive and initiative to radically transform local political culture and institutions. The first challenge for U.S.-Africa policymakers is to identify enterprising individual public leaders and nascent government institutions that appear promising in terms of transparency, accountability, and effectiveness. Policymakers must also recognize the need for incorporation of indigenous African models and not attempt to impose mirror images of U.S. institutions. These models may include something like Botswana's House of Chiefs as an integral part of a democratic government, but in whatever form, the approach must be individually appropriate for each state's unique political culture. As Tanzania's President Mkapa recently said, "After all those years of colonial rule and the five decades or so of self-rule, with its mistakes of all colors and shades, the time has now come for Africa to go back to the drawing board and try to engender a new democracy for Africa with African characteristics . . . I am convinced that Africa needs a home-grown new democracy."[6]

With the current high level of U.S. involvement in the Gulf of Guinea, the opportunity is especially ripe for policymakers to help African reformers push their democratization agenda in order to pursue long-term stability. Stability, as a specific policy goal, is difficult to define, especially as there are big differences between economic and political stability. In terms of governance, it is perhaps more useful to think about structural stability—the ability of government institutions to deal with crises and handle conflicts of interest peacefully and effectively within a stable system. To achieve this goal, our analysis suggests three major focus areas in which new efforts can be directed: transparency, to build legitimacy and effectiveness in governments; military professionalization, as a catalyst for cultural and institutional transformation; and leadership, for the development of institutions, legislation, and processes for the rule of law.

Transparency

In order to build legitimacy and effectiveness in Africa's governments, the U.S. and its allies must demand transparency in everything. Although admittedly a gross generalization, African politics are usually blinded by ethnicity and money—i.e., people vote for their group and their provider, regardless of policies and principles. Part of this is due to ignorance and apathy, but a larger part of it is due to endemic, systemic corruption. Transparency is the antidote to such corruption. In Gulf of Guinea governments, officials take advantage of the system at every level, yet this is not a genetic African problem; it is a cultural and institutional one. However, it is very difficult for external policymakers to directly affect the culture and norms of masses of corrupt individuals; thus, we believe that if the system itself can be changed, the people will change correspondingly.

In order to help change the system, U.S.-Africa policymakers must aggressively and publicly promote transparency and accountability in government on several different levels. First and foremost, the United States must encourage budget transparency to ensure that local populations of the oil-producing states in the Gulf of Guinea are given a complete understanding of where their country's oil revenues are spent. As described in the previous chapter, oil revenue transparency is good for U.S. business, economy, and access to oil, as well as being honestly representative of American values of fairness, governmental accountability and the rule of law. Oil revenue transparency is necessary for regional stability and sustained economic development. On a practical level, fiscal transparency in places like Nigeria will reduce attacks on pipelines and transfer flow stations by those who feel disenfranchised as they come to see personal benefits from allowing the unencumbered flow of oil. Further, transparency is needed to ensure that huge oil revenues are never used to support criminal organizations or other transnational threats like al Qaeda. As discussed earlier in the book, the presence of terrorism in Africa (particularly in the realm of money laundering) demands a full disclosure about where oil monies are spent.

As Wirth, Gray and Podesta (2003) noted in a 2003 *Foreign Affairs* article, the "mismanagement of energy resources contributes to impoverishment and inequity, breeding unrest and violence and making the delivery of sustainable energy even more difficult."[7] The international community is already moving in a promising direction—the Extractive Industries Transparency Initiative (EITI), a British proposal endorsed in 2003 by the Group of 8 countries, calls upon all oil companies to demonstrate a commitment to fiscal transparency by reporting information on revenue transfers.[8] The global "Publish What You Pay Campaign," which is sponsored in part by George Soros and the Open Society Institute, has also called on oil, gas and mining companies to reveal the extent of their payments to resource-rich countries.[9] The U.S. should strongly back these initiatives, and incorporate their principles of transparency and accountability into every political and economic interaction with Gulf of Guinea governments.

Another critical venue in which transparency is paramount, but glaringly absent, is the system of checks and balances that is needed between various institutions of government and civil society so that they may hold each other accountable to the population. In most Gulf of Guinea states, there are no real checks and balances on presidents and their executive arms. This is exacerbated in the Francophone states (Cameroon, Chad, Gabon, and Congo) because the exceptionally powerful presidencies are modeled on the French "super-presidential" system. In addition to budget transparency, increased objectivity and empowerment of government oversight commissions is essential to transparency and accountability. This is especially true for election, anti-corruption, and judicial watchdog agencies.

As mentioned in the previous chapter, Nigeria has begun a genuine concerted effort to empower objective economic anti-corruption units, but these institutions are still in their infancy and are the exception in the sub-region. The U.S. should strongly encourage and provide support to such anti-corruption organizations, focused on economic, political and legal accountability, within each Gulf of Guinea state. For example, several of the sub-region's constitutions require public declaration of government officials' private assets; but in actuality this is not enforced. Where some governments claim to provide "statistical transparency" on revenue allocation decisions, these figures are not independently checked with reality, and in fact there is almost always serious "skimming" by corrupt individuals. Several of the sub-regions governments have official anti-corruption units, some down to the level of each major ministry, but almost none of them are in fact impartial. Presidents in the Gulf of Guinea usually personally appoint all ministers, governors, prefects, judges, senior election oversight officials, and anti-corruption chiefs with little or no opportunity for parliaments, independent commissions, or civil society groups to seriously weigh in on the decisions. Therefore, there is no real objectivity of institutionalized "constraints on power," and subsequently, no real accountability to the people.

In addition to strong diplomatic pressure from high-level U.S. officials, U.S.-Africa policymakers should emphasize public diplomacy programs that overtly promote African government accountability and transparency. Methods should include direct information campaigns and indirect public awareness initiatives that are realistic and consistent across all levels of U.S. Embassy engagement. The U.S. should also support more professional and educational exchanges directly related to good governance practices and procedures. For example, talented young leaders from Gulf of Guinea administrations could be supported to attend specifically focused executive programs at institutions like the John F. Kennedy School of Government or other equivalent schools. Professional training and education exchanges could also be arranged with counterpart U.S. government agencies—not to transfer U.S. methods verbatim, but to expose key individuals to a variety of processes and ideas that may be adaptable to promote good governance at home. And finally, public diplomacy programs should also be aimed at empowering indigenous civil society groups so that local populations have the information, space, and means to get involved and begin to hold their own governments accountable.

Military Professionalization

One of the most tangible ways to improve governance in the Gulf of Guinea is to invest heavily in the development of the military. This may seem incredibly counterintuitive for states with such a checkered history of military dictatorships and disproportionate and corrupt military influence. Yet this is exactly why this approach would be so effective. We are not referring here to investment in terms of buying new, more, and better tanks, planes, and guns, etc. Rather, we are talking about investing in military professionalism as a direct method of positively influencing leadership, governance, and democracy.

In Samuel Huntington's classic *The Soldier and the State,* which examines the importance of good civil-military relations in a democracy, the author calls for the requirement of a "politically neutral" military to support a democratic system. In the United States, for example, the military swears allegiance to the Constitution, not to any individual or political group. This is significant. Our research has led us to conclude that unless the military establishment is truly focused on supporting the government as an institution—as opposed to a specific government—it cannot be relied upon to ensure smooth democratic transitions of power. Unless the military is consciously serving the people as a whole, as opposed to a particular ethno-linguistic subset, it cannot establish the trust required between a democratic society and the state.

In Chapter 8 of this volume, we discussed in some detail the security and stability benefits of more professional military establishments in the Gulf of Guinea. Without revisiting many of the similarly relevant requirements and methods, the arguments raised earlier hold true for democratization as well. Military engagement with questionable regimes should not be prevented, interrupted, or rendered ineffective by overcautious lawmakers who do not understand how a truly professional military can be a catalyst for significant cultural and institutional transformation. On the contrary, U.S.-Africa policymakers should leverage the sub-regional security agendas and genuine desires to engage with the U.S. military in order to make a profound impact on good governance. Again, U.S. military engagement with Gulf of Guinea states should not be perceived as a nice reward for past performance; rather it should be utilized as a powerful tool for shaping and influencing the future.

In most Gulf of Guinea states, the military is both revered and feared. Despite their often-corrupt tendencies, African militaries are certainly one of the most organized and effective institutions among an array of weak and ineffective ones. Young men generally look up to soldiers, and officers are regarded as an elite class within society. Due to this perception, the actions and values of military leaders play an especially significant role in shaping the attitudes and perspectives of their societies. Precisely because of this disproportionate influence, the U.S. must work hard to professionalize the Gulf of Guinea militaries as an important first step towards good governance.

It is worth discussing briefly how a professional military is essential for democratization and simultaneously contributes hugely positive externalities to national stability and development in general. Without a politically neutral military, real democratization cannot take place. Even the bare minimum "electoral democracy" is unachievable if the incumbent regimes retain the loyalty of powerful, biased militaries. For an election to be "fair," there must be a reasonable possibility of opposition victory. And in reality, to have a stable government transition to an opposition plurality party, the state must have a professional, integrated, neutral military—not corrupt incumbent affiliates. Otherwise, the new government stands no chance of success and may even be ripe for a military coup d'etat.

It is fair to say that the Gulf of Guinea militaries are all politically influential and exert inappropriately prevailing effects on domestic politics. Whereas in the United States, there are clear legal constraints on the words, actions, and behavior of active duty soldiers regarding political activities, nothing like this is enforced in the Gulf of Guinea. In fact, it is often prominent and wealthy military officers who weigh in heavily on appointments of public officials and back particular political candidates, either overtly or behind the scenes.

These challenges of unprofessional militaries are best addressed through direct, continuous U.S. military engagement, using the variety of ODC tools outlined earlier in this volume. Continued professional military education and exchange programs do have a significant impact on the perspectives, values, and capabilities of select individuals. And if these individuals are carefully chosen beforehand, and closely followed and supported afterwards, they can have a dramatic impact on the systems to which they return.

In addition to gradually changing the political mentality and loyalties of military institutions in the Gulf of Guinea, there are many other potentially positive results from increased and continuous U.S. military engagement. A professional military and good civil-military relations can advance many of the essential, but less tangible aspects of a development agenda. Women are egregiously underempowered in most Gulf of Guinea states, and ethnic rivalries and mistrust are the norm. A truly professional military is an institution that rapidly advances integration and gender empowerment. This is evident in U.S. history, where the military led the nation with integration of African-Americans and equality of women. A non-corrupt, merit-based military can be a great economic equalizer and a vehicle for social advancement. A professional military provides education, vocational job skills, and a common language, all of which are lacking to some extent in Gulf of Guinea states. Finally, and very importantly, a professional military contributes to a sense of nationalism that may begin to supersede ethnic factionalism and contribute directly to increased security.

The Critical Role of Leadership

Governance in the Gulf of Guinea is riddled with problems including corruption, nepotism, weak institutions, lack of accountability, mismanagement, external interference, etc. This chapter has so far discussed the potential for better governance via increased transparency and more professional militaries. Yet there is an even more basic element that is absolutely essential for real security, economic development, and democratization in the sub-region; and that is good leadership.

Leadership is one of the most intangible variables for social scientists to measure; yet it is arguably the most critical in terms of government effectiveness and legitimacy. National leaders are the players from which a country takes direction. They are the heads of state, the implementers of policy, and the determinants of priorities. The effectiveness of a leader is critical in solving the problems that face a particular people, and in facilitating the nation's development progress. Effective leadership provides "political goods" such as security, infrastructure, a framework for commercial activities, and positive international representation. Effective leadership results in the improved human condition of a nation's population, to include health, education, prosperity, peace and stability, and freedom from corruption.

Leadership, both U.S. and African, is arguably the primary determinant for the success or failure of U.S.-Africa policy. Though in reality politically sensitive and difficult to influence, leadership must not be the "elephant in the corner" that nobody wants to talk about. That is how it used to be with corruption before the World Bank, Transparency International, and others had the courage to publicly identify corruption as a scourge to development policy. This is not a call for externally initiated regime change as in the case of Iraq, but it is a clear message that leadership matters tremendously and should be addressed accordingly. For U.S.-Africa policymakers, it must be a primary and stated goal to encourage good leadership for the development of institutions, legislation, and processes for the rule of law that will lead to increased security and better governance in the Gulf of Guinea.

For a variety of security, energy, and development reasons, the U.S. and the rest of the G-8 now have the distinct opportunity to make Africa more of a priority. The effects of poor leadership—government waste, mismanagement, and corruption, combined with external interference for external gain—have been tolerated for too long. There is a great need for: enlightened leadership; public and transparent competition of ideas and government; innovation and change in public policy formation and implementation; education reform; and the recognition that elections do not equal democracy.

Policies focused on encouraging media transparency and education throughout the Gulf of Guinea are essential, particularly in countries where freedom of expression is resisted by an historically authoritarian regime. Institutions are needed to strengthen the rule of law—for example, energy policy regulatory frameworks are needed to thwart corruption in the region that threatens to undermine U.S. energy interests. Civil societies require the empowerment of people to enable peaceful regime transformation—thus, African countries can no longer be allowed to produce ballot-stuffed election results as the "will of the people." Term limits in accordance with constitutional intentions must be imposed on senior positions throughout the region, and attempts to hastily change constitutional requirements should not be allowed to perpetuate authoritarian regimes. And even more importantly, there is a need to instill in society the "enough is enough" principle required to develop a generation of responsible public leaders.

One of the biggest challenges for Gulf of Guinea leadership is how to overcome the classic "Big Man" politics of Paul Biya in Cameroon, Omar Bongo in Gabon, Teodoro Obiang in Equatorial Guinea, Denis Sassou-Nguesso in Congo-Brazzaville, and Jose Eduardo Dos Santos in Angola.[10] This is not an impossible task, and one can examine U.S. history for a parallel example. During the U.S. evolution of democracy, the big political party "machines" dominated the politics of the late nineteenth and early twentieth centuries. Extremely undemocratic, they consisted of embedded patronage systems that often provided jobs, money, and housing in return for political loyalty, not unlike systems found in Africa today. It was the development of democratic institutions, legislation, and processes for rule of law that assisted the U.S. democratic evolution, and it is the same approach that can aid Africa.

It is imperative that senior U.S. leadership publicly supports good, sincere leaders that are legitimately trying to move their states forward in terms of security and development, and it is equally vital to publicly denounce the actions of those who do not. The newly formed African Leadership Council has created a Code of African Leadership[11] that consists of 23 "commandments" to guide public figures (Figure 10.1). An indigenously developed initiative, much like the African Union's Peer Review Mechanism, this code may be a wonderful step forward in the gradual evolution of African governance. But unfortunately, in reality, unless there is some kind of objective enforcement or significant external encouragement, these efforts are doomed to be rendered ineffective.

Strong, focused U.S. leadership is required to assist in the implementation of the kinds of indigenous initiatives mentioned above. From high level official visits to professional and government reciprocal exchange programs, incentives can be leveraged to make an impact. Implicit encouragement of poor governance is another danger that good U.S. leadership can help avoid. When U.S.-Africa policy is poorly coordinated or even counterproductive, it often sends the wrong message and is never very effective. When U.S. diplomats try to work towards better governance while U.S. corporate interests are undermining these efforts in order to pursue unscrupulous business interests, firm leadership is needed to rectify the differences in de facto U.S. policy. When overzealous and shortsighted legislators are sabotaging legitimate corporate or military interests, attentive U.S. leadership is indispensable to providing coherency and vision. There are many cases where a failure of U.S. leadership results in poor policy coordination, but these will be discussed in more detail in the next chapter.

Figure 10.1: Code of African Leadership

Mombasa, 20 March 2004

African leaders serve their peoples and their nations best when:
1. They offer a coherent vision of individual growth and national advancement with justice and dignity for all.
2. They seek to be transformational more than transactional leaders.
3. They encourage broad participation of all levels of society, including all minorities and majorities, and emphasize the deliberative nature of the best democratic practices.
4. They demonstrate in their professional and personal lives deep respect for the letter and the spirit of all of the provisions of the national constitution, including strictly abiding by term limits.
5. They lead by example and teaching to acquaint their peoples with respect for dissent, the ideas of others, and the importance of disagreement between political parties and individuals.
6. They enforce rulings of all courts and independent tribunals and emphasize and strengthen the independence of the judiciary, so as to bolster the rule of law.
7. They respect international conventions and international laws.
8. They promote transparency and encourage and adhere to internationally common forms of accountability.
9. They recognize that they are accountable for their actions and that no one is above the law nationally and internationally.
10. They accept peer review.
11. They promote policies aimed at eradicating poverty and enhancing the welfare and livelihood of their people within an appropriate macroeconomic framework.
12. They strengthen and improve access to education and health care.
13. They respect all human rights and civil liberties.
14. They demand and work for the peaceful and lawful transfer of power.
15. They promote and respect the separation of powers by ensuring financial autonomy of the judiciary and parliament, and ensure that the judiciary and parliament are free from unlawful interference by the executive.
16. They adhere to a strong code of ethics and demand the same from all subordinate officials and cabinet ministers.
17. They do not use their office for personal gain and avoid (or declare) all conflicts of interest; they declare their personal and immediate family assets yearly.
18. They specifically eschew corrupt practices and expose those in their official capacities that violate national laws and practices against corruption.
19. They ensure human security.
20. They respect freedom of religion.
21. They respect freedom of the press and media.
22. They respect freedom of assembly.
23. They respect freedom of expression.

Source: Council for a Community of Democracies, online at: http://www.ccd21.org/news/alc_code.htm

Strong U.S. leadership is necessary, but not sufficient for improving governance in the Gulf of Guinea. Many of the sub-region's political institutions need to be significantly restructured and strengthened in order to be effective, and this requires determined and enlightened African leadership. Leaders who cling to power and preserve the status quo at the expense of their populations are detrimental to future security and development. The U.S. should do all it can to encourage African leaders to accept real competition of ideas in government, and to promote innovation and change in public policy.

There is probably too much focus on the electoral component of democracy, and not enough on the institutional aspects. Elections are neither truly free nor fair in any of the Gulf of Guinea states, and most of the "independent" electoral commissions are not actually independent at all. Despite generous external funding for items like transparent ballot boxes, and considerable outside assistance with election monitoring, elections in the sub-region have not improved considerably. Part of this is because an election is relatively easy to rig when the incumbent exerts dominant control over all aspects of the state. In fact, dispatching western observers all over a country to verify the freeness and fairness of an election on the day of the poll does very little to identify the inherently undemocratic systemic problems. This is like evaluating a Broadway show by watching the final performance without having ever observed any of the rehearsals. The outcome of an election can be determined well before election day, and in most Gulf of Guinea states, this is the norm. Because of this unfortunate reality, U.S.-Africa policymakers would do better to allocate resources to indigenous capacity building programs and make overt efforts to champion the pro-transparency and anti-corruption institutions within each state. When objective checks and balances have been created to limit the power of autocratic rulers, free and fair elections are then more likely to follow as part of the natural democratic evolution.

Another major challenge for African leadership is to allow decentralization of power and to trust more traditional institutions of governance. As mentioned earlier, most African countries experienced a violently interrupted state formation process with the introduction of external institutions of conquest and domination. Some of the semi-authoritarian regimes that persist today in the Gulf of Guinea are no more well suited to good governance than were the historically extractive colonial regimes. A small minority segment of the population continues to benefit from natural resource wealth extraction while the majority of the remainder suffers in poverty and insecurity. Enlightened U.S. and African leaders need to finally encourage real indigenous institutional development under the general principles of federalism and liberal democracy.

Based on our research, we are convinced that a fundamentally "Africanized" democracy requires decentralization away from the current "Big Man" power centers, with much more autonomy at local levels for socio-political decisions and revenue allocation. This is in part due to the diverse nature of the populations in the Gulf of Guinea states, and in part due to the historical domination of power by select groups. Within Nigeria and Cameroon, for example, there are well over two hundred and fifty distinct ethno-linguistic groups, the majority of which have been historically disenfranchised and marginalized. In Angola, Equatorial Guinea, Gabon, and Congo, there has also been ascendancy to power of elite ethnic sub-groups who have exerted monopolistic control over energy revenue streams for quite some time. The advancement of liberal democratic ideals of individual rights and freedoms, combined with the rule of law, would eliminate some of the political inequalities and economic injustices that lend to sub-regional instability. And the devolution of central power to subnational entities would put some authority back into the hands of the people, allowing them to resolve political and economic crises at the lowest levels.

Some of the logic for this argument goes back to one of the U.S.' founding fathers, James Madison. In *The Federalist Papers,* Madison argued that in a pluralistic society, factions will form naturally around political, economic, and social issues; and that factions are not good for democracy because a majority faction can "democratically" suppress the rights of minority factions.[12] However, a democracy cannot forbid or destroy factions, for to do so would be in itself counter to democratic principles. Therefore, factions must be encouraged to proliferate to the extent that none can be politically dominant over the others, and their free competition of ideas will lead to an effective democracy. This argument for a decentralized, republican form of government for a plural society is relevant and useful for the Gulf of Guinea states, and can be applied using indigenous African political models.

Simply dividing up a large state into smaller components is not enough. The Nigerian federal state and 36 sub-states are artificial creations that do not reflect ethno-linguistic identity and therefore must struggle to be legitimate in the eyes of many citizens. This is a real challenge for governance. This legitimacy sword cuts both ways, and a government that is not legitimately connected to all its constituents through a strong sense of identity may not exhibit the sense of ownership required of responsible governments. In fact, as observed in the previous discussion on corruption, because of this lack of a legitimate state-society connection, many civil servants do not question their right to act selfishly with state resources, at the expense of the public.

By decentralizing political power appropriately, African governments can increase their legitimacy and effectiveness, reconnecting the state and the society. One way to do this is to relinquish decision-making authority to legitimate sub-national governments at the state or provincial level. Current sub-national governments may be legitimate if they were actually elected freely and fairly, but there are many cases in which they were not. Another way to decentralize decision-making is to empower traditional rulers, who often retain more legitimacy in the eyes of local constituents than do elected governments. For example, in many regions of Cameroon, traditional rulers are not officially empowered by the constitution, nor funded by the national government, yet they have real power to resolve disputes at the local level and are directly involved in resource allocation decisions. They are more integrated with local populations, more connected by a sense of identity to a community, and have more authority to handle local affairs. Therefore they are often more effective at conflict resolution and governance than their elected counterparts. Traditional rulers have been a key to Cameroon's unusual internal stability, and are perhaps an indication of how a distinctly "African democracy" may evolve more effectively.

A word of caution is necessary at this juncture. Some traditional rulers are easily co-opted by powerful central authorities, and sometimes there exist no local checks and balances to reign in corrupt or abusive individuals.[13] We are certainly not advocating traditional governance over elected democracies. However, in cases where the elected governments are hopelessly corrupt and ineffective, there may be room to capitalize on well-functioning traditional institutions of governance in the short term. Eventually, indigenously formed African liberal democracies may incorporate elements of both elected and traditional governance, perhaps along the lines of Botswana or South Africa. One thing is certain—the evolution of African liberal democracy in the Gulf of Guinea will depend heavily on the quality of African and U.S. leadership, and the corresponding policies and priorities regarding the transformation of governance.

A Case Study of Good Governance, Democracy and Leadership

Trinidad and Tobago provides an excellent example of how good leadership in an underdeveloped, energy-producing state can turn oil and gas revenues into successful economic development while simultaneously pursuing an agenda of democratization. Trinidad and Tobago achieved independence about the same time as the Gulf of Guinea states, and its people suffered from prior colonial domination in much the same way as the people of Africa. Yet today Trinidad and Tobago boasts a literacy rate of about 98% and a UNDP Human Development Indicator (HDI) ranking of 54 out of 177 nations, whereas the Gulf of Guinea states rank considerably lower.[14] The key difference in the levels of current development is the presence of good leadership. Starting with Dr. Eric Williams, the first Prime Minister, Trinidad and Tobago's leaders have consistently exhibited liberal democratic tendencies, pursued balanced economic development, and embarked upon visionary public policies for the benefit of the population.

Trinidad and Tobago has an established democratic system, experiencing only constitutional changes of government since independence. This stable democracy has even weathered two recent insurrection attempts, resolved through its solid legal system, based on British Common Law. The media is free, and government decisions are transparent. The currency is liberalized, and the healthy economy is characterized by a very low unemployment rate, solid real GDP growth, a current account surplus, and strong foreign exchange reserves.

Like the Gulf of Guinea states, Trinidad and Tobago's economy is based primarily on the energy sector, but there are some critical differences. Rather than monopolizing the energy revenue streams, stealing the public funds for minority benefit, and neglecting national development priorities, solid leadership has transformed this energy economy into a model for others to follow. The government started by constructing port facilities and gas pipelines to support industry, and then diversified into more value-added industries such as iron and steel, petrochemicals, liquefied natural gas (LNG), power generation, oil refining, and light industry. Recognizing that very cheap and reliable electricity was good for both people and businesses, the government capitalized on oil production and natural gas for local electrification projects. This has resulted in relatively strong local firms, with many more up and coming. Even within the energy sector, the government has emphasized diversified value-added products and services for export such as oil platform engineering and fabrication, energy infrastructure design capabilities, and energy sector consulting services. Today, raw energy represents only roughly one-third of GDP and employs only about three percent of the population.

Trinidad and Tobago's honest, democratic and visionary leadership has enabled the country to use energy resources to empower the population and to promote stable development. Corrupt governments did not simply sit back and just reap the benefits of oil income while focusing on selfish consumption spending for an elite minority. Instead, the government has produced a plan to be "developed" by 2020, and is working hard to push the economy towards tertiary and quaternary sector employment. Unlike some of its selfish, kleptocratic counterparts in the Gulf of Guinea, the leadership of Trinidad and Tobago is actively seeking optimal wealth distribution among its population through emphasis on local ownership and increased growth of indigenous human capital. The government originally sought strategic partnerships with international businesses and other countries, but is now seeking to redefine "local content" in the energy sector through more local financing, investment, management, ownership, and control of production. The government has established many initiatives to train and lift underprivileged youth up on to their feet as entrepreneurs, and has drastically increased expenditure on education—even building a new local university. In addition to a robust program of government-sponsored university scholarships for top high school graduates, the government also leverages private corporate entities to promote education. Technically related scholarships and energy sector research and development projects are now mandatory items in oil block bidding contracts.

Trinidad and Tobago's progressive, responsible, and accountable leadership has also demonstrated admirable foresight by planning for the future inevitable decline of oil wealth. A great example of this is the Heritage and Stabilization Fund, which allocates a large proportion of government energy revenues into specifically designated accounts for the future. One is intended to stabilize oil shocks in the short term; another is to be used for a strategic economic development plan, in areas where private capital will likely not flow; and yet another is to plan and invest for future generations in the long term. This visionary fund was created after extensive, transparent dialogue with academics and policy-makers and serves as a wonderful example of the benefits of good leadership and democratic governance. In sum, this case study is useful in demonstrating how a small, formerly colonized nation has faced challenges similar to its Gulf of Guinea counterparts, and has overcome these challenges through wise leadership and a commitment to good governance.

Conclusion

This discussion of democratization's challenges and potential is admittedly oversimplified. However, it illustrates the important point that shortsighted pursuit of U.S. energy interests at the expense of fundamental U.S. values would be an enormous policy blunder. Emphasis on good governance and transparent, accountable African leadership must be a priority for U.S.-Africa policymakers, so that foreign policy mistakes of the past are not repeated today. U.S. support of regimes that simply cooperate in the War on Terror or provide unfettered access to strategic resources (as seen in the Persian Gulf) does not engender long-term, sustainable energy security or national security. Our commitment to democratization in Africa must go beyond rhetoric, toward initiatives that produce real, tangible results. Earlier chapters have highlighted the importance of broad, public ownership of a nation's problems and solutions. In a nutshell, this is what democracy is all about. It is sorely needed in the oil-rich countries of the Gulf of Guinea.

Unfortunately, according to some observers, "United States engagement with security and democracy issues in African countries is driven more by geopolitical considerations, in a dangerous replay of cold war disregard for African concerns."[15] This is a mistake the U.S. cannot afford to repeat. As Joseph Nye has argued, "hard power, the ability to coerce, grows out of a country's military and economic might. Soft power arises from the attractiveness of a country's culture, political ideals, and policies. When U.S. policies appear legitimate in the eyes of others, American soft power is enhanced . . . emphasis on democracy and human rights can help make U.S. policies attractive to others when these values appear genuine and are pursued in a fair-minded way."[16] Now is our chance to undo decades of neglect on the African continent and apply the nation's energies toward a strong, vibrant democratization agenda. It is clearly in the U.S. national security and energy security interests to nurture the development of mature democracies in the Gulf of Guinea.

Notes

1. Ghana's Minister of Defense, in an address to students at the Kofi Annan International Peacekeeping Training Centre, Accra, Ghana, 13 June 2005.

2. Richter and Tsalik.

3. Kaplan, 66.

4. Country ratings available at: http://www.freedomhouse.org/ratings/index.htm

5. Democracy is expensive! Consider the Malawi example: $20 million was needed for elections in 2005, but the government had to consider postponing them until 2006 due to a shortage of funds. Malawi's 2000 elections would not have been possible had Germany and the UN not funded them. Many Malawians argue that this money could be much better used to directly improve their lives if it were used for economic development instead.

6. President Benjamin Mkapa of Tanzania, in a pre-retirement address given in Kampala, Uganda on 25 August 2005.

7. Wirth, Gray, and Podesta, "The Future of Energy Policy," *Foreign Affairs* (July/August 2003), p.138.

8. Richter and Tsalik.

9. Richter and Tsalik.

10. Each of these have held power in their countries for long tenures, often decades. Please see Chapter 2 for more on this.

11. See Robert Rotberg, Strengthening African Leadership, Foreign Affairs, Jul-Aug 2004. This and other documents pertaining to the African Leadership Council can be found online at Harvard University's Belfer Center website: http://bcsia.ksg.harvard.edu/publication.cfm?ctype=event_reports&item_id=126.

12. *The Federalist Papers* were a series of articles written under the pen name of Publius by Alexander Hamilton, James Madison, and John Jay. Madison, widely recognized as the Father of the Constitution, would later go on to become President of the United States. Jay would become the first Chief Justice of the US Supreme Court. Hamilton would serve in the Cabinet and become a major force in setting economic policy for the US. The full text of the Federalist Papers is available online at: http://www.law.ou.edu/hist/federalist/federalist-papers.

13. It is a myth that traditional African governance, prior to colonialism, consisted simply of "Big Men" serving as autocratic chiefs with a monopoly on power. Traditional institutions such as a Council of Elders existed to provide a check and balance on Chiefs; and Chiefs could be removed from their positions if they failed to satisfy their constituents.

14. For this and other statistics pertaining to development in the Gulf of Guinea, please see the country profiles provided in Chapter 2.

15. Booker, Salih, William Minter, and Ann-Louise Coigan, "America and Africa," *Current History* (May 2003), p.199.

16. Joseph Nye, "U.S. Power and Strategy After Iraq," *Foreign Affairs,* July/ August 2003, 66-67.

Chapter 11
The Policy Coordination Imperative

One of the most challenging aspects of U.S.-Africa policymaking—indeed of policymaking in general—is to turn good ideas into reality. The implementation phase of policymaking is by far the most difficult and important step in the process, without which, good ideas remain just that. It doesn't take a flash of brilliance to recommend that U.S.-Africa policy needs to emphasize increased internal security as a precondition for economic development and democratization; however, turning that recommendation into something tangible and implementable on the ground in the Gulf of Guinea is quite another matter.

Many good policy ideas concocted in Washington never actually play out in reality. Some policy metamorphosis and degradation is to be expected, as practitioners have to account for cultural differences, financial constraints, and competing local priorities, etc. However, many of the obstacles to effective policy implementation are self-induced and potentially quite easily avoidable. Lack of coordination between various U.S. government agencies and branches, between the private and public sectors, and between major international stakeholders are to blame for many U.S.-Africa policy problems. This chapter will explore how critical policy coordination mechanisms can help alleviate unnecessary impediments, thereby contributing directly to more efficient energy and security policy in the Gulf of Guinea.

Interagency Coordination

There is a considerable need among U.S. policymakers to recognize and tear down barriers to intra-governmental cooperation. Domestic constraints include policy misalignments that stem from philosophical differences and bureaucratic turf wars between agencies and branches of government. Overall, national security must drive the train, but energy security is a key component, and U.S. foreign policy must be integrative, consistent, sustained, and well coordinated. Strong leadership is required to break down the barriers and cross-organizational boundaries between various U.S.-Africa policymakers. Turf wars and "not my job" attitudes have no place in the Global War on Terrorism (GWOT) or in future U.S. energy and security challenges.

It must be acknowledged that most of the U.S.-Africa initiatives discussed in this text receive strong bipartisan support, perhaps more so than in most other regions of the world, and in fact, the overarching policy goals have been common to both the Clinton and Bush administrations.[1] Policy agreement is relatively simple at the macro scale because the scope of Africa's problems is so enormous—who would not be in general support of fighting disease, poverty, and terrorism? Yet there are a few fatal flaws that may explain the U.S.' continued policy ineffectiveness in sub-Saharan Africa. There have been many initiatives aimed at treating the symptoms of Africa's problems, but not as many focused on addressing the root causes. Many times, adequate funding is not delivered consistently over time. Additionally, all too often policy is not integrated synergistically across sectors of influence, and certain "soft power" instruments are neglected almost entirely. Policymakers need to consider how government/diplomatic, corporate/economic, and military/security foreign policy levers can be executed in concert, where the whole is greater than the sum of its often-disjointed parts.

Unfortunately, it is not common for U.S. agencies to strive for policy integration. "We don't integrate very much—we look at oil in Africa but don't do much here in [the Department of Defense] to secure it," said one senior defense official. There is no correlation between oil and International Military Education and Training (IMET), Joint Combined Exchange Training (JCET), or other similar programs. Acknowledging that there are not a lot of immediate threats to the U.S.' dominant role as a market for West African oil ends up leaving de facto energy security policy to the Departments of Commerce and Energy, as well as the private sector. Yet the policies of the Departments of Commerce and Energy, and the actions of U.S. energy companies, have a direct impact on the Department of Defense's ability to ensure national security in the long run. Just as the Departments of State, Defense, and Homeland Security, and the CIA, FBI, and local law enforcement agencies are working more closely than before in the GWOT, the U.S. must ensure that business and energy policy stakeholders and foreign assistance programs support—rather than undermine—the nation's long-term national security strategy.

A major part of the U.S.-Africa policy challenge is to connect the key players under a universal set of long-term goals, and then leverage each component based on its strengths, weaknesses, and appropriate capabilities. Many well-intended legislative policy restrictions are due to human rights concerns, but ironically are often a hindrance to realistic, effective long-term democratization policy. And African energy itself doesn't seem to be much of an interest yet at the interagency level, but should be a fundamental reason for more coordination. The U.S. currently has relatively unfettered access to African oil de facto, and has not had to apply significant government resources to secure that supply. But this is not the real issue at all—long-term regional stability is. Disjointed operations based on often competing short-term interests will never do this properly. Integrated actions based on consistently overarching common values, like security, economic development, and good governance, are far more likely to be effective in the long run.

Within and around the executive branch, there are an amazing variety of departments, offices, and independent agencies that work to further U.S. interests in security, development, and democracy; but there is a real lack of coordination in achieving synergy in policy implementation, especially in Africa. Peter Watson, the Chairman, President, and CEO of the Overseas Private Investment Corporation (OPIC) explains that, "Achieving a real break-through [in economic development], however, would require the coordinated efforts of a number of different agencies. The U.S. Agency for International Development (USAID), the U.S. Trade and Development Agency (USTDA), the Millennium Challenge Account (MCA), the Export-Import Bank of the U.S., and the Office of the U.S. Trade Representative all have important roles to play in cajoling countries to adopt the right policies and institutions for mobilizing the energies and creativity of private investors. While each of these organizations have different roles to play in managing U.S. international economic policy interests, they generally pursue compatible aims with respect to the promotion of a market-oriented policy framework . . . however, they pursue these aims independently of each other . . . it would be highly desirable to establish a development-oriented coordination mechanism."[2]

Economic development is only one component of the security, development, and democratization agenda required to promote long-term energy security and national security in the Gulf of Guinea. Without consistency, efficiency, and continuity based on a common strategic end state across each of these components, what chance is there of realizing effective policy implementation through the application of so many disparate programs?

Poor policy coordination results in inefficient policy implementation, and at times is downright counterproductive to stated policy goals and objectives. For example, when U.S.-Africa policymakers attempted to promote development of the Kofi Annan International Peacekeeping Training Centre (KAIPTC) in Ghana, they were challenged by disparate approaches.[3] Although very well intended, generous funding for enhanced peace support operations training fell through in part due to compartmentalization between various departments and agencies. The U.S. offered funding for a computer simulation system for KAIPTC, but the Departments of Defense and State were working on parallel, redundant initiatives to do this—actually competing with each other. State pushed a new flexible peace support operations system called "ABACUS" while Defense pushed the standard war-fighting "JANUS" system it uses in conjunction with the African Contingency Operations Training and Assistance (ACOTA) program. Each department offered funding by pushing their own program, and arguing convincingly against the other's. In the end, the KAIPTC received neither. This lack of coordination was completely counterproductive and inefficient, but potentially quite avoidable. Is the U.S. government just so big and doing so much that it can no longer coordinate effectively?

A great part of the interagency coordination challenge stems from the incredibly complicated nature of U.S.-Africa policy, and the lack of priority U.S. embassies in Africa have received for staffing and resources. There are in fact so many different U.S. agencies, departments, organizations, and agendas working on issues related to Africa that it is truly difficult to get a handle on all levels of engagement. For example, in any given country, there might be a U.S. State Department program emphasizing democratization, a Commerce Department program advancing small business interests, an Energy Department program working towards rural electrification, a Justice Department program aimed at improved law enforcement capabilities, a USAID mission working on infrastructure projects, a Defense Department program to assist with border security, a Treasury Department program to counter money laundering, an FBI program to combat drug trafficking....and the list goes on. In strategically "important" countries, there are often representatives on the ground from each of these organizations that work with the Ambassador and the country team to effectively coordinate and implement their programs, especially when they are potentially complementary. In reality, in most Gulf of Guinea countries there is not this level of U.S. engagement, and there is certainly not a coordinating representative from each organization on the ground full time to oversee policy implementation. Rather, where various departments and agencies do have interests relevant to the Gulf of Guinea, their policies are usually created in separate offices in Washington with very little coordination or regard for potentially mutually supporting or conflicting programs from other offices. In some cases, the situation is even worse. For example, there is no permanent U.S. Ambassador residing in Equatorial Guinea or in São Tome and Principe, despite the tremendous U.S. energy and security interests and corporate investments in each of them. U.S. policy for Equatorial Guinea is coordinated by the U.S. embassy country team in Cameroon, while policy for São Tome and Principe is coordinated from Gabon. Despite talented and capable embassy staffs in both Cameroon and Gabon, it is extremely difficult to properly synchronize and implement effective U.S. policy on a part-time basis.

The U.S. should establish permanent missions in all of the Gulf of Guinea states, and should staff them to levels commensurate with their importance to U.S. energy and security concerns. (Not to mention economic development and democratization agendas.) And in order to effectively harness more of the elements of national power (diplomatic, information, military, and economic), a greater number and diversity of relevant U.S. agencies and organizations should become directly involved with achieving and coordinating U.S.-Africa policy goals in the Gulf of Guinea. For example, the Department of Energy has many potential and ongoing programs in the sub-region, but they are not well coordinated outside that department. The Department of Commerce's International Trade Administration has an excellent Good Governance Program and anti-corruption agenda, but it is not yet active in Africa—why not? The Department of Homeland Security's Federal Law Enforcement Training Center offers great potential for police training and professionalization in the Gulf of Guinea and should be an important component of each embassy's country team. The Department of Justice's Office of Justice Programs has tremendous expertise on rule of law implementation, but is only marginally involved in West and Central Africa. The Department of Transportation's Financial Crimes Enforcement Network could be used to bolster anti-corruption and transparency efforts in the sub-region, perhaps lending support to programs like Nigeria's Economic and Financial Crimes Commission. The Export-Import Bank, the Overseas Private Investment Corporation (OPIC), the U.S. Trade and Development Agency (USTDA), and the U.S. Agency for International Development (USAID) are all very important for promoting economic development, but are not well integrated into energy and security policy coordination and implementation on the ground. The Voice of America (VOA) should be better used to bolster public diplomacy and could be directly linked to policymakers and country teams in order to get the message out about democracy, development, and security in the Gulf of Guinea. There are also numerous potential partners for professional education and training exchange programs (similar to the Department of Defense's IMET program). These include the Federal Election Commission, the Federal Energy Regulatory Commission, the Small Business Administration, and so many others.

This chapter does not seek to prescribe in detail how each of these important government departments and agencies can best contribute to U.S. energy and security policy in the Gulf of Guinea. However, the main point here is that there is so much more that U.S.-Africa policymakers could do to be effective in securing U.S. interests in the sub-region if they could only harness and coordinate the extensive network of relevant organizations and programs.

In addition to having a more robust interagency approach and a stronger policy implementation presence on the ground, there is a macro-level requirement to coordinate diverse programs more effectively. There must be a way to better focus all the elements of national power on a common strategic end state, like energy security. Though the overarching responsibility primarily lies with the President and his National Security Council, there should be some institutionalized mechanisms to guarantee better coordination at lower levels. Of course, there are some very simple ideas that could improve policy coordination within and around the executive branch, especially since most of the stakeholder organizations have a common boss (the President) and leadership appointed for both their capability and loyalty.

At the risk of sounding like proponents for a bigger government (which we are not), our analysis suggests the need for an interagency body specifically constructed and tasked to oversee policy coordination, and to increase efficiency of resources and efforts during policy implementation. We have recently witnessed the creation of an interagency body to deal with the nation's intelligence gathering and analysis needs (NCTC, the National CounterTerrorism Center), so why not a similar kind of entity to focus on coordinating development and security policies in Africa? One working group within such an agency might be responsible for coordinating energy security programs, with a representative specifically focused on the Gulf of Guinea. It may surprise readers to know that within the executive branch, there is not even a common division of responsibility for African countries, by region. That is, no two "maps" look the same. For example, the administrative boundaries for "East Africa" and "Central Africa" overlap with the "Horn of Africa" when viewed from the perspectives of the Departments of Defense, State, Commerce, Energy and the International Trade Administration. Unfortunately, this is not just a question of semantics, but in fact contributes to increased coordination difficulties between offices and representatives with varying policy implementation responsibilities. (As discussed in Chapter 6, these types of challenges are even an issue within the Department of Defense with the division of responsibility for Africa between EUCOM, CENTCOM, and PACOM resulting in additional bureaucratic coordination requirements when coping with crises in places like Darfur, for example.)

After establishing a basic, common division of regional responsibilities between executive departments and agencies, a unified vision is necessary for all the dogs to pull the sled in the same direction. Given the multiple lines of operation (State, Defense, Energy, USAID, OPIC, etc.), the best document to link all the players together is the *National Security Strategy* (NSS). Perhaps the NSS just needs to be read more closely by executive branch constituents, and used explicitly to develop the charters, missions, and priorities of each suborganization. More importantly, policy implementation at each level should be regularly checked to verify that it is indeed directly supporting the higher agenda outlined in the NSS. Specific programs and resource allocation decisions should be in alignment with priorities, goals, and objectives of·the NSS, or else corrective action should be taken immediately.

Within certain executive branch departments and agencies, there are some institutionalized mechanisms that may serve as models for better policy coordination. The combined Department of State and USAID *Strategic Plan* describes five separate mechanisms used to evaluate their performance:

1) Mission Performance Plans (MPP) and Annual Reviews—where 25% of all missions' MPPs are reviewed annually by the Assistant Secretary for Resource Management to evaluate intended goals, priority initiatives, and performance indicators for each country team;

2) Bureau Performance Plans (BPP) and Senior Reviews—where the Bureau of Resource Management evaluates each BPP and provides recommendations to improve programs;

3) Internal Bureau Assessments—these are self-evaluation rating tools utilized by program managers to assess specific performance results;

4) Performance Assessment Rating Tool (PART)—this is a program of the Office of Management and Budget's (OMB), used by State to evaluate selected programs;

5) Office of Inspector General (OIG) and General Accounting Office (GAO) evaluations—these are independent government bodies for inspection, auditing, and evaluation of all diplomatic missions and domestic bureaus.

If appropriately implemented at the interagency level, these types of mechanisms may be used to comprehensively assess and evaluate the effectiveness of diverse programs from a variety of agencies. Findings could be used to check on the effective use of applied resources, as well as to identify further opportunities for policy synchronization. For an example of ways to ensure that policy goals and programs are better aligned in principle and in implementation, consider the three principal mechanisms for coordination of the Army International Activities Plan (AIAP):

1) HQDA (Headquarters, Department of the Army) back-brief conference—which is an annual Army conference with HQDA staff, Major Commands (MACOMS), and Army Service Component Commands (ASCC) that serves as an opportunity for horizontal and vertical integration, synchronization, and coordination of policy as Army elements formally present their programs to HQDA and receive briefings on new and emerging strategies;
2) HQDA coordination visits—during which international activities personnel conduct annual on-site visits to HQDA staff elements, MACOMs, and ASCCs to review and integrate their international programs and provide guidance for future direction;
3) Resource discussions—where Army elements may request to meet with HQDA to solve resource issues in the year of program execution, and for most activities, resource assistance is normally contingent on demonstrated compliance with the AIAP goals, objectives, and priorities.

This is a wonderful set of coordination mechanisms, some semblance of which should be considered at the interagency level to ensure consistency and efficiency of U.S.-Africa policy. Another place to turn for good potential examples of improved coordination mechanisms is the private sector. Although generally much more competitive by nature, the private sector is also more efficient and often finds creative and effective ways to achieve complementary goals with disparate constituencies. For example, the Corporate Council on Africa established an Equatorial Guinea working group to leverage ideas and business opportunities in the newly energy-rich country. The private Center for Strategic and International Studies (CSIS) also established a working group under the leadership of an Africa expert, Dr. J. Stephen Morrison, in order to consider foreign policy imperatives regarding energy and security in the Gulf of Guinea. Recently, the Department of State seems to have learned from these examples and has organized some new interagency policy meetings on Equatorial Guinea, chaired by the Bureau of African Affairs, to better coordinate policy between various executive branch departments and agencies.[4]

These kinds of interagency working groups should be institutionalized to ensure more effective policy coordination mechanisms are the rule and not the exception. In the absence of an interagency agency, policymakers should consider the Africa Center for Strategic Studies (ACSS) as an excellent potential policy coordination institution for U.S.-Africa policy in the Gulf of Guinea. ACSS is well organized and well run and has great credibility as an objective policy agent. Its leadership does a terrific job of incorporating stakeholders from the private and public sector, consulting with practitioners and academics, and bringing together Africans, Americans, and other key international players.

Additional models for improved interagency coordination can be taken from the U.S.' international partners. For example, the United Kingdom (UK) has established a Post-Conflict Reconstruction Unit (PCRU), which is an interagency agency that serves as the highest-level coordination mechanism for all post-conflict reconstruction efforts. The PCRU is used to coordinate efforts of the Foreign and Commonwealth Office (FCO), the Defense Ministry, the Department for International Development (DFID), and others. The U.K.'s Africa Conflict Prevention Pool (ACPP) is a collection of funds from the FCO, the Ministry of Defense, and DFID that removes the need to "pass the hat" each time a project or initiative arises that relates to all three agencies. Funding from the ACPP is what supports the KAIPTC in Ghana, and due to its inherent interagency characteristics, U.K. policy funding is more streamlined and effective than that potentially delivered by the current U.S. approach.

These examples demonstrate synergy of interdepartmental coordination for a common goal, created by visionary leadership and the establishment of effective institutions. Why not create something along these lines for U.S. security and development efforts in general, and perhaps for the Gulf of Guinea more specifically? An institution structured to promote synergy like this is not simply another layer of bureaucracy, but is a mandatory coordination and synchronization mechanism that will immediately enhance the effectiveness of U.S.-Africa policy.

Policy coordination becomes even more challenging when considering the additional requirements of synchronization across branches of government. Accepting the fact that in the U.S. system the legislative branch was intentionally designed to check the power of the executive branch, and vice versa, there is still too much unintentional policy obstruction. Often, well-intended legislators (or their staffers) set out to accomplish a noble task without really grasping the far-reaching effects on overall U.S. policy continuity and effectiveness. Some policy obstruction is clearly intentional and is based on philosophical and ideological differences, but some of it may simply be due to ignorance of potential interference or an immediate focus that is too narrow.

Congressional "holds" or "restrictions" are a good example of how well-intended individual Representatives may temporarily obstruct larger foreign policy goals, thereby rendering them incoherent and ineffective. Take for example the case of U.S. military engagement with Nigeria. The Department of Defense used military training in Nigeria as part of Operation Focus Relief (OFR), in order to promote regional peacekeeping capabilities to address the crises in Liberia and Sierra Leone in 2000. This was an effective program that resulted in more professional African peacekeepers and managed to effectively stop the hemorrhaging without having to commit significant U.S. troops to the subregion. The Department of Defense, through EUCOM, is trying to build on earlier success like OFR to continue to make Nigeria's military smaller and more professional. One of the most effective ways to influence the culture, values, and leadership of a military institution is through consistent, long term exchange programs like IMET (discussed in more detail in earlier chapters). In 2003, according to the office of Senator Feingold, the Nigerian Army provided an insufficient explanation concerning an element that was accused of a massacre, and warranted immediate sanctions. Feingold's "509 sanctions" resulted in the prohibition of U.S. IMET engagement with Nigeria. Now, we are not suggesting that the Nigerian Army did not deserve some tough, public attention regarding the issue of the alleged massacre, but we are arguing that to cut off an effective professional education exchange program as a form of punishment is not wise. Remember, our argument is that IMET should not be seen as a reward for good behavior; rather, is should be used as an important policy tool for influencing foreign military institutions.

Interruptions and inconsistencies in U.S.-Africa policy render it far less effective than it could be, and this is a frustrating reality to practitioners in the field. Apparently because of convincing military and political pressure on Senator Feingold's office, his restrictions were lifted so that IMET could continue to have a positive impact on Nigerian military reform. However, after Feingold's sanctions had been lifted, U.S. military engagement was again rerstricted with Nigeria due to the imposition of sanctions by Senator Leahy. This time the sanctions were due to Senator Leahy's displeasure at the refuge granted to Liberia's ex-president Charles Taylor by Nigeria's president Obasanjo—and again, IMET was forbidden. We agree that Charles Taylor is a terrible man and should be brought to justice for the chaos and misery he brought to Liberia and the subregion. However, we again find these types of sanctions ineffective as a punishment and extremely detrimental to consistent U.S. policy implementation. This particular example is especially ironic because it was the U.S. president who asked Nigeria to accept Taylor in the first place, in order to help bring an end to the conflict in Liberia. This is a classic case of internal U.S. political disagreement negatively affecting consistency of foreign policy.

This example of U.S. policy discontinuity in Nigeria is only one of many that have frustrated policymakers on the ground in the Gulf of Guinea. Clearly, one cannot expect to prevent contentious disagreement about U.S. foreign policy in Africa, and we recognize that such a competition of ideas is a healthy part of an effective democracy. However, we do argue that these types of individually imposed sanctions have no real punishment effect on the states in question, but rather serve only to unnecessarily tie U.S. policymakers' hands, constrain the effectiveness of important long term programs, and frustrate policy continuity.[5]

Public-Private Partnerships

Another critical area for improved coordination that would favorably impact U.S.-Africa policy in the Gulf of Guinea is in private-public partnerships. As discussed in Chapter 9, the private sector is the real engine of growth for economic development for a variety of reasons. Private companies are generally more competitive, more efficient, more results-oriented, and more entrepreneurial than government organizations. They also have clear financial incentives to invest in lucrative growth sectors and to maximize profits. However, despite their tremendous potential to create wealth, private companies are infamous for extractive modus operandi in underdeveloped countries, capitalizing on cheap labor and/or natural resources at the expense of local populations. Therefore, the policy challenge is to ascertain the best way for a public-private partnership to harness and shape the private growth engines for maximum public good without constraining them out of profitable operation.

The private sector has been especially ignored as a critical component of U.S. influence, from both a domestic and foreign perspective. In the Gulf of Guinea, the biggest multinational corporations are the energy extractors, and they have tremendous potential to contribute significantly to economic growth in the sub-region while still making a healthy profit. In fact, we are convinced that by contributing more to local security and economic development, the energy majors are actually creating conditions for long-term stability that over time will allow them to reap greater profits with lower risk. As non-state actors, oil companies are already playing an influential role in the political, social and economic development of Gulf of Guinea states. However, these companies are naturally driven by a profit agenda (rather than the core democratic values of the NSS), and their short-term actions may inadvertently threaten the U.S.' long-term energy and national security interests. The nation's energy and security agenda demands a recognition that the private sector serves as a true engine of development and a driving force behind policies that must be integrated into government efforts. The challenge for policymakers is to find ways to identify and capitalize on incentives that are common to both public and private stakeholders.

To begin with, U.S. government agencies must work more closely with national and multinational corporations to ensure that the development of the oil industry in the Gulf of Guinea does not undermine the nation's security agenda. This is a serious consideration for U.S.-Africa policymakers because corporate actions, decisions, and policies often end up dominating perceptions of U.S. policy, despite the best efforts of government programs. For example, if an embassy country team spends tens of thousands of dollars on a public diplomacy campaign focused on anti-corruption, while a corporate giant pays millions of dollars in shady oil contract kickbacks that support the status quo, not much progress will be made on the democratization and transparency front. One has only to look at the French example, where the corporate leaders of the conglomerate ELF suffered public, legal consequences for corruption in relation to their activities in Africa. Arguably, ELF's actions in the Gulf of Guinea were justified by immediate profit motives and the "realities" of business and government relations in Central Africa. However, they in effect served to undermine long-term stability objectives like good governance. On the other hand, if private companies recognize the financial benefits and business efficiencies of transparent and public oil contracts, they may become the strongest advocate of government reform. This logic applies to security, economic development, good governance, environmental concerns, public health, human rights, etc. In sum, wherever U.S. public and private energy and security interests can be aligned, there is potential for a powerful partnership that can be used to advance U.S.-Africa policy in the Gulf of Guinea.

Of course, it must be recognized that a good deal of effort is already spent by specific U.S. government agencies to assist multinational oil firms working in the region, and to assist host-nation governments. For example, the U.S. Department of Commerce's International Trade Administration (Energy Division) promotes a variety of international opportunities for U.S. businesses.[6] This agency helps facilitate meetings between U.S. oil executives and senior African administration officials, and sponsors trade missions to help U.S. businesses stay on top of new opportunities. The U.S. Department of Energy, Office of Policy and International Affairs assists directly with energy infrastructure development, including both physical infrastructure projects and supporting legislation (for example, posting an energy regulatory expert at USAID in Nigeria to help with a rural electrification project.) This agency also capitalizes on its technical assistance policy experts and consults with African energy ministers, private companies, and other various organizations in order to offer a clearinghouse of best practices on how to manage and run the energy infrastructure of a developing country.[7]

Advisory boards and other avenues exist for companies to have input to Department of Energy initiatives—a key component of business-government relations. And when transparent and accountable, these serve as a critical state-society link, not a corrupt corporatist arrangement. The opportunities for mutually beneficial business-government relations have clearly been recognized by the current administration. For example, there are currently only a limited number of oilrigs capable of extracting oil from some of the Gulf of Guinea's deep water reserves. To address this, recent energy bill discussions in Congress have included support for deep and ultra-deep water technology development for oil extraction—a promising sign of public-private cooperation needed to ensure the nation's long-term energy security interests.

These examples demonstrate the current networks and partnerships that already exist between the U.S. government, private energy companies, and African governments. However, the U.S. government and private energy companies should work more closely together to influence African governments, emphasizing communication and cooperation to advance local development more aggressively. For example, USAID is currently working with Chevron-Texaco in Angola on microfinance projects to reinforce the private sector as the primary vehicle for indigenous development. The U.S. partners should insist that their aid contributions be matched by funds from Angola's burgeoning government oil revenues in order to establish more domestic ownership of the development agenda.[8] Pressure from both the U.S. diplomatic and corporate fronts would be far more effective than diplomatic pressure alone.

There are also cases where more U.S. government involvement can support private U.S. corporate initiatives. Some U.S. companies already support a variety of "indigenization" projects to increase job participation, especially in management. These corporate programs should be more directly encouraged via tax incentives and leveraged advantages available through applicable U.S. government agencies such as: the U.S. Overseas Private Investment Corporation (OPIC), for political insurance and financial guarantees; the U.S. Export-Import Bank, for loan guarantees; and the U.S. Trade and Development Agency, for feasibility studies, etc. And in yet another example of potential public-private partnership, during his visit to Nigeria in July 2003 President Bush called on U.S. financial institutions, like Fannie Mae and the Overseas Private Investment Corporation, to help strengthen and broaden capital markets on the African continent, with the objective of helping Africans get loans for businesses and homes.[9]

There is some public disagreement on the assignment of responsibility for government reform and economic development in the cases of poor, corrupt oil states. That is, how much of the burden should be shouldered by private companies, how much by U.S. leadership, and how much by local African governments? Famous environmental cases like those of Shell Nigeria really highlight this dilemma. Without evading the question, we submit that the burden of responsibility lies in part with all three of the stakeholders above, and that without cooperation from any one of them, real security and development will remain elusive. U.S. energy companies should not be expected to take on the traditional role of USAID, but should work in transparent partnership with local governments for accountability of oil revenues and emphasis on development. The real onus is on African governments to stop abusing positions of access to undisclosed energy revenue streams, and to start using the enormous mineral wealth to promote security and economic development for local populations. But corruption surely works both ways, and strong U.S. leadership can assist by holding companies accountable for appropriate corporate ethics and transactions, while pressuring and advising local governments for better stewardship of financial resources.

An example of good public-private cooperation between a U.S. company and an African government may be found in the case of Marathon Energy and Equatorial Guinea.[10] Marathon Energy is the second biggest investor in Equatorial Guinea (after Mobil), and has invested approximately $12 billion in energy development projects, including a world-class liquefied natural gas processing complex. Marathon is the only U.S. energy company with a significant onshore presence, which may explain its relatively progressive relationship with the local government, compared to other U.S. firms.[11] The bottom line is that interests are clearly aligned, and stability and development in Equatorial Guinea is good for the government and good for Marathon. Subsequently, Marathon has embarked on numerous development programs in partnership with the public sector, to include working with the IMF and World Bank to participate in the Extractive Industries Transparency Initiative, and to encourage the Equatorial Guinean government to do the same. Marathon recruits seventy percent of its workforce from the local population; has created a construction craft training facility for local labor; chairs the committee for the National Technology Institute (an EG government flagship education initiative); initiated a five year, $8 million roll-back-malaria program; and sponsors numerous other local social programs focused on health, education, environmental, and infrastructure improvements.

In addition to this example of a public-private partnership focused on local development in economic, social, and human capital terms, there are also great opportunities for public-private cooperation in the area of security. Both host nation governments and U.S. energy firms have a strong interest in improving local internal security institutions and capabilities. Therefore there exists the possibility of burden sharing between them, to include assistance from external international donor states with an interest in sub-regional security. Rather than oil companies simply spending money on provision of private security, they should consider corporate investment in public security, again in tandem with local governments and external donors. Admittedly complicated and difficult, it is these kinds of potential public-private partnerships that U.S.-Africa policymakers should seek out and encourage through strong leadership and clear economic and diplomatic incentives. There is a lot of room for synchronization of programs between the private sector oil majors, the new oil-rich African governments, and U.S. government funding. It is in the nation's best interests—and in the best interests of U.S. multinational corporations—to support strong public-private partnerships, collaboration on local security and development, and clear long-term energy policy integration.

Multilateral Cooperation

The final critical coordination area for effective U.S.-Africa policy implementation is probably the most difficult to influence—and that is multilateral cooperation. The United States requires the cooperation of other states, international government organizations (IGOs), and regional organizations in order to achieve its energy security and national security goals in the Gulf of Guinea. This is especially relevant because the U.S. is only the third largest consumer of African energy, after Europe and Asia, and should work more closely with these other major stakeholders to advance common interests.

Of course, interests vary tremendously between potential multilateral partners, and this deserves brief attention in this discussion. Regional organizations like the African Union, ECOWAS, and CEMAC quite closely share the basic U.S. interests in security, economic development, and democratization, as do the major IGOs like the World Bank, the IMF, and the UN. The dominant U.S. role in these IGOs (in terms of financial contributions and policy influence) helps align basic interests more easily. However, in terms of potential multilateral partners that are independent states, things are not quite so clear. Based on political relations and corporate energy investment, France has arguably been the most influential external power in the Gulf of Guinea, followed by the UK and the Netherlands. Although perhaps perceived as competitors in an economic and energy extraction sense, these nations are close allies of the U.S. and also share common interests in security, economic development, and democratization in the sub-region. However, when rapidly developing economies like India and China continue to seek enormous new energy sources, and have clearly turned toward Africa, their interests may not be so neatly aligned.

China is an especially interesting and important case. Based on current activity in the sub-region, and in fact, across Africa, the Chinese clearly have an agenda of economic development, most likely driven by an intense need for access to cheap and vast natural resources. The Chinese government is building highways, constructing public buildings, and supporting a wide variety of social programs for Gulf of Guinea governments in exchange for relationship building and market access. Chinese professional and educational exchanges are offered for university students, businessmen, and military officers. Arguably, the Chinese share common U.S. interests with African security and economic development, but perhaps not with democratization. In fact, one of the reasons that Chinese foreign aid is so welcomed in Africa is that, unlike U.S. or World Bank aid, it does not come with strings attached. China does not make demands for political reform, human rights improvement, or transparent financial transactions in exchange for development assistance. Therefore, for certain African leaders who may have a lot to lose through increased transparency and accountability, it is much easier to work with China.

This is not an alarmist reaction to natural Chinese expansion in the world economy, but simply a reminder of the potential difficulties policymakers may encounter when trying to align interests in key multilateral relationships. Having said that, it is still essential for U.S.-Africa policymakers to work hard to secure and capitalize on cooperation with China, France, the UK, and others in order to pursue our own interests in the Gulf of Guinea more effectively.

Economic development is probably the easiest realm within which U.S. policymakers can begin more serious coordination with multilateral partners. This is due in part to the noble perceptions of development assistance, and also to the currently ongoing bilateral (national) and multilateral (IGO) programs already in existence. At least one lesson learned from analyzing past nation-building efforts is directly relevant to a Gulf of Guinea development strategy. As observed in a recent study by Rand, "multilateral nation-building can produce more thoroughgoing transformations and greater regional reconciliation than can unilateral efforts . . . Additionally, a regional approach is necessary for ensuring the cooperation of a nation's neighboring states. It is nearly impossible to put together a fragmented nation if its neighbors try to tear it apart."[12] Given the chaotic regional security environment and the dearth of human development in West and Central Africa, this point is well taken. Focused on economic development, the U.S. should cooperate more closely with the major foreign stakeholders, the IGOs, and the relevant African regional organizations

As described in an earlier chapter, the Millennium Challenge Account holds promise as a revolutionary way for administering development aid to reward good leadership and sensible, accountable local development programs. Ideally, this type of approach will foster better governance, which will surely lead to greater stability in the long run. The U.S. should try to institutionalize this methodology and rationale via increased cooperation and coordination with the other major external powers involved in African development programs. The British, French, German, Scandinavian, Chinese, and Japanese aid organizations are already heavily involved in various parts of sub-Saharan Africa, yet there is no institutional mechanism to ensure that all the well-intended programs are pointing in the same direction. Foreign aid programs often unintentionally work at cross-purposes, neglect entire sectors or geographic regions, or duplicate efforts unnecessarily. Given the common interest in stable, developing African states, (whether that is based on moral-philosophical grounds, pragmatic natural resource extraction rationale, or mass-immigration-prevention logic is irrelevant); improved coordination between the relevant external players is essential.

The U.S. also needs to coordinate more closely with specific IGOs, especially those that are effectively pursuing our common interests. The International Finance Corporation (IFC), the private-sector sibling of the World Bank, has imposed rules on its lending which require an environmental impact study and full compensation for those who are displaced in the course of an IFC-funded project. Standards may soon include measures to avoid violence against civilians by security forces and the provision of health clinics and schools.[13] Even more encouraging is the World Bank-sponsored Chad-Cameroon oil pipeline project that uses international private and public funds to develop Chad's energy sector in a novel way that requires transparency and accountability of the oil revenues so that they are used to directly benefit Chad's population. These are the types of policies that the U.S. should aggressively support and enable as part of a comprehensive multilateral approach to energy and security in the Gulf of Guinea.

Potential multilateral cooperation for economic development also extends into the realm of the private sector, despite inherent competition. With improved political stability and internal security conditions, many multinational corporations could invest and thrive in the underdeveloped markets of the Gulf of Guinea. Downstream production that spawns ancillary industries from the petroleum and gas sector are very important for long run economic sustainability (as in Trinidad and Tobago), and could be induced by multilateral FDI and increased cooperation for international business opportunities. Additionally, U.S.-Africa policymakers should avidly pursue a standardization of international corporate ethics via multilateral cooperation with programs like the Extractive Industries Transparency Initiative (EITI). This would provide tremendous benefits to U.S. companies who have to currently compete with those of other nations who may not necessarily acknowledge or enforce anti-corruption laws. Increased transparency also feeds directly into better accountability of energy revenues for economic development and good governance.

African regional organizations are also exhibiting new potential for effective economic and political development measures, and deserve vastly increased U.S. financial and public relations support. Positive indigenous developments are emerging through the AU, ECOWAS, CEMAC, and others, which may lead to significant improvements in the security environment. To begin with, South Africa and Nigeria have taken the lead in launching the African Union's New Partnership for African Development (NEPAD), the continent's massive multilateral poverty-reduction initiative—a sign that major African states are beginning to work together. Broadly modeled on the U.S. ' post-WWII Marshall Plan, NEPAD seeks an annual commitment of $64 billion from the developed world (through a combination of increased aid, investment and debt relief) to achieve a 7 percent annual growth rate, and in return African nations commit to the pursuit of good governance and the rule of law.[14] Peer scrutiny is a key part of NEPAD. A voluntary "peer review" process has been launched, through which experts will visit individual countries to assess their performance on human rights, corruption, and democracy.[15] The AU is also pursuing a conflict resolution and peacekeeping strategy based on regional cooperation within Africa's five major sub-regions, and is taking the lead with peacekeeping operations in Sudan's troubled Darfur region. These types of internally driven, regionally supported, multilateral initiatives should be strongly supported by the U.S. in a continent virtually devoid of the domestic institutional capability to sustain economic, political, and military reform.

U.S. policy partnerships with African regional organizations and reputable IGOs can be especially productive in areas where international legitimacy and objectivity is highly valued. Despite many Americans' aversion to and distrust of the United Nations, for example, it is still the highest hope for representation and fairness from the perspective of poor African countries. With help from IGOs like the UN or the AU, U.S.-Africa policymakers may be more successful in promoting the use of independent, international auditing firms to oversee and verify macroeconomic reforms and revenue distribution schemes. Equitable, transparent distribution of new energy wealth is critical to maintaining development momentum, and so is expectation management. It is very important that burgeoning civil societies are not aggravated by misperceptions and false expectations of reform.

Multilateral cooperation in the area of security is perhaps a bit more complicated than in economic development because of the sensitivity of divergent interests amongst potential partners (i.e., mistrust between neighboring African states, and competition between western states due to national pride and defense contracts). However, if focusing primarily on developing improved internal security mechanisms (as suggested in chapter 8), some of the tensions and misgivings between individual Gulf of Guinea states and potential external partners may be avoided. To begin with, U.S. policymakers should examine the experiences of the French and British security relationships more closely to learn from their mistakes and successes. The vast French network of military and police schools could be a terrific cooperation entry point for more robust U.S. involvement and influence. Additionally, the French RECAMP program has an awful lot in common with the U.S. ACOTA and GPOI programs, yet there seems to be very little coordination to promote real synergy in their application. The French Ministry of Defense has tentatively announced that France will soon execute a major military force realignment in Africa.[16] Responding to political pressure at home and in Africa, France plans to realign its troops to more closely correspond with and lend support to the AU's ASF regional brigade concept. This should hopefully encourage the U.S. and the European Union to think and act along the same lines in order to leverage a strong multilateral approach to regional security. Increased (and more visible) U.S. support for the Koffi Annan International Peacekeeping Training Centre (KAIPTC) would be another opportunity to influence African professional military ethics, and coordinate on the ground with French and British security stakeholders. And the U.K.'s Africa Conflict Prevention Pool may be a great mechanism for the U.S. to replicate or support where it has complementarities with U.S. security goals.

A gaping hole in potential multilateral African security cooperation at this point is China. With the biggest army in the world, and huge economic interests in terms of natural resources and markets, why doesn't China help out more with peacekeeping operations and internal security reform? The U.S., Europeans, and Japanese pay most of the UN's security bill, and India and Pakistan each sent an entire brigade to the DRC, but China has contributed almost nothing to address the internal or regional security issues. Perhaps this is an area where skillful U.S. diplomats can find incentives and demonstrate common interests to influence China to play a greater role. Given that there are nowhere near enough resources to adequately provide for sustained internal and regional security in the Gulf of Guinea, it would be an advantage to have more multilateral partners pursuing the same goals.

Regionally, multilateral cooperation is complicated somewhat by the maze of overlapping regions and institutions (CEMAC, CEAC, SADC, ECOWAS, GOG Commission, etc.). However, a regional approach offers some distinct advantages. If there is unexpected turbulence within any particular Gulf of Guinea state (a coup for example), U.S. investments in regionally supported security institutions and mechanisms are less likely to be completely wasted. There is also the increased appearance of an African solution when regional bodies are empowered to tackle their own problems. And in fact, this approach is far more likely to promote real regional ownership and commitment to resolving security issues that inevitably cross (artificial) state boundaries. The Gulf of

Guinea Commission provides some opportunities for introducing and discussing regional security issues, but is unlikely to produce any real security cooperation in terms of intelligence sharing between countries like Nigeria and Cameroon. Obstacles to regional maritime security cooperation include political questions of sovereignty and the fact that there is almost no domestic political constituency for issues of maritime security. Therefore, the U.S. would be better off to strongly support the regional security initiatives already under way in the AU, ECOWAS, CEMAC, and SADC, and to try and influence those accordingly (like the AU's five regional standby brigades). Despite the relatively feckless history of the OAU, there are reasons for optimism when examining the new AU and ECOWAS' recent history of successful military and political interventions, and there are promising signs of commitment to democratic norms as well. Other African regional organizations have also recently demonstrated real progress with attempts to tackle difficult problems (like the AU in Sudan, or SADC in Burundi, for example).

To initiate increased multilateral cooperation on sensitive security issues, it may be advisable to consider a few different less sensitive approaches. U.S.-Africa policymakers must make it clear to other stakeholders that to profoundly attack insecurity, it is essential to pursue economic development in order to improve the lives of the most disenfranchised individuals, who are often the immediate causes of energy sector disruption. As discussed earlier, a development focus may generate solid preliminary international cooperation that can be gradually expanded into the security sector. International cooperation to deal with environmental disaster response may be another good first step towards further regional cooperation along more sensitive military and economic lines. For example, the communications infrastructure, technical competencies, and international cooperation necessary to establish a search and rescue capability for storm-damaged ships, or an emergency oil spill response capability, may be a great base from which to build future maritime security cooperation. To support cooperative multilateral initiatives like those mentioned above, a revision of local legal frameworks might be necessary to ensure that initiatives are actually implemented and that multilateral donor funds are appropriately utilized. With continued, unified external multilateral pressure, these legal frameworks may become the basis for more robust legal requirements that help ensure better governance and the rule of law (for example, to publish energy contract payments between companies and governments).

Although perhaps somewhat naively optimistic, the important point here is that there are many key external players involved in the Gulf of Guinea who do in fact have common security and development interests with the U.S. For U.S.-Africa policymakers, it is imperative that we approach problem solving from a multilateral perspective, capitalizing on the strengths of our potential partners. It is important to include stakeholders from all sectors in planning, coordinating, and executing reforms, especially where the local capacity is egregiously lacking to actually implement reforms that require high levels of capital, equipment, and/or technology. It may also be useful to involve multinational organizations as "honest brokers," to help implement sensitive or difficult reforms and to overcome popular mistrust of national governments.

Conclusion

In sum, multilateral cooperation is an absolute requirement for any effective foreign policy agenda. There are so many international stakeholders that play a role in economic, security, and governance challenges, and that offer prospective solutions, it is pure foolishness not to work together more closely when policy goals align. Unfortunately, for political reasons, too many practical opportunities for synergy are completely missed. Closely coordinated, mutually supporting multilateral approaches can be extremely effective in achieving a desired policy outcome. And when policy goals are at odds between significant international actors, it is essential to address these discrepancies head-on and upfront in order to avoid unnecessary confrontation, misunderstanding, and collateral damage to local third-party constituents.

As with the previous chapters on security, economic development and democratization, this discussion emphasizes the importance of outcomes over the bureaucratic and political squabbles that have all too often created obstacles for real progress in U.S.-Africa relations. Our nation's leaders must remain focused on the long-term considerations of U.S. policy in Africa. All levels of policy planning and implementation need to understand the linkages between the essential foundations and the desired security end states. All stakeholders need to realize the synergy achievable by effectively synchronized and thoroughly coordinated policy implementation practices. And overall, national leadership and key department and agency leadership needs to be consistent and harmonized in focusing all efforts to achieve the desired policy outcomes in two interdependent arenas: long-term energy security and national security. Further, in achieving these policy outcomes, our generation should take advantage of new and emerging opportunities to secure a positive long-term future for Africa. Now is the time for us to work together in turning good ideas—from the U.S., Africa, and elsewhere—into reality.

Notes

1. Susan Rice, former Assistant Secretary of State for African Affairs, comments made during a WIIS Policy Forum (US Policy Towards Africa: Principles and Practice), Brookings Institution, Washington, DC, 16 September 2003.

2. *Private Sector Investment in Development*, Peter Watson, Chairman, President, and CEO of the Overseas Private Investment Corporation (OPIC), Aspen Institute, 31 July 2004, 9.

3. Interview with Mr. Derek Warby, Resource Accounts and Budgeting Director, KAIPTC, 7 July 2005.

4. It is interesting to note that the State Department's Bureau of African Affairs official website lists links and information for HIV issues, NEPAD, AGOA, education, and other "topics of interest", but nothing at all for energy in Africa. The Department of Energy, however, has quite a bit of information available about African energy sources, but no significant caveats about security or governance in the region. Perhaps this is indicative of the unhealthy compartmentalization of US-Africa policy.

5. Neither Feingold nor Leahy sanctions applied to other Department of Defense programs such as JCET, HA, EDA, or FMS, or to EUCOM's Africa mil-to-mil engagement program. This really begs the question of why withholding IMET would be considered an effective punishment from an African perspective? And because IMET is arguably the most important program for influencing an institutional culture, the effects are especially counterproductive.

6. Aaron S. Brickman, Energy Division, International Trade Administration, US Department of Commerce, Interview in Washington D.C., 23 Sep 2003.

7. Person, George L. Jr., Director for African and Middle Eastern Affairs, Office of Policy and International Affairs, US Department of Energy, Interview in Washington D.C., 24 September 2003.

8. Eviatar.

9. U.S. Department of State, "Bush Outlines Areas for Continuing US Support of Africa," 12 July 2003.

10. From briefing by Rich Paces, CEO of Marathon Energy in Malabo, Equatorial Guinea, 4 May 2005.

11. Some will argue that strictly offshore energy extractors have no real interest in onshore stability, as it does not immediately affect resource extraction and therefore corporate profits. We disagree strongly with this, and submit that irresponsible corporate attitudes like this will only lead to future instability.

12. James Dobbins, et. al. *America's Role in Nation Building: From Germany to Iraq.* Santa Monica: RAND, 2003.

13. "How Banks Do Well by Doing Good" (editorial), *New York Times* (November 18, 2003), Section A, p. 24.

14. Jonathan Stevenson, "Africa's Growing Strategic Resonance," *Survival,* vol. 45, no. 4 (Winter, 2003), 165.

15. David Merger, "Africa to Review 16 Nations' Governance by 2006," *The Washington Post* (Feb. 14, 2004).

16. "France Tinkers with its African Troop Deployment," *IRIN News Service*, 30 September 2005.

Chapter 12
Conclusion

The observations and analysis presented in this volume lead to a single conclusion: the U.S. must adopt a long-term, integrated strategy for achieving the nation's energy and security goals in sub-Saharan Africa. Long-term national security for the U.S. will prove elusive unless our energy security interests are pursued alongside coordinated efforts to increase state legitimacy and good governance in oil-producing countries worldwide. This argument is particularly salient when building our relationships with the oil-rich countries of West and Central Africa, and particularly in the Gulf of Guinea, where a complex history of external and internal factors have led to an overall decline in the standard of living for most people.

Based on an historical analysis of oil extraction in the Middle East, it becomes clear that securing unfettered access to oil for multinational extraction corporations without commensurate investments in socioeconomic and political improvement does not bode well for achieving long-term energy security and national security goals. Thus, as the U.S. moves forward in developing the energy extraction industry in the Gulf of Guinea, it must demand transparency in public financial transactions, respect for human rights, and a social and economic environment governed by the rule of law. Further, the U.S. must be prepared to take decisive action when states fail to make progress in these areas. We have already seen what happens when an over-reliance on a particular region's petroleum results in a lack of commitment to such basic principles.

Indeed, the annals of oil extraction are an uninterrupted chronicle of naked aggression, exploitation, and the violent mores of the corporate frontier.[1] Decades of oil extraction in the Middle East have resulted in a widespread image of the U.S. as a global parasite, feeding off Middle Eastern petroleum reservoirs and propping up malevolent and greedy autocratic states, and this has undoubtedly contributed to the challenges of global terrorism. The U.S. did not demand transparency or infrastructure development in the Middle East, nor was there much visible policy integration or interagency cooperation. Various security-related initiatives, particularly in Saudi Arabia and Kuwait, were not pursued alongside a democratization agenda. Overall, as the past several years have demonstrated, the goals and objectives of U.S. national security have to some degree been jeopardized by the achievement of our energy acquisition goals.

This is not a call to closely regulate the oil industry's activities in Africa. Nor is this a treatise for interfering in the affairs of the sovereign state governments of sub-Saharan Africa. Rather, we offer a rationale for ensuring that the transactions of U.S. oil companies and the approaches by the U.S. government's energy policy communities in Africa do not lead to long-term negative impacts on U.S. national security. Given some of the lessons learned from the recent history of the Middle East, it is clearly in the nation's best interests to do so. Throughout sub-Saharan Africa, a combination of economic failure, high birth rates, disease, corruption, and crumbling infrastructure threaten social disintegration and governmental collapse. And yet, this is the century in which we will witness great political, social and economic advancements throughout the African continent. The U.S. can and should be a vital and supportive partner in this process. The current situation in the Gulf of Guinea, and in other key regions of the developing world, offer a significant opportunity to avoid repeating the mistakes made in the Middle East that have contributed to the current environment of global insecurity. The extraction of oil should no longer result in the same patterns of theft, greed, corruption, and authoritarianism. This is not an opportunity to be lost; this is a chance to get it right.

Confronting the Challenges

The Gulf of Guinea has lots of oil and gas, but plenty of challenges to overcome before the people of the region can truly benefit from the revenues these energy resources will bring. There are numerous security challenges throughout the region that must be addressed before good governance can truly be achieved. Unfortunately, because of the authoritarian regimes, corruption, and other challenges discussed in this volume, there are a range of broad political, social, and economic grievances that create a climate of unrest and dissatisfaction in the region. As individuals become dissatisfied and angry with their regimes, some resort to violence. Weaker, smaller states—particularly those in which oil discoveries are relatively recent—are particularly vulnerable to instability. Equatorial Guinea, São Tomé and Príncipe, and Chad are countries of significant concern to most observers. Here, a huge influx of cash in local markets will offer new, tempting targets for theft and corruption. As the U.S. is poised to be the main provider of this influx of cash, we must take into account the way in which these challenges (and our potential for exacerbating them) could undermine our energy security objectives.

Like other regions of the continent, the Gulf of Guinea suffers from chronic armed conflict, extremely high rates of poverty, porous border security, and governmental inefficiency and corruption. These conditions have permitted the growth of numerous armed insurgent groups; an extensive narcotics trafficking network centered in Nigeria; trafficking in women and children; misappropriation of natural resources such as timber, precious metals, and diamonds; and an enormous arms trafficking industry that is supplied from Eastern Europe and the former Soviet Union and regionally centered in Liberia. A strong driver of criminal conduct in West and Central Africa is the region's rich supply of natural resources, which has attracted unscrupulous entrepreneurs from Europe and financed an array of criminal activity.[2] The wealth derived from these natural resources has also fueled corrupt, authoritarian regimes in several countries of the region, whose citizens come to view their national institutions as "prizes" to be won and exploited, rather than as forums for national government.[3] Criminal cartels routinely take advantage of governmental corruption throughout the continent, giving bribes to poorly paid officials and security forces in return for their turning a blind eye toward the illicit trade in drugs, weapons, and humans.

These security challenges underscore an environment that offers a host of potential opportunities for terrorist activity. Throughout the conflicts described in this volume, various groups of insurgents, rebel factions, and government security forces have routinely used violence to terrorize local populations into submission and acquiescence. In some instances, attackers used systematic rape, or chopped off the limbs of innocent civilian noncombatants, for the main purpose of compelling some form of action on the behalf of their opponents. Such individuals can reasonably called both criminals and terrorists. While acts of terrorism in West and Central Africa have been limited to local conflicts, the increasing importance of this region to the world's oil markets can transform such attacks into acts of global terrorism.

Overall, this analysis suggests that the oil-rich countries of the Gulf of Guinea are highly vulnerable to a terrorist attack from globally-oriented groups like al Qaeda and its affiliates. The incapacity of security forces throughout much of the region to protect targets threatened by terrorism is in stark contrast with the great variety of potential targets such as embassies, the numerous agencies and projects of international development organizations, subsidiaries of American and European companies (including those related to the oil industry), and international tourist hotels.[4] According to Stefan Mair, deputy director of the German Institute for International and Security Affairs, "The U.S. embassies and offices of the development organizations already resemble 'wild west' forts of the 19th century. Oil and mining companies have resorted to protecting their property with private, paramilitary security services. Americans, Europeans and Africans who can afford to are increasingly withdrawing to heavily guarded and elaborately protected gated communities."[5] African countries, along with many others of the developing world, lack the resources to effectively prevent or respond to acts of terrorism. Of course, the primary targets of such attacks might be an institution of (or private corporation headquartered in) the United States, Israel, or some other Western country, but as the 1998 embassy bombings in Kenya and Tanzania clearly demonstrated, many Africans will likely die in any major terrorist attack on Western targets in Africa.

The militant Islamist dimension to terrorist violence in Africa is particularly worrisome given the aforementioned interest expressed by al Qaeda in destabilizing the region and attacking its oil infrastructure. According to the Council on Foreign Relations, a non-profit think tank in the U.S., "any African nation with the combustible mix of a weak central government, widespread poverty, and an increasingly politicized Muslim population is at risk" of becoming a potential haven for terrorists.[6] The combination of weak central government and widespread poverty is already present throughout the Gulf of Guinea. Further, as the West increases its involvement with—and physical presence within—the countries of West and Central Africa, these countries run the risk of becoming new targets of the global terrorists who seek to attack the West wherever it can. For example, in Chad—where 52% of the population are Muslims—the newly discovered oil wealth and Western-built oil infrastructure offer several new and tempting targets for anti-American terrorists.

Learning from the Past

In the Gulf of Guinea, states are both potential victims and enablers of terrorism. Because similar patterns of political repression, corruption and underdevelopment are common in the Persian Gulf, and because we have seen a rise in terrorist organizations operating in (and coming from) that region, a review of U.S. foreign policies in this region is warranted. History has taught the West that the objective of Middle Eastern stability is important, but the need for stability should not be used to indefinitely postpone political and civil reform. By supporting corrupt and dictatorial regimes for immediate economic and strategic advantages, the West has actually prevented the kind of change necessary to stabilize these countries through representative government.[7] As U.S. intelligence expert Paul Pillar (2005) has observed, "Many Arabs feel stifled . . . by their own governments, which preside over unreformed economies and unresponsive political systems . . . [and] Washington is seen—and resented—as providing support to prop up the local oppressor."[8]

Overall, the backlash from the nation's foreign policy and energy security approaches in the Persian Gulf has led to greater insecurity for the U.S. Our continued support for undemocratic regimes, coupled with our willingness to do virtually anything to maintain open and reliable access to the oil resources of the Middle East, has produced increasing animosity throughout the region that will take years of hard work to reverse. The current administration appears to recognize this, as reflected in Secretary of State Rice's observation in June 2005, when she remarked that, "For 60 years, my country, the United States, pursued stability at the expense of democracy in this region, here in the Middle East, and we achieved neither . . . Now, we are taking a different course. We are supporting the democratic aspirations of all people . . . It is time to abandon the excuses that are made to avoid the hard work of democracy."[9]

From our analysis of the history of U.S.-Persian Gulf relations, the following lessons can be derived, which should inform our future policies toward the oil-rich countries of the Gulf of Guinea:

- Economically, regimes that focus on capital-intensive development of a single industry, rather than diversifying their economy, run afoul of fundamental economic principles, particularly in a globally interdependent environment;
- Regimes that remain in power not because of a popular mandate from the people they govern, but solely because of U.S. backing, are destined for trouble;
- When the main source of wealth in the country is the largesse of the ruling family, there is clearly a recipe for under-investment in economic diversification, meritocracy, innovation, creative/critical thinking, etc.;
- Lack of transparency, rule of law, good governance—these problems which now plague the regimes of the Persian Gulf are directly related to the oil extraction industry.

The history of U.S. foreign relations with the Persian Gulf was largely driven by the Cold War, bipolar struggle with the Soviet Union for regional influence. With China's growing reliance on oil imports (it is already the world's second largest consumer of oil),[10] coupled with its rapidly modernizing military and economy, will the U.S. default to similar competitive strategies and conflict, only this time with African players as the new pawns in the game? In the Persian Gulf, unequal distribution of opportunities for advancement coupled with political corruption and governmental incompetence has led to political unrest and a reservoir of recruits for groups such as al Qaeda. Can we avoid encouraging a similar fate for the oil-exporting countries of the Gulf of Guinea?

Clearly, problems arise when the pursuit of U.S. short-term interests conflicts with broader U.S. values. One could argue that much of the anti-American sentiment in the Middle East is in part caused by the perceived hypocrisy between American values and national economic interests. How can a nation that trumpets freedom and democracy above all else justify support for oppressive, authoritarian regimes simply to ensure the consistent extraction of strategic minerals, specifically oil and natural gas? Why is there so much instability in petroleum-rich regions where the U.S. engages with the underdeveloped world? These questions frame an important discussion for the nation's burgeoning energy relationship with Africa, and should impact U.S.-Africa policymakers accordingly.

Framing Policies for the Future

This volume has identified a variety of politicizing factors that lead individuals to become actively opposed to their regimes and to the presence of Western oil extraction firms. As the historical record shows, U.S. support for regimes that are not taking adequate care of all their citizens contributes to anger toward these regimes as well as toward the U.S. Thus, as we increase our involvement in the affairs of western and central African nations, we must be careful to avoid

contributing to triggering factors that can quickly transform oppressive governments, opposition groups, or individual anger into more active violence and increased long-term instability. Consequently, we have offered a broad U.S.-
Africa policy framework through which our nation can contribute to a better
future for the Gulf of Guinea—a future of peace, prosperity and security.

Security is the fundamental cornerstone upon which all other policy framework elements must be built, and there is much the U.S. can do to strengthen the
security environment in the Gulf of Guinea. Internal threats faced by these nations include criminals, mercenaries and war profiteers who take advantage of
weak governments, porous borders, widespread poverty and a history of corruption. They also face problems within the security institutions themselves, where
there is urgent need for law enforcement training, professionalism, and equipment. For the oil-rich countries of this region, special training is needed for the
complicated array of security requirements essential to safeguarding energy resources, production facilities, and transport infrastructure. While national governments should take primary fiscal responsibility for their own security, most
are relatively incapable due to the poor status of equipment and training, while
debt burdens inhibit the capability of most African nations to pay the high costs
of new security equipment.

The situation calls for new public/private security ventures, involving all
stakeholders who have a vested interest in protecting the energy infrastructures
of this region. Through a more coordinated approach to security assistance and
development, the U.S. can build the capacity of these states to effectively tackle
their security challenges, creating a more hospitable environment not only for
U.S. interests but for all the region's citizens. Private corporate involvement is
vital: if oil companies do not establish good relations with local communities in
energy source areas, this will continue to create instability and may lead to terrorism. Security training and execution should be conducted by a combination of
military, law enforcement, and private security companies that are well supervised and coordinated by national governments. Beyond training military and
police forces, U.S. contributions could include intelligence and surveillance to
counter smugglers, bandits, oil thieves, and terrorists.

Beyond an individual country's challenges, there are also a number of regional threats to security which require cooperation between countries. These
include transnational criminal and terrorist organizations, the cross-border flow
of weapons and drugs, piracy and other maritime security challenges. International maritime security is a global public good, and the costs for it should be
covered by all those who both benefit and have the means—including the U.S.
and its allies. In tackling these and other regional security challenges, we should
support the network of multinational organizations which Africans have established for themselves. The African Union should take the lead on overall continental security improvement, while regional organizations like ECOWAS and
CEEAC should take the lead in their respective regions.

Overall, true security of a country's energy infrastructure can only be realized when it is seen as beneficial to (and a responsibility of) everyone. The U.S.

cannot and should not focus its energy security efforts on protecting oil pipelines and extractive industries in sub-Saharan Africa. Rather, the focus should be on ensuring that the local populations of Nigeria, Angola and other countries have it in their best interests to protect these pipelines themselves. Algeria provides a good case in point. Here, despite years of terrible internal violence, the gas pipelines and other potential terrorist targets have seldom been attacked because—unlike Nigeria—there is a widespread perception throughout the population that the country as a whole derives benefits from the energy resource industry. Building this perception—and by extension, confidence in the government—should be a key component in the U.S. *National Security Strategy*. This can only be done by empowering these populations to reap the benefits of their natural resources and facilitating a secure environment in which to pursue the individual opportunities of economic and political freedom.

Conflict prevention is always better and usually cheaper than any conflict resolution option. The best conflict prevention is to intervene in weak states before they fail, by promoting security, economic development, and democratization. Security (in all its forms) is an absolute prerequisite for economic development and democratization, not least because stakeholders need institutionalized means to solve political differences without violence. Efforts to prevent governmental corruption and develop a country's infrastructure are sure to fail unless a secure operating environment is provided by a professional military and police force. Indeed, internal security plays a critical role in economic growth. Thus, the reformation of African militaries and police forces can help lead the way for real societal transformation in the Gulf of Guinea.

At the most fundamental level, development assistance is futile if businesses and households are constantly at risk of seeing their goods appropriated by armed groups. In a lawless environment, neither production nor trade can proceed.[11] At a macro level, insecurity translates into states that may directly or indirectly enable transnational terrorist threats to emerge. The U.S. should implement security programs in tandem with economic development programs, as both are absolutely essential to long term stability.

Human security and economic development are part of the essential foundations upon which energy security and national security are built. In addition to qualified debt relief, elimination of western agricultural subsidies, and the development of human capital and strong education systems, the private sector has an enormous role to play in African economic development. An augmented private sector can empower entrepreneurs and lead to economic diversification, enabling Africans to free themselves from dependency and pull themselves out of poverty. For the private sector growth engines to function properly, motivated individuals need adequate security, infrastructure and capital. Additionally, economic development will not be achievable in the Gulf of Guinea unless the glaring problem of corruption is tackled head-on by the U.S., and more importantly, by the African governments themselves. In the Gulf of Guinea states, corruption is intrinsically linked and anathema to both economic development and good governance. A critical component of anti-corruption and development initiatives is the reform of energy revenue stream management processes and institutions. Insecurity, poverty, political instability and inadequate governance currently threaten the tremendous potential benefits of the energy sector. An integrated, long-term approach is thus needed to address key issues and to ensure long-term stability in support of U.S. energy security goals.

In turn, human security and economic development can only be truly institutionalized through good governance—loosely defined as encompassing quality democratic institutions, a supportive political culture, and trustworthy, effective leaders. There can be no long-term energy security in states that are not politically stable. Democracy, adapted to local culture and unique national factors, is what will guarantee this stability by institutionalizing peaceful mechanisms for political compromise and thereby strengthening the relationship between the society and the state. Unfortunately, the current lack of democratic institutions and culture in the Gulf of Guinea poses a serious threat to our nation's long-term energy security and national security interests.

Although this volume's discussion of democratization's challenges and potential is admittedly oversimplified, it illustrates the important point that short-sighted pursuit of U.S. energy interests at the expense of fundamental U.S. values would be an enormous policy blunder. Emphasis on good governance and transparent, accountable African leadership must be a priority for U.S.-Africa policymakers, so that foreign policy mistakes of the past are not repeated today. U.S. support for regimes that simply cooperate in the War on Terror or provide unfettered access to strategic resources (as seen in the Persian Gulf) does not engender long-term, sustainable energy security or national security. Our commitment to democratization in Africa must go beyond rhetoric, toward initiatives that produce real, tangible results.

Unfortunately, according to some observers, "United States engagement with security and democracy issues in African countries is driven more by geopolitical considerations, in a dangerous replay of cold war disregard for African concerns."[12] This is a mistake the U.S. cannot afford to repeat. As Joseph Nye has argued, "hard power, the ability to coerce, grows out of a country's military and economic might. Soft power arises from the attractiveness of a country's culture, political ideals, and policies. When U.S. policies appear legitimate in the eyes of others, American soft power is enhanced . . . emphasis on democracy and human rights can help make U.S. policies attractive to others when these values appear genuine and are pursued in a fair-minded way."[13] Now is our chance to undo decades of neglect on the African continent and apply the nation's energies toward a strong, vibrant democratization agenda. It is clearly in the U.S. national security and energy security interests to nurture the development of mature democracies in the Gulf of Guinea.

Multilateral cooperation is also a requirement for any effective foreign policy agenda. There are so many international stakeholders that play a role in economic, security, and governance challenges, and that offer prospective solutions, it is pure foolishness not to work together more closely when policy goals align. Unfortunately, for political reasons, too many practical opportunities for synergy are completely missed. Closely coordinated, mutually supporting multilateral approaches can be extremely effective in achieving a desired policy outcome. And when policy goals are at odds between significant international actors, it is essential to address these discrepancies head-on and up-front in order to avoid unnecessary confrontation, misunderstanding, and collateral damage to local third-party constituents. As the world's only superpower, the U.S. has a unique opportunity to provide leadership here, to ensure a better future for all countries—both the consumers and the producers of energy.

This volume emphasizes the importance of outcomes over the bureaucratic and political squabbles that have all too often created obstacles for real progress in U.S.-Africa relations. Our nation's leaders must remain focused on the long-term considerations of U.S. policy in Africa. All levels of policy planning and implementation need to understand the linkages between the essential foundations and the desired security end states. All stakeholders need to realize the synergy achievable by effectively synchronized and thoroughly coordinated policy implementation practices. And overall, national leadership and key department and agency leadership needs to be consistent and harmonized in focusing all efforts to achieve the desired policy outcomes in two interdependent arenas: long-term energy security and national security.

Final Thoughts

Further study of the challenges and possibilities discussed in this volume is clearly warranted, both in sub-Saharan Africa and in other regions vital to the long-term security interests of the U.S. While our research has focused primarily on the Gulf of Guinea, the integrated policy strategy proposed in this volume could also be applicable to a wide variety of regions with similar characteristics (e.g., large reservoirs of oil and natural gas, corrupt and non-democratic governments, weak institutions, and severe underdevelopment), such as Central Asia, the Caspian Sea region, and certain segments of Latin America. Generally speaking, the history of U.S. foreign policy toward energy resource-endowed countries suggests that new thinking is needed. With the exception of Canada and a few others, the countries to which the U.S. has tied its energy security needs are not models of good governance, economic development, or human security. Instead they are fraught with an array of political, economic, social and security challenges, some of which have influenced followers of a radical strain of Islamic fundamentalism to call for terrorist attacks against the U.S. and its allies. Given the social, economic and political forces currently at play in the Gulf of Guinea (and in other regions where trouble is brewing), we should learn from this past and avoid creating similar national security challenges for ourselves in the future. Of course, the world's security challenges are constantly evolving, and can be rather unpredictable. However, what is predictable—and highly likely—is that in the world of U.S. energy security and foreign policy, failure to learn from the past will lead us to repeat our mistakes in the future.

Notes

1. Oronto Douglas, Von Kemedi, Ike Okonta, and Michael Watts, "Alienation and Militancy in the Niger Delta: A Response to CSIS on Petroleum, Politics, and Democracy in Nigeria," Foreign Policy in Focus Special Report, July 2003. Available online at: http://www.fpif.org/papers/nigeria2003_body.html.

2. Congressional Research Service, "Nation's Hospitable to Organized Crime and Terrorism," Library of Congress, Federal Research Division, October, 2003.

3. Congressional Research Service, "Nation's Hospitable to Organized Crime and Terrorism," Library of Congress, Federal Research Division, October, 2003.

4. Stefan Mair, "Terrorism and Africa: On the Danger of Further Attack in Sub-Saharan Africa," *African Security Review,* 12(1) (2003), 109.

5. Stefan Mair, "Terrorism and Africa," 109.

6. Council on Foreign Relations, "Africa: Terror Havens," December 30, 2003. Online at http://www.cfr.org.

7. Dominique Moisi, "Tragedy that Exposed a Groundswell of Hatred," *Financial Times* (London), September 24, 2001, referenced in Noreng, 10.

8. Paul Pillar, "Superpower Foreign Policies: A Source for Global Resentment," in *The Making of a Terrorist* (vol. 3), ed. J. Forest (Westport, CT: Praeger, 2005).

9. U.S. Secretary of State, Condoleezza Rice, in a speech given at the American University in Cairo, 20 June 2005.

10. "Balanced Energy Supply-Demand Market for China in 2004," *People's Daily* (Beijing), 30 March 2004. Accessed at http://english.peopledaily.com.cn/200403/30/eng2/0040330_138924.shtml.

11. James Dobbins, et. al. *America's Role in Nation Building: From Germany to Iraq.* Santa Monica: RAND, 2003.

12. Salih Booker, William Minter, and Ann-Louise Colgan, "America and Africa," *Current History* (May 2003), p.199.

13. Joseph Nye, "U.S. Power and Strategy After Iraq," *Foreign Affairs,* July/ August 2003, 66-67.

Global Oil Reserves, Production and Consumption

Table A-1: Consumption of Oil, 1984 and 2004
(thousand barrels per day)

	1984	2004	% of 2004 total
USA	15,725	20,517	24.9%
Canada	1,554	2,206	2.6%
Mexico	1,195	1,896	2.3%
Total North America	**18,474**	**24,619**	**29.8%**
Argentina	442	393	0.5%
Brazil	1,093	1,830	2.2%
Chile	102	232	0.3%
Colombia	170	223	0.3%
Ecuador	70	140	0.2%
Peru	122	153	0.2%
Venezuela	370	577	0.7%
Other S. & Cent. America	800	1,192	1.5%
Total S. & Cent. America	**3,171**	**4,739**	**5.9%**
Austria	201	284	0.4%
Azerbaijan	n/a	91	0.1%
Belarus	n/a	150	0.2%
Belgium & Luxembourg	422	779	1.0%
Bulgaria	226	98	0.1%
Czech Republic	219	202	0.3%
Denmark	212	189	0.2%
Finland	216	224	0.3%
France	1,813	1,975	2.5%
Germany	2,581	2,625	3.3%
Greece	237	411	0.5%
Hungary	211	136	0.2%
Iceland	10	19	♦
Republic of Ireland	82	181	0.2%
Italy	1,737	1,871	2.4%
Kazakhstan	n/a	192	0.3%
Lithuania	n/a	52	0.1%
Netherlands	624	1,003	1.2%
Norway	189	209	0.3%
Poland	332	462	0.6%
Portugal	194	325	0.4%
Romania	285	212	0.3%
Russian Federation	n/a	2,574	3.4%
Slovakia	126	74	0.1%
Spain	956	1,593	2.1%
Sweden	360	319	0.4%

Table A-1 (cont.): Consumption of Oil, 1984 and 2004
(thousand barrels per day)

	1984	2004	% of 2004 total
Switzerland	250	258	0.3%
Turkey	368	688	0.8%
Turkmenistan	n/a	98	0.1%
Ukraine	n/a	348	0.5%
United Kingdom	1,851	1,756	2.1%
Uzbekistan	n/a	120	0.2%
Other Europe & Eurasia	8,754	500	0.6%
Total Europe & Eurasia	**22,455**	**20,017**	**25.4%**
Iran	812	1,551	1.9%
Kuwait	159	266	0.4%
Qatar	20	84	0.1%
Saudi Arabia	894	1,728	2.1%
United Arab Emirates	118	306	0.4%
Other Middle East	730	1,354	1.7%
Total Middle East	**2,733**	**5,289**	**6.7%**
Algeria	173	242	0.3%
Egypt	409	566	0.7%
South Africa	307	525	0.7%
Other Africa	778	1,314	1.6%
Total Africa	**1,667**	**2,647**	3.3%
Australia	611	858	1.0%
Bangladesh	32	86	0.1%
China	1,733	6,684	8.2%
China Hong Kong SAR	110	314	0.4%
India	822	2,555	3.2%
Indonesia	477	1,150	1.5%
Japan	4,619	5,288	6.4%
Malaysia	192	504	0.6%
New Zealand	83	151	0.2%
Pakistan	145	296	0.4%
Philippines	168	336	0.4%
Singapore	228	748	1.0%
South Korea	500	2,280	2.8%
Taiwan	349	877	1.1%
Thailand	243	909	1.2%
Other Asia Pacific	190	411	0.5%
Total Asia Pacific	**10,502**	**23,446**	28.9%
TOTAL WORLD	**59,002**	**80,757**	**100.0%**

Source: *BP Statistical Review of World Energy, 2005.*

Table A-2: Proven Oil Reserves, 1984 and 2004
(thousand million barrels)

	1984	2004	% of 2004 total
USA	36.1	29.4	2.5%
Canada	9.4	16.8	1.4%
Mexico	56.4	14.8	1.2%
Total North America	**101.9**	**61.0**	**5.1%**
Argentina	2.3	2.7	0.2%
Brazil	2.0	11.2	0.9%
Colombia	1.1	1.5	0.1%
Ecuador	1.1	5.1	0.4%
Peru	0.7	0.9	0.1%
Trinidad & Tobago	0.6	1.0	0.1%
Venezuela	28.0	77.2	6.5%
Other S. & Cent. America	0.5	1.5	0.1%
Total S. & Cent. America	**36.3**	**101.2**	**8.5%**
Azerbaijan	n/a	7.0	0.6%
Denmark	0.5	1.3	0.1%
Italy	0.6	0.7	0.1%
Kazakhstan	n/a	39.6	3.3%
Norway	4.9	9.7	0.8%
Romania	1.5	0.5	*
Russian Federation	n/a	72.3	6.1%
Turkmenistan	n/a	0.5	*
United Kingdom	6.0	4.5	0.4%
Uzbekistan	n/a	0.6	*
Other Europe & Eurasia	83.2	2.5	0.2%
Total Europe & Eurasia	**96.7**	**139.2**	**11.7%**
Iran	58.9	132.5	11.1%
Iraq	65.0	115.0	9.7%
Kuwait	92.7	99.0	8.3%
Oman	3.9	5.6	0.5%
Qatar	4.5	15.2	1.3%

Table A-2 (cont.): Proven Oil Reserves, 1984 and 2004
(thousand million barrels)

	1984	2004	% of 2004 total
Saudi Arabia	171.7	262.7	22.1%
Syria	1.4	3.2	0.3%
United Arab Emirates	32.5	97.8	8.2%
Yemen	0.1	2.9	0.2%
Other Middle East	0.2	0.1	*
Total Middle East	430.8	733.9	61.7%
Algeria	9.0	11.8	1.0%
Angola	2.1	8.8	0.7%
Chad	-	0.9	0.1%
Rep. of Congo (Brazzaville)	0.8	1.8	0.2%
Egypt	4.0	3.6	0.3%
Equatorial Guinea	-	1.3	0.1%
Gabon	0.6	2.3	0.2%
Libya	21.4	39.1	3.3%
Nigeria	16.7	35.3	3.0%
Sudan	0.3	6.3	0.5%
Tunisia	1.8	0.6	0.1%
Other Africa	1.0	0.5	*
Total Africa	57.8	112.2	9.4%
Australia	2.9	4.0	0.3%
Brunei	1.5	1.1	0.1%
China	16.3	17.1	1.4%
India	3.8	5.6	0.5%
Indonesia	9.6	4.7	0.4%
Malaysia	2.9	4.3	0.4%
Thailand	0.1	0.5	*
Vietnam	-	3.0	0.2%
Other Asia Pacific	1.1	0.9	0.1%
Total Asia Pacific	38.1	41.1	3.5%
TOTAL WORLD	761.6	1,188.6	100.0%

Source: *BP Statistical Review of World Energy, 2005.*
Note: Less than 0.05%

Table A-3: Production of Oil, 1984 and 2004
(thousand barrels per day)

	1984	2004	% of 2004 total
USA	10,509	7,241	8.5%
Canada	1,775	3,085	3.8%
Mexico	2,942	3,824	4.9%
Total North America	**15,226**	**14,150**	**17.3%**
Argentina	509	756	1.0%
Brazil	473	1,542	2.0%
Colombia	173	551	0.7%
Ecuador	261	535	0.7%
Peru	185	93	0.1%
Trinidad & Tobago	170	155	0.2%
Venezuela	1,853	2,980	4.0%
Other S. & Cent. America	95	152	0.2%
Total S. & Cent. America	**3,719**	**6,764**	**8.8%**
Azerbaijan	n/a	318	0.4%
Denmark	47	394	0.5%
Italy	44	104	0.1%
Kazakhstan	n/a	1,295	1.6%
Norway	752	3,188	3.9%
Romania	249	119	0.1%
Russian Federation	n/a	9,285	11.9%
Turkmenistan	n/a	202	0.3%
United Kingdom	2,632	2,029	2.5%
Uzbekistan	n/a	152	0.2%
Other Europe & Eurasia	12,833	496	0.6%
Total Europe & Eurasia	**16,557**	**17,583**	**22.0%**
Iran	2,043	4,081	5.2%
Iraq	1,228	2,027	2.6%
Kuwait	1,229	2,424	3.1%
Oman	419	785	1.0%
Qatar	353	990	1.2%

Table A-3 (cont.): Production of Oil, 1984 and 2004
(thousand barrels per day)

	1984	2004	% of 2004 total
Saudi Arabia	4,534	10,584	13.1%
Syria	162	536	0.7%
United Arab Emirates	1,283	2,667	3.3%
Yemen	-	429	0.5%
Other Middle East	50	48	0.1%
Total Middle East	**11,301**	**24,571**	**30.7%**
Algeria	1,137	1,933	2.1%
Angola	204	991	1.3%
Cameroon	146	62	0.1%
Chad	-	168	0.2%
Rep. of Congo (Brazzaville)	117	240	0.3%
Egypt	816	708	0.9%
Equatorial Guinea	-	350	0.4%
Gabon	174	235	0.3%
Libya	1,022	1,607	2.0%
Nigeria	1,388	2,508	3.2%
Sudan	-	301	0.4%
Tunisia	115	69	0.1%
Other Africa	60	92	0.1%
Total Africa	**5,179**	**9,264**	**11.4%**
Australia	568	541	0.6%
Brunei	172	211	0.3%
China	2,292	3,490	4.5%
India	583	819	1.0%
Indonesia	1,505	1,126	1.4%
Malaysia	456	912	1.0%
Thailand	24	218	0.2%
Vietnam	-	427	0.5%
Other Asia Pacific	102	184	0.2%
Total Asia Pacific	**5,702**	**7,928**	**9.8%**
TOTAL WORLD	**57,683**	**80,260**	**100.0%**

Source: *BP Statistical Review of World Energy, 2005.*

Table A-4: Selected Statistics on Gulf of Guinea Countries

	ANGOLA	CAMEROON	CHAD	CONGO	EQUATORIAL GUINEA	GABON	SAO TOME & PRINCIPE	NIGERIA
Population (July 2005 est.)	11,190,786	16,380,005	9,826,419	3,039,126	535,881	1,389,201	187,410	128,771,988
Median Age	18.12 years	18.6 years	16.02 years	20.7 years	18.83 years	18.57 years	16.12 years	18.63 years
Avg. Life Expectancy	36.61 years	47.84 years	47.94 years	48.97 years	55.56 years	55.75 years	66.99 years	46.74 years
GDP	$35.1 billion (2004 est.)	$30.17 billion (2004 est.)	$15.66 billion (2004 est.)	$2.324 billion (2004 est.)	$1.27 billion (2002 est.)	$7.966 billion (2004 est.)	$214 million (2003 est.)	$125.7 billion (2004 est.)
GDP Per Capita	$2,525 (2004 est.)	$1,900 (2004 est.)	$1,600 (2004 est.)	$800 (2004 est.)	$2,700 (2002 est.)	$5,900 (2004 est.)	$1,200 (2003 est.)	$1,000 (2004 est.)
GDP Growth, 2004	11.7% (2004 est.)	4.9% (2004 est.)	38% (2004 est.)	3.7% (2004 est.)	20% (2002 est.)	1.9% (2004 est.)	6% (2004 est.)	6.2% (2004 est.)
Population below poverty line	70% (2003 est.)	48% (2000 est.)	80% (2001 est.)	n/a	n/a	n/a	54% (2004 est.)	60% (2000 est.)
External Debt	$10.45 billion (2004 est.)	$8.46 billion (2004 est.)	$1.1 billion (2000 est.)	$5 billion (2000 est.)	$248 million (2000 est.)	$3.804 billion (2004 est.)	$318 million (2002 est.)	$30.55 billion (2004 est.)
Literacy	42%	79%	47.5%	83.8%	85.7%	63.2%	79.3%	68%
UN Human Development Index Ranking[2]	166	141	167	144	109	122	123	151
Probability at birth of not surviving to age 40 (% of 2000-2005 cohort)	49%	44%	43%	32%	36%	28%	10%	35%
Population without sustainable access to an improved water source	62%	42%	73%	49%	56%	14%	n/a	38%
Physicians per 100,000 people[3]	5	7	3	25	25	n/a	47	27
Malaria cases per 100,000	8,733	2,900	197	5,880	2,744	2,148	n/a	30
Public Expenditures:								
on education (2001)	2.8%	5.1%	2.0%	3.2%	0.5%	3.9%	n/a	n/a
on health (2001)	2.8%	1.2%	2.0%	1.4%	1.2%	1.7%	1.5%	0.8%
on the military (2002)	3.7%	1.4%	1.4%	n/a	n/a	n/a	n/a	1.1%
on debt service (2002)	7.7%	3.9%	1.5%	0.8%	0.2%	8.3%	12.1%	3.4%
Armed Forces (2002)	100,000	23,000	30,000	10,000	2,000	5,000	n/a	79,000

Sources: *2005 CIA Factbook*, 2004 UN Human Development Index, and U.S. Department of State, Bureau of Africa Affairs

Selected Bibliography

Abb, Madelfia A. and Cindy R. Jebb. "Human Security and Good Governance: A Living Systems Approach to Understanding and Combating Terrorism." In *The Making of a Terrorist: Recruitment, Training and Root Causes*, edited by James JF Forest. Westport, CT: Praeger, 2005.

Ake, Claude. *Democracy and Development in Africa.* Washington, DC: Brookings Institution, 1996.

Ayittey, George B. N. *Africa in Chaos.* New York: St Martin's Press, 1999.

Booker, Salih, William Minter, and Ann-Louise Colgan. "America and Africa," *Current History* (May 2003).

Byman Daniel L., and Jerrold D. Green. *Political Violence and Stability in the States of the Northern Persian Gulf.* Santa Monica: RAND Corporation, 1999.

Carafano, James Jay and Nile Gardiner. "U.S. Military Assistance for Africa: A Better Solution," Heritage Foundation Backgrounder #1697. Available online at: http://www.heritage.org/Research/Africa/bg1697.cfm

Cillers, Jackie. "NEPAD's Peer Review Mechanism," Institute for Security Studies, Occasional Paper No. 64 (November 2002). Available online at: http://www.iss.co.za/Pubs/Papers/64/Paper64.html.

Collier, Paul, and Anke Hoeffler. *Greed and Grievance in Civil War.* Policy Research Working Paper 2355. Washington, DC: World Bank, Development Research Group (May 2000)

Collier, Paul. *Economic Causes of Civil Conflict and their Implications for Policy.* Washington, DC: World Bank, June 2000.

Commission of the European Communities. "Communication from the Commission to the Council: The EU-Africa Dialogue." Available online at: http://europa.eu.int/eur-lex/en/com/cnc/2003/com2003_0316en01.pdf

Commission for Africa. *Our Common Interest: Report of the Commission for Africa.* London: Commission on Africa (London, March 2005). Available online at: http://www.commissionforafrica.org

Congressional Research Service. *Nation's Hospitable to Organized Crime and Terrorism.* Library of Congress, Federal Research Division (October, 2003). Available online at: http://www.loc.gov/rr/frd/terrorism.html

Corey, Charles W. "Gulf of Guinea of Increasing Importance: West African Nations Critical to U.S. Energy Security." *The Washington File,* 22 July 22 2004. Washington, DC: U.S. Department of State, Bureau of International Information Programs. Online at: http://usinfo.state.gov.

Corporate Council on Africa. "A Ten-Year Strategy for Increasing Capital Flows to Africa" (June 2003). Available at: http://www.africacncl.org.

Crocker, Chester A. "Engaging Failed States," *Foreign Affairs* (September/October 2003).

Daly, John C.K. "The Threat to Iraqi Oil." *Terrorism Monitor* 2, no. 12, 17 June 2004.

Davidson, Basil. *The Black Man's Burden: Africa and the Curse of the Nation State.* New York: Random House, 1992.

Deegan, Heather. "Elections in Africa – The Past Ten Years." Elections in Africa Briefing Paper No. 2. London: Royal Institute of International Affairs, April 2003.

Diamond, Jared. *Guns, Germs, and Steel: The Fates of Human Societies.* New York: W.W. Norton & Company, 1999.

Dickson, David. "Political Islam in Sub-Saharan Africa: The Need for a New Research and Diplomatic Agenda." Special Report 140. Washington, DC: United States Institute of Peace (May, 2005). Available online at: http://www.usip.org

Dobbins, James, et. al. *America's Role in Nation Building: From Germany to Iraq.* Santa Monica: RAND, 2003. Available online at: http://www.rand.org/publications/MR/MR1753.

Ellis, Stephen. "West Africa and its Oil." *African Affairs* 102 (January 2003).

Engendering Bold Leadership: The President's Emergency Plan for AIDS Relief, First Annual Report to Congress (March 2005). Available online at: http://www.state.gov/documents/organization/43885.pdf

Ero, Comfort, and Angela Ndinga-Muvumba. "Small Arms and Light Weapons." In *West Africa's Security Challenges,* edited by Adekeye Adebajo and Ismail Rashid. Boulder, CO: Lynne Reinner, 2004.

Farneth, Molly. "Powering Foreign Policy: The Role of Oil in Diplomacy and Conflict." Energy Security Initiative Report. New York: Physicians for Social Responsibility, October 2004.

Fisher-Thompson, Jim. "U.S. Officials Cite Importance of African Oil to U.S. Economy," U.S. Department of State, Washington File, February 1, 2002.

Flanary, Rachel. "The State in Africa: Implications for Democratic Reform." *Crime, Law and Social Change* 29 No. 2 (1998): 179-196.

Forest, James J.F., ed. *Teaching Terror: Knowledge Transfer in the Terrorist World.* Boulder, CO: Rowman & Littlefield, 2006.

—, ed. *The Making of a Terrorist: Recruitment, Training and Root Causes.* Westport, CT: Praeger, 2005.

Games, Dianna. *An Oil Giant Reforms: The Experience of South African Companies Doing Business in Nigeria.* Pretoria: The South African Institute of International Affairs, 2004.

Gary, Ian and Nikki Reisch. *Chad's Oil: Miracle or Mirage?- Following the Money in Africa's Newest Petro-State.* Catholic Relief Services and Bank Information Center, February 2005. Available online at: http://www.bicusa. org/bicusa/issues/chad_oil_report.pdf.

Goldwyn, Daniel L. "Extracting Transparency." *Georgetown Journal of International Affairs* (Winter/Spring 2004).

Goredema, Charles. "Organized Crime and Terrorism: Observations from Southern Africa." Pretoria, South Africa: Institute for Security Studies, *ISS Paper 101* (March 2005).

Hagel, Chuck. "A Republican Foreign Policy," *Foreign Affairs,* 83, no. 4 (July-August 2004): 64-76.

Handy, Russell J. "Africa Contingency Operations Training Assistance: developing training partnerships for the future of Africa." *Air and Space Power Journal,* Fall 2003. Available online at:
http://www.airpower.maxwell.af.mil/airchronicles/apj/apj03/fal03/handy.html.

Hawley, Susan. *Turning a Blind Eye: Corruption and the UK Export Credits Guarantee Department.* London: The Corner House, June 2003.

Hazem Beblawi and Giacomo Luciani, eds. *The Rentier State.* New York: Croom Helm, 1987.

Henk, Dan. "U.S. National Interests in Sub-Saharan Africa." *Parameters* (Winter, 1997-98) : 92-107.

Hodges, Tony. *Angola from Afro-Stalinism to Petro-Diamond Capitalism.* Bloomington: Indiana University Press, 2001.

Hourani, Albert. *A History of the Arab Peoples.* Cambridge University Press, 1991.

Human Rights Watch, *Some Transparency, No Accountability: The Use of Oil Revenue in Angola and Its Impact on Human Rights* (January 2004). Available online at: http://www.hrw.org/reports/2004/angola0104/index.htm

Ibeanu, Okechukwu. "(Sp)oils of Politics: Petroleum, Politics and the Illusion of Development in the Niger Delta, Nigeria." *ACAS Bulletin* 64 (Fall 2002).

Institute for Advanced Strategic and Political Studies. *African Oil: A Priority for U.S. National Security and African Development.* Washington, DC: Institute for Advanced Strategic and Political Studies, 2002. Available online at: http://www.israeleconomy.org/strategic/africatranscript.pdf

International Crisis Group. "Angola's Choice: Reform or Regress." ICG Africa Report No. 61, Brussels: International Crisis Group, 7 April 2003.

Juma, Monica, and Aida Mengistu. *The Infrastructure of Peace in Africa: Assessing the Peacebuilding Capacity of African Institutions.* A report submitted by the Africa Program of the International Peace Academy to the Ford Foundation, September 2002.

Kaplan, Robert D., *The Coming Anarchy.* New York: Random House, 2000.

Karl, Terry Lynn. *The Paradox of Plenty: Oil Booms and Petro-States.* Berkeley: University of California Press, 1997.

Kaufmann, Daniel, Aart Kraay, and Massimo Mastruzzi. *Governance Matters IV: New Data, New Challenges.* Washington, DC: The World Bank, May 2005.

Keay, Malcolm. "Oil and Governance: Focus on West Africa." London: Royal Institute of International Affairs, July 2002.

Klare, Michael T. "Fueling The Fires: The Oil Factor in Middle Eastern Terrorism." In *The Making of a Terrorist: Recruitment, Training and Root Causes (vol. 3),* edited by James JF Forest. Westport, CT: Praeger, 2005.

—. "The Deadly Nexus: Oil, Terrorism, and America's National Security." *Current History* (December 2002).

—. *American Arms Supermarket.* Austin: University of Texas Press, 1984.

—. *Blood and Oil: The Dangers and Consequences of America's Growing Petroleum Dependency.* New York: Metropolitan Books, 2004.

—. *Resource Wars: The New Landscape of Global Conflict.* New York: Henry Holt and Company, LLC, 2001.

Klitgaard, Robert. "International Cooperation Against Corruption." *Finance and Development* 35 no. 1 (March 1998).

—. *Tropical Gangsters: One Man's Experience with Development and Decadence in Deepest Africa.* New York: Basic Books, Inc., 1990.

Korin, Anne, and Gal Luft. "Terrorism Goes to Sea," *Foreign Affairs* (November/December 2004).

Krueger, Jessica. "U.S. Oil Stakes in West Africa." *Africa Notes* 11 (December 2002). Available online at http://www.csis.org

Landes, David S. *The Wealth and Poverty of Nations: Why Some Are So Rich and Some So Poor.* New York: W.W. Norton & Company, 1999.

Le Billon, Philippe. "Angola's Political Economy of War: The Role of Oil and Diamonds (1975-2000). *African Affairs* (2001): 55-80

Lia, Brynjar, and Ashild Kjok. "Energy Supply as Terrorist Targets? Patterns of 'Petroleum Terrorism' 1968-1999." In *Oil in the Gulf: Obstacles to Democracy and Development,* edited by Daniel Heradstveit and Helge Hveem. London: Ashgate, 2004.

Long, David E. *The United States and Saudi Arabia.* Boulder, CO: Westview Press, 1985.

Lovins, Amory B. *Energy Security Facts: Details and Documentation.* Snowmass, CO: Rocky Mountain Institute, 2 June 2003

Lyman, Princeton N. and J. Stephen Morrison. "The Terrorist Threat in Africa." *Foreign Affairs,* 83, no. 1 (Jan/Feb 2004): 75-86.

Luft, Gal and Anne Korin. "Terrorism Goes to Sea," *Foreign Affairs* 83, no. 6 (Nov-Dec 2004): 61-71

Mair, Stefan. "Terrorism and Africa: On the Danger of Further Attack in sub-Saharan Africa." *African Security Review,* 12, no, 1 (2003).

Manby, Bronwenn. "The Role and Responsibility of Oil Multinationals in Nigeria." *Journal of International Affairs* (Fall 1999).

Messiant, Christine. "The Eduardo dos Santos Foundation; or, How Angola's Regime is Taking Over Civil Society." *African Affairs,* 100 (2001): 287-309.

Miller, Aaron Dean. *Search for Security.* Chapel Hill: University of North Carolina Press, 1980.

Minter, William. *Apartheid's Contras: An Inquiry into the Roots of War in Angola and Mozambique.* St. Martin's Press, 1994.

Mitchell, John, with Koji Morita, Norman Selley and Jonathan Stern. *The New Economy of Oil: Impacts on Business, Geopolitics and Society.* Royal Institute of International Affairs/Earthscan, London, 2001.

Neethling, Theo. "Shaping the African Standby Force," *Military Review* (May-June 2005): 68-71.

New Partnership for Africa's Development (NEPAD). "A Summary of NEPAD Action Plans." Online at: http://www.nepad.org/2005/files/documents/2.pdf

Noreng, Oystein. "The Predicament of the Gulf Rentier State." In *Oil in the Gulf: Obstacles to Democracy and Development,* edited by Daniel Heradstveit and Helge Hveem. London: Ashgate, 2004.

Nwankwo, Arthur A. *Nigeria: The Stolen Billions.* Enugu, Nigeria: Fourth Dimension Publishers, 1999.

Nye, Joseph. "U.S. Power and Strategy After Iraq," *Foreign Affairs* 82, no. 4 (July-August 2003): 60-73.

Painter, David S. *Oil and the American Century.* Baltimore: Johns Hopkins University Press, 1986.

Pauly, Jr., Robert J. *U.S Foreign Policy and the Persian Gulf.* London: Ashgate Publishers, 2005.

Pegg, Scott. "Globalization and Natural Resource Conflicts." *Naval War College Review* 61, no. 4 (Autumn 2003).

—. "The Cost of Doing Business: Transnational Corporations and Violence in Nigeria. *Security Dialogue* (December 1999).

Pillar, Paul "Superpower Foreign Policies: A Source for Global Resentment," in *The Making of a Terrorist: Recruitment, Training and Root Causes* (vol. 3), edited by James J.F. Forest. Westport, CT: Praeger, 2005.

Pollack, Kenneth M. *The Persian Puzzle.* New York: Random House, 2004.

Porto, Joao Gomes. "Coup D'Etat in Sao Tome and Principe." *African Security Review,* 12, no. 4 (2003).

Rashid, Ismail. "West Africa's Post-Cold War Challenges." In *West Africa's Security Challenges,* edited by Adekeye Adebajo and Ismail Rashid. Boulder, CO: Lynne Reinner, 2004.

Renner, Michael. "Fueling Conflict." In *PetroPolitics Briefing Book.* Washington, DC: Interhemispheric Resource Center/Institute for Policy Studies/SEEN (January 2004).

Robbins, James S. "No Blood for Oil." *National Review Online,* 12 July 2005. Online   at: http://www.nationalreview.com/robbins/robbins200507120857.asp

Ross, Michael. "Does Oil Hinder Democracy?" *World Politics* 53, no. 3 (April 2001): 325-61.

Rotberg, Robert I. "Strengthening African Leadership: There is Another Way," *Foreign Affairs* 83, no. 4 (July-August, 2004): 14-19.

Sachs, Jeffrey D. "The Development Challenge, *Foreign Affairs* 84, no. 2 (March/April, 2005): 78-90.

Schneidman, Witney W. "The Commission on Capital Flows to Africa." *The Africa Journal* (Aug/Sep 2003). Available online at: http://www.africacncl.org/AfricaJournal/index.asp.

Schramm, Carl. "Building Entrepreneurial Economies," *Foreign Affairs* 83, no. 4 (July-August 2004): 104-115.

Serafino, Nina M. *The Global Peace Operations Initiative: Background and Issues for Congress,* February 16, 2005. Available online at: http://www.fas.org/sgp/crs/misc/RL32773.pdf.

Silverstein, Ken. "U.S. Oil Politics in the 'Kuwait of Africa.'" *The Nation* 274, no. 15 (22 April 2002).

Singer, P.W. *Corporate Warriors: The Rise of the Privatized Military Industry.* Cornell University Press, 2003.

—. "Corporate Warriors: The Rise of the Privatized Military Industry and its Ramifications for International Security." *International Security* (Winter 2001/2002).

Stevenson, Jonathan. "Africa's Growing Strategic Resonance." *Survival* 45, no. 4 (Winter, 2003).

Stoff, Michael B. *Oil, War and American Security.* New Haven: Yale University Press, 1980.

Suarez, Alfredo Rangel. "Parasites and Predators: Guerillas and the Insurrection Economy of Colombia." *Journal of International Affairs* (Spring, 2000).

Swanson, Philip. *Fueling Conflict: The Oil Industry and Armed Conflict* (Fafo report 378). Oslo, Norway: Program for International Cooperation and Conflict Resolution, Fafo Institute for Applied Social Science, March 2002.

The Economist. "What Oil Can Do to Tiny States." 23 January 2003.

Thurow, Roger. "Africa's Problems Move to Top of Global Agenda." *Foreign Policy,* 9 June 2005.

Transparency International. *Corruption Perceptions Index 2004.* Online at: http://www.transparency.org

—. *Report on the Transparency International Global Corruption Barometer 2004.* Online at: http://www.transparency.org

U.S. Department of Energy. *International Energy Outlook 2005.* Available online at: http://www.eia.doe.gov/oiaf/ieo/oil.html

U.S. Department of State. *International Narcotics Control Strategy Report 2005.* Available online at: http://www.state.gov/g/inl/rls/nrcrpt/2005

—. 2003. Patterns of Global Terrorism, 2002. Available online at: http://www.state.gov/s/ct/rls/pgtrpt/2002

United Nations Development Program. *Arab Human Development Report.* New York: United Nations Development Program, 2002. Available online at: http://www.undp.org/rbas/ahdr

United Nations Office on Drugs and Crime. *Crime and Development in Africa.* New York: United Nations, June 2005. Available online at: http://www.unodc.org/unodc/index.html

—. *Transnational Organized Crime in the West African Region.* New York: United Nations, June 2005.

Volman, Daniel. "Oil, Arms, and Violence in Africa." Washington, DC: African Security Research Project, February 2003. Available online at: http://www.prairienet.org/acas/military/oilandarms.pdf

Waas, Murray. "What Washington Gave Saddam for Christmas." In *The Iraq War Reader: History, Documents, Opinions,* edited Micah L. Sifry and Christopher Cerf. New York: Simon and Schuster, 2003.

Williams, Phil, and Doug Brooks. "Captured, Criminal, and Contested States: Organized Crime and Africa in the Twenty-First Century." *South African Journal of International Affairs* 6, no. 2 (Winter 1999): 86-96.

Wirth, Timothy E., C. Boyden Gray, and John D. Podesta. "The Future of Energy Policy." *Foreign Affairs* 82, no. 4 (July/August 2003): 132-155.

World Bank. *The Role and Effectiveness of Development Assistance: Lessons from World Bank Experience* (March 2002). Available online at: http://www.gm-unccd.org/FIELD/Multi/WB/WB_lessons.pdf

—. *World Development Report 2006: Equity and Development* (2005). Available online at: http://econ.worldbank.org.

Yates, Douglas. *The Rentier State in Africa: Oil Rent Dependency and Neocolonialism in the Republic of Gabon.* Trenton, NJ: Africa World Press, 1996.

Yergin, Daniel. *The Prize: The Epic Quest for Oil, Money, and Power.* New York, NY: Simon and Schuster, 1991.

Useful Online Resources

Africa Center for Strategic Studies
  http://www.africacenter.org
Africa Growth and Opportunity Act
  http://www.agoa.gov and http://www.agoa.info.
Africa Policy of the Bush Administration: An Overview
  http://www.whitehouse.gov/infocus/africa
African Coastal Security (ACS) Program
  http://www.globalsecurity.org/military/ops/acsp.htm
African Union Peace and Security Council
  http://www.africa-union.org
Center for Strategic and International Studies, Africa Program
  http://www.csis.org/africa
Commission for Africa
  http://www.commissionforafrica.org
Corporate Council on Africa
  http://www.africacncl.org
Economic Community of Central African States (ECCAS or CEEAC)
  http://www.ceeac-eccas.org
Economic Community of West African States (ECOWAS or CEDEAO)
  http://www.ecowas.int
Export-Import Bank of the United States
  http://www.exim.gov
G8 Africa Action Plan
  http://www.g8.gc.ca/2002Kananaskis/kananaskis/afraction-en.pdf
G8 Summit Information
  http://www.whitehouse.gov/g8 and http://www.g8.gc.ca
The Global Fund to Fight HIV, Malaria, and Tuberculosis
  http://www.theglobalfund.org
Harvard University's Belfer Center for Science and International Affairs
  http://bcsia.ksg.harvard.edu
Institute for Security Studies (South Africa)
  http://www.iss.co.za
International Monetary Fund
  http://www.imf.org
International Trade Administration, Good Governance Program
  http://www.ita.doc.gov/goodgovernance
Kofi Annan International Peacekeeping Training Centre (KAIPTC)
  http://www.kaiptc.org/kaiptc
Maghreb Union
  http://www.maghrebarabe.org

Millennium Challenge Account
   http://www.mca.gov/about_us/overview/index.shtml
National Military Strategy of the United States of America (March 2005)
   http://www.defenselink.mil/qdr/docs/2005-01-25-Strategic-Plan.pdf
National Security Strategy of the United States (2002).
   http://www.whitehouse.gov/nsc/nss.pdf
Office of the U.S. Global AIDS Coordinator
   http://www.state.gov/s/gac
Overseas Private Investment Corporation
   http://www.opic.gov
Security Cooperation and Education Center
   http://scetc.tecom.usmc.mil.
Societe Nationale Des Hydrocarbures (National Hydrocarbons Corporation)
   http://www.snh.cm
Southern African Development Community (SADC)
   http://www.sadc.int
Southern African Regional Poverty Network (SARPN)
   http://www.sarpn.org.za
UN Millennium Goals
   http://www.unmillenniumproject.org
U.S. Department of State and USAID Strategic Plan (2004)
   http://www.state.gov/s/d/rm/rls/dosstrat/2004
U.S. Department of State, Bureau of African Affairs
   http://www.state.gov/p/af
U.S. Department of State, Patterns of Global Terrorism, 2003
   http://www.state.gov/s/ct/rls/pgtrpt/2003
U.S. Trade and Development Agency
   http://www.ustda.gov
USAID Development Experience Clearinghouse
   http://www.dec.org
USAID Policies
   http://www.usaid.gov/policy
USAID Presidential Initiatives, FY2004 Status Report
   http://www.usaid.gov/about_usaid/presidential_initiative
USAID Primer: What We Do and How We Do It (March 2005)
   http://www.usaid.gov
World Bank
   http://www.worldbank.org
World Bank Heavily Indebted Poor Countries Initiative
   http://www.worldbank.org/hipc
World Trade Organization
   http://www.wto.org

Index

About the Authors

James J.F. Forest is director of terrorism studies and assistant professor at the U.S. Military Academy, where he teaches courses in the Department of Social Sciences and directs research projects for the Combating Terrorism Center. Recent publications include *The Making of a Terrorist: Recruitment, Training and Root Causes* (3 volumes: Praeger, 2005); *Homeland Security and Terrorism: Readings and Interpretations* (McGraw-Hill, 2005, with Russell Howard and Joanne Moore); and *Teaching Terror: Strategic and Tactical Learning in the Terrorist World* (Rowman & Littlefield, 2006). His research has also appeared in the *Cambridge Review of International Affairs* and the *Journal of Political Science Education,* and he has been an invited speaker at numerous conferences and workshops worldwide on terrorism and counterterrorism. He received his graduate degrees from Stanford University and Boston College, and undergraduate degrees from Georgetown University and De Anza College.

Matthew V. Sousa is currently serving as a Foreign Area Officer in the U.S. Army, specializing in Sub-Saharan Africa. Previously, he was an Assistant Professor in the Department of Social Sciences at the U.S. Military Academy, where he taught *Politics and Development of Sub-Saharan Africa* and *Comparative Politics.* He served the first half of his career as an Armored Cavalry Officer, and has lived, worked, and traveled in 21 African countries, and 30 others around the world. He received his graduate degree in Public Administration and International Development from Harvard University, and undergraduate degree in Human/Regional Geography from West Point.

329